NETWORK+
CERTIFICATION

ISBN 0-13-016895-5

90000

9 780130 168955

TIM HOFFMAN
KOSTYA RYVKIN
DAVE HOUDE

NETWORK+ CERTIFICATION

Prentice Hall PTR
Upper Saddle River, New Jersey 07458
www.phptr.com

Library of Congress Cataloging-in-Publication Data

Ryvkin, Kostya.
   Network+ certification/Kostya Ryvkin, Dave Houde, Tim Hoffman.
      p. cm.
   ISBN 0-13-016895-5
      1. Electronic data processing personnel—Certification. 2. Computer
   networks—Examinations—Study guides. I. Houde, David. II. Hoffman, Timothy. III.
   Title.

   QA76.3 R99 1999
   004.6'076—dc21   99-056523

Editorial/production supervision: *Vincent Janoski*
Acquisitions editor: *Mary Franz*
Marketing manager: *Lisa Konzelmann*
Developmental editor: *Jim Markham*
Manufacturing manager: *Maura Goldstaub*
Editorial assistant: *Noreen Regina*
Cover design director: *Jerry Votta*

© 2000 by Prentice Hall

 Published by Prentice-Hall PTR
Prentice-Hall, Inc.
Upper Saddle River, NJ 07458

Prentice Hall books are widely used by corporations and government agencies
for training, marketing, and resale.

The publisher offers discounts on this book when ordered in bulk quantities.
For more information, contact: Corporate Sales Department, Phone: 800-382-3419;
Fax: 201-236-7141; E-mail: corpsales@prenhall.com; or write: Prentice Hall PTR,
Corp. Sales Dept., One Lake Street, Upper Saddle River, NJ 07458.

All products or services mentioned in this book are the trademarks or service marks of their
respective companies or organizations. Screen shots reprinted by permission from
Microsoft Corporation.

Printed in the United States of America
10 9 8 7 6 5 4 3 2 1

ISBN: 0-13-016895-5

Prentice-Hall International (UK) Limited, *London*
Prentice-Hall of Australia Pty. Limited, *Sydney*
Prentice-Hall Canada, Inc., *Toronto*
Prentice-Hall Hispanoamericana, S.A., *Mexico*
Prentice-Hall of India Private Limited, *New Delhi*
Prentice-Hall of Japan, Inc., *Tokyo*
Prentice-Hall Asia Pte. Ltd.
Editora Prentice-Hall do Brasil, Ltda., *Rio de Janeiro*

To Giulia, Sandy, and Tatiana, for cheerfully providing support and continuing to endure the loneliness while we developed this book.

CONTENTS

Acknowledgments   xv

About the Authors   xvii

Comptia Network+ Exam Requirements Matrix   xix

Introduction   xxv

1

Introduction to Networking   1
  What Is Networking?   2
    Why Do We Need Networking?   3
  Network Planning   4
  Types of Networks   5
    The Peer-to-Peer Network   6
    Server-Based Networks   8
  Network Topologies   11
    Logical Topologies   12
    Physical Topologies   13
    Segments and Backbones   17
  Summary   19

2

Major Operating Systems   23
  Novell NetWare   24
    Novell NetWare 3.1x   25
    Novell NetWare 4.1   29
    Performance   31
    Security Services   34
    Novell NetWare Version 5   35
  Microsoft Windows NT Server 4.0   39
    Resources Required   40
    Installation   40
    Performance   41
    Fault Tolerance Support   41

Network Services   42
Directory Services   45
Microsoft Windows 2000 Server   45
Resources Required   46
Performance   46
Fault Tolerance Support   46
Network Services   47
Directory Services   47
Security Services   48
Support for Hardware   48
Wizardry   48
UNIX   49
Sun Solaris   49
Linux   50
UNIX Features and Functionality   50
IBM Operating System/2 (OS/2)   53
Clients   53
*Microsoft Windows 95/98 and Windows NT
4.0 Workstation   53*
Connecting to the Server   55
Summary   57

3

Introduction to Standards   63

What are Standards?   64
Standards and Models   65
Protocols   66
Standards for Network Interface Cards   67
DoD Four-Layer Model   67
Network Interface Layer   68
Internet Layer   69
Transport Layer   70
Application Layer   70
Open Systems Interconnect Model   72
Application Layer   73
Presentation Layer   74
Session Layer   75
Transport Layer   76
Network Layer   76

Data Link Layer 76
Physical Layer 77
Putting it all Together 78
Protocol Mapping 78
IEEE 802 MODEL 80
Media Access Control (MAC) Sublayer 81
Logical Link Control (LLC) Sublayer 82
Encapsulation 82
Summary 83

4

Cables, Access Methods, and Network Architecture 87

Types of Cables 88
Coaxial Cable 89
Twisted Pair 98
Fiber Optic Cable 107
Choosing the Right Cable Type 110
Access Methods 112
Carrier-Sense Multiple Access with Collision Detection (CSMA/CD) 113
Carrier-Sense Multiple Access with Collision Avoidance (CSMA/CA) 114
Token Passing 114
Demand Priority 115
Network Architecture 116
Ethernet 116
10BASE-T Ethernet 118
Token Ring 127
ArcNet 132
Cabling 134
Summary 134

5

Wide Area Networks 141

Introduction to Wide-Area-Network Technologies 142
Connecting Two or More LANs 142
Segmenting the Existing LAN 143
Connecting Your LAN to Other Foreign Systems and Environments 145

LAN Expansion Equipment   146
    Repeaters   147
    Bridges   151
    Switches   159
    Routers   167
    Gateways   171
Wide Area Network Technologies   174
    What is a WAN?   175
    WAN Devices   176
    T1   176
    Digital Data Service   177
    Frame Relay   178
    ATM   179
    ISDN   181
    Digital Subscriber Line   182
Summary   183

6

TCP/IP Fundamentals and Configuration   193
TCP/IP Basic Information   195
    Standards and How They Appear   195
    Advantages of TCP/IP   196
    TCP/IP Utilities and Services   197
TCP/IP Architecture   203
    Address Resolution Protocol   204
    Internet Control Message Protocol   206
    Internet Group Management Protocol   206
    Internet Protocol   207
    Transmission Control Protocol   207
    User Datagram Protocol   209
    Ports and Sockets   210
IP Addressing Basics   211
    Dotted Decimal Notation   211
    Two Parts of an IP Address: Network ID and Host ID   214
    Address Classes   215
    Valid and Invalid Host IDs and Network IDs   220
    Subnet Mask   221

How Does the Computer Use the Subnet Mask?   222
Automating IP Address Assignment Using DHCP   224
The DHCP Process   225
DHCP Lease Duration   226
DHCP Scopes and Options   227
DHCP Relay Agents   228
NetBIOS over TCP/IP   230
NetBIOS Names   231
NetBIOS Name Registration, Discovery, and Release   232
NetBIOS Name Scopes   233
NetBIOS Name Resolution   235
Standard Name Resolution Methods   235
Name Resolution Methods Specific to Microscoft   236
Name Resolution Nodes   237
The LMHOSTS File   238
Host Name Resolution   241
What Is a Host Name?   242
Standard Name Resolution Methods   243
Name Resolution Methods Specific to Microsoft   244
Name Resolution Using a HOSTS File   244
Name Resolution Using a DNS Server   245
Summary   246

7

Troubleshooting TCP/IP   253

General Considerations   254
Diagnostic Tools Overview   254
TCP/IP Troubleshooting Guidelines   256
Subnet Mask Problems   260
Testing IP Communications   261
Routing Problems   264
Testing TCP/IP Name Resolution   267
NetBIOS Name Resolution Problems   267
Host Name Resolution Problems   270
Session Communications Problems   272
Troubleshooting Tools   272
Event Viewer   273
Performance Monitor   273

Using Microsoft Network Monitor   274

Summary   279

8

Remote Connectivity   285

Hardware and Software   286

Modem Types   287

Modem Installation and Configuration   288

Modem Transmission Rates   291

Modem Connection Requirements   292

Media   294

Public-Switched Telephone Network   294

Integrated Services Digital Network   296

Other Connection Options   297

Protocols   298

Serial Line Internet Protocol   298

Point-to-Point Protocol   299

Point-to-Point Tunneling Protocol   301

Summary   303

9

Network Administration   309

Installation   310

Planning   312

Performing the Installation   315

Administration   316

Security   318

Physical Security   318

Logical Security   319

Summary   323

10

Maintaining the Network   327

The Physical Environment   328

Line Power   328

Electrostatic Discharge   329

Electromagnetic Interference   330

Radio Frequency Interference   330

Climate   330

Physical Placement   *331*
Monitoring the System   **331**
The Virus Threat   **334**
   Anti-virus Policies and Training   *334*
   Backup Program   *334*
   Anti-virus Software   *334*
Backup Program   **336**
   Backup Equipment   *337*
   What and When to Backup   *338*
   Backup Methods   *339*
   Backup Strategy   *340*
   Tape Management and Storage   *340*
   Testing and Logging   *341*
   Managing the Program   *342*
Fault Tolerance   **343**
   Disk Mirroring   *343*
   Stripe Set with Parity   *345*
   Other RAIDs   *348*
   Sector Sparing   *348*
   Volume Sets   *348*
   Hardware RAID   *349*
Uninterruptible Power Supply   **349**
Software Patches   **350**
   Where Should I Obtain Patches?   *351*
   How Can I Tell What the Patch Does and How It Will Work on My System?   *351*
   How Do I Install the Patch?   *352*
   When Will I Need to Reinstall the Patch?   *352*
Summary   **353**

11

Network Troubleshooting   359

Troubleshooting Methodology   **360**
   STEP 1: Identify the Exact Issue   *361*
   STEP 2: Recreate the Problem   *362*
   STEP 3: Isolate the Cause   *363*
   STEP 4: Formulate a Correction   *365*
   STEP 5: Implement the Correction   *366*
   STEP 6: Test the Correction   *366*

STEP 7: Document the Problem and the Solution   366
STEP 8: Give Feedback   367
Wire to Application   371
Go Easy Early   372
Walk Through the Protocol Stack   373
Network Interface Cards   374
Network Analysis Resources   379
Crossover Cables   380
Tone Generator/Tone Locator   380
Time-Domain Reflectometers   380
Protocol Analyzers   381
Summary   381

Appendix   385

Glossary   435

Index   453

ACKNOWLEDGMENTS

This book is for the technical student seeking certification. Several dedicated professionals collaborated to write, review, and coordinate the publishing.

The authors, Tim, Kostya, and Dave acknowledge the guidance, patience, support and watchful eyes of the team at Prentice Hall: Acquisitions Editor Mary Franz, Technical Editor Jorge Martinez, and our task master, Development Editor Jim Markham.

Together we encourage the student to learn as much as possible about the technology and wish you well with your certification exam.

ABOUT THE AUTHORS

Tim Hoffman, MCP, MCSE, MCT, PSS   Tim is the president of the Alida Connection and provides consulting and training full-time in Microsoft Windows NT Server and BackOffice environments. His professional career dates from 1969 with exceptional depth in telecommunications and computer fields. His expertise includes systems analysis, protocol definition / information transfer (X.25 and TCP/IP), network modeling, certification and accreditation of sites, networks and systems, and systems test. He regularly provides troubleshooting and analysis on networks, messaging systems and data repositories.

Tim holds a masters degree and has attended specialized military training in troubleshooting, multi-channel signals processing, off-line cryptography, high speed cryptographic secure systems and satellite communications. He also authors courseware, trainer materials, presentations, lab manuals and test questions. He recently co-authored MCSE Study Guide: Internetworking with Microsoft TCP/IP on Microsoft Windows NT 4.0 and the MCSE Study Guide - Proxy Server 2.0.

Kostya Ryvkin, MCP, MCSE +I, MCT, Network+   Kostya is a consultant, trainer and network engineer. He recently co-authored the MCSE Study Guide: Internetworking with Microsoft TCP/IP on Microsoft Windows NT 4.0 and the MCSE Study Guide Microsoft Proxy Server 2.0. He provides customers with network installation, sophisticated web design, messaging system integration, and advanced technical support.

As a Microsoft Certified Trainer, he teaches these skills and is adept at developing courseware, student and trainer kits, lab manuals and test questions. He is a PhD Candidate, Graduate Student-Teacher, and holds a masters degree from St. Petersburg, University; thesis on TCP/IP.

Dave Houde, MCP, MCSE, MCT   Dave is a consultant, trainer and network engineer. He recently co-authored the MCSE Study Guide: Internetworking with Microsoft TCP/IP on Microsoft Windows NT 4.0 and the

MCSE Study Guide: Microsoft Proxy Server 2.0. He has written and delivered several courses such as Microsoft SQL 7.0, Microsoft Windows NT, and Networking Essentials. He provides consulting services including advanced messaging solutions and data recovery programs and he has developed courseware, student and trainer kits, presentations, lab manuals and test questions.

Dave retired from the US Air Force where he was involved with information technology since the early 1970s as a programmer/analyst and operating system/network support engineer. As a programmer, Dave delivered mainframe and microcomputer software ranging from simple accounting and database software to complex navigation and modeling applications. His work with the Internet spans many years.

COMPTIA NETWORK+ EXAM REQUIREMENTS MATRIX

Objectives		Chapter
I.1 BASIC KNOWLEDGE		
I.1.1	Demonstrate understanding of basic network structure including the characteristics of star, bus, mesh, and ring topologies, their advantages and disadvantages; the characteristics of segments and backbones.	1 & 4
I.1.2	Identify the following: the major network operating systems including Microsoft Windows NT, Novell NetWare, and Unix, the clients that best serve specific network operating systems and their resources, the directory services of the major network operating systems.	2
I.1.3	Associate IPX, IP, and NetBEUI with their functions.	2 & 3
I.1.4	Define the following terms and explain how each relates to fault tolerance or high availability: Mirroring Duplexing Striping Volumes Tape backup	10
I.1.5	Define the layers of the OSI model and identify the protocols, services, and functions that pertain to each layer.	3
I.1.6	Recognize and describe the following characteristics of networking media and connectors: the advantages and disadvantages of coax, Cat 3, Cat 5, fiber optic, UTP, and STP and the conditions under which they are appropriate; the length and speed of 10Base2, 10BaseT, and 100BaseT; the length and speed of 10Base5, 100Base VGAnyLan, 100Base TX, the visual appearance of RJ45 and BNC and they are crimped.	4
I.1.7	Identify the basic attributes, purpose, and function of the following network elements: full- and half-duplexing WAN and LAN Server, workstation, and host	5
	Server-based networking and peer-to-peer networking.	1
	Cable, NIC, and router.	4
	Broadband and baseband. Gateway, as both a default IP router and as a method to connect dissimilar systems or protocols.	5

(*continued*)

Objectives	Chapter
I.2 Physical Layer	
I.2.1 Given an installation, configuration, or troubleshooting scenario, select an appropriate course of action if a client workstation does not connect to the network after installing or replacing a network interface card. Explain why a given action is warranted. The following issues may be covered:	10
Knowledge of how the network card is usually configured, including EPROM, jumpers, and plug-and-play software.	11
Use of network card diagnostics, including the loopback test and vendor-supplied diagnostics.	11
The ability to resolve hardware resource conflicts, including IRQ, DMA, and I/O Base Address.	11
I.2.2 Identify the use of the following network components and the differences between them: Hubs MAUs Switching hubs Repeaters Transceivers	5
I.3 Data Link Layer	
I.3.1 Describe the following data link layer concepts: bridges, what they are and why they are used; the 802 specs, including the topics covered in 802.2, 802.3, and 802.5; the function and characteristics of MAC addresses.	5
I.4 Network Layer	
I.4.1 Explain the following routing and network layer concepts, including: The fact that routing occurs at the network layer.	5
The difference between a router and a brouter.	5
The difference between routable and nonroutable protocols.	3, 5, 7
The concept of default gateways and subnetworks.	5
The reason for employing unique network IDs.	5 & 6
The difference between static and dynamic routing.	6
I.5 Transport Layer	
I.5.1 Explain the following transport layer concepts: the distinction between connectionless and connection transport; the purpose of name resolution, either to an IP/IPX address or a network protocol.	6
I.6 TCP/IP Fundamentals	
I.6.1 Demonstrate knowledge of the following TCP/IP fundamentals: The concept of IP default gateways. The purpose and use of DHCP, DNS, WINS, and host files. The identity of the main protocols that make up TCP/IP suite, including TCP, UDP, POP3, SMTP, SNMP, FTP, HTTP, and IP. The ideas that TCP/IP is supported by every operating system and millions of hosts worldwide.	6
The purpose and function of Internet domain name server hierarchies (how email arrives in another country).	7

Objectives		Chapter
I.6.2	Demonstrate knowledge of the fundamental concepts of TCP/IP addressing, including: The A, B, and C classes of IP addresses and their default subnet mask numbers. The use of port number (HTTP, FTP, SMTP) and port numbers commonly assigned to a given service.	6 & 7
I.6.3	Demonstrate knowledge of TCP/IP configuration concepts including: The definition of IP proxy and why it is used.	7
	The identity of the normal configuration parameters for a workstation, including IP address, DNS, default gateway, IP proxy configuration, WINS, DHCP, host name, and Internet domain name.	6 & 7

I.7 TCP/IP Suite: Utilities

I.7.1	Explain how and when to use the following TCP/IP utilities to test, validate, and troubleshoot IP connectivity: ARP Telnet NBTSTAT TRACERT NETSTAT Ipconfig/winipcfg FTP PING	6 & 7

I.8 Remote connectivity

I.8.1	Explain the following remote connectivity concepts: The distinction between PPP and SLIP. The purpose and function of PPTP and the conditions under which it is useful. The attributes, advantages, and disadvantages of ISDN and PSTN (POTS).	8
I.8.2	Specify the following elements of dial-up networking: The modem configuration parameters that must be set, including serial port IRQ, I/O address and maximum port speed. The requirements for a remote connection.	8

I.9 Security

I.9.1	Identify good practices to ensure network security, including: Selection of a security model (user and share level). Standard password practices and procedures. The need to employ data encryption to protect network data. The use of a firewall.	9

(continued)

Continued

Objectives	Chapter
II. KNOWLEDGE OF NETWORKING PRACTICES	
II.1 Implementing the Installation of the Network	
II.1.1 Demonstrate awareness that administrative and test accounts, passwords, IP addresses, IP configurations, relevant SOPs, etc., must be obtained prior to network implementation.	9
II.1.2 Explain the impact of environmental factors on computer networks. Given a network installation scenario, identify unexpected or atypical conditions that could either cause problems for the network or signify that a problem condition already exists, including:	10
Room conditions (e.g., humidity, heat, etc.).	10
The placement of building contents and personal effects (e.g., space heaters, TVs, radios, etc.). Computer equipment. Error messages.	10
II.1.3 Recognize visually, or by description, common peripheral ports, external SCSI (especially DB-25 connectors), and common network componentry, including: Print servers Peripherals Hubs Routers Brouters Bridges Patch panels	4 & 5
UPSs	4 & 10
NICs	5 & 11
Token ring media fillers	5
II.1.4 Given an installation scenario, demonstrate awareness of the following compatibility and cabling issues: The consequences of trying to install an analog modem in a digital jack.	4
That the uses of RJ-45 connectors may differ greatly depending on the cabling.	4 & 5
That patch cables contribute to the overall length of the cabling segment.	4 & 5
II.2 Maintaining and Supporting the Network	
II.2.1 Identify the kinds of test documentation that are usually available regarding a vendor's patches, fixes, upgrades, etc.	10
II.2.2 Given a network maintenance scenario, demonstrate awareness of the following issues: Standard backup procedures and backup media storage practices. The need for periodic application of software patches and other fixes to the network. The need to install anti-virus software on the server and workstations. The need to frequently update virus signatures.	10

Objectives	Chapter

II.3 Troubleshooting the Network

II.3.1 Identify the following steps as a systematic approach to identifying the extent of a network problem, and, given a problem scenario, select the appropriate next step based on this approach: — 11

1. Determine whether the problem exists across the network.
2. Determine whether the problem is workstation, workgroup, LAN or WAN.
3. Determine whether the problem is consistent and replicable.
4. Use standard troubleshooting methods.

II.3.2 Identify the following steps as a systematic approach to determining whether a problem is attributable to the operator or the system, and, given a problem scenario, select the appropriate next step based on this approach: — 11

1. identify the exact issue
2. recreate the problem
3. isolate the cause
4. formulate a correction
5. implement the correction
6. test
7. document the problem and the solution
8. give feedback

II.3.3 Identify the following steps as a systematic approach to determining whether a problem is attributable to the operator or the system, and, given a problem scenario, select the appropriate next step based on this approach. — 11

1. Have a second operator perform the same task on an equivalent workstation.
2. Have a second operator perform the same task on the original operator's workstation.
3. See whether operators are following standard operating procedure.

II.3.4 Given a network troubleshooting scenario, demonstrate awareness of the need to check for physical and logical indicators of trouble, including: — 10 & 11
link lights
power lights
error displays
error logs and displays
performance monitors

II.3.5 Given a network problem scenario, including symptoms, determine the most likely cause or causes of the problem based on the available information. Select the most appropriate course of action based on this inference. Issues that may be covered include: — 10 & 11
Recognizing abnormal physical conditions.
Isolating and correcting problems in cases where there is fault in the physical media (patch cable).
Checking the status of servers.

(continued)

Continued

	Objectives	Chapter
	Checking for configuration problems with DNS, WINS, HOST file.	7
	Checking for viruses.	10
	Checking the validity of the account name and password.	9
	Rechecking operator logon procedures.	11
	Selecting and running appropriate diagnostics.	10 & 11
II.3.6	Specify the tools that are commonly used to resolve network equipment problems. Identify the purpose and function of common network tools, including: crossover cable hardware loopback tone generator tone locator (fox and hound)	10 & 11

INTRODUCTION

Welcome to Network+. If you are like many IT professionals, you have decided to upgrade your job skills by becoming professionally certified. This book is designed primarily for network professionals preparing for the Computer Technology Industry Association (Comptia) testing program for Network+. Passing this examination is recognition by the computer industry that you have acquired knowledge equivalent to that of networking technicians with 18–24 months experience. The examination covers a wide range of vendor and product neutral network technologies so don't be intimidated by the wide variety of test questions. Keep studying and your efforts will pay off.

Who Is This Book For?

This book is designed to provide concise and comprehensive information about networks. This book gets right to the point and provides all you will need to know to pass the examination. It will also benefit computing professionals who are responsible for the management of network-based computing environments because it has been designed to be both a training guide and reference resource. Many aspects of client and server, TCP/IP, installation, configuration, network administration, and security are covered. The readers of this book should have a good working knowledge of the hardware requirements of the A+ certification and familiarity with the graphical interface of the network operating systems discussed.

What You Will Need

Through the use of numerous illustrations and CD-ROM-based training supplements, we have endeavored to make this book as self-contained as possible. Nevertheless, we acknowledge that there is no substitute for hands-on experience. To fully practice the concepts explained in this book, you will need at least three Intel 486/66 (or better) computers with at least 32 Mbytes of RAM (64 Mbytes recommended), 450MB of free hard disk space, three network adapter cards, three mice (or other pointing device), four port UTP 10baseT hub, three sections of 10baseT twisted pair with RJ45 connectors, two VGA monitors, CD-ROM drive, and a 1.44MB 3.5-inch floppy diskette drive. Also, you will need an evaluation copy of either Novell NetWare or Microsoft Windows NT. Optional equipment includes a modem or ISDN adapter, a printer, and a tape drive.

How This Book Is Organized

This book is divided into 11 chapters, which cover issues such as Network types, planning, upgrading, topologies, major operating systems, clients and servers, standards and protocols, TCP/IP, IPX/SPX, NetBEUI, DLC, AppleTalk, cabling, connectors, routers, hubs, bridges, ATM, ISDN, Frame Relay, DSL, remote connectivity, network administration, security, back up, anti-virus, fault tolerance, UPS, and plenty of troubleshooting.

Conventions Used in This Book

This book uses different features to help highlight key information.

Chapter Syllabus

This book's primary focus is to address those topics that are to be tested in the Network+ exam. Therefore, each chapter opens with a syllabus that lists the topics to be covered, and each topic directly corresponds to the main section headings in the chapter.

Icons

Icons represent called-out material that is of significance and that you should be alerted to. Following are some icons that are included in this book:

This icon is used to call out information that deserves special attention; one that the reader may otherwise run a highlight marker through.

This icon is used to flag particularly useful information that will save the reader time, highlight a valuable technique, or offer specific advice.

 This icon flags information that may cause unexpected results or serious frustration.

Chapter Review Questions

Each chapter ends with a series of review questions. These questions are designed to simulate part of an actual exam and to reinforce what you have just learned. The number of questions will vary depending on the length of subject matter in the individual chapter. All of the questions are taken directly from the material covered in the chapter, and the author's answers can be found in the Appendix.

About the Examination

Step 1 is to register to take the Network+ examination. To do this, you should either call 1–800–909–EXAM (3926) or use the Registration Wizard found at http://www.2test.com. The online registration can be performed at any time day or night. Once registered to take the examination, you simply show up at the testing center at the right place and time. The examination is given at the Sylvan Prometric examination centers around the country. The folks at the number given have information about the costs, closest center, the center's hours, and availability. Although we've provided the outline and shown how the chapters of this book map to the objectives of the examination, you can view the objectives and related information at http://www.comptia.org/

Introduction to Networking

▲ **Chapter Syllabus**

What Is Networking?

Network Planning

Types of Networks

Network Topologies

The computing power of a single computer has become an awesome force as smaller and smaller boxes are delivering more and more power. Computers have a tremendous capacity for storing, working with, and sharing data. Put these computers together on a local area network (LAN) and you have either a work of art or a scientifically proven workhorse that delivers many times its value in the workplace by enabling workers to do more, work faster and easier, and share information with each other. As computer networks grow, they can become increasingly more complex. As a result, you will not be a stranger to maintenance tasks, which we will talk about later in the book.

We find the general characteristics of the network-computing environment at a number of companies to be the focus of hard choices such as cost tradeoffs, equipment and software failures, and a great deal of troubleshooting. If poor choices were made during the system's implementation, cycles of work that require early mornings, late nights, and weekend work for the system administrator are sure to develop.

Fortunately, with proper planning, good network design, and adequate training for the information technology (IT) staff, the effectiveness of the network can be improved and stability can be achieved. Our computer networks need many things to run well, and a good network administrator can make a huge difference. Sometimes this is overlooked or good personnel may simply cost too much for smaller companies to afford. Sometimes there are not enough people available or trained to do the job. Sometimes practices are not performed consistently enough to handle attendant network problems. Whatever the reason, the result is felt in poor performance, less than adequate network support, and a staff that is always busy with brush fires instead of planning the next upgrade.

LAN systems are becoming much more sophisticated so it takes many months, and even years, to master the processes required for supporting networks. LAN administrators must, therefore, become increasingly sophisticated. This means that they must be careful about introducing network changes as well as cautious with the methods used for introducing those changes. The result can either be a well-run ship or a sinking feeling that the whole company is going to be down hard for the entire year. Throughout this book we describe the best practices and expect that a novice LAN administrator will use caution and good judgment when making changes. The experienced administrator already knows the result of failed planning.

In this chapter, we introduce the types of networks that you might find in a company or organization and discuss how they would be used and upgraded.

After completing this chapter, you will be able to do the following:

- Describe Networking
- Identify the important steps required for effective network planning
- Discuss the features of the major network types
- Identify the characteristics of star, bus, mesh and ring topologies

What Is Networking?

Even as fledgling business computers began making the scene between the late 1950s and early 1970s, paper record keeping continued as the order of the day because not all companies could afford to put their information on computers. Computers were large, complex, and expensive. A considerable amount of planning was required before a company purchased one, and the business case for having computers was a big issue in those early days. Once the business community understood the benefits and the machines became more affordable, central mainframe computers and host terminals became much more popular.

Local area networks (LANs) began to show up as an alternative to large mainframe systems during the 1970s and grew in use throughout the 1980s. The smaller computers were less costly so it was easier to budget for one or more. The next logical step was to link them together, but integration of different hardware and software vendor products was difficult due to a lack of standardization from one manufacturer to another. (To a lesser extent, this can still be a problem today, although much of the integration work has been made easier by a variety of industry standards.)

As we will discuss later, there are several types of cabling typically found in the makeup of a LAN. These include twisted pair, coaxial, and fiber optic. Each of these has its benefits and disadvantages. The most common configurations are called *ring*, *star*, and *bus*. There are also many networks built on combinations of these basic configuration types. We will begin by investigating the standards that permit data exchange over the basic network configurations and determine why each would be used for a particular networking scenario.

Why Do We Need Networking?

The need to share information is based on the goal of an organization to succeed. By having everyone on the team know what is going on, each person can more effectively contribute to the success of the business. The LAN represents one of the most significant investments related to sharing information that a company has. LANs handle all types of important business data. Placing information in a directory, volume, or folder on one computer and creating a "share" point is the first step. Assigning permissions to users or groups completes the process of sharing. The administrator on a large network or a user with administrative duties on a small network usually does this. Depending on the type of network and the amount of control that is given to users, once the share is created, users with the proper rights may access the share, make copies of the information, or modify it as needed. To further extend the reach of the corporate network, wide area networks (WANs) now connect many LANs across the country and the world.

Valuable company information is placed on many servers throughout the organization and can be found in the file system, electronic mail systems, calendars, and in project planning and scheduling software. The network, with all its resources, and the professionals who keep it running achieve such benefits as

- Cost cutting through sharing data and peripherals
- Standardization of applications
- Central administration and security
- Timely data acquisition
- Central database management
- More efficient communications and scheduling

Network Planning

Planning, or the lack of it, generally shows up as a network starts to expand beyond the original two to four computers. Doing the proper planning while the network is still small may result in saving a great deal of time and money as it grows. Peer-to-peer LANs are likely to be less expensive than a server based network because there is no need for large, expensive servers. Planning is sometimes overlooked in these diminutive networks because the computers are similar or identical to what we have in our homes. Once computers are networked they function in a manner that is similar to a home computer but they now differ from their home-bound counterparts in several important ways. (In addition to the information presented here, the Appendix provides a comprehensive guide for network planning.)

The first aspect of planning is to answer the basic question: "Do we really need a network?" For example, if there are two users and one printer, you may be able to install a switch to route each user to the printer sequentially instead of installing a network—a cheaper and easier solution.

Next, identify the benefits that will be derived from the network installation to permit you to articulate the value, cost, cost savings, and expectations of improved performance to company decision makers. Company leaders are likely to ask the following: "Will we save money?" "Is the installation worth the expense?" "How will the network be used?" "How will the company benefit by having a network?" An additional question that you should answer, even if your leadership doesn't ask, is "Who will administer the network?"

Actual network planning considerations must start with user needs. First, determine how many users need computers and what IT activities the users need to accomplish now and during the next one to three years as the system grows. By doing this first, you will have an idea of what type of hardware and software is needed. The applications you select must be compatible with the computer and network operating systems you choose (we'll talk about operating systems in the next chapter).

The next thing you need to determine is a list of resources you currently have in use. Your choice of cabling, hubs, network adapters, and network type must be matched. For example, if the signaling types between two different network adapters were different, the two would not communicate properly. Since network adapter cards must be installed in each computer, it is your job to ensure that they are properly matched, installed, and configured to communicate. Of course, if you're starting from scratch, this step is pretty easy.

Once the hardware path is established, the networking protocols must match and the applications must be able to support networking functionality. This means that you now must consider the purchase of network ready software. In order to remain within legal boundaries, you will need to ensure that you have purchased the correct license for what is being done on the network. Licensing is specific to the vendor of the software for both the operating system and application, so be sure to check. (Although you may have licensed the applications and computer and network operating systems, most vendors expect you to pay a licensing fee to permit the legal connection of a client computer to a server or other network resource.)

The decision on what to install on your network should be guided by your needs for quality and performance. The purchase of low quality computer hardware, software, and peripherals may cause your environment to suffer.

It is a good idea to map or diagram your computer environment and document the operating systems, versions, patches, and applications that are on the network. This will save a lot of time in troubleshooting. It is always a good idea to know about the resources on the network that need attention, but it is more important to know where something is during a crisis. You should be certain to document all printers and other specialty items like integrated FAX scanners and so forth.

Types of Networks

There are two major types and various combinations of LANs in use today. Variations that mix both types usually require extensive planning and more user training for maximum productivity. Our discussion will center on the server-based and peer-to-peer LANs, and we will offer information on how to plan, upgrade, and use them.

The Peer-to-Peer Network

A basic description of the peer-to-peer network type might be best found in the Model of a small UNIX environment or a small Windows 95 style LAN where each user is responsible for managing his or her own host computer as well as its resources and security. Peer-to-peer networks are typically found in smaller organizations because of some of the model's limitations. An example of the peer-to-peer network is shown in Figure 1–1.

Using a Peer-to-Peer LAN

Using a peer-to-peer LAN is easy. Each user logs onto his or her workstation and begins to work. The user at the local machine is limited to using the applications on his or her machine in most cases. The question of who will administer the network is answered because no one and everyone must administer. That is that there is no central administrator so each user is responsible for maintaining his or her computer, peripherals, and share points. This also means that users are responsible for the general security of their machines. This generally works well in very small networks of up to 15 to 20 people who have been properly trained to understand the significance of password length, uniqueness, and password changing. Once there are 10 or 12 users that lack training, don't understand how to perform sharing, or who do not understand security, there will be difficulties encountered that

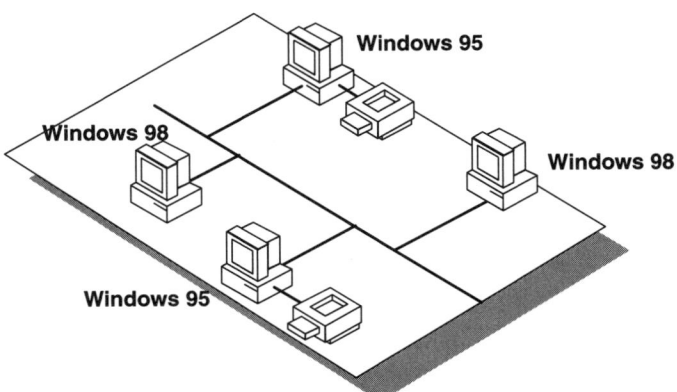

Figure 1–1 *Windows 95 and Windows 98 mixed peer-to-peer network.*

point up the need for a skilled administrator. When your peer-to-peer network has reached this point, it is time to start thinking about upgrading to a server-based network.

Advantages and Disadvantages

Some of the advantages of a peer-to-peer network are as follows:

- Each host (computer) serves as both server and client
- There are no dedicated servers
- Requires less planning and administration than a server-based LAN
- Each user manages security for own machine and peripherals
- Each user acts as both user and administrator
- Works best in areas where only 10 or fewer computers are expected
- Adequate if central security and central administration not an issue

Some of the disadvantages of a peer-to-peer network are as follows:

- Limited to small number of users
- More difficult to manage as the numbers of users grow
- Security is an issue when there are large numbers of users
- Does not scale well when multiple technologies are present

Upgrading a Peer-to-Peer LAN

The question of whether to simply add machines or upgrade from a peer-to-peer network to a server-based network is generally one of numbers. Costs are always important but the number of users is also a serious consideration. As the peer-to-peer network moves beyond a dozen machines, the use of workstation-level sharing gets more and more difficult. Trying to remember one password is difficult. Keeping up with 30 or 40 passwords is almost impossible. Many times users start to write their passwords on post-it notes and place them on the front of their monitors, which eliminates any chance for security.

When a network has more than a dozen machines, the requirement for someone to administer a share or printer increases. If each user knows a good deal about computing, there may still be no need to centralize administration. When considering a centralized server-based network, include needs for the following:

- Standardization
- Central security

- Ensured data availability (through central backups)
- Management of specialized equipment (router, hub, etc.)

In planning for an upgrade, consider the following factors:

- Existing and planned hardware (cables, hubs, switches, routers)
- Network configuration (remains the same or changes?)
- Application subset (suite or individual?)
- What types of peripherals are needed
- Who will be the administrator
- How much training is needed for the administrator
- How much training is needed for the users

You should collect information about what is already in place in the peer-to-peer network. Are you adding to the existing system or will your expansion result in a major upgrade such that compatibility with existing resources must be considered? What about the existing cables? Are they already at their maximum length? Will they support new signaling or faster signals? How many hubs are on the wire already and are we exceeding a maximum? When the network is upgraded, are the network adapters to be matched? What is the overriding concern for this upgrade—cost? Is the configuration capable of supporting the upgrade? Are the signaling types different? Will the protocol remain the same or are we changing it? Is there a need to maintain compatibility with the Internet? Is there a need to match the networking protocols to the applications? Do the applications support networking functionality?

Server-Based Networks

Having a server-based network simply means that a central computer, which is usually more powerful than the other machines on the network, handles the administrative tasks and security for the whole network. On server-based networks where the administration and security are centralized, you might find special features in the central server such as dual processors, dual power supplies, and some form of integrated fault tolerance for the hard drives as well. The server-based LAN contains one or more specialized servers such as a print server, FAX server, communications server, mail server, or application server. Other differences may include scripts that run from a server when the user performs a login/logon, management of peripherals and computers by one or more administrators, and policies to govern the network's use and operation. An example of a server-based network could be either a Novell NetWare® or Microsoft® Windows NT LAN. The model in Figure 1–2 which follows depicts a modern business environment with a mixed network that uses both Windows NT and Novell NetWare as well as remote and Internet connectivity. This server-based LAN is only an example. The configuration could be any number of possible combinations that might include various UNIX stations, OS/2®, and other network operating systems in addition to those shown.

Planning a Server-Based LAN

Planning for a server-based LAN includes all the steps discussed at the start of this chapter but requires greater attention to detail. In contrast to the peer-to-peer LAN, client-server LANs can demand a lot more from applications. As in any network planning, user needs must drive the process. The computers that are put on the network must be able to provide users with the proper functionality and permit them to do their jobs more efficiently

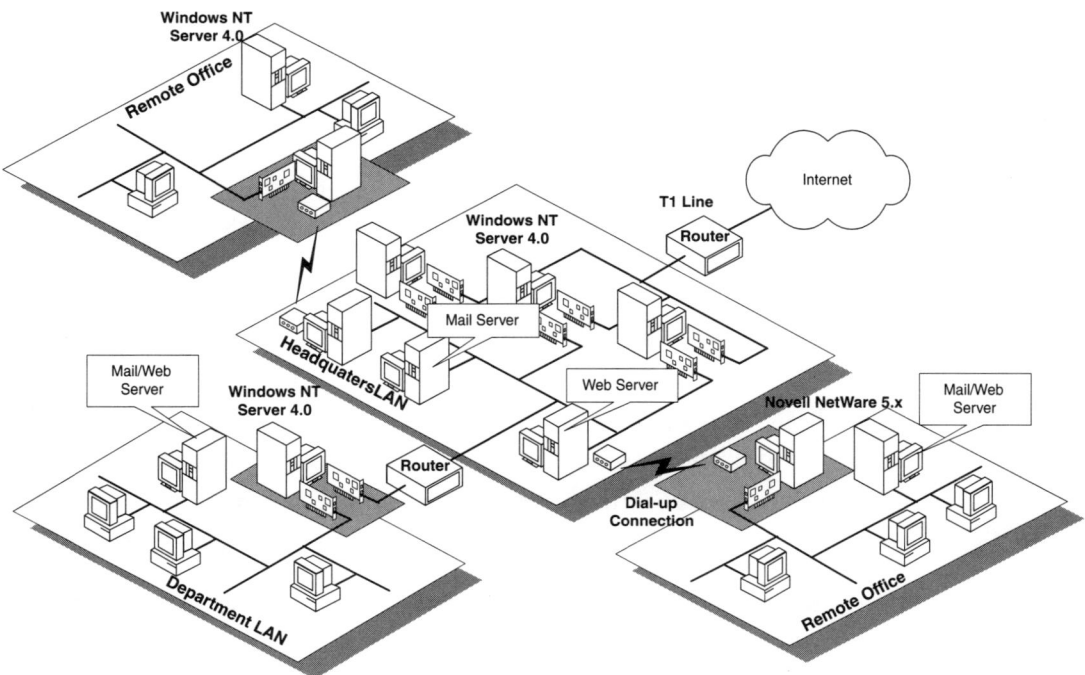

Figure 1–2   *Novell NetWare and Microsoft Windows NT server-based LAN with remote connectivity.*

and/or provide the company with savings over the cost of manual processing methods. Otherwise, why use networked computers at all?

In addition to the general questions concerning savings and benefits of networking discussed at the beginning of this chapter, you should be able to answer the following additional questions:

- Has security been properly considered?
- Are there security issues with the existing network that will be fixed by upgrading to a server-based network?
- What training is needed to understand security?
- Is the licensing proper for this environment?

Remember you will have to ensure the proper number of client access licenses has been purchased and that training for administrators and users has been planned.

In server-based networks, mapping or diagramming the network to document the operating systems, versions, patches, and applications takes on even greater importance than in the peer-to-peer network. This will save a lot of time in later upgrades or when something goes wrong on the network. You should be certain to document all printers and other specialty items like integrated FAX machines, scanners, wiring closets, hubs, patch panels, and so forth.

Advantages/Disadvantages of a Server-Based LAN

Some of the advantages of a server-based LAN include the following:

- Sharing resources (servers are typically larger and more powerful so they are capable of supporting many users without sacrifice to performance)
- Improved security (often this may be the main reason to migrate to a server-based LAN)
- Easier to manage a large number of users
- Standardization of the application set, which results in cost savings
- Centralized backup (more planning in general is done)

Some of the disadvantages of a server-based LAN are as follows:

- Servers typically cost more than desktop machines and require more knowledge to maintain
- Security and application use must be taught to users
- Requires experienced administrator to perform more complex tasks

Upgrading a Server-Based LAN

The upgrade *to* a server-based LAN was covered in the last section. Here we will ask the question about whether to upgrade components or add WAN capabilities to an existing LAN. The need to centralize security and administration becomes more evident as the number of users increases. Some of the reasons for upgrading your LAN include the need for

- Standardization
- Central administration
- Central security
- Ensuring total data availability (through central backups)
- Managing specialized equipment (router)

In addition to the general planning steps mentioned at the start of this chapter, planning for a server-based upgrade must consider additional factors such as

- Compatibility with existing hardware and planned hardware (cables, hubs, switches, routers)
- Configuration (remain the same or change?)
- Application subset (suite or individual?)
- Peripherals
- Procedural changes
- Training (administrators)
- Training (users)

Network Topologies

What is a topology? In essence, it is the way that the equipment is organized or laid out. You might think of a topology as a structural indication of that meaning. In other words, the physical topology is simply the arrangement of network components. This arrangement must provide the desired network functionality. As you know, the relative cost of providing reliable network operations has continued to decrease. We mentioned that peer-to-peer and client/server are the two most predominant types of local area network in use today. If you were to design a network, you would have to give serious thought to the physical layout of the components so that machines that do certain jobs could be put close to the machines that need that job done. For example, you would want machines that use a certain printer to be physically close to the machine that has the printer connected to it.

The network physical media have a big impact on the number and layout of the devices on the network. What types of cables and connections would you use? How far are the most distant ends of the circuit? What devices are on the network? What is needed to extend the reach of the network? The design or arrangement of the network can be termed the topology; and although many different designs are possible, most common are the bus, ring, and star topologies. Much less common is the mesh topology. Remember that, once in place, it will be *very* costly to remove the entire cable plant and replace it, so businesses are not likely to do this very often.

Let's discuss the types of topologies that you are likely to encounter on most corporate networks and begin by identifying the difference between a *logical* topology and the physical reality of the wiring. The logical topology will provide the reference point for how the signals travel around the wires and through the components on the network. The reason for describing both physical and *logical* topologies is because it is possible to have a physical topology that uses a different internal or logical topology.

Logical Topologies

The logical topologies provide us with the means to understand how the signals move around the network regardless of how the wires are placed or connected. They use the same names as their physical counterparts. The logical topologies can best be described as

- **Bus topology** indicates that the source computer puts information on the wire. The information then travels out from the source to all computers on the network. Although all computers listen for signals sent out this way, only the computer that was addressed actually responds.
- **Star topology** indicates the source of information which creates a transmission that travels to a central concentrator of signals and then down one cable or wire leg to the receiver. (Although listed here for consistency, the star topology is actually a physical variation of the bus topology, as we'll see later in this chapter.)
- **Ring topology** indicates that a source of information creates a transmission that travels in one direction around the circle, and the intended recipient removes or strips off the data during its turn.
- **Mesh topology** indicates an overlapping of paths such that a signal can take any number of different paths. This is a complex topology that uses multiple connections to tie each computer to *every* other

computer in the network. A complex and expensive technology, the mesh features a high degree of fault tolerance.

Physical Topologies

Although similar to the logical topologies, physical topologies are concerned with where the wires go and how the signals really get to the computers. While logical topologies provide a good entry point to understand networks, physical topologies put us on line!

Bus Topology Characteristics

The bus topology began with the use of a single thick coaxial cable run that permitted multiple machine connections through the use of taps (or vampire connectors as they were known). The computers are all attached to this single cable. Both ends are terminated to attenuate the network adapter signals on the wire. Without the use of terminators, the ends of the cable would be said to be *open*. An open wire produces signal bounce, which can keep the rest of the network from transmitting. The thicknet bus proved to be difficult to work with since the vampire taps are not practical. For example, when a machine has to be moved to another location on the wire, another tap has to be put on the wire, the old tap does not move, and so on. Although the applicability of this model is somewhat limited, you might find this type of bus on older backbone installations or building-to-building connections that don't frequently change. Figure 1–3 depicts a thicknet bus used as a backbone.

An improvement over the original thicknet bus cabling took the form of thinner coaxial cable, called thinnet. Thinnet permits easier machine movement by using T-connectors instead of taps. A T-connector could be placed in the cable to accommodate a cable run to an individual computer. Should you need a machine at another location, simply cut a cable, install a

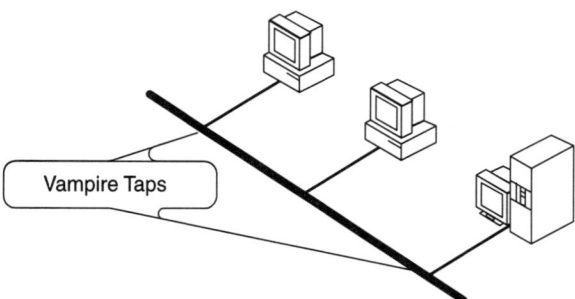

Vampire Taps

Figure 1–3 *Thicknet backbone coaxial cable.*

new T-connector and connect the machine. The cable can run from computer to computer, twist around corners and through the ceiling, and make its way to the next computer with ease because it can be pre-cut to the right length. Design of this type of network makes it very simple to install and maintain. It is also easy to remove a machine from the network and join the two open ends with a barrel connector. (We'll discuss T-connectors, barrel connectors, and other network "plumbing" a bit later in this book.) The cost is relatively low, so it was used for years as the standard way to create a local area network.

Advantages of the bus topology are:

- Simplest and most common
- Uses less cable than other topologies
- Inexpensive
- Single coaxial cable runs or pieces connect all computers in a line
- Passive: the computers are not responsible for moving data
- Easy to install and terminate
- If a computer fails, the network keeps working

Disadvantages of the bus topology are

- If wires or coaxial cable are installed inside walls, it is difficult to change and move
- Proper termination is required because once the signal reaches the end of the bus, it will bounce if the cable is not properly terminated, which effectively shuts down the whole network
- Every cable on the network must be plugged into something
- If the cable, connectors, or terminators fail, the entire network goes down (not much in the way of fault tolerance)
- Can slow down in heavy traffic
- Can be difficult to troubleshoot

Star Topology Characteristics

The star topology is installed so that all of the computers are connected individually to a central point or hub. Figure 1–4 shows a physical star topology. At the center of the star is the hub with wires radiating out to connect each computer individually. As in the bus topology, all of the computers receive the signal but only the intended recipient accepts it. The functional difference is that each computer has its own cable run. Distinct from bus topology, a break

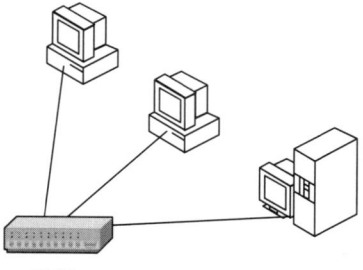

HUB

Figure 1–4 *Star topology.*

in any of the star's cable runs will not take the entire network down but will affect only the computer to which it is attached. Because each machine gets its own cable run, the amount of cable required to create the star topology is greater than that used in the bus topology. Typically, the type of cable used for the runs is twisted pair, which is less expensive than coaxial cable and easier to put connectors on. Twisted pair is thinner and bends better than coaxial cable, so it is useful in tight areas that require the cable to be bent around angles or corners. The hub that is used can either be active or passive and may have any number of ports. The most common hubs have an average between 4 and 24 ports. In an active hub, a signal may get regenerated and be retransmitted. In passive hubs, the hub simply provides a connection point for the cable runs. Because the hub is the central point of the network, if the hub fails, the entire network fails. Although it is rare for this to happen, the loss of a hub can quickly take down an entire network. The acquisition of hubs, therefore, is one area where cost cutting may be imprudent.

When more ports are required, hubs may be connected together in a bus (shown in Figure 1–5) or a star (shown in Figure 1–6). These hybrid topologies are know as the star bus and cascaded star respectively.
Advantages of the star topology are

- A single cable break will affect only the computer to which it is connected (the rest of the network continues to function)
- Easy to wire, modify wiring, and attach connectors
- Permits centralized management from a managed hub
- Usually quite reliable

Disadvantages of the star topology are

- If the hub goes down, the entire network fails
- Total cost of ownership can be high since hubs must be purchased and cables must be run from the hub to each machine

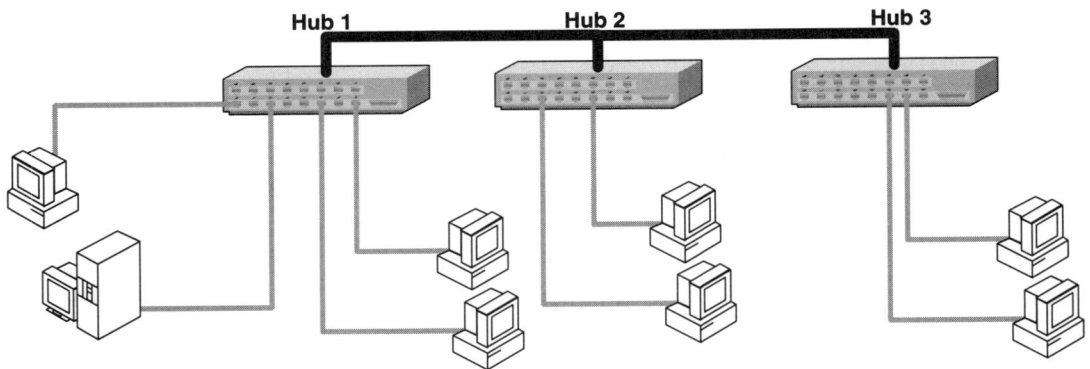

Figure 1–5 *Star bus.*

Ring Topology Characteristics

The ring topology provides equal access for all computers by connecting each computer to its upstream and downstream neighbors to ultimately form a ring. This type of topology provides good performance even when there are many computers on the network. Data moves from computer to computer sequentially in one direction. In the ring, each attached computer is considered a repeater and the network interface card installed inside the computer is responsible for both receiving and sending the information. The

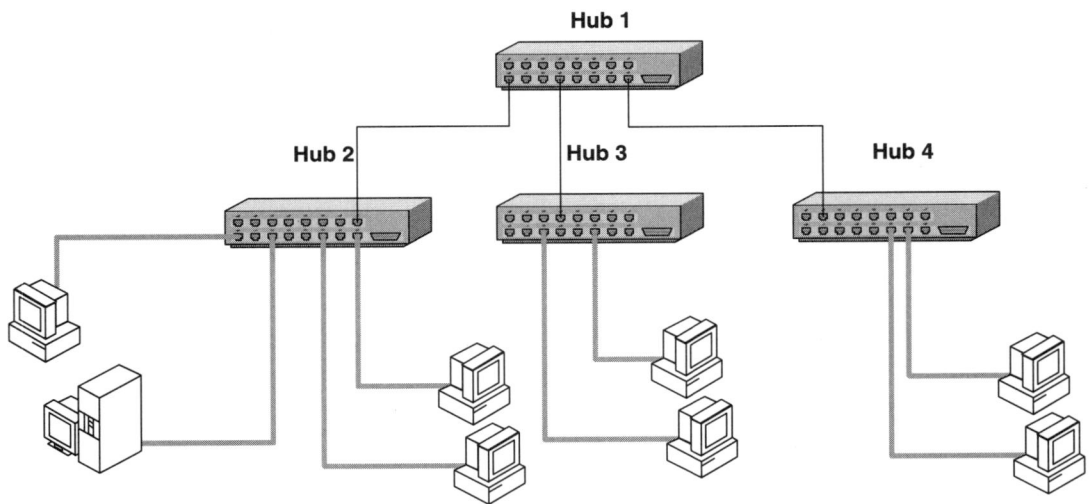

Figure 1–6 *Cascaded star.*

LAN is a closed loop and there are no endpoints as in the bus topology. What we see in practice is a star-wired ring, which is a combination of the physical star topology and logical ring topology. The equivalent of a hub in the ring topology is known as a multistation access unit (MAU or MSAU). The MSAUs can be connected together to permit the connection of many computers. Figure 1–7 shows the physical star and the logical ring that the signal takes for a path.

Mesh Topology Characteristics

The mesh topology, as its name suggests, is a wiring scheme that permits each computer to be interconnected to every other computer in the network. This type of topology is complex and much more expensive to install, configure, and troubleshoot but features a high degree of fault tolerance. Its cost and complexity mean that it is not likely to be found in today's local area networks. A concept similar to the mesh topology is the way the Internet is connected in multiple paths through routers. (The Internet is not a mesh network in the true sense since all computers do not directly connect to all other computers on the network.) Figure 1–8 depicts the complexity. You will notice that as the number of computers increase, the number segments required to connect them is represented by $N(N-1)/2$, where N represents the number of computers in the mesh.

Segments and Backbones

Large networks are typically divided into smaller segments to increase efficiency by reducing the amount of chatter and to ease the administration of larger sites. The individual smaller segments are then connected together by

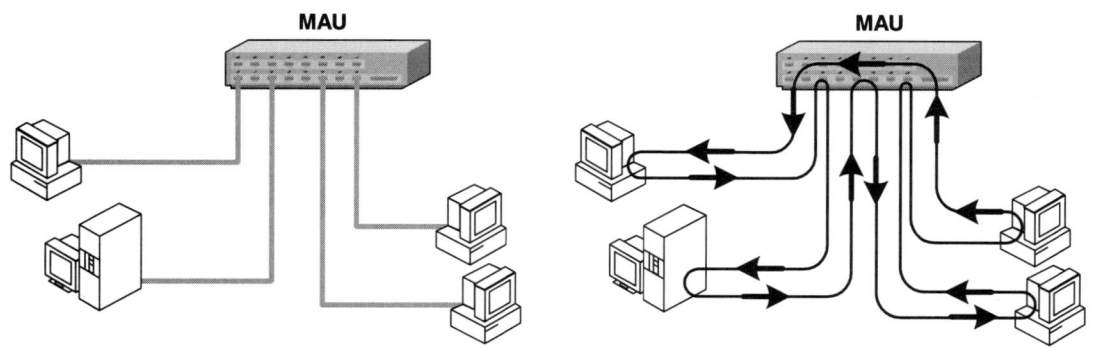

Figure 1–7 *Physical connections and logical signal flow around a MAU.*

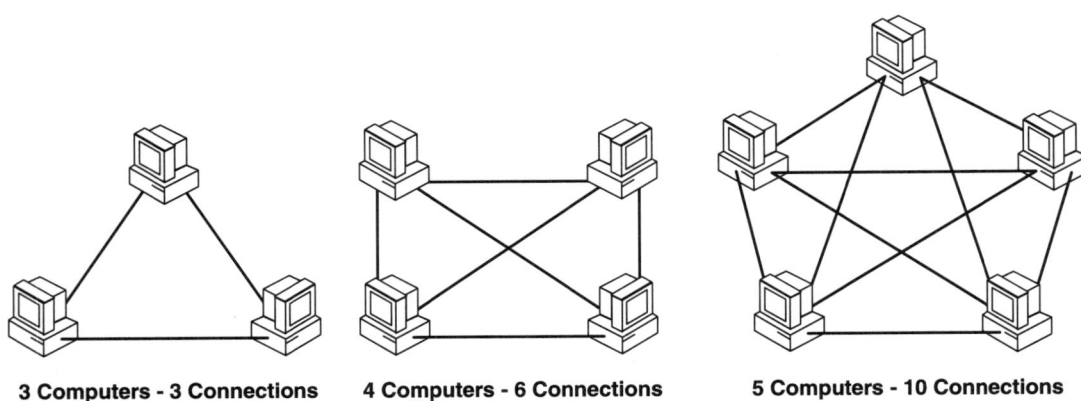

3 Computers - 3 Connections   **4 Computers - 6 Connections**   **5 Computers - 10 Connections**

Figure 1–8   *Mesh topology.*

a backbone. Figure 1–9 depicts a small LAN with servers and segments attached to the backbone.

Segments contain groups of computers that are physically linked together on the same network. The backbone connects the segments and company-level servers. By doing this, we can ensure no segment is ever more than one hop or segment away from any company-level server. A network configured in this manner is more efficient than if it were connected in the cascaded style shown in Figure 1–6. The backbone is the central part of the

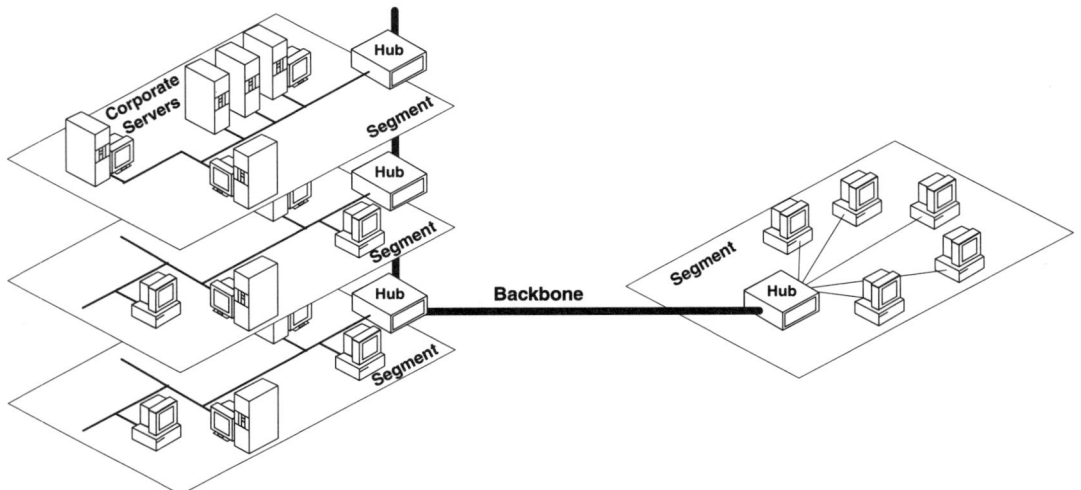

Figure 1–9   *Segments and backbone.*

network that all segments and servers connect to. This part of the network structure is considered the main part of any network topology. An example might be where the company network is housed in two buildings. The two-building network segments may have already been connected with a thicknet coaxial connection.

Summary

This introductory chapter traced the history of business computing beginning with a few stand-alone machines to today's robust networked computing environment. We moved on to discuss the critical importance of proper network planning, stressing the importance of tailoring the environment to the tasks and needs of the network's users. We started with the question, "Is a network necessary?" We then looked at the need to determine the business benefits of the network and who will manage the system. We saw the importance of determining current hardware and software resources and deciding if we should augment them or start over. The need to select hardware, software, and licensing consistent with the organization's facilities, needs, and operations was stressed.

We then turned our attention to the major types of network. We reviewed peer-to-peer and server-based networks and saw peer-to-peer as simply a grouping of equivalent computers with no central administration. The server-based network, on the other hand, featured servers and workstations, and central administration.

With the major network types in mind, we then turned our attention to network topologies, or the way machines are wired together. The major topologies were the bus, star, ring, and mesh. The bus and star topologies function in essentially the same manner with signals going to all computers but being accepted only by the computer(s) to which they are addressed. The bus topology places all computers on a single wire run—a break anywhere on the line will bring down the entire network. In contrast, the star topology features a wire run from a central hub to each computer. Although a hub malfunction will bring the network down, a single wire break will affect only the computer to which the wire is connected.

We looked at the ring topology and discovered that ring computers were connected in a circle with each computer responsible for receiving and transmitting each signal on the wire—Although computers only "read" signals addressed to them. Although this topology can handle very high traffic, the failure of a single computer or wire run can take the entire network down.

In the mesh topology, each computer had an individual connection to every other computer in the network. A complex and expensive network solution, the mesh provides a high degree of fault tolerance because signals may take many different paths through the mesh to reach their destinations.

Finally we looked at segments and backbones. We saw that networks may be divided into individual segments connected together with cable runs called backbones. This method of cabling increased efficiency by keeping local communications within individual segments while permitting quick access to company-level servers.

▲ REVIEW QUESTIONS

1. *What are the two major types of LANs?*
    A. Sneakernet and NETBIOS
    B. Server based and client server
    C. Peer-to-peer and server-based
    D. Centralized and remote

2. *Which type of LAN is better for a large company?*
    A. Sneakernet
    B. NetBIOS
    C. Server based
    D. Peer-to-peer

3. *Who is the central administrator in a peer-to-peer LAN?*
    A. No one
    B. The proxy administrator
    C. The server administrator
    D. The person using NWADMIN

4. *What is the main advantage of peer-to-peer networking?*
    A. Requires more planning
    B. Requires multiple segments
    C. Requires no servers
    D. Requires only one administrator

5. *What are the main advantages of a server-based network? (Select all that apply.)*

   A. Greater freedom for the user

   B. Increased security

   C. Less standardization

   D. No centralization of protocols

6. *What is topology?*

   A. Packet transfer process that includes encapsulation

   B. A form of routing

   C. Multiple network cards

   D. The physical arrangement of the equipment or the logical flow of the traffic on the wires

7. *What are the three most common topology designs?*

   A. Bus, star, token ring

   B. Ring, star, bus

   C. Bus, closed loop, token ring

   D. Standard bus, looped bus, star

Major Operating Systems

▲ **Chapter Syllabus**

Novell NetWare 3.x, 4.1, and 5.0

Microsoft Windows NT 4.0

Windows 2000

UNIX

OS/2

Clients

This chapter identifies some of the more prominent features, requirements, and functions of the major network operating systems such as Novell NetWare®, Microsoft® Windows NT, UNIX, and OS/2®. The focus of our discussion covers performance, networking services, directory services, and security services. We will also discuss "wizardry," cross operating system support, and network clients.

After completing this chapter, you will be able to do the following:

- Identify the features and functions of Novell NetWare, Microsoft Windows NT, Unix, and OS/2
- List available Network Client software and explain the issues involved in connecting to network servers

A network operating system (NOS) is specialized software that is installed on computers that make up a network to permit them to communicate with each other. A typical network consists of powerful, fault-tolerant, backup-enabled machines called servers and workstations (called clients) that allow users to access the servers. Configuring the server involves considerable planning and decision making along the way. You must know the details of your hardware, the network where you are placing the server, the type of connectivity you want, and the configuration details of the clients or peers to which you are connecting the server.

You will also need to decide on the characteristics of each protocol you are going to use over a local-area-network (LAN) interface. You make these decisions based on the topology used and the existing characteristics of the network. Some of the things you will want to consider are routing and tunneling (we will talk about both of these in later chapters).

As we discuss the network operating systems in the next sections, remember, when we speak about the SERVER, we are discussing the place that holds the databases, files, messaging system, administrative functions, and management console (for maintaining and configuring the network). When we speak about the CLIENT, we are speaking about a desktop machine that a user would operate to perform word processing, electronic mail, data entry, and other related tasks. To complete many of these tasks, the user may have to access resources on one or more servers.

Novell NetWare

Novell NetWare has been the most popular NOS for many years and, with the development of NetWare 5, continues this heritage by providing a superior set of tools and features for the use and administration of a LAN. We will compare some of the features and functionality of the server and then move into the client side.

The most notable features offered by NetWare 4 and beyond are as follows:

- A sturdy network directory service (NDS)
- A simple user interface
- Minimal hardware requirements
- Scalable hardware support
- Third-party support
- Interoperability with many other NOS

The history of NetWare contains an interesting list of accomplishments and dates back to the early 1980s. Both Advanced NetWare 86, and then Advanced NetWare 286, were exceptionally complex to install with their hardware-based security systems to prevent copying of the software. NetWare version 2.12 introduced the removal of all keycard copy protection, and NetWare Version 2.15 integrated support for the AppleTalk® Filing Protocol®. NetWare 3.1 added TCP/IP support, while the installation of the server became much easier. NetWare 3.12 introduced a protocol change, making the default IPX/SPX frame type 802.2 (versus the original 802.3).

Novell's design goal for NetWare was always to be the most competitive and the highest performance NOS in the LAN environment. NetWare has grown very popular because it built a product that had, and still has, exceptional file and print services. NetWare captured the attention of many early networkers because it was able to support multiple manufacturers' Network Interface Cards—rare in the early days of networking because most manufacturers were busy building proprietary hardware.

Novell NetWare provided a bridge between ARCnet, Ethernet, and Token Ring networks and offered the services that enabled connections to UNIX, Apple®, and IBM® SNA and OS/2 environments. This interoperability was very attractive because of the dissimilar systems in place in most large environments at the time and it remains a selling point of NetWare products.

Novell NetWare 3.1x

The benefits of Novell NetWare 3.1x were compelling. Necessary hardware drivers for just about all types of equipment were available and the software was available and reasonably easy to install. While the ease of installation was not what you would find with today's integrated software packages, it was measured in minutes and not hours, which had been the case for everything up until then. With a few exceptions, Novell provided accurate, up-to-date documentation, step-by-step instructions, and device drivers for everything needed.

Resources required were small, the NOS performed file and print services very well, system crashes were rare, and the support for many hardwares made it the file server of choice in many organizations. In fact, you will find a number of NetWare 3.1x servers still in the field.

Resources Required

To install NetWare 3.12 server, Novell recommends a *minimum* of 4 MB RAM for the NetWare 3.12 OS and drivers, 1 to 4 MB RAM for file caching, and 2 MB RAM for the NetWare loadable modules (NLMs) that perform file, print, routing, or system functions such as PSERVER.NLM, CLIB.NLM,

STREAMS.NLM, BTRIEVE.NLM, NetWare for Mac, or NetWare NFS. The required hard drive space is 75 MB; but you would want to use the server capability for file and print services, so a larger hard drive would be in order. NetWare servers with 32MB RAM and 600 MB to 1GB of hard drive space are not uncommon. NetWare 3.1x uses the file server's memory for many different functions and stores details such as user connection information, open and locked files, and NetWare loadable modules. By storing the directory information, the file allocation table (FAT), and most frequently used files in memory, NetWare reduces the number of disk reads, which increases the server speed.

Performance

The 386 CPU and small hard drive space requirement was minimal when compared to just about any other NOS of the day but as with any file server, more than adequate performance was achieved by installing more than the minimums.

As noted above, with the critical files loaded into memory, NetWare 3.1x is a fast network operating system for most uses and is reasonably well benchmarked. A 486/66 with 40 MB RAM and about 1 or 2 GB of hard drive space was considered to be quite a powerful machine and could support simple file and print services for a 75-to-100-user environment without difficulty.

Network Services

The network services to provide interoperability with other operating systems worked well. NLMs to support MAC, OS/2, and UNIX were available and, in larger environments, were depended upon to get the job done. Interoperability with a wide variety of network technologies, such as Ethernet, Token Ring, FDDI, and Mac, was easily achieved.

NetWare traffic considerations were improved through the use of packet burst mode which provides for a single read or write request for up to 64KB of data. This is built into NetWare 3.12 through the use of PBURST.NLM on the server and BNETX or VLM on the workstations.

Earlier network applications were monolithic, that is, they were written with the drivers incorporated for a particular network interface and protocol. This severely limited the use of an application to "standard" configurations. The introduction of the Novell Open Data-Link Interface (ODI™) driver specifications permitted multiple protocols to be bound to one NIC. The availability of support modules and the sharing of sample code sped the development and implementation of applications compliant with the ODI specification. Compliance with ODI sharply increased the number of applications available for network use because compliant applications didn't need to know about the network card at all but only had be able to comply with the standard.

Another item of interest is the MONITOR utility, which is a NetWare loadable module that provides a great deal of information about the health and status of the disk, LAN, and system modules as well as statistics on resource and processor utilization. The server memory statistics, for example, can be accessed through the resource utilization option in MONITOR. This shows the size of the server's memory pools, which derive their memory from file cache buffers.

Directory Services

The BINDERY is the central administration point in a NetWare 3.1x server. It contains a representation of users, groups, printers, and devices and permits the administrator to easily control them. This is where the database of user accounts that permits user authentication during logon is found. The limitation of the NetWare 3 bindery is that it only supports operation from a single NetWare server. This is called the *preferred server,* and it must be available for a user to log onto the network. A login script is used in conjunction with the user and group properties contained in the bindery this maintains consistency for the user. Once the user logs into the preferred server, a LOGIN script is run and the properties or preferences, such as mapped drives, become available.

Security Services

There are many levels of software security provided by NetWare. We will discuss only a few of the basic features. One place that NetWare implements its security is at the user level, which means that in order to access the shared resources of a NetWare server, there must be a defined user account on the server with a valid password and sufficient rights to the share. Any unauthorized access will be recorded in the error log, and the associated user account can be locked.

To prevent unauthorized access to the server console, there is a keyboard lock feature in the MONITOR utility program. A SECURE CONSOLE command can be used to prevent the loading of a "Trojan horse" module. SECURE CONSOLE can be included in the AUTOEXEC.NCF file as the last statement. It prevents the following:

- The use of DOS.
- NLMs from being loaded anywhere but SYS\SYSTEM, which is accessed by administrators *only*.
- Access to the operating system debugger, which prohibits remote boot and any change to the date and time.

The most effective security is to ensure that only authorized access is possible. Once you have booted the server, you can remove the keyboard and monitor and use the NetWare Remote Console (RCONSOLE) utility to remotely access the console screen. This can be enabled by loading the REMOTE and RSPX (or RS232) NLMs on the server.

Support for Hardware

As we mentioned earlier, Novell truly led the pack with support for a wide variety of hardware products behind the vanguard of the Novell Open Data-Link Interface (ODI™) driver specifications. Novell ODI support modules and sample source code were well received and encouraged vendors to build compliant products. Novell later introduced the *Yes, Tested and Approved*™ program, which meant that a product could receive the Novell *Yes* logo if it was designed and ran according to the specification.

We mentioned earlier that most hardware of the day was supported, and this was the chief selling point of NetWare in the era when proprietary hardware was everywhere. Certain hardware vendors started selling more equipment as their products became more standardized, which garnered more support for standardization. A great deal of improvement in LAN communication took place as a result of standardization, which actually sold more LAN equipment as it got easier to install, configure, and operate. Of particular note was the notion that NLMs need to be updated from time to time to take advantage of advances in software or to support newer hardware. (Although these patches or updates may be called by different names, such as service level patches, updates, or engineering changes, they are a central theme in all the NOS we will look at.)

Cross Operating System Support

By now, you have heard that NetWare 3.1x was a good NOS for its day and that it is still around. One of the reasons you are likely find NetWare 3.1x in place is because it is able to support interoperability with other operating systems. That is, support for connectivity with OS/2, Apple networks, and IBM SNA (using SAA) is all built into the NetWare server product, which could operate on Ethernet, AppleTalk, Token Ring, and IBM SNA networks. These features were not trivial, and they are still important today because getting to the place where the data is stored is imperative in most business scenarios.

Another interoperability tool, NetWare Connect, provides a capability for remote Windows 95/98, Windows 3.1, Mac OS, and DOS users to dial into NetWare networks to access network resources.

Novell NetWare 4.1

New product features in NetWare 4 added functionality to make it another excellent product. With NetWare 4, file system improvements include automatic file compression, block suballocation, NetWare peripheral architecture support, and extended storage capacity. With file compression, NetWare 4 can compress user files as they are saved to a server's hard drive to make more efficient use of the server's disk space. (File compression won't save any network traffic because the data is compressed when it gets to the hard drive and expanded when it is read from the hard drive, not while in transit.)

Block suballocation permits the part of a file that exceeds a volume's default block size to share a disk block with another file or files. Data is written to hard drives in blocks; and, by being able to more closely control the size of the block, NetWare can make more efficient use of the hard drive.

NetWare peripheral architecture (NWPA) provided a wider variety of drivers for host adapters and connected hardware devices such as the newer standards of peripheral component interconnect (PCI) and PCMCIA, now simply called PC Card.

NWPA separates NetWare driver support into two components: a host adapter module (HAM) and a custom device module (CDM). The HAM drives the host adapter hardware (bus). The CDM drives hardware devices attached to a host adapter bus. The advantage to this modular approach is that NWPA is better designed for scalability and the CDMs enable hardware autodetection. If you wanted to add a new hardware device to the host bus adapter, you would only need to load the appropriate HAM. NWPA.NLM is automatically loaded and the computer is scanned for new devices. If a new device is found, the appropriate CDM is loaded.

Although we don't have sufficient space to cover every detail of every operating system, it is useful to know how utilities change between versions. Table 2.1 shows the utilities that have been consolidated from version 3.11 to NetWare 4.

When the NetWare 4.11 package was released, Novell decided to call it *IntranetWare.* The thought was to capture the Internet craze that was sweeping the country. The release included a Web Server, FTP Server, an IPX to IP

Table 2.1 *Lineage of NetWare Utilities Between Versions 3.11 and 4.1x*

NetWare 3.11	NetWare 4.1x
BINDFIX, BINDREST	DSREPAIR
FCONSOLE	MONITOR
NBACKUP	SBACKUP
RCONSOLE, ACONSOLE	RCONSOLE

gateway, and many other enhancements to NetWare. While this might have seemed like a good thing from the marketing standpoint, changing the product name may not have helped as much as expected and actually created some confusion with LAN Administrators. The product name reverted to *NetWare* with the release of version 5.

The most significant difference between NetWare 3.x and NetWare 4 is the use of NetWare directory services (NDS). NDS provides a distributed database containing records for users, groups, and network resources such as printers, servers, and volumes. NDS keeps the information in a hierarchical tree structure, independent of the physical location of any of the objects. This permits users to access any network service without having to know the physical location of the server providing the service. NDS replaces the bindery, which required a system database in NetWare 3.x for each server.

Novell improved NetWare installation a great deal by allowing the installation utility to automatically detect the server's hardware devices (such as the CPU, RAM, hard disk drive, CD-ROM drives, LAN cards and so on). Once hardware devices are detected, the installation scans for the applicable device drivers, which are .dsk and .ham files, and selects the appropriate driver for the specific hardware identified. This type of automated setup is what LAN administrators had been asking for and was a welcome change from the lengthy setup that required a nontrivial amount of machine watching.

Another feature released with NetWare 4.11, Storage Management Services (SMS), introduced improved backup capability with SBACKUP. This utility permits creation of session files from tape, allows for the searching of log files for specific character strings, and shows a running count of up to 4.2 terabytes of data as it is backed up (previous versions went only to 4.2 GB). NDS target service agents (TSAs) for Windows 95, Windows NT, and Macintosh permit backup of information that resides on those client machines.

NetWare 4.11 includes improved extended name space support for Windows 95, Windows NT, and OS/2 workstation platforms using NetWare Volumes. This is accomplished through the use of the LONG.NAM NLM, which is loaded as part of the default server configuration. LONG.NAM is a special type of NLM that enables non-DOS filenames. In previous versions of NetWare 4, the OS/2 name space was supported by OS2.NAM, which is replaced by LONG.NAM in NetWare 4.11.

Resources Required

NetWare 4 can run with a minimal amount of RAM, but a good starting point is 64 MB for most environments with 20 to 30 users requiring only file and print support. If you have more users or expect to add services or applications, your environment would likely benefit from additional efforts of LAN planning. In fact, unless otherwise indicated, it is a good idea to have extra memory installed in advance as requirements tend to grow not shrink. Like its predecessor, NetWare 4 will run on an 80386 machine but will benefit from a more powerful computer. Installation requires at least 105 MB of hard-drive space.

Performance

NetWare 4.1x and NetWare 4.1x SMP (the SMP variant provides support for multiple processors) both provide excellent file, print, and application server performance on the LAN. If you start adding services or running applications on the server, however, you will need to go beyond Novell's minimal hardware recommendations and add resources such as more RAM and more processing power to retain the desired performance.

One of the most important performance improvements is in the way the product responds to server crashes (known in the Novell world as an *abnormal end* or *ABEND*). In NetWare 4.11, additional information about the source is displayed on the server console and automatically written to a text file called ABEND.LOG, which is initially written to the DOS partition. This information identifies the NLM or hardware problem to permit the LAN administrator to take quick corrective action. There is also the capability to permit "Auto Restart After Abend." This enables the server to automatically reboot after experiencing a crash. The feature is enabled by default.

Fault Tolerance Support

Support for a redundant array of inexpensive disks (RAID) and server fault tolerance (SFT) is built into the NetWare 4.1x products. (We will cover both RAID and fault tolerance more thoroughly in Chapter 10.) As the name implies, RAID features the use of multiple disks on which some or all of the data is stored redundantly—if a single disk is lost, the data is still available elsewhere in the array.

Three levels of server fault tolerance are supported by NetWare 4:

- SFT I–Duplicate copies of FAT and DET, read after write verification, hot fixing (also called sector sparing)
- SFT II–Mirrored/duplexed disks
- SFT III–Mirrored servers

SFT I combines three items. The NetWare operating system creates and provides a second copy of the File Allocation Table (FAT) and the Directory Entry Table (DET). *Read after write verification* is used to ensure each block of data written to a disk is properly stored. If the verification fails, the block is assumed to be a bad block, which causes the *hot fix* process to establish a hot fix redirection area.

SFT II provides additional protection against loss of data through the creation of a disk mirror. This makes a copy of the entire contents of a primary disk on a secondary drive. *Disk duplexing* adds a disk controller for each mirrored drive to provide additional redundancy.

SFT III costs the most but is often used in large organizations that require higher reliability numbers than the standard server would offer. This features the use of two servers connected through a shared small computer system interface (SCSI) bus. The two machines share name space; and, if a failure occurs, the standby server accepts the full responsibility for operation. This requires special hardware, and you should consult the IBM, Compaq®, Dell®, Hewlett-Packard®, or other hardware vendor for their implementation.

NetWare 4.11 also provides the NetWare Symmetric Multiprocessing (SMP) technology, which enables the NOS to use a multiprocessor computer. NetWare SMP runs resource-intensive services, such as large databases, document management software, and multimedia applications on a NetWare server. Depending on the hardware platform, SMP can take advantage of the increased processing power of up to 32 processors. Most hardware vendors currently offer multiprocessor models. The IBM 720, for example, provides support for up to six processors while models in the IBM 500 series support up to four.

NetWare Symmetric Multiprocessing (SMP) software support includes multiprocessing-enabled NetWare and third-party NLM programs that are specifically written to support multiprocessors. These can take advantage of the increased processing power available with SMP servers from IBM, Compaq, HP, and others. NetWare SMP will also allow LAN interrupts to be distributed across the multiple processors which improves performance and permits the routing of multiple segments. During the installation or upgrade of NetWare 4.11, the process automatically determines whether your server contains multiple processors. If it does, you are given the option of installing NetWare SMP. If you choose not to install SMP during the installation, it can be installed at a later time.

SMP applications are written to permit their threads of execution to run across all the processors in the server. When software that is not SMP capable runs, its threads are executed on processor 0 just as they would be in a uniprocessor (single-processor) system. Since multithreaded processes are split among the additional processors, additional processing time is available on processor 0 for nonmultithreaded processes.

NetWare 4.11 also provides support for advanced programmable interrupt controllers (APICs). This function ensures that if any processor (except processor 0) fails, the server will continue to function. This permits the loading and unloading of APIC processors without bringing the server down.

Network Services

The network services that provided interoperability with other operating systems in previous NetWare versions worked well. Under NetWare 4.1x they continued to be improved and expanded. Support is available for MAC, OS/2, and Unix, DHCP Server service (we will cover DHCP in Chapter 6) and NetWare-to-Unix printing. Under this version, large internet packets (LIP) can be sent, which means support for packets over 512 bytes is built in and will function with routers that support LIP.

The MONITOR utility provides the same robust support found in Version 3.

Directory Services

Novell Directory Services (NDS) is the information database in both NetWare 4 and 5 that organizes the network resources such as users, groups, printers, servers, volumes, and all of the other physical network devices into an easy to use, hierarchical tree structure that operates as a name service.

The Directory Services feature replaces the NetWare 3 bindery with greatly enhanced support. You will remember the bindery was able to support only a single server.

NDS, on the other hand, can support the entire enterprise. NDS is separated into compartments as a distributed database. These compartments are called partitions and can be distributed across many servers through a process called replication. In this way, NDS provides increased reliability and accessibility because the information is stored across many computers instead of being held in a single computer. The process that maintains the consistency of information is called the *replica synchronization process.* Replica synchronization involves updates to all of the replicas (replicated databases) for a specific partition, which includes all of the changes that have been made to the partition since the last synchronization cycle.

Security Services

Enhanced security is introduced in NetWare 4.11, which is designed to meet the Controlled Access implementation (Class C2) requirements of the Trusted Network Interpretation (NCSC-TG-005) of the Trusted Computer System Evaluation Criteria (DoD5200.28-STD). While this sounds exciting and very secretive, it is actually an open criteria that has been used by the National Security Agency for years to evaluate whether a site, server, or system is "trusted." (We will talk more about some of these security concepts in Chapter 9.)

NetWare provides several features that work together to provide enhanced security including the following:

- AUDITCON, which is a utility that provides C2 compliant auditing
- Audit Log files which are represented and managed as Directory objects
- Enable SECURE.NCF SET parameter, which enables the server to be set at boot time as an Enhanced NetWare Server or launched from the console at any time after boot.

Support for Hardware

During the installation of a NetWare 4.11 server, the Install utility will automatically detect hardware devices in a server, including hard disks, CD-ROM drives, LAN cards, and so on. It will then scan for and select the appropriate device drivers such as the .DSK and .HAM files for the hardware it has found. In rare cases, the installation might not automatically detect a particular device. When this occurs, the appropriate device driver(s) may be loaded manually.

Wizardry

A wizard is a piece of software that asks questions to which you supply the answers. The outcome is a configured application, server, or client. Because of wizards, the NetWare 4 server installation is much more user friendly than under previous versions. Installation requires less intervention, and screens that require information are easy to read and deal with. Prompts have been designed to make data entry quick and nearly painless.

Novell NetWare Version 5

NetWare 5 is Novell's latest network server software. It provides a LAN-to-Internet interface, superior management tools for a heterogeneous network with a mixed protocol environment, and excellent support capability for a diverse group of desktop clients. It is fast, secure, and easier to use than previous versions. It scales to large environments fairly easily and provides the LAN administrator with proven performance. Version 5 supports mixed environments of version 4.1 and 5 servers in the same network and supports communications with most other NOSs. While it might seem like a laundry list, the NetWare connectivity listing is another feature of a good NOS:

- Windows NT (workstation and server)
- Windows 95/98
- Mac OS
- VMS
- OS/400
- Unix
- OS/2

If, for instance, you were looking at the NetWare server across the network while seated at a Macintosh client machine, the NetWare server would look just like another Macintosh server.

Resources Required

The resources required for installing NetWare 5 are as follows:

- Pentium-level 100 MHz or greater processor
- 64 MB of RAM
- The SYS volume should be at least 550 MB
- The DOS partition should be at least 50 MB with sufficient space for creating a core dump for technical support.

If you plan to install other products, you will need to increase the resources accordingly:

- Use at least 128MB of RAM and provide a few extra gigabytes of storage space depending on the function of the server.

- Use 1998 or newer ODI compliant network cards and run the certified NetWare 5 LAN drivers that are bundled with the server software.
- Ensure the NetWare Loadable Modules are kept current to avoid problems associated with outdated software. (You can view the list of patches on the Novell Web site: www.novell.com.)

Warning

With the implementation of the Virtual Memory feature in NetWare 5, LAN drivers that assume that logical addresses are equal to physical addresses can cause intermittent data corruption. This issue is most likely to manifest itself in DMA adapters certified before November 1, 1997.

Performance

Novell NetWare has always had a reputation as an excellent file and print server platform with support for a variety of applications and clients. NetWare 5 maintains this distinction and provides support for many of the latest applications (such as Netscape FastTrack, Web Server, and the Oracle 8 Database).

Network Services

A new feature in this newest release of NetWare is *ConsoleOne,* which is a Java utility that provides for managing and administering network resources. It can run on either a NetWare 5 server or a NetWare 5 client workstation (Windows 95 or NT) and can be started from the server command prompt, the GUI, or from a client workstation with a drive mapping to the SYS volume. A Pentium 200 class machine with at least 128MB of RAM is recommended to run ConsoleOne.

A second tool is an updated version of ManageWise®, which is an open platform management solution, based on the simple network management protocol standard. This tool permits the system administrator to accomplish management tasks from a single point of administration, including NDS monitoring, NetWare and Windows NT server management, network traffic analysis, desktop management, software distribution, virus protection, network inventory, and network health reporting. A ManageWise Agent™ for Windows NT server exists and it is capable of managing NetWare and NT servers and Windows 95/98 desktop clients. The tool works on Ethernet,

Fast Ethernet, Token Ring, and FDDI segments and functions under both IP and IPX protocols.

Another management tool, ZENworks™ 2, is an enhanced version of Novell's directory-based management solution for Microsoft Windows' desktops. This provides for desktop management through the use of customized individual user profiles. The feature permits central administration for large network environments and permits each user access to their personal desktop from anywhere on the network.

Directory Services

NetWare Directory Services appears able to handle about a half-billion objects, and tracks not only devices and user names, but also routers, security, applications and switches. NDS 8 is Novell's next generation directory service for NetWare 5. NDS 8 features a new larger data store that allows NDS 8 to accommodate millions of objects in a directory tree.

NDS works best with time synchronization configured correctly but will work without synchronized time. Partition operations such as split, join, change type, add, remove, and such are sensitive to proper time synchronization, which is important in an enterprise environment.

Security Services

Security features protect network and local resources, and the Version 5 NOS does a good job of it. New features include discretionary access controls, memory protection, auditing, and mandatory login to access network resources. NetWare 5 has a graphical secure console utility to keep unauthorized users from accessing the GUI *servertop*.

As with any utility that provides local security, the use of the secure console utility does not preclude someone from doing physical damage to the server. You should always place servers in an area that is physically inaccessible to the general public.

The standard network security services that are provided include user, group, port, and service-level access security. There are security provisions for both network and remote access security. These provisions permit restrictions on network or remote users based on privilege, time, group membership, or other factors. (Remote access is a feature that permits users to join a network over telephone lines or other WAN carriers. We will thoroughly discuss this networking concept in Chapter 8.) Remote access third-party security products that implement token-based challenge/response security through the use of additional hardware and software are available from a number of different vendors. The hardware components are installed between the remote access port and the modem, and any configured security for a service is applied to the call before the session is established. These security providers increase assurance that unauthorized users are not getting into the network. Remote access security includes the following defaults:

- All users have access to all services and ports.
- All services have access to all ports at all times.
- Users can remain connected for an unlimited amount of time.
- User sessions can remain idle for an unlimited amount of time.
- Users can dial out to any number.
- There are no restrictions on defining remote client passwords.
- After the remote client establishes a connection, it must log into the NetWare network. The system does not prompt for a NetWare login until the user runs the login command.

As an administrator, you can customize the level of security for remote access clients by restricting

- Users from accessing certain ports
- Users from accessing specific services
- Ports to a particular service for a specified time

Study Break

Cryptography

No discussion about security would be complete without a discussion of cryptography, which is the ciphering, or encoding and decoding of data so that sensitive information remains protected from view or use by anyone who does not have the proper authority. Cryptography is used to implement the NetWare 5 security services. United States export and local government regulations control this cryptography. The cryptographic services are provided in at least three NetWare 5 editions, which are U.S./Canada, World Wide, and Null. The World Wide edition supports only the permissible strength of cryptography that can be exported from the U.S. (for example, 40-bit). The U.S./Canada version provides the stronger 128-bit cryptography. If you have the Null edition, the Cryptography Security Services will not be available and IP packet signing will be disabled.

Support for Hardware

In addition to the comprehensive hardware support found in previous versions, NetWare 5 includes support for the new I20 standard[1] as well as updated support for mass storage systems, RAID devices, CD ROM and so on.

Wizardry

New installation wizards allow the NetWare 5 to proceed with much less intervention than ever before and provides easy access screens that have prompts for entering information. In addition, the release notes for the Novell Upgrade Wizard are easily installed from the CD-ROM installation set.

Cross Operating Systems Support

As in previous releases, support for Unix, Apple, IBM SNA with SAA, and OS/2 and long file names is present. While the IPX protocol remains as the default protocol, for more standard use with other operating systems, you can set the TCP/IP protocol to load first by issuing the following command:

```
SET NCP Protocol Preferences = TCP IPX
```

Microsoft Windows NT Server 4.0

The Microsoft Windows family includes Windows 3.x, Windows 95, Windows 98, Windows NT (New Technology) Workstation, Windows NT Server and Windows NT Server (Enterprise Edition). The original Windows was not a network operating system until the addition of the networking components in Windows for Workgroups version 3.11. Windows NT version 3.1 was released as Microsoft's first 32-bit operating system, and Windows 95 followed soon after. According to Microsoft, Windows 98 represents the last release of the Windows 9x line. Future Microsoft OS releases will feature Windows NT architecture and will be the Windows 200x product line. This section will concentrate on Windows NT server software. We will cover Windows NT Workstation later in the *client* section.

The Windows NT Server 4.0 software optimizes network server as a scaleable file, print, and application server. Because the interface is the familiar Windows interface already installed on many home and office desktops,

---

[1]The I20 standard provides intelligent input/output (I/O) over a fiber channel. This technology uses a dedicated processor with its own memory to lighten the CPU's I/O load.

this NOS is easy to learn and use, sharply reducing the time and effort required to train new users and administrators.

Windows NT Server 4.0 has been developed with support for Intel 80486, Pentium, and Pentium Pro computers. In addition, reduced instruction set computing (RISC) based computers, such as MIPS R4x00, DEC Alpha AXP, and PreP-Compliant PowerPC-based systems, are supported. Multiprocessor support is built into Windows NT for all of these platforms.

Microsoft SNA Server is a gateway application that runs on Windows NT Server. It allows a Microsoft client (such as Windows 95 or Windows 98) that is using a standard terminal emulation package to emulate the 3270 or 5250 terminal. This permits the Microsoft client to connect via the SNA server gateway directly to an IBM midrange (such as an AS/400) or mainframe computer.

Resources Required

Microsoft Windows NT Server can run with as little of 16MB of RAM on a 486DX/33 or higher microprocessor and at least 125MB of hard drive space. If you want to use this operating system in the way it was intended, you will definitely want a much more powerful computer and the additional resources to support the environment you are designing.

Installation

A major selling feature of Windows NT rests with its ease of installation, configuration, and maintenance. You can get the NOS up and running with a full selection of connectivity and fault tolerant services in about an hour's time. With a little fine tuning similar to what you do with other NOS, the server can be tuned to your exacting specifications and can work for years without any need to go back and tinker.

Configuration is dependent on how sophisticated you want to get; but for the most part, the easy-to-use graphical interface replaces the bulk of command prompt configuration changes with ICONS that are easy to use and understand.

Maintenance is rare unless you absolutely must add service packs[2]. If you are experiencing any difficulties with Windows NT Server, check the Microsoft Web Site or TechNet CD to start.

---

[2]Service pack installation should be done with caution. Service packs are generally issued by Microsoft to repair problems that have been experienced in some implementations or with some applications. Experience with service packs shows, however, that if you don't have any problems, don't look for solutions. If, on the other hand, you are experiencing a problem the pack is designed to correct or could benefit from an advertised feature of the service pack, back up your system and add the pack.

Performance

Analogous to oil in an automobile, RAM helps make your computer run smoothly and efficiently. A Microsoft Windows NT Server should, like other NOS in this class, use about 64MB of RAM for starters and go up from there. Microsoft Windows NT Server 4.0 is tuned as a file, print, and application server. The retail version of the product supports up to four processors in a symmetric multiprocessing environment. Original equipment manufacturers' (OEM) implementations of Windows NT Server support up to 32 processors. Some of those manufacturers include ACER, Compaq, Dell, IBM, NCR, Sequent, and WYSE.

With the appropriate amount of memory, Microsoft Windows NT Server can provide exceptional network, remote access services (RAS), and application performance. Even with less memory, it can provide good performance through the use of a virtual memory manager. The virtual memory manager can relocate applications anywhere within the machine's 32-bit flat memory address space[3] to increase efficiency. It can even write portions of RAM to disk (to a file called *pagefile.sys*) to "create" additional memory when the machine runs low on RAM. (There is, of course, an attendant penalty when this feature functions since the disk time required to access pagefile.sys is significantly greater than that required to access data in RAM. Although virtual memory makes Windows NT a very robust operating system, it is always better to add more physical memory than to consistently depend on significant amounts of virtual memory.) This feature permits users to run more applications at one time than could otherwise be run.

Fault Tolerance Support

Fault tolerance is built into the Windows NT server by way of support for RAID 1 (mirroring) and RAID 5 (stripe set with parity). (We will cover these fault tolerance methods is some detail in Chapter 10.) This is a *software* implementation, which is not as fast as corresponding hardware RAIDs. Software RAID requires a nontrivial measure of CPU time to support it—a factor that will impact other applications on the system. The built-in software RAID is, however, available at no additional cost and can be set up quickly and easily.

---

[3]This is just a fancy way of saying the memory is wide open. In other words, the memory is not segmented into smaller pieces but is fully accessible to the operating system.

Network Services

Windows NT Server features a plethora of network services that are both interesting and useful. This section will outline some of those services to acquaint you with how to work with Windows NT in the many environments it is capable of supporting. Through its network services, Windows NT server can provide support to other operating systems such as Novell, Macintosh, and UNIX.

At the core of the Windows NT network services, we find the Network Driver Interface Specification (NDIS) discussed in Chapter 1. Windows NT 4.0 uses the NDIS 4.0, which is both a driver library and a driver wrapper, which serves to isolate the driver from both the protocol and network card. Keeping the network adapter cards and corresponding drivers independent from one another permits smooth transition from one protocol to another and does not require a reconfiguration of network adapter cards when a protocol is changed.

Protocols

The most significant protocols supported by Windows NT Server 4.0 include the following:

- TCP/IP—The default and most widely used protocol. This permits interoperability with Unix systems and the Internet.
- NWLink—The 100% NDIS 4.0 compatible version of IPX/SPX and the protocol that permits communications with Novel NetBIOS IPX/SPX, MS-DOS, OS/2, Windows, or Windows NT.
- NetBEUI—The fast and non-routable protocol used for LAN operations and interoperability with LAN Manager, IBM LAN Server, Windows 95, and Windows for Workgroups.
- AppleTalk—Used with services for Macintosh to permit connections to and from Macintosh clients.
- DLC—Data Link Control is used to connect to network printers such as Hewlett-Packard printers with jet direct cards or as a tool to connect with systems network architecture (SNA) IBM mainframe computers.

Microsoft Windows NT Server Services

In addition to the protocols, which are used for interoperability, there are a variety of standard services along with some specialized services that can be added during or after system installation.

An example of some of these services includes the following:

- Computer Browser
- DHCP Relay Agent
- Microsoft DHCP Server
- Microsoft DNS Server
- Gateway (and Client) Service for NetWare
- Microsoft Internet Information Server 2.0
- Microsoft TCP/IP Printing
- NetBIOS Interface
- NETLOGON
- Network Monitor Agent
- Network Monitor Tools and Agent
- Remote Access Service
- Remoteboot Service
- RIP for Internet Protocol
- RIP for NWLink IPX/SPX compatible protocol
- RPC Configuration
- RPC Support for Banyan
- SAP Agent
- Server
- Services for Macintosh
- Simple TCP/IP Services
- SNMP Service
- Windows Internet Name Service
- Workstation

COMPUTER BROWSER • The Computer Browser Service continually collects information about resources (e.g. computers, shared directories, and printers) available on the network. This information is displayed through the Windows *Network Neighborhood* icon as well as through a myriad of Windows-based applications. The information displayed is the current browse list.

DHCP • Dynamic Host Configuration Protocol (DHCP) service permits automatic assignment of the IP address and a host of other TCP/IP configuration information. We will look at DHCP in greater detail in Chapter 6.

DNS • The domain name system, (DNS), is a distributed database method to provide a hierarchical naming system for identification of hosts on the Internet. This is the system that permits mapping, for example of a uniform resource locator (URL) such as www.alidatrain.com, to an IP address. The Windows NT version of DNS server is fully graphic user interface (GUI) based, making installation, configuration, and maintenance very easy. We will look more deeply into DNS in Chapter 6.

NETWORK MONITOR • Before any optimization or capacity planning can be done on the LAN, the administrator must know how much traffic is being generated. Analysis involves determining what effect each of the Windows NT services has on the network. The network monitor is a software tool that provides a significant amount of information on the network about the types of traffic, timing, sizing, and available bandwidth.

REMOTE ACCESS SERVICE • Clients, such as Windows 95/98 and Windows NT, can use dial-up networking to establish connectivity over telephone lines to the LAN. A Windows NT Server with RAS services installed can be configured to answer the dial-up networking calls and to make the dial-up client a member of the network. RAS can also be used to dial out to an Internet service provider or other WAN link to provide Internet or WAN access to the LAN. This is a functional equivalent to the NetWare Connect on NetWare networks—the NetWare server service that supports remote connectivity.

SERVICES FOR MACINTOSH • Services for Macintosh can provide access to a shared Windows NT directory for Macintosh clients. This shared directory can allow your Macintosh client computers to save work to that location. At the same time, the Windows 95/98 and Windows NT computers running on the LAN can view, access, and modify the saved documents through the use of a standard drive mapping to the same shared directory.

SERVICES FOR NETWARE INTEGRATION • Microsoft Windows NT Server, 4.0 has a very solid set of integration and connectivity services for NetWare products.

- Client services for NetWare permit any Windows NT server or workstation computer running the NWLink protocol to connect to a NetWare server.
- Gateway services for NetWare may be installed on a Windows NT server along with the NWLink protocol to permit it to operate as a gateway to a NetWare server for any client that can connect to the Windows NT server. Clients of the Windows NT server need not run

any special hardware or software but only need to be able to connect to the Windows NT gateway. This gateway is not intended to be a high-volume or high-performance gateway but is designed for occasional use by a few clients.

- File and Print Services for NetWare is a product, available at extra cost, which, when loaded on the Windows NT server, enables NetWare clients to access file and print services on the Windows NT server. This feature requires no additional client hardware or software.

- Directory Service Manager for NetWare is a product, available at extra cost, that permits management of the NetWare 2.x, 3.x and 4.x (using bindery emulation) environments. Management of NetWare users, groups, account information, and migration of that information to a Microsoft Windows NT server is all possible.

Directory Services

Microsoft Windows NT Server 4.0 provides a secure, distributed directory database and services for end users and network administrators through the use of NT directory services (NTDS). Windows NT operates on the concept of a *domain*. A domain is a logical grouping of computers that share common user and computer account information. Through Windows NT directory services, domain users may be granted access to resources anywhere in the domain through only a single user account in the security accounts manager (SAM) database. The first machine installed in a domain is installed as a primary domain controller (PDC). The PDC maintains the master copy of the SAM database. Each domain may also contain one or more backup domain controllers (BDC). The SAM database is periodically replicated to the BDC(s) to provide load balancing and fault tolerance. When users attempt to log onto a domain, their logon may be handled by the PDC or one of the BDCs.

Microsoft Windows 2000 Server

Windows 2000 is a multi-threaded, multi-tasking, multi-purpose operating system that represents the next generation of Windows NT. This server is reliable and features enhanced security. Because it maintains the same look and feel of the familiar Windows interface, it remains quite easy to install, implement, manage, and use.

Resources Required

Like Windows NT 4.0, Windows 2000 supports multiple platforms such as the 32-bit x86, and DIGITAL Alpha. The minimum requirements should be compared to the real world the same way a thimble of gasoline and the purchase of a new red FERRARI can be compared. If you want to see your performance improve, give it more gas! In this case, the gas is equal to the amount of RAM, the number and speed of the processor(s), and the amount of hard disk space.

The Windows 2000 Server product will run on a Pentium 133 or Digital Alpha computer. The x86 version requires 64MB RAM while 96MB RAM is needed for the Digital Alpha. The client product (Windows 2000 Professional) will run on a 66Mhz 80486-class machine with 32MB RAM. A similar class of Digital Alpha will require 48MB RAM. The server requires 510MB hard drive space on x86 and 630MB for Digital Alpha. The client requires 470MB hard drive space on x86 and 590MB for Digital Alpha computers. VGA video support is required and a CD-ROM is recommended (unless a network installation is used, which requires a NOS already be operational on the installation target).

Performance

Enhanced performance is possible through the use of 64-bit memory addressing. Current Intel CPUs such as the Pentium Pro and Pentium II do not offer 64-bit memory addressing. Thus they cannot support memory in excess of 4GB, known as very large memory (VLM).

The Windows 2000 Enterprise Edition provides access to VLM on systems that use the 64-bit Digital Alpha CPU. The purpose of VLM is to support applications that deal with large amounts of data such as databases. VLM can result in significant performance gains for these applications.

A new feature in Windows 2000 is *disk quotas*. Disk quotas can be set up to limit the utilization of disk space on a per-user basis. [The use of disk quotas is possible only on partitions formatted under the proprietary New Technology File System version 2000 (NTFS2000).]

Fault Tolerance Support

Previous levels of fault tolerance support remain in Windows 2000 but the Distributed File System (DFS 2000) brings new capabilities. DFS 2000 replicates shared information to other participating servers. Should one of these shares become unavailable, Windows 2000 Active Directory Services (which we will discuss shortly) automatically locates the desired information from one of the other replicated shares.

Network Services

Windows 2000 provides a dynamic DNS name server, compliant with open Internet standards, that reduces the need for manual edits. It replicates the DNS database each time a change occurs in a DNS client's configuration.

Windows 2000 provides for efficient bandwidth use through quality of service (QoS) standards that reserve bandwidth and establish priority for transmission of data for QoS compliant applications.

The routing and remote access service (RRAS) permits routing over IP and IPX networks on LANs and WANs. Support for asynchronous transfer mode networking is built into Windows 2000. This enables voice, data, and video transmission over LANs, WANs, and the Internet.

Directory Services

Windows 2000 Active Directory stores information about all objects on the computer network and makes this information easy for administrators, developers, and users to find and use. The use of Active Directory provides a consistent set of interfaces for performing common administrative tasks, such as adding new users, managing printers, and locating resources throughout a distributed computing environment. Active Directory automatically installs DNS, which integrates the network with the Internet and uses Internet domain names. In fact, under Windows 2000, Windows domain names and Internet domain names are the same (this eliminates a significant point of confusion found in Windows 2000 predecessors). Active Directory services and DNS also support the universal naming convention (UNC) used in Windows NT server-based networks to refer to shared volumes, printers, and files. A user can refer to a shared file published in the Active Directory by a UNC name, for example;

```
\\alidatrain.com\product.Sys.DocVol\Word\BigContract.doc
```

The Windows 2000 Active Directory Services maintain directory information in a hierarchical database (distinct from the earlier flat directory services database) and eliminate the distinction between primary domain controllers and backup domain controllers. Under the Active Directory all domain controllers (DC) are peers. A change to any DC is automatically replicated to the others.

Another important directory-related functionality is found in the Microsoft Directory Service Migration Tool. This permits discovery, offline modeling, and migration of NetWare resources such as users, groups, and data to the Windows 2000 Active Directory from both Bindery- and NDS-based NetWare systems.

Security Services

Unlike its predecessors, Windows 2000 security is based on the Kerberos protocol. Kerberos is a well-known industry standard based on RFC1510. The combination of Active Directory services and Kerberos results in faster authentication and greater flexibility in accessing shared information across Windows 2000 domains while maintaining a high degree of security.

A new file encryption feature, available on NTFS2000-based files, provides protection for sensitive data. It can be enabled on a per-file or per-directory basis.

Support for Hardware

Windows 2000 supports plug and play, which makes it easy to install and troubleshoot new hardware. The plug and play support in Windows 2000 includes a new hardware wizard, the device manager, and improved support for laptops.

Built in fiber channel (FC) support provides high-speed data transfer between servers and storage devices for large volumes of information. The IEEE 1394 standard for high-speed peripheral interconnect offers simple connectivity combined with bandwidth for multimedia.

Wizardry

The Hardware Wizard has a new Win32® Device Manager Model (WDM) that enables new devices to have a single driver for both Windows NT and Windows 98. It makes device management easier and faster by consolidating commonly used hardware-related tools and functions into a single wizard.

The Windows 2000 Server Configuration Wizard simplifies configuration and provides an unattended setup feature to allow creation of the entire setup configuration before beginning a roll out. There are backup and restore wizards and the active directory has several wizard-like features to simplify directory services management.

UNIX

Today we are faced with a myriad of varieties of UNIX Operating Systems. UNIX predates most of the other operating systems currently in use. Over UNIX's rich history, vendors such as AT&T®, BSD, Cray®, Dec, HP, IBM, SUN®, and others have created different variants of the UNIX. These operating systems were designed to fit customer needs back when hardware and software were generally proprietary with very little cross-vendor applicability. Customers are still purchasing these products for their utility, strength, security, and fault tolerance. This continued popularity is notable in an era characterized by attractive, easy to use, GUI-based networking products.

Generally the UNIX OS can be put into classifications such as UNIX System V and Berkley Software Distribution (BSD). UNIX was originally developed by AT&T Bell Laboratories, but another variety, BSD UNIX, was quickly created and distributed at the University of California, Berkeley. Sun Microsystems had yet another version, which was merged with the AT&T version to become UNIX System V. System V became the "standard" UNIX system, but the standard failed to elicit the full support of all vendors resulting in today's plethora of variants.

UNIX administration has mostly required the use of a command prompt, which necessitates memorization of commands, switches, and the use of various complex command combinations. Installation, configuration, and interoperability can be challenging under many circumstances. There is now a common desktop environment (CDE), which provides a UNIX GUI. Although it is not always used by hard core UNIX administrators who have become accustomed to the command prompt, it is now accepted as an industry standard with a consistent end user look and feel from all major UNIX environments. CDE supports customization with multiple workspaces and a single supported applications programming interface (API) to which software developers may write. It is standards based and has an extensive online help system.

Sun Solaris

One of the UNIX variants, produced by Sun Microsystems, is known as Solaris. Although it has limited hardware support, Solaris' performance and scalability make it a NOS worth consideration for many heavy-duty tasks. The Sun product line is generally a high-end line with excellent network-computing environment support. Solaris is based on support for 64-bit chipset, mainframe-like reliability and binary compatibility with all Solaris

2.x releases on both SPARC and Intel processors. The SPARC platform is a high-power, yet versatile, workstation based on proprietary hardware.

In spite of its generally proprietary nature, Solaris enjoys a fair amount of interoperability. Products such as SunLink connect PC desktop clients to a Solaris server. Such products enable Solaris to act as a file, print, and applications server in an existing Apple Macintosh, Novell NetWare, or Microsoft Windows NT network. The Solaris Easy Access Server product makes it easy to set up and run Solaris systems in a Windows NT network.

Linux

Another UNIX variant, Linux, has not had the support necessary from the application community but has received widespread acceptance for Internet-based work and among hobbyists. Application vendors have a very difficult time trying to build applications to suit the wide variety of UNIX operating systems, but some vendors are starting to offer Linux support. Oracle®, for instance, has recently made an announcement to port a version of Oracle to Linux. Linux improvements, such as symmetric multiprocessing (SMP) capabilities in version 2.2, will demand that non-SMP applications be rewritten to take advantage of the new capability. Linux is a true workhorse, fully capable of tasks such as file and print services in a major network environment. Linux can be purchased in CD-ROM format or downloaded from a variety of sites (e.g., www.linux.org).

The Internet has always been a UNIX stronghold. The introduction of Linux with its *Apache Web Server*, has increased the popularity of UNIX for Web application making UNIX and Linux words common to most vocabularies.

UNIX Features and Functionality

Now that we have seen some of the UNIX variants, we will look at some generic UNIX features and functions

Resources

Historically, UNIX system requirements for both CPU and RAM have been consistently lower than other operating systems. These requirements are based on the kernel, the central part of the operating system, directly interacting with the hardware and a very light load from the console. As applications and operating systems become more robust and complex, requirements increase. As with the other operating systems we discussed, exceeding the minimum requirements is prudent and will provide much better support for applications and network operations. Since there are a multitude of UNIX versions in the world, it is impossible to provide a comprehensive list of UNIX hardware requirements. The following minimum criteria are for UnixWare 7, a current NOS product from Santa Cruz Operation (SCO), Inc.:

- Processor: 80486/DX (Pentium recommended)
- Hard drive space: 300MB
- RAM: 32MB (64MB when using common desktop environment)

Performance

UNIX delivers good performance on standard hardware and exceptional performance for mission-critical tasks with a multiprocessor kernel when fine tuned on vendor specific hardware.

Fault Tolerance Support

Sequent DYNIX, a UNIX variant, regularly sees implementations of 32 processors and a seemingly unending list of different RAID implementations. Many custom installations of this type are used for mission critical application operations such as large databases and enterprise processing.

Network Services

The TCP/IP protocol is the central focus for nearly all UNIX services. With the proliferation of Novell NetWare, Windows 95/98, and Windows NT, however, UNIX has benefited from support for other protocols, gateways, and services. Although most of these services started out as third-party, add-on products, many are now built into UNIX and are fully functional.

Directory Services

The UNIX-based Network Information System (NIS) is a network naming and administration system for smaller networks developed by Sun Microsystems. NIS+ is a later version that provides additional security and other facilities. Using NIS, each host, client, or server computer in the system has knowledge about the entire system. A user at any host can get access to files or applications on any other host in the network with a single user identification and password. Intended for use on local area networks, NIS is similar to the Internet's Domain Name System (DNS), but somewhat simpler and designed for a smaller network.

NIS uses the client/server model and remote procedure call (RPC) interface for communication between hosts. It consists of a server, a library of client programs, and some administrative tools. NIS is often used with the Network File System (NFS).

Although Sun and other vendors offer proprietary versions, most NIS code has been released into the public domain and there are a number of freeware versions available. NIS was originally called *Yellow Pages* but, because someone already had a trademark by that name, it was changed to Network Information System. It is, however, still sometimes referred to by the initials: "YP."

Sun offers NIS+ together with its NFS product as a solution for Windows PC networks as well as for its own workstation networks.

Security Services

Third-party products, such as SATAN, provide intelligent information about security holes and give recommended courses of action for repairs and updates. UNIX is one of the few operating systems with different varieties that have been documented under the *Trusted Computing Base* and the *Trusted Network Interpretation* as being secure.

Support for Hardware

Intel based computers have benefited from free copies of BSD Unix and several free iterations of Linux. Most of the UNIX operating systems built for specific proprietary hardware are complex and do not lend themselves to easy movement to other platforms or good operability with hardware from outside vendors. HP-UX is a proprietary UNIX operating system written for Hewlett Packard servers and workstations. IBM AIX is a proprietary UNIX operating system written for IBM RS6000 servers and workstations.

<hr>

Study Break

Software Base

Installed base is important, and in 1998 the Santa Cruz Operation (SCO) gave away free copies of Open Server (another UNIX variant) for nearly two months. FreeBSD is a free UNIX operating system available for Intel compatible computer platforms. In the user software arena, Sun has made a free copy of StarOffice available. This product is an office suite for UNIX, Windows, OS/2 and Macintosh that can exchange documents with Microsoft Office version 4.x.

IBM Operating System/2 (OS/2)

Microsoft and IBM created OS/2 in 1990 as a joint venture. The marriage lasted until code swapping stopped sometime between late 1992 and early 1993. It seems likely that IBM wanted OS/2 to be built to compete with Windows on MS-DOS and eliminate the need to use DOS and Windows altogether. As it was built and refined, OS/2 became a network operating system with excellent capabilities as a powerful desktop operating system or as an application or gateway server.

The latest version, OS/2 WARP, is a stable, robust NOS with interesting features that include a nice graphical interface and ability to support dual booting. It provides excellent support for 16-bit Windows programs and provides some 32-bit Windows support also.

Since OS/2 has greater resource requirements than the operating systems it was competing against, it did not attract as wide a following of software developers and never won a significant market share. What IBM and Microsoft set out to accomplish was, however, fairly well received. You will likely find OS/2 somewhere in the installed base of most large organizations. The NOS is frequently used, for example, as a gateway for older mail systems.

Clients

Network servers wouldn't do much good without network clients. We will start by discussing the Microsoft software that is most frequently used in client applications. The operating systems we will overview are able to operate in a Microsoft Windows NT 4.0 environment, as a client in a NetWare Bindery based or NDS environment, and as a peer or a client of most any other NOS with the appropriate protocol support.

After we have outlined some of the products that will get you on line, we will discuss how to connect to the server.

Microsoft Windows 95/98 and Windows NT 4.0 Workstation

Microsoft Windows 95, Windows 98, and Windows NT Workstation all support file and print services and perform exceptionally well as network clients. These products are tuned to support local applications and quick and efficient access to both local hard drives and network shares. Each product features a nearly identical graphical user interface to permit easy operation by inexperienced users while hiding the software's sophisticated architecture. (Windows NT Server can also perform as a client, but it is optimized for use as a server platform.)

Windows 95/98

Windows 95 and Windows 98 require less hardware support (RAM and disk space) than Windows NT and can best be used as desktop network clients or home user machines. These operating systems offer the best compatibility with and support for older MS-DOS applications and games that require direct access to the hardware. These are 32-bit operating systems with sharply improved stability over Microsoft Windows 3.x (the 16-bit version of Windows).

Both products include a user interface that provides the user with a clean desktop from which to operate. This GUI permits a standardized or customized appearance while hiding many administrative features (hidden, but easily accessible when required). The architecture is such that the networking components are built-in, not added on. The capability to use system policies for effective centralized security, combined with user and hardware profiles, remote administration and built-in backup make this an interesting OS. The dial-up networking, accessibility options, and support for a wide variety of legacy hardware and both DOS- and Windows-based software make this the client of choice in many situations.

Windows 95/98 offer such key networking features as follows:

- Support for infrared device drivers & applets
- Microsoft service for NetWare directory services
- Internet Explorer 3, NetMeeting, Internet Mail, Internet News and Personal Web Server, all designed for improved Internet connectivity and interoperability
- Supports for Java Script
- Multiple protocol support, which includes the ability to bind multiple network clients

The Windows 98 product also includes

- Modem sharing to permit more than one computer to share a single connection to the Internet.
- Web TV
- A media player, which permits you to view multimedia content as it is delivered over the Internet to your computer

Windows NT Workstation

Windows NT 4.0 Workstation is considered one of the most powerful 32-bit network operating systems in use today because it provides built-in support for multitasking, multithreading, and dual processor hardware. It has the ability to act as a remote access server (RAS) for one inbound session from another dial-up networking client and built-in support for multiple platforms such as X86 and RISC hardware. When the hard drive is formatted with the NTFS file system, local security is available and an account must be created on the local machine for every user if it is used outside of a Windows NT domain. The graphical user interface is the same as Windows 95/98, and the hardware requirements are only slightly above that for Windows 95/98.

Connecting to the Server

The Microsoft client software we have just covered will provide a great look and feel and will give you superior computing capability. There is, however, considerably more to the story. If you expect to connect to a particular type of server, you need two more pieces of software (assuming your networking hardware is connected and functioning properly): a *protocol* and a *redirector*.

To properly "talk" to the server, it is critical that your client use a network protocol the server will understand. You may remember, for example, that NetWare products typically use the IPX/SPX protocol while most Windows products and UNIX networks use TCP/IP. Whatever the protocol to be used, both client and server must both be configured to use it!

But wait! There's more! Even with the proper protocol in place, the client computer must have a *redirector* to properly communicate with the server. A redirector is the software that permits the client and server to communicate using the rules (protocol) the server understands. (You will remember we indicated in Chapter 1 that protocols are frequently transmitted over other protocols. To properly network, you need to get both the network protocol and the server protocol correct!) Windows NT, for instance, communicates via server message blocks (SMB) while NetWare uses the NetWare Core Protocol (NCP). We mentioned in Chapter 1 that computers can use multiple network cards and that network cards may use more than one protocol. In like manner, client computers may use multiple redirectors to access more than one type of network server.

Microsoft Redirectors

If you are going to access Windows NT servers from Windows NT workstations, you will find the redirector is already built in. The Windows NT redirector is called the Workstation Service, and it is running and waiting for you. Client services for NetWare is a redirector to permit your Windows NT client to connect to a NetWare server. Services are also available to connect the client to Banyan–Vines servers. If you are using a Windows 95/98 client, you must load the *Client for Microsoft Networks* to access a Windows NT server. Although this does not load automatically, it is available on the distribution disk and easily installed. There are also client services (redirectors) for Banyan–Vines and Novell networks.

Although Microsoft doesn't provide any software to permit clients using non-Microsoft operating systems to connect to Windows NT servers, services for Macintosh and file and print services for NetWare may be loaded on a Windows NT server to allow clients from these networks to connect to the Windows NT server.

NetWare Redirectors

Although the Microsoft client operating systems come with a host of redirectors, these products are available from the network system vendors also. The product was originally named Client32 for DOS, Windows 3.x, Windows 95, and Windows NT, but later versions are simply called Novell Client for Windows 3.x (includes DOS), Windows 95/98, and Windows NT. This 32-bit package is capable of supporting TCP/IP and has been available as a free download from several places on the Internet for quite some time. The Client32 permits manual or automatic assignment of TCP/IP address, enables the use of TCP/IP utilities such as ftp and telnet, and comes with a desktop SNMP agent. NetWare redirectors may also be obtained for Macintosh and OS/2 clients.

UNIX Redirectors

Although many proprietary UNIX installations operate with dumb terminals, client software is also used for UNIX access. In working with UNIX clients and servers, we find the network file system (NFS), which is a client/server application that lets a computer user view and optionally store and update files on a remote computer as though they were on the user's own computer. In order for this to work, the user computer must have the NFS client and the server needs to have the corresponding NFS server software loaded and running.

Both systems are also required to have TCP/IP properly installed. NFS can be installed on Windows 95/98, Windows NT, and some other operating systems using products such as Sun's Solstice Network Client.

DOS Support

What if we didn't have any of the fancy network client systems we discussed? How could we access a network through DOS? DOS is *not* a network operating system all by itself, so client software such as NETX in the NetWare environment or MS-Network Client in the Microsoft environment needs to be added with the correct drivers for the network card and the correct protocol. It is some amount of work to configure a standard DOS computer with the proper drivers for either NetWare or Microsoft client connections. The proper configuration requires a shell created as a terminate and stay resident (TSR) program that needs a fair amount of memory. This shell is the set of commands that permit using the network functionality such as mapping drives, using printers, and such. The NETX shell, for instance, is a typical network configuration used with DOS or more likely with Windows 3.x to access NetWare products.

Summary

In this chapter we provided an overview of the major network operating systems in use today. We looked at the three latest versions of Novell NetWare to find an excellent network operating system with good directory services, an easy-to-use interface, and a wide degree of acceptance in the marketplace. We found the chief difference between NetWare 3.x and 4.x was in how their directory services were configured. NetWare 3.x servers featured the *bindery*. This central administration point contained the database used to authenticate users and track groups, printers, and other devices. Because the bindery is machine specific, the designated logon server (the preferred server), must be available when users attempt to log onto the network.

NetWare 4.x and later features a distributed directory database that is synchronized among NetWare servers. Any machine with an appropriate directory services database is able to authenticate users.

Next, we turned our attention to Windows NT 4.0. Similar to later versions of NetWare, we found Windows NT Server 4.0 to be a GUI-based product. Like NetWare, Windows NT is a high-performance operating system with excellent hardware support and a very good set of fault tolerant features.

Windows NT directory services are based on the Windows NT *Domain*. This logical grouping of computers permitted users and groups to store authentication information on a central server.

Windows 2000 is the follow on to Windows NT. Although both products are similar, Windows 2000 features active directory services. The active directory functions with an automated domain name system (DNS) server that makes Windows 2000 domains look like Internet domains. In another departure from its predecessors, Windows 2000 features security based on the industry standard Kerberos protocol.

The next operating system we reviewed was UNIX. Here we discovered a multitude of different UNIX variations. Most variations were proprietary and developed to support a particular vendor's hardware. In spite of the apparent confusion between variants, we saw UNIX as a very popular and robust networking tool.

Although originally a command line-based product, the common desktop environment (CDE), provides an excellent graphical user interface to manage and monitor the product. CDE enjoys excellent API support and sharply increases the usability of UNIX-based products.

UNIX has good fault tolerance support, has lower resource usage than Novell or Windows products, and benefits from strong third-party security support. Directory services are provided by the Unix-based network information system.

Looking at OS/2, we saw a powerful desktop operating system developed as a joint venture between Microsoft and IBM. Because of increased resource requirements, OS/2 never found favor with software developers and was unable to acquire the market share to win universality. Still, OS/2 is a strong, high-performance NOS. To its credit, OS/2 machines are likely still operating in portions of major corporate networks, providing support, for instance, as mail gateways.

We next turned our attention to the client operating systems that allow users to interact with network servers. We looked at the features and functions of Windows 95/98 and Windows NT Workstation operating systems. These products featured a nearly standard graphical user interface and were easily committed to the network client role.

Once we were familiar with the client operating systems, we looked at the issue of connecting the client to the server. We were reminded that a common protocol is required and also discovered the need for *redirector* software to communicate with the server. We saw that the Microsoft clients had fairly robust redirector support, which included not only Windows networks, but also Novell and Banyan–Vines networks. Although Microsoft doesn't provide redirector software for other operating system clients, we saw that Windows NT servers could be configured to support Novell and Macintosh clients.

Novell client software was found to provide redirector support to machines running DOS, all versions of Windows, Macintosh, and OS/2. Unix uses the network file system (NFS) protocol. NFS support is available from many UNIX vendors for most current operating systems.

▲ REVIEW QUESTIONS

1. *A Server computer*

   A. Holds databases, files, messaging systems, and management console products

   B. Permits users to log on and access resources found on other computers

   C. Is a machine a user operates to perform word processing, electronic mail, and other related tasks

   D. Must have a redirector

2. *Novell NetWare server products support (Select all that apply.)*

   A. ARCnet and token ring networks

   B. Unix and Apple environments

   C. Ethernet networks

   D. IBM and OS/2

3. *NetWare 3.x is*

   A. A monolithic application

   B. ODI compliant

   C. NDIS compliant

   D. Microsoft networking compliant

4. *The Novell Bindery is*

   A. A NetWare 3.x function that permits the use of multiple servers for user log on

   B. A NetWare 4.x feature that allows NetWare domains to look like Internet domains

   C. A NetWare 3.x feature that creates a preferred server

   D. A NetWare 5.x feature that creates a preferred server

5. *NetWare 4.x NDS*

   A. Relies on primary and backup domain controllers

     B. Is the networking protocol that must be installed on clients to permit them to connect to the server

     C. Maintains network information in a hierarchical tree

     D. Provides enhanced features for the bindery

6. *Windows NT fault tolerance support includes (Select all that apply.)*

     A. RAID1

     B. RAID2

     C. RAID3

     D. RAID4

     E. RAID5

7. *Windows NT provides (Select all that apply.)*

     A. Client services for NetWare

     B. Gateway services for NetWare

     C. Message retrieval services for NetWare

     D. File and print services for NetWare

8. *Windows NT directory services (Select all that apply.)*

     A. Are based on a domain structure

     B. Maintain a SAM database

     C. Are found under a default tree and context

     D. Require a primary domain controller

9. *Windows 2000 Server is*

     A. The server equivalent to the Windows 95/98 operating system

     B. The follow-on product to Windows NT 4.0 Server

     C. A y2k compliant version of Windows NT 4.0 Server

     D. A client program for accessing NetWare 2000 software

10. *Active Directory Services (Select all that apply.)*

     A. Eliminate BDCs from Windows 2000 networks

     B. Create a hierarchical database

     C. Work with an automated DNS product

     D. Maintain the distinction between Windows 2000 domains and Internet domains

11. *Unix operating systems*

    A. Come in only one variation

    B. Are found in many varieties because the product is always being improved and rereleased

    C. Are found in many varieties because many vendors provide a proprietary version to go with their hardware.

    D. Are outdated and no longer used in major networks.

12. *Linux (Select all that apply.)*

    A. Was the forerunner of UNIX

    B. Is a new UNIX version that has had slow acceptance with software vendors

    C. Is the next version of Apple networking

    D. Has found solid support in Web-related operations

13. *OS/2*

    A. Provides connectivity between Windows NT and Apple networks

    B. Is still found in many large networks performing gateway functions

    C. Is a Novell/IBM product designed to compete with Windows 2000

    D. Is not a NOS.

14. *Windows 95/98 and Windows NT Workstation (Select all that apply.)*

    A. Are not suited as client operating systems unless they run with Windows NT Server

    B. Have nearly identical graphical user interfaces

    C. Operate with TCP/IP only

    D. Do not support 16-bit software

15. *Once server and client software has been installed and the machines connected with the appropriate hardware, what two items must be functioning on the client to provide a network connection?*

    A. Network monitor

    B. Redirector

    C. Protocol

    D. Remote access server

Introduction to Standards

▲ **Chapter Syllabus**

What Are Standards?

Standards and Models

Protocols

Standards for Network Interface Cards

DoD Model

OSI Model

IEEE 802 Model

Encapsulation

Standards, created by many organizations, are all around us. This chapter will focus on many of the standards that apply to today's computer networks—specifically, the rules by which we measure certain network properties. While the task may seem to demand a considerable amount of study, it is not as difficult as it appears and brings with it the reward of a deeper understanding of what goes on inside the "box" and on the wire.

We will discuss the origin of some of the standards we find today, explain the Department of Defense (DoD) four-layer model, Open Systems Interconnect (OSI) seven-layer model, and Institute of Electrical and Electronics Engineers (IEEE) 802 model. Finally, we will map the protocols you commonly find on networks to get a better understanding of what connects to what.

After completing this chapter, you will be able to do the following:

- Define *protocol*
- Outline the advantages of using the NDIS and ODI specifications
- Explain the components of the DoD four-layer model
- Explain the components of the OSI seven-layer model
- Describe how the IEEE 802 model impacts the OSI model
- Understand where different protocols work within the OSI model.

What are Standards?

A standard is a regulation or a rule that gives us the means to measure compliance with regard to specific or stated properties of a process. In clearer terms, standards are what give us the ability to figure out if we are "getting it right" when it comes to the necessary communications on a wire. Proper application of standards permits us to reliably exchange information between and among computers on a network. There are a lot of steps to getting it right, so we need to have some sort of idea or framework (perhaps a model) that gives us the perspective to investigate and learn what goes on inside the process.

Let us start by asking a few questions about communications on a network:

- Are we sending and receiving what we are supposed to?
- Is the format right?
- Are there requirements for what comes first?
- How many pieces of information can we send at one time?
- Where do I start to look if there is a problem?

Before we can jump to the end of the book and have all of the questions answered, we need to frame the information and show communications between computers on a network as a process. Next, we study the process so we are clear on what makes it up and how it works. The very last part is to figure out how to deal with problems.

A piece of string and two cans can be a communications system. Such a system will provide crude communications over fairly short distances. If, however, we need to have a system that will carry communication for miles or if we need error checking and correction, a more sophisticated system is in order. To implement such a system, we would be well advised to begin by constructing a model for long-distance communication. Our model should, ultimately, explain the rules for making the sophisticated communications system we need. Initially, the communications model would be very simplistic—adding rules for features such as error checking and correction would then add successive layers of complexity.

Thinking back to our original tin can communications system, if we try going around a corner of a building or take tension off the string, the signal (the voice of the other person) simply stops. If we were building a model for this communication, one of our standards would be to keep the string tight for communications to take place. This is no different from the standards we are about to discuss. If the equipment and software adhere to the standards, communication takes place.

Now that we understand what a model is, we move on to some real-world networking models. We will see that the concept is identical to modeling our tin can telephone—state the rules, and we know what it takes to communicate; adhere to the rules, and we get good solid communication with a minimum of errors and delays.

Standards and Models

Standards exist for just about everything networks. As mentioned above, a standard is used much like a yardstick or a type of measuring device. You can compare the actual physical layout of a network with the rest of the hardware and software including the applications and appropriate computing standards.

A critical concept in the computer world is how a single space, capital letter, or missing character can mean the difference between communications and frustration. The purpose for having standards is to permit both sides of the communications channel to adapt vendor-specific hardware and software to a known model. By comparing both sides to the theoretical model, communications are standardized and connectivity is achieved between similar or different types of hardware and software.

There are many different standards that apply to the computing environment such as those for type, size, and length of cables; those for voltages, signals on the wire, duration of calls, and size of packets; and many more.

In the early days of computing, the Department of Defense (DoD) used a model that consisted of four layers to design equipment that was to communicate with other equipment. A model was deemed necessary to standardize communications between devices supplied by a number of different manufacturers. The DoD model is useful because it groups network functions and allows us to see the items that must be identified for effective communication.

Later, when it proved to be financially attractive for business to get involved in computer communication, several of the largest companies started to create their own standards, which led to inconsistencies and incompatibilities. Digital Equipment Corporation (DEC) had a digital network architecture (DNA) that could not directly communicate or exchange information with IBM's system network architecture (SNA). The standards organizations such as the Institute of Electrical and Electronic Engineers (IEEE) and the International Standards Organization (ISO) created models for networking. These models were recognized globally and gained acceptance as the standards for designing anything that was to communicate on a network.

Each of the models we will discuss offers a framework that will permit us to understand the network communication process. As we make our way through the rest of the chapter, keep in mind that we are discussing framework and that the various protocols and properties of each do not necessarily map directly to the models. Keep the focus on what it takes to get two sides to communicate and you will be on the right track.

Protocols

The term "protocol" is perhaps the most over used term in networking today. A protocol is simply a standard for network communication. Spoken language is an excellent analogy for a network protocol. Both are simply rules for encrypting and decrypting information. If I meet you on the street and say: "Hello, how are you?" you know what I am saying because you possess the "English Protocol." That is, you are able to translate the sounds I make into actual information. If you didn't have the "English Protocol," you would simply hear a series of tones and pauses making little or no sense. In the same manner, a computer that uses a particular protocol can make sense out of the ones and zeroes sent to it by a computer using that protocol. In addition to merely interpreting the network's bits, most protocols provide some sort of error checking, and many provide an acknowledgement that a message has actually been received.

Unfortunately, network protocols come in far greater variety than spoken languages. It is possible for one protocol to "ride" on another protocol. For instance, a TCP/IP communication might use the transmission control protocol (TCP) to carry the actual information. The TCP communication might actually be carried as *data* by the Internet protocol (IP) across the Internetwork, and the IP communication might be found as *data* within the Ethernet protocol on the local area network. When the message reaches its destination, each of these protocol layers will need to be peeled back until the communicated information is revealed. (We will talk more about specific protocols later in this book and will discuss ways of modeling the way protocols ride on protocols later in this chapter.)

Standards for Network Interface Cards

Before the late 1980s there were no industry-wide standards for network interface cards (NICs). In those days, a NIC was designed to work with only a few computers and only one network protocol. Every NIC had to have its own set of proprietary drivers. This made network operations inflexible, severely limiting interoperability and growth.

By the end of the decade, standards had been developed to define a communications interface to permit the manufacture of NICs and development of protocols that would work with each other without proprietary restriction. The process of establishing a channel between the protocol driver and the NIC is called binding. Through use of the NIC standards, we can now bind multiple protocols to a single network interface, bind multiple addresses to the same protocol, or place multiple network interfaces in the same computer. This is all made possible because any NIC that conforms to the standard can communicate with any protocol meeting the same standard. The flexibility and growth potential made possible by modern NIC standards have been a major factor in the development of contemporary computer networks.

There are two major sets of NIC standards currently in use today. These are the *Network Device Interface Specification* (NDIS) and *Open Datalink Interface* (ODI). NDIS was developed by 3Com and Microsoft while ODI was a Novell/Apple venture. Most network hardware available today is compliant with both NDIS and ODI.

DoD Four-Layer Model

While more than one theory can be used to identify how computer components connect dissimilar systems, the DoD four-layer model was the original example. Let us take a look at how we can use a standard protocol like TCP/IP and have each component or utility make the connection as it relates to the model.

In Figure 3–1, we see that the DoD four-layer mode contains the following:

- Network interface layer
- Internet layer
- Transport (also known as host-to-host or transmission) layer
- Application layer (known earlier as the process layer)

In the next few sections we will study the DoD model, starting at the place where the signals go to and come from (the wire) and working our way

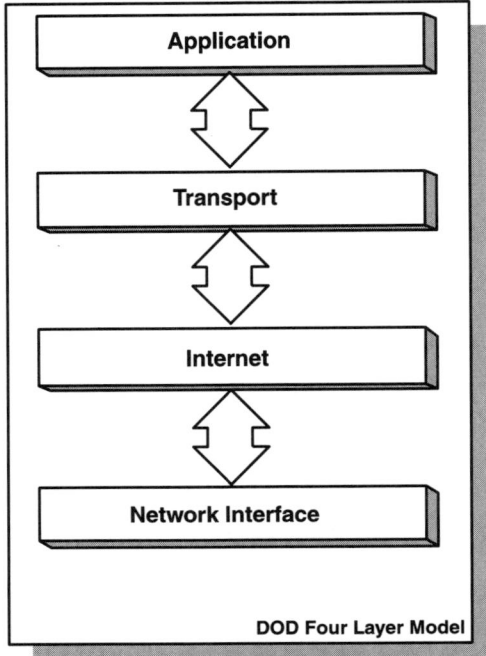

Figure 3–1 *DoD Four-Layer Model.*

up the protocol stack from there. Before we get into the details, however, let us take a moment to define a couple of terms you will see a lot as you read this book: *frames* and *packets*. These terms are often used interchangeably and refer to a "parcel" of data. When data is sent over a network, the bits that comprise the information are typically divided into chunks called frames or packets. As we will see by the end of this chapter, the frames or packets are really more than chunks of bits. In addition to the information they transmit, frames and packets have additional protocol information attached. The models we are about to discuss will show you when and where the data parcels have information such as *addressing, handling instructions,* and *error checking* attached to them during their journey across the network.

Network Interface Layer

The lowest layer in the model is responsible for putting frames on the wire and pulling frames off the wire. In order to get information to the next higher level, which is where the routing and switching take place, there must be information that permits computers to find each other on the subnetwork or subnet. This most basic piece of information is the network interface card's hardware address. The network interface card (NIC) contains a hardware address that is mapped to and used by higher-level protocols to pass the information up and down the stack and back and forth across the wire. The NIC address must be unique, otherwise the resulting ambiguity would make it impossible to find the correct interface with which to establish communications. (Fortunately, there are manufacturing standards developed by the IEEE to ensure NIC addresses *are* unique.)

Internet Layer

Internet layer protocols provide three specific services:

- A connectionless delivery service
- A mechanism to break the data up into individual packets or frames on the transmitting side and to put them back together on the receiving side (fragmentation and reassembly)
- The routing functions necessary to interoperate with other networks

Using only TCP/IP as a point in the discussion, we find that five protocols are implemented at this layer:

1. The Internet protocol (IP), which addresses and routes packets
2. The address resolution protocol (ARP), which determines the hardware address of the hosts
3. Reverse address resolution protocol (RARP), which provides reverse address resolution at the receiving host[1]
4. Internet control message protocol (ICMP), which sends error messages to IP when problems crop up
5. Internet group management protocol (IGMP), which informs routers of the availability of members of multicast groups

The aforementioned protocols do their job by encapsulating packets into Internet datagrams and running all the necessary routing algorithms (a datagram is a connectionless or one-way communication—it is sent with no confirmation of arrival, much as when you send a letter to someone). The user data originates in one of the higher-level protocols and is passed down to the Internet layer. The router then examines the IP address of the datagram to determine if the destination is local or remote. If both machines are on the same network (local), the datagram is forwarded directly to the destination host. If the destination host is on a different network (remote), the

---

[1]RARP is not supported by Microsoft

datagram is forwarded to the default gateway (locally attached gateway—router—to remote networks).

When a network joins the Internet, the administrator must apply for and receive a valid IP network and host number from the Internet Information Center (InterNIC), so the hosts on the network can carry out the functions mentioned here. The combination of a valid IP network and host number is called your IP address. We discuss this, as well as valid domain names (which also must be requested from the InterNIC), in a later chapter.

Transport Layer

Transport protocols provide communications sessions between connected computers. The desired method of data delivery determines the transport protocol. Continuing to use TCP/IP as our example protocol, there are two transport protocols provided within TCP/IP. These are the transmission control protocol (TCP) and the user datagram protocol (UDP). TCP provides the virtual circuit service to make the end-to-end connection for user applications. Data transfer is made reliable through the use of connections (specified channels for communication) and acknowledgements. The user datagram protocol provides delivery but does not use connections or acknowledgements making it less reliable but faster.

The terms *host-to-host* or *transmission layer* are used interchangeably with *transport layer*. The transport layer is responsible for error detection and correction in the DoD model and is analogous to the transport layer in the *OSI model*, as we will see shortly.

Application Layer

Both Microsoft and Novell implement two program interfaces at the application layer to allow the applications to utilize the services of the TCP/IP protocol stack. These are sockets and NetBIOS. These interfaces are standardized such that a Microsoft client properly configured with TCP/IP will have no difficulty communicating with a Novell server running the correct TCP/IP service. An example would be an FTP (file transfer protocol) session where the client retrieves files from the server by using FTP.

The Windows sockets interface provides a standard application-programming interface (API) under Microsoft Windows to transport protocols such as IPX and TCP/IP. This open standard library of function calls, data structures, and programming procedure permits Windows applications to take advantage of TCP/IP. This interface enables Windows NT to exchange data with non-NetBIOS systems.

NetBIOS provides a standard interface to protocols that support Net-BIOS naming and message services such as TCP/IP and NetBEUI. NetBIOS is used in Microsoft products to permit application communication with the lower protocol layers as well. Three TCP ports provide NetBIOS support. These are port 137 for NetBIOS name service, port 138 for datagram service, and port 139 for session service. NetBIOS support is a built-in feature of the Microsoft TCP/IP protocol stack and a standard add-on feature of the Novell IPX/SPX and Microsoft NWLink (IPX/SPX) protocols[2].

Several standard TCP/IP utilities and services exist at the application layer:

- File transfer protocol (used for transferring large files between remote machines)
- Simple mail transfer protocol (used by mail servers to exchange mail)
- Standard network monitoring protocol (used by network monitoring machines to determine the health and status of the network)
- Telnet (used by your machine to connect to a remote host and use its services)

Study Break

What Are Ports and Sockets?

The terms **ports** and **sockets** (or Windows Sockets — also known as WINSOCK) may seem a little foreign. A port provides a location for sending messages. It functions as a multiplexed message queue, which means that it can receive more than one message at a time. Ports are identified by a numerical value between 0 and 65,536.

Sockets refer to a connection-oriented interprocess communication protocol. An interprocess communication is the way programs communicate with each other. A connection-oriented protocol is distinct from a connectionless protocol because in connection-oriented communications, the transmitter gets a positive response from the receiver when it sends a communication. (We use a telephone call analogy for a connection-oriented protocol and a letter for a connectionless one.) Under sockets, each participant in the communication agrees on a logical data location (the "socket") at each end of the communication channel. Communications are sent to these sockets, which are kept open for the duration of the communication session.

---

[2]NetBIOS support is available for many other protocols and network operating systems through the addition of third-party products.

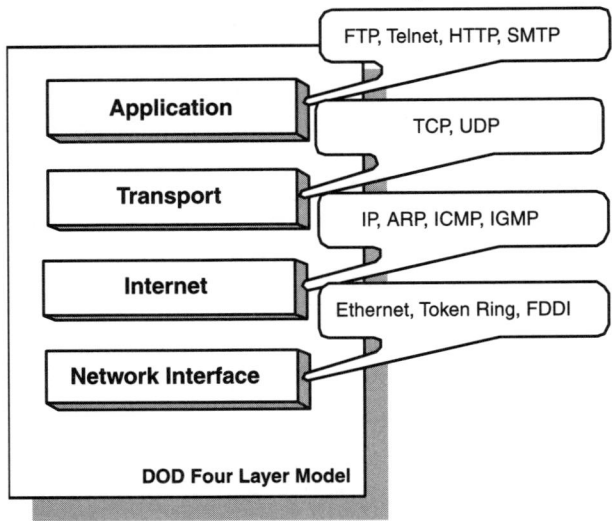

Figure 3–2   *DoD Layers Showing the TCP/IP Protocol Stack.*

Figure 3–2 provides you with an idea of what the DoD model looks like with the listed protocols in place. Visualizing the protocols at work, you might be able to trace how an application such as Mail could use the layers to get down the protocol stack. On the other side of the communication, the signal would travel up through those same layers to connect to the mail server to process the subject of the data communication—a message.

Study Break

How Can I Remember the DoD Model?

The easy way to remember the DoD model's layers is with a simple phrase: *"Networking is truly amazing."* Notice how the words represent the *network interface, internet, transport,* and *application* layers.

Open Systems Interconnect Model

The open systems interconnect (OSI) model was developed by open comment of many people and adopted by the International Standards Organization (ISO). It has been the most widely used model to explain network communications. A large part of its success stems from its ability to identify in a far more granular way than previous models how the functions of network protocols relate to each other to establish communications.

As we look at the OSI model, remember it is just a concept—we don't actually see the model when two hosts work together. (That is to say, not every communication between hosts nor every network protocol utilizes *all* aspects of the model.) The model, however, *is* the standard, and in order to communicate, we must adhere to the standard. If both computers trying to establish communications are configured according to the standard, communications will take place. If they are not, you may end up getting error messages, failure to initialize services, or no communications at all.

The OSI Model consists of seven layers. Each layer is said to shield the layers above and below it from the networking details it covers. Although data is processed through the layers sequentially, you can envision communications between the layers such that each layer on the sending computer corresponds with its counterpart on the receiving computer and vice-versa. The layers are typically numbered with the layer closest to the wire receiving the lowest number. Using that convention, the OSI layers are as follows:

7. Application layer
6. Presentation layer
5. Session layer
4. Transport layer
3. Network layer
2. Data link layer
1. Physical layer

Figure 3–3 compares the layers of the International Standards Organization open systems interconnect model to the layers of the DoD model. This helps us see how the expanded newer standards stack up.

In the OSI model, the application, presentation and session layers provide services useful to applications in general. These services are separate from similar but distinct functions that take place at the lower levels. Error detection and correction, for instance, may take place at two different points in the protocol stack. We now look at the individual layers and see what they offer an application.

Application Layer

The topmost layer of the OSI model is the application layer, or layer 7; and it provides support to end-user network applications by providing application programming interfaces (sets of procedure calls). These are the engines that drive actual user applications and provide support to them. They serve as a

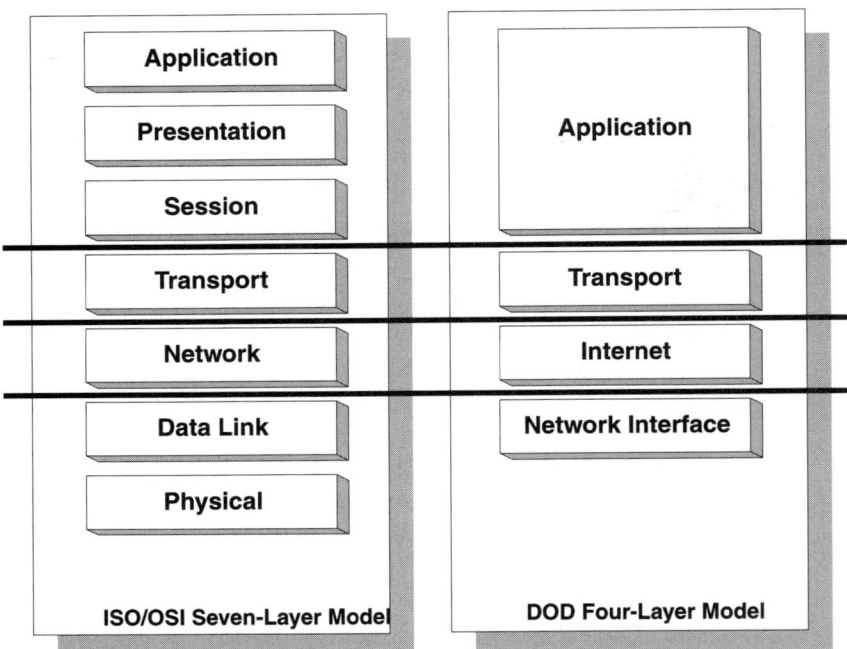

Figure 3–3 *Comparison of OSI and DoD models.*

window or portal through which we pass data to lower layers that provide more direct support to the operations we are trying to perform including mail, data bases, terminal emulation, or file transfers. This layer is responsible for working with, or bridging, the gap between the originated data stream and the lower layers. Some examples of applications programming interfaces (APIs) would be Mail API (MAPI), MS FAX API (FAPI), Telephone API (TAPI), and Internet Server API (ISAPI).

Presentation Layer

The presentation layer, or layer 6, expresses the format that must be used to exchange information between networked computers. The layer provides for data formatting and encryption, which is the platform-to-platform translation of syntax for the purpose of data exchange. Modification of the position of the data inside a data stream is done according to a common set of rules at this layer.

On the side that is sending the data, a process to place the data into a commonly recognized intermediary format is undertaken. On the side that is receiving the data, this layer is responsible for taking the intermediary data stream and putting it in the proper format so that it can correctly deal with the data according to the requirements of the application layer. A common utility found at this layer is known as the redirector. This is useful for any application that requires network access because it is the function that permits basic input/output redirection, for example when you are placing a file on another machine on the network, the redirector is used. Redirectors are very common and may be thought of as the "client" portion of the network transmission. When you wish to contact another machine on a network, you use a redirector to initiate that contact. (Some common examples of redirectors are the Client for Microsoft Networks found on Windows 9x systems and the Windows NT Workstation Service.) Other functions that are accomplished at layer 6 are compression and encryption. Compression is useful because it reduces the amount of data that needs to be sent over the wire to save transmission time. Encryption is useful because it provides data security through the use of codes and formulas to change the data so it cannot be understood without the key to unlock the code.

Session Layer

Layer 5, the session layer, provides for the negotiation, establishment, and maintenance of sessions between applications including failure recovery. This layer allows applications on different computers to open, use, and close a connection. This connection is referred to as a *session*. The session permits sharing data, controls the flow and direction of data, and ensures the recovery of missing or corrupt data. The dialog is controlled through the use of checkpoints in the data stream so both sides can recover quickly in the event of a failure. A checkpoint is a marker that helps each side understand what data has been sent and received. Although it adds more information to the communication, which might seem to slow things down, it really speeds up the process because, when a failure occurs, only the data after the last correctly received checkpoint needs to be retransmitted. This significantly reduces the amount of data that must be retransmitted. (Sadly, data error and retransmission is still a way of life on today's networks. Anything that can be done to minimize the degree of retransmission is a significant help to communication.)

Depending on the type of application, you might see a simplex, half-duplex, or full-duplex data flow. Simplex is a one-way data flow. Half-duplex provides two-way data flow, but only one host may transmit at a time. Full duplex allows two-way data flow without the half-duplex restriction. That is to say both hosts can send information to each other at the same time. By providing the appropriate checkpoint methods, the wire between the two computers can stay full of data; and only the data that does not correctly make it to its destination need be retransmitted.

Transport Layer

The transport layer, layer 4, guarantees end-to-end reliable delivery of data, which means the data is delivered in the right order and in a reliable manner. Here again, we consider error checking and correction as a means to put the information in the right order and to make certain the whole message is received. Some of the rules for correct data exchange require that the information be delivered in an error-free state, in the right sequence, and without duplication of data or any data loss.

The transport layer is responsible for repackaging as necessary, which might mean dividing long data streams into shorter lengths if the packets are too big, or collecting smaller packets into a single large packet so that efficient use is made of the network medium. At the computer that receives the data, the same process takes place in reverse so corresponding data may be found at each machine.

Network Layer

The network layer is layer 3, and it is responsible for the routing of packets of information across multiple networks. This layer must provide addressing for routing between internetworks. It does this by translating logical addresses and names into physical addresses for the lower layers. It also shields the layers above from the details of the lower layers (the physical topology, for example).

It is at this layer that we first find addressing (for example, the IP address), and this is where the path our data will take is selected. Factors such as the conditions on the network, service priority, and problems or outages, might cause our data to be routed differently each time we put information on a wire.

When two different network types are involved, the traffic being sent may have a data size too large for the destination network or host. In that case, the data can be broken into smaller fragments, numbered (so that they can be put back into the same order), and shipped out to the destination station. On the receiving end, the process is reversed and the reassembled data, in larger chunks, is passed up the stack to the application needing it.

Data Link Layer

Layer 2, the data link layer, is responsible for placing data frames on the wire outbound and taking the data frames off of the wire inbound. This layer provides reliable transfer of data across the physical link using data frames. A data frame is an organized piece of information that has structure into which the data can be placed. If you looked inside a data frame, you would find the following:

- Sender ID
- Destination ID
- Control information (frame type, routing and segmentation information)
- Data (the information that you want to get from computer A to computer B)
- Cyclical redundancy check (CRC is used for error correction and verification of the information to ensure error-free transmission and reception)

The data link layer functions to provide all the necessary elements for the physical medium such as formatting, error detection, link management, and data flow control so the network layer above can assume a virtually error-free network environment. Again we find addressing—this time at the hardware layer. The hardware address of the network interface card is a unique network address, and it is how information actually arrives at the correct computer on a network. A hardware address, for example, might be expressed as 00–60–08–29–31–AA.

Physical Layer

The physical layer, layer 1, accepts data from the data link layer and puts it in the right format for the physical medium. This layer deals with the rules for handling binary data or the raw bitstream of zeros and ones to and from the wire. A bitstream would have no meaning unless there were some way of understanding when the signals started, when they stopped, how they had to clear the channel, and how they could be broken into some form of package for use higher up the protocol stack.

At the physical layer, requirements are specified for

- The wire—voltage levels and other electrical properties
- Timing & sizing—how long each bit should last and the space between bits
- Electrical signals—how each bit is translated into electrical or optical impulses for use on the wire or other medium
- Physical connectivity—connector types and mechanical specifications
- Handshake—the procedural specifications of how to connect

To maintain reliable communications, there are requirements for how long the cables can be, what the electrical or optical voltages/parameters can be, and mechanical specifications such as how the cables attach to NICs or hubs. This layer deals with transmitting *pluses* and *minuses*, *oFFs* and *oNs* or *highs* and *lows* to represent *ones* and *zeroes* from one computer to another that would have no meaning without the data encoding and bit synchronization specifications that the physical layer model provides.

Study Break

How Can I Remember the Layers of the OSI Model?

There are a few easy ways to memorize the OSI model. As with the DoD model, the best involve the use of simple phrases. The phrases *"**A** **p**riest **s**aw **t**en **n**uns **d**oing **p**ushups"* and *"**A**ll **p**eople **s**eem to **n**eed **d**ata **p**rocessing"* will each help you remember the seven layers (*application, presentation, session, transport, network, datalink,* and *physical*) in the correct order.

Putting it all Together

Now that we have seen each layer of the OSI model, it might be useful to see how all the steps fit together during a typical network operation. Figure 3–4 shows how network activities involved with saving a Microsoft Word file to a network drive would fit the OSI model.

Protocol Mapping

Now that we have seen how the layers of the OSI model work during a typical operation, let us look at the layers from the network protocols' point of view. As we go through the layers, you may want to refer to Figure 3–5 to better visualize the different levels of functionality. We will start at the wire and work our way up the stack.

Physical and Data Link Layers

It is sometimes difficult to separate these layers in practice since much of what goes on here overlaps. At the very lowest levels of the physical layer, we find specifications for wire types and connectors. Traversing the layers, we see LAN protocols such as Ethernet and Token Ring. As we climb through the data link layer, we discover rules for how the LAN protocols share the wire and other network devices.

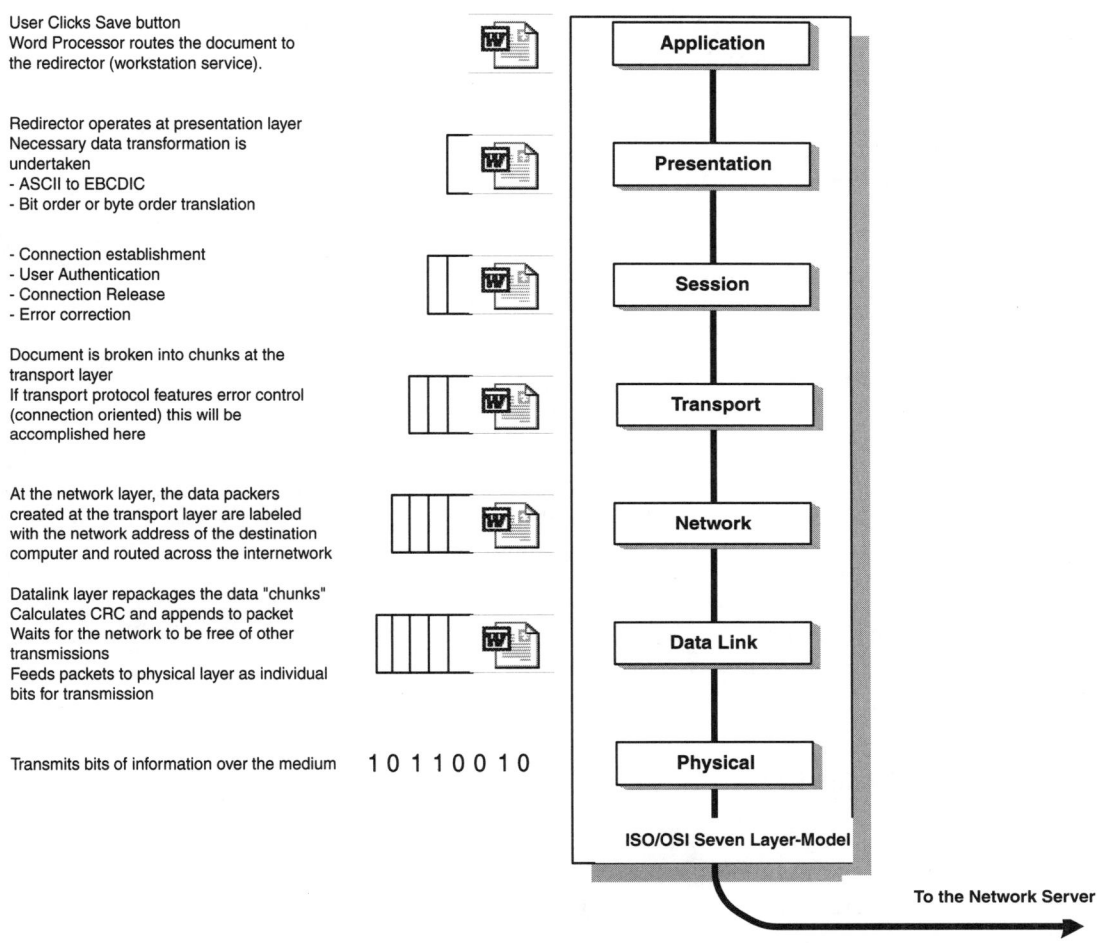

User Clicks Save button
Word Processor routes the document to
the redirector (workstation service).

Redirector operates at presentation layer
Necessary data transformation is
undertaken
- ASCII to EBCDIC
- Bit order or byte order translation

- Connection establishment
- User Authentication
- Connection Release
- Error correction

Document is broken into chunks at the
transport layer
If transport protocol features error control
(connection oriented) this will be
accomplished here

At the network layer, the data packers
created at the transport layer are labeled
with the network address of the destination
computer and routed across the internetwork

Datalink layer repackages the data "chunks"
Calculates CRC and appends to packet
Waits for the network to be free of other
transmissions
Feeds packets to physical layer as individual
bits for transmission

Transmits bits of information over the medium   1 0 1 1 0 0 1 0

Application

Presentation

Session

Transport

Network

Data Link

Physical

ISO/OSI Seven Layer-Model

To the Network Server

Figure 3–4 *Saving a Word document to a server-based file from the perspective of the OSI model.*

Network Layer

As you might expect, the network layer is the domain of the network protocols that can carry messages over large WANs and small LANs alike. Here we
find the NetWare Internet Packet Exchange (IPX) protocol and the TCP/IP
Internet protocol (IP). Here, TCP/IP uses the address resolution protocol
(ARP) to determine hardware addresses.

Transport Layer

Protocols at the transport layer are responsible for delivering data. They
"ride" over the network and LAN protocols to make their way across the

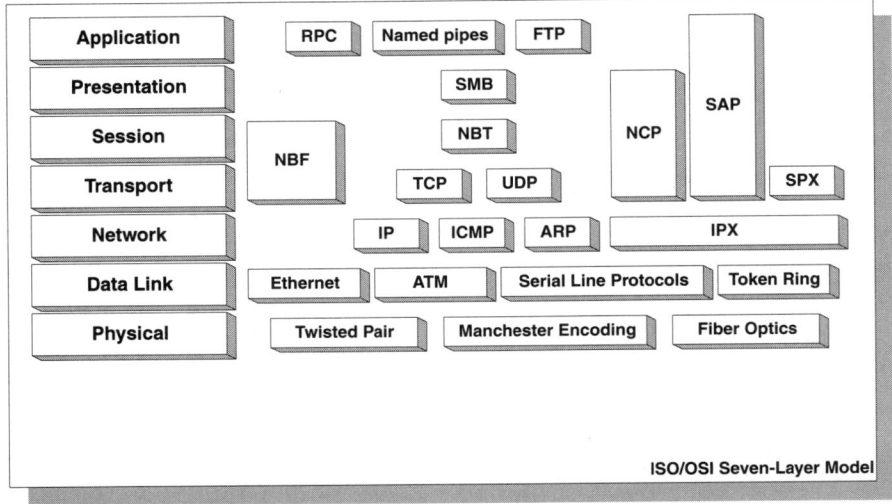

Figure 3–5 *The OSI model and some popular protocols.*

wire. Here we see the TCP/IP transmission control protocol (TCP) and user datagram protocol (UDP) as well as NetWare's sequenced packet exchange protocol (SPX).

Session Layer

Of all the OSI layers, the session layer is the hardest one to map. As you know, it is at the session layer that "sessions" are established. Here we find application and presentation layer protocols conversing with transport layer protocols to hammer out the rules they will use to communicate. The Network Basic Input/Output System (NetBIOS), although not strictly a protocol, defines naming conventions and a software interface that provide guidelines for establishing sessions.

Application and Presentation Layers

Just as with the physical and data link layers, the boundary between the application and physical layers has become somewhat obscured. Much of the data translation expected to be performed at this level is actually performed by application layer protocols. It is reasonable to conclude, therefore, that most of today's application layer protocols operate at both layers. We have already identified the application layer as the home of the *redirector*. Some of the protocols that support the redirector are NetWare's Service Advertising Protocol (SAP) and NetWare Core Protocol (NCP), as well as the Microsoft

Server Management Blocks (SMB) protocol. SAP provides network users with a list of available IPX services while NCP responds to network requests from users. Like NCP, SMB supports user requests in Microsoft networks. At the application layer's upper levels, we find network services like the TCP/IP file transfer protocol (FTP) and domain name system (DNS).

IEEE 802 MODEL

With the proliferation of computer networking, the IEEE became involved in defining LAN standards. The actual title of this "definition project" is Project 802, which refers to the year (1980) and month (February) that the project was started. Project 802 concerned itself with creation of LAN standards that have had far-reaching effects and are still in use today. The 802 project and OSI model were under development at about the same time, resulting in a considerable amount of overlap between the two. IEEE and ISO shared a lot of information with each other so that the two models are roughly compatible.

IEEE 802 is a data-link protocol that controls the link between two stations. The most significant impact on the OSI model was the 802.2 standard. This refers to logical link control (LLC) which is a subset of the high-level data-link control (HDLC) protocol. LLC works with the media access control (MAC) layer to reduce the LAN's susceptibility to errors and provide an interface more compatible with wide area networks. Although this increased the level of complexity by introducing two new sublayers, the benefits outstrip the disadvantage. (We will cover LLC and MAC shortly.)

In addition to IEEE 802.2, the 802 project produced several other important standards; such as

- IEEE 802.3, which defines the standards for bus networks.
- IEEE 802.4, which defines the standards for token-passing bus networks.
- IEEE 802.5, which defines the standards for token-passing ring networks.

Media Access Control (MAC) Sublayer

The MAC sublayer is defined in the 802 specification as the lower portion of the data link layer. The MAC sublayer provides a form of shared access from the computer's network card(s) to the physical layer. For shared access, the MAC layer is protocol specific and communicates directly between the network card and the physical layer. It has the responsibility to provide error-free transmission between the two networked computers. It is this sublayer that is responsible for how individual devices share the wire; and, based on protocol, dictates whether access is controlled systematically or simply given to the first device that transmits. If you hear of a MAC layer address, it is referring to the unique hardware address of a network card. The terms "MAC address" and "hardware address" are used interchangeably. (You will remember that a MAC address is specified as a series of hexadecimal numbers such as 00–60–08–29–31–AA.) The MAC layer can and does provide the framing, addressing, and error detection for the IEEE 802.x series. This means that the MAC layer performs the same services for Ethernet & token ring types (such as 802.3, 802.4, and 802.5) according to the protocol it has to support.

Logical Link Control (LLC) Sublayer

The LLC sublayer, or upper sublayer, manages data-link communications according to the 802.2 specification. This sublayer manages the links between communicating hardware devices on the network. Logical interface points, better known as service access points or SAPs, provide a reference for the exchange of information between the LLC sublayer and remaining upper layers.

Encapsulation

The way information is handled under the DoD, OSI, or IEEE models is often referred to as *encapsulation*. Encapsulation is the process of adding a header to the data accepted from a higher level protocol. When the application originates the data or sends a request to get data, the data or the request moves down through the protocol stack, and at each level a new header is added. This increases the total size of the information until it reaches the wire. The individual zeros and ones are sent via the wire to the remote computer where each of the headers is opened and peeled off, much like peeling the skin off an onion. The header information is stripped off at each layer, and the information is sent upward through the layers to reach the intended application. In Figure 3–6 we see how this process works to create the final form that is transmitted by the network card to the wire. Notice that the application at the top and the network wire at the bottom are considered to be *outside* of the OSI Model.

At the top of the process, the application sends data to or makes a request of the OSI application layer. Network components at this layer append application layer header information to the data or request and pass the package to the next layer. Presentation layer components then place

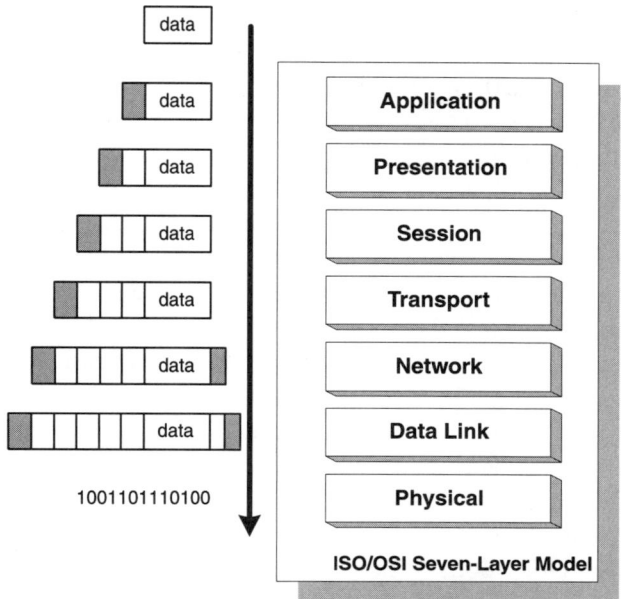

Figure 3–6 *OSI Layers showing how header and trailer information is added.*

presentation layer header information in front of the application layer header and pass the package to the session layer. At each successive layer the information is added to the front until we get to the network layer. From here on both header and trailer information are added (the trailer information is used for error checking). This continues down to the physical layer where the frame preamble and frame postamble are both added and the information is passed directly to the wire. After running along the wire at nearly the speed of light, the frame arrives at the other side where it is unwrapped by each successive layer and presented to the correct application for use.

Summary

This chapter covered the rules by which network communications can take place. We began by defining the terms *standard* and *model*. We saw that in the network context, standards are a way of describing how the network should function, while models provided us with a framework we could use to visualize the application of the standards.

The first standards we discussed were *protocols*. We discovered that protocols are nothing more than a set of rules to tell us how to interpret the ones and zeroes transmitted over the network wire. We also noted that protocols may provide error checking and acknowledgement and that protocols are typically carried by other protocols to travel on WANs and LANs.

We then turned our attention to the *Network Device Interface Specification* and *Open Datalink Interface*. These standards provided rules for the manufacture of network interface cards (NICs) and the creation of network protocols that would work together regardless of who made them. We found the specifications allowed us to put multiple NICs in a single computer and/or bind multiple protocols and addresses to a single NIC.

After reviewing the important network standards, we explored the three network models commonly in use today. We saw that each model defined network operations from signals on the network wire right up to the software that supports user applications. We saw that network models use a layering concept where each successive step in the model adds more information to, or removes information from, the communication (depending on which way the information is going). We started our exploration of models with the DoD model. The four layers of that model explained everything from the wire to the application. We then looked at the open systems interconnect (OSI) model and saw that it provided better granularity than the DoD model because it defined the same network operation in seven, rather than four, steps. We saw how a typical network communication would look from the model's viewpoint and looked closely at where different protocols might be found within the model.

After the OSI model, we looked at the IEEE 802 model. We learned that this model is essentially identical to the OSI model except that it divides the OSI model's data link layer into the logical link control sublayer and media access control sublayer to better define network device access in WANs and LANs.

Finally, we considered *encapsulation*. This is the way information is added to or removed from a message during the transmission process. We referred to this as wrapping and unwrapping the data.

▲ REVIEW QUESTIONS

1. *What are the four layers of the DoD Model?*
    A. Application, transport, internet, and network
    B. Application, transport, network, and data
    C. Application, transport, network, and physical
    D. Application, central, transport, and remote

2. *Which layer in the DoD Model is responsible for pulling frames off and putting them on the wire?*

    A. Application

    B. Transport

    C. Data

    D. Network

    E. Internet

3. *Which layer provides connectionless delivery, routing, fragmentation and reassembly?*

    A. Application

    B. Transport

    C. Central

    D. Network

    E. Internet

4. *What five protocols are used at, and map to, the Internet layer?*

    A. GGP, IGRP, ICMP, PARP, and IP

    B. IGMP, RARP, ARP, ICMP, and IP

    C. ARP, IP, PARP, ICMP and IGMP

    D. IP, PARP, ARP, ICMP and IGMP

5. *When a host recognizes that the source and destination addresses are on the same LAN, it will (Select one.)*

    A. Apply a decrement of at least 1 and forward the datagram directly to the host

    B. Forward the datagram directly to the host

    C. Reject the datagram for having the same source and destination network numbers

    D. Suspend processing until the LAN ID is resolved

6. *When a host recognizes that the source and destination addresses are on different LANs, it will (Select one.)*

    A. Reject the datagram for having incorrect network numbers

    B. Suspend the processing until the LAN ID is resolved

    C. Forward the datagram directly to the host

    D. Forward the datagram to the default gateway

7. *What is encapsulation?*

    A. A tunneling protocol that can be used on bus, star, and token ring networks

    B. A process for tunneling through the layers to provide for Ethernet and token ring compatibility with the OSI and DoD models

    C. A process where the data is wrapped with layer-specific information

    D. A process for wrapping the layers with the data to place more information in a frame than could otherwise be transmitted

8. *At what layer of the OSI model does the NIC operate as it exchanges data with the wire?*

    A. Network

    B. Transport

    C. Session

    D. Data link

9. *What is an interprocess communication?*

    A. A tunneling protocol that can be used on bus, star, and token ring networks

    B. The way that programs communicate with one another

    C. The way an application can encapsulate data

    D. A process for tunneling through the layers to provide for Ethernet feedback

10. *What is a socket?*

    A. A tunneling protocol

    B. The Ethernet connector that permits hub attachment

    C. A connection-oriented interprocess communication

    D. Transport layer host ID that is used to identify each computer

    E. Network layer host ID that is used to identify each process

11. *IEEE 802.2 introduces the specification for (Select one.)*

    A. Logical link control

    B. Connection-oriented interprocess communication

    C. Tunneling protocols

    D. Encrypted datagram, media access controlled Ethernet

Cables, Access Methods, and Network Architecture

▲ Chapter Syllabus

Types of Cables

Access Methods

Network Architecture

The chapter presents the heart of the network, the cabling system. We will learn about the different cable types and their advantages and disadvantages. We will study popular cable types such as twisted pair and fiber optic and see real-world examples of their usage. This chapter also introduces different network architectures, such as Ethernet and token ring.

After completing this chapter, you will be able to do the following:

- Describe different cable and connector types
- Explain the differences in cabling systems and choose the suitable cabling type based on the network needs
- Discuss network media access control methods
- Explain features and functionality of Ethernet class networks
- Explain features and functionality of token ring class networks
- Explain features and functionality of ArcNET class networks

Modern networks can be large and complex. They consist of hundreds of computers, dozens of network devices, and megabytes of software. The basis of every network, however, is its communication equipment. Good communication equipment permits smooth and reliable data travel from one computer to another. Communication equipment is found in both active and passive varieties. Active communication equipment requires an external power supply to operate, while passive devices do not. Examples of active communication equipment are as follows:

- Network adapter cards—serve as end points for network communications, form the signal, and responsible for sending and receiving data from the communication channel
- Repeaters—boost and regenerate attenuated signals
- Concentrators—connect multiple devices together
- Bridges and switches—help to guide network traffic by directing it along the channel
- Routers—able to make intelligent decisions about the optimal path between the source and the destination
- Multiplexers— combine multiple communication channels into one

In contrast, passive communication equipment requires no external power. Examples of the passive communication equipment are cabling systems, jacks, wall plates, passive hubs, communication closets, etc.

We will discuss all of the communication equipment in the following chapters but for now will focus on the cabling system.

Types of Cables

Cables rank as one of the most important parts of the network. All network operations depend on how good the cabling system is, how well it was installed, how reliably it functions, and at what speed it can transmit data.

Perhaps you have already seen that computers can be connected using different types of cable and are wondering what kind of cables can be used for computer networking. You may be surprised to learn that leading cable manufacturers' catalogues contain more that 2,000 types of cabling. As you can see, cabling can be confusing. Fortunately, cables used in the majority of modern networks can be divided into three main categories:

- Coaxial (coax) cable
- Twisted pair
- Fiber optic cable

By understanding the difference between these groups of cables, you will be able to make decisions concerning what cable type is appropriate in certain situations.

Coaxial Cable

Coaxial cable (or coax) is the simplest cable type to install. Coax consists of a copper core surrounded by a layer of dielectric insulation, a braided metal shielding, and an outer cover. Some types of coaxial cable have double shielding that provide better protection from external interference. Double shielding consists of one layer of foil insulation and one layer of braided metal shielding. In environments subject to high interference, quad shield coax cables can be used. They consist of two layers of foil insulation and two layers of braided metal shielding.

Shielding is typically used to protect the transmitted data from external electrical interference, often called noise. Good shielding prevents noise signals from getting into the cable to distort the data. Shielding will also prevent crosstalk (signal overflow from adjacent wires).

In coaxial cable, the data is transmitted through the core. This core can be stranded or solid. Different core types result in different electrical characteristics and can limit cable usage to certain areas. Because the resistance of the stranded cable is less, this type of conductor is more desirable for data transmission.

As we mentioned before, the core is separated from the wire mesh by a dielectric insulation layer. Without this layer of insulation, the cable's core and the wire mesh will touch, resulting in a short circuit that will destroy data traveling in the core and make network communications impossible.

The outer layer of standard coaxial cable is covered by the outer shield, which is usually made of plastic, Teflon, or rubber. Unfortunately, when standard coaxial cable burns, it gives off poisonous gases. This is because a typical coaxial cable contains Polyvinyl Chloride (PVC)—a type of plastic that is used for the cable's insulation and/or outer covering. For this reason, standard PVC-coated coaxial cable is not allowed in plenums. Plenums are the short spaces found in many buildings between the false ceiling and the floor above. Because plenums are often used for circulating warm and cold air through the building, poisonous smoke in the plenum will eventually become a part of the building's breathing air. Fire codes specify a special type of coaxial cable for use in plenum areas. This so called plenum-grade cabling contains special materials in its insulation and cover that are resistant to fire and, if burning, produce only a minimum amount of smoke. The chief drawbacks to the plenum cable are expense and less flexibility. The lack of flexibility makes it difficult to route in exposed office areas.

Aside from fire rating, coaxial cable used in computer networking is typically divided into two main groups:

- Thin coaxial cable, or thinnet
- Thick coaxial cable, or thicknet

Thin Coaxial Cable

Thin coaxial cable is about .25 inch (.5 mm) thick. This rather flexible cable is easy to work with and can be used for nearly any type of network. The thinnet cable is included in the RG-58 group. Thin coaxial cable has 50-ohm impedance.

Impedance is the resistance that a conductive cable offers to the transmission of alternating electric current. Impedance is measured in ohms (Ω). Cables with higher values of impedance are highly resistant to the transmission of electrical signals, while cables with lower impedance typically show a lower signal loss with distance. Most network standards and network devices require using cables with a specific impedance level. If the impedance value for the cable is different from that described in the standard, the network may not work properly.

Thinnet can carry signals for distances up to 607 feet (185 meters). This does not mean a segment 608 feet in length will not work but specifies a distance at which all equipment should work properly all the time. Greater distances may be supported by some manufactures, but acceptable results are not guaranteed in all cases.

The RG-58 group includes several types of coaxial cable. Each of them has different electrical characteristics, and some of them cannot be used for digital network communications. Table 4.1 shows what is included in the RG group.

Table 4.1 *RG-58 Group of Coaxial Cables*

Cable	Description
RG-58 /U	Solid copper wire
RG-58 A/U	Stranded copper wire
RG-58 C/U	Military specification of RG-58 A/U
RG-59	Used in broadband transmission like cable television
RG-6	Used for broadband transmissions, but is rated for higher frequencies than RG-59
RG-62	Used in the ArcNet networks

Broadband and Baseband Transmission

There are two techniques that can be used to transmit an encoded signal over a cable: baseband and broadband. Baseband transmission uses digital signals over a single frequency. Signals in baseband transmission are electrical or optical *pulses*. They occupy the entire communication channel capacity, thus making it impossible for two simultaneous signals to coexist on one cable at the same moment.

The other type of transmission is known as broadband. Broadband uses analog signals which are continuous and nondiscrete. In contrast to the pulses found in baseband, broadband signals take the form of electrical or optical waves. These signals occupy a range of frequencies; and if enough bandwidth is available, multiple data channels can exist simultaneously on a single wire. A good example of broadband is cable television, where you can receive multiple channels from a single cable.

One of the key differences between baseband and broadband transmissions is that baseband uses a digital signal and broadband uses analog signaling. Another big difference is that broadband technologies need analog amplifiers to strengthen the signal over distances while baseband systems use simple repeaters. The problem with amplifiers is that they can transmit a signal in one direction only. When a computer receives a packet from a neighbor that is located upstream from the amplifier, the recipient computer is not able to answer back. The amplifier will not propagate the signal in the reverse direction.

To work around this one-way problem, both dual- and single-cable solutions were developed. Under the dual-cable solution, two separate wires are used: one for sending and one for receiving. A special device, called a *headend*, is used to manage the signal. With single cable, different frequency bands are allocated for inbound and outbound transmissions. For example, if the computer wants to send a signal, it can use a high frequency range (e.g., from 40 to 300 MHz); and to receive data, it can use a low frequency range (e.g., 5 to 30 MHz). To translate the frequency from the sending device to the receiving device, the same headend devices used in the dual-cable solution are used.

The advantage of baseband transmission is that it is relatively simple and inexpensive to install and does not require complex equipment and interfaces. Broadband transmission, on the other hand, offers multiple channels; and although the bandwidth of each individual channel is usually lower than its baseband counterpart, the aggregate bandwidth can be significantly higher. For most applications, however, the additional bandwidth of broadband does not justify its complexity and the cost of equipment to support it. Because of this, baseband is the more widely used technology.

Thick Coaxial Cable

Thick coaxial cable is about .5 inch (10 mm) in diameter. Thick coaxial cable or thicknet is often referred to as *standard Ethernet*, because it was the first cable to be used in the Ethernet-type networks. The main difference between the thick and the thin coaxial cable is that the copper core of the thick coaxial cable is thicker. The thicker the cable core, the farther the cable can carry a signal without significant attenuation.

Attenuation is the reduction of signal strength in a cable as a result of absorption or dispersion of the electrical or optical impulse traveling through the cable. Attenuation is measured in decibels (dB). From a networking point of view, the attenuation characteristics of a cable are important. It is expressed in dB/m, dB/km, or dB/ft. The rule of thumb is as follows: the lower this value is, the better the cable is.

Thick coaxial cable is able to carry a signal for 1,640 feet (500 meters). Again these numbers are what the standards say. You may build working networks that use longer pieces of thick coaxial cable; however, reliability cannot be assured in these cases.

Because thick coaxial cable is able to transmit a signal over greater distances than thin coaxial cable, it is often used as a backbone to connect several thinnet networks together. Thick coaxial cable is thicker than its thin analog and is, therefore, less flexible and more difficult to work with. Because of this, thick coaxial cable is not typically used in the tight places such as conduits and troughs.

Connecting Coaxial Cables

The cable itself is not a network. You must connect computers and other network devices to the cable to create a network. You might be curious how you can connect a computer to a cable segment. Computers may be connected to coaxial cables in two basic ways. The first way is to cut the cable and insert a special T-junction often referred to as a "T-"connector. Computers and other network devices are connected to this T-connector.

Another way of connecting a device to the coaxial cable is to use a *vampire tap*. (See Figure 4–1.) During the installation of a vampire tap, a hole of exceedingly precise depth is drilled into the cable's core. A special connector is screwed into the hole to perform essentially the same function as the T-junction. The advantage of the vampire tap is there is no need to cut the cable to install a connector.

Thick coaxial cable uses the vampire tap method with an external transceiver. Connection from the transceiver to the network adapter card is made using a transceiver cable (often known as a drop cable). The transceiver cable has special plugs called AUI connectors (attachment unit interface), which plug into an AUI port on the network adapter card.

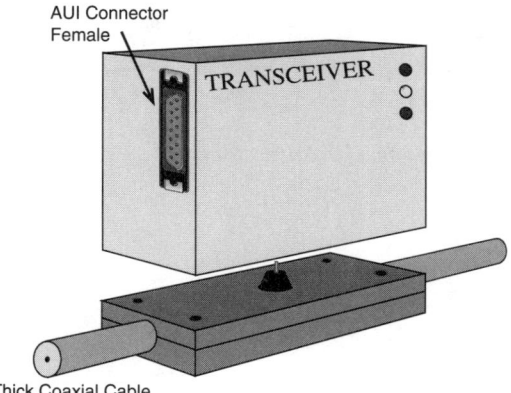

AUI Connector
Female

TRANSCEIVER

Thick Coaxial Cable

Figure 4–1 *Vampire tap technology.*

> **Note**
>
> The AUI port connector is also known as a DIX connector. The DIX (Digital Intel Xerox) connector is named after the three companies that developed it and the related standards. Yet another term for an AUI connector is DB-15. The number fifteen corresponds to the number of pins that the connector uses.

The computer is connected to the external transceiver with the help of a special AUI cable. An AUI cable should be used for no purpose other than connecting network devices to external transceivers. AUI cable is made up of four individually shielded pairs of wire surrounded by an overall cable-shielding sheath. Because it is double shielded, AUI cable is more resistant to electrical signal interference than other, lighter cables. An AUI cable should be terminated on one end by a male connector and on the other end by a female connector as shown in Figure 4–2.

Any AUI cable that uses a male/male or female/female configuration is a non-standard cable and should be avoided. AUI cables were originally designed to attach transceivers to computers or other active network equipment. Transceivers, of course, require power to operate and that power can be supplied by a pair of wires in the AUI in the cable[1]. A male/male or female/female AUI cable does not properly supply power and grounding to the transceiver. If connected by female/female, both devices will try to draw power from each other and the configuration will not function.

[1]Or by an external power supply, of course.

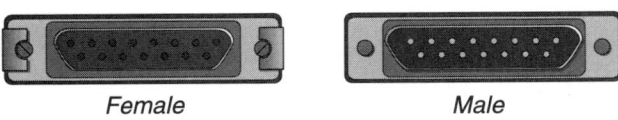

Female   Male

Figure 4–2 *Male and female AUI connectors.*

AUI Connector Pin Numbering

Some network operations require a network administrator to identify the pin order in the AUI connector. The general rule is: the channel located at the upper right-hand corner of the female DB15 connector is identified as channel 1. (See Figure 4–3.)

Further numbering continues across the top of the connector to Channel 8 at the upper left-hand corner. Channels 9 to 15 are the seven channels at the bottom of the connector, with channel 9 at the lower right-hand corner and channel 15 the lower left-hand corner.

The male DB15 connector reverses the left-right order of numbering, placing pin 1 at the upper left-hand corner, then following the path across and down to pin 15 at the lower right-hand corner. (See Figure 4–4.)

Another type of connector used in the world of the coaxial cable is Thinnet, which uses BNC (British Naval Connector) components to connect cables and computers together. BNC represents the whole family of connectors. Among them there are the following:

Channel 15   Channel 1

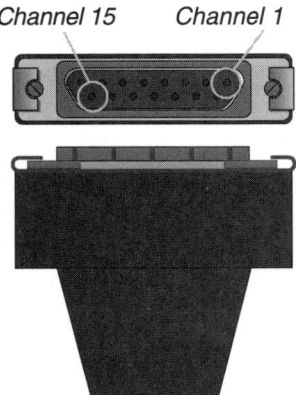

Figure 4–3 *AUI (DB15) Female connector numbering.*

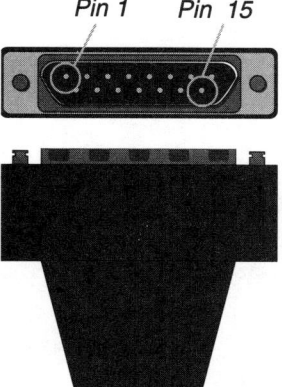

Pin 1   Pin 15

Figure 4–4 *AUI (DB15) Male connector numbering.*

- BNC cable connector
- BNC T-connector
- BNC barrel connector
- BNC terminator

There are varieties of BNC cable connectors that can be soldered, screwed, or crimped onto the end of the cable. Many network equipment manufactures recommend the use of the crimp-on BNC connectors for more stable and consistent connections. Typically, thinnet cable is built with a male BNC cable connector at either end. (See Figure 4–5.)

A BNC barrel connector (also known as a BNC female/female connector) is used to join two lengths of thin coaxial cable. The installation of a BNC barrel connector, however, causes some signal loss. You should not use an excessive number of barrel connectors when constructing your network. (See Figure 4–6.)

A BNC T connector is used to join the computer's network interface card to the network cable. The two female parts of the T-connector are attached to the thinnet coaxial cable though the standard BNC connectors.

Figure 4–5 *BNC cable connector.*

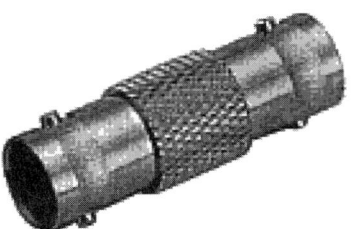

Figure 4–6 *BNC barrel connector.*

The male part of the T connector is attached directly to female BNC plug on the network adapter card. (See Figure 4–7.)

Although it is physically possible to do so, you should never attach the BNC cable directly to the network adapter card. Such a configuration will not work and will bring down your network. Additionally, you should always attach the T-connector directly to the computer. Attaching the T-connector through a coaxial jumper cable of any length may cause the coaxial-based network to go down. (See Figure 4–8.)

The BNC T-connector of the first and last computers in the bus must be connected to a BNC terminator.

BNC T-connectors should not be confused with the so-called BNC three male or BNC three female connectors that look very similar but are not usually used to connect thin coaxial cable to the network adapter. (See Figure 4–9.)

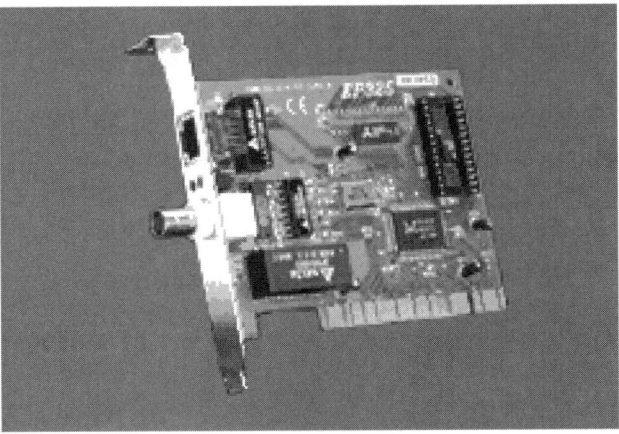

Figure 4–7 *Network adapter with the BNC connector.*

Figure 4–8 *BNC T-connector.*

A BNC terminator closes each end of the bus cable. (See Figure 4–10.) The reason for using terminators, is to absorb the transmitted signal at the end of the bus. Without BNC terminators, transmitted signals will reflect from the ends of the cable and the network will not function. Network standards strictly define the resistance values for terminators. The terminator resistance must match the cable's impedance. (For thicknet/thinnet the value is 50 ohms.) If you use terminators with different values, your network may not function. One BNC terminator on a bus must be grounded. Ensure you ground only one terminator, grounding both ends of the bus may do what we call "ground loops" and bring the network down.

Some network equipment is capable of performing internal termination. If a network device supports internal termination, and that device is located at one end of the thin coaxial cable, no external terminators need to be added to the cable segment.

Some BNC connectors provide an ability to connect thick coaxial cable.

Figure 4–9 *BNC Three male and three female connectors.*

Figure 4–10 *BNC terminator.*

Note Thick coaxial cable uses connectors similar to BNC connectors, but they are not compatible with the BNC connectors used in the thinnet. Thick coaxial cable uses N-series connectors. (See Figures 4–11 and 4–12.)

Twisted Pair

A twisted pair consists of two insulated copper wires. Typically the wires are 1 mm thick and may be solid or stranded. The wires are twisted together in a helical form, just like a DNA molecule. The reason for the twists is to reduce external electrical interference in the wires.

Let us say that a transceiver or computer network adapter card wants to send a signal using two twisted wires, which form a twisted pair. The means by which the ones and zeroes of network communications are turned into these signals is called encoding. In a twisted pair world, the signal is sent along one wire of the twisted pair; but at the same time, an inverted signal is sent along the second wire. (See Figure 4–13.)

The two signals that are sent along a single twisted pair are mirrors of each other. Since the pairs are twisted together, any outside electrical interference that affects one member of the pair will have the same effect on the

Figure 4–11 *Male connector N-series for thick coaxial cable.*

Figure 4–12 *Female connector N-series for thick coaxial cable.*

other member of the pair. At the destination transceiver, both signals are read in. The signal that had previously been inverted is reinverted and returned to its original state. The two signals are added together. Since the encoded transmissions are now identical, there is no change to the data content. Line noise spikes, however, are combined with noise spikes of their exact opposite polarity, causing them to cancel each other out.

The effect described above is known as CMR–common mode rejection.

The goal of twisting is to make sure all external interference has the same effect on both wires of the twisted pair by exposing them as equally as possible to any outside fields. That would not be the case if the pairs were not twisted, since one conductor would always be likely to be closer to the interference source than the other. Knowing this, we can say that the

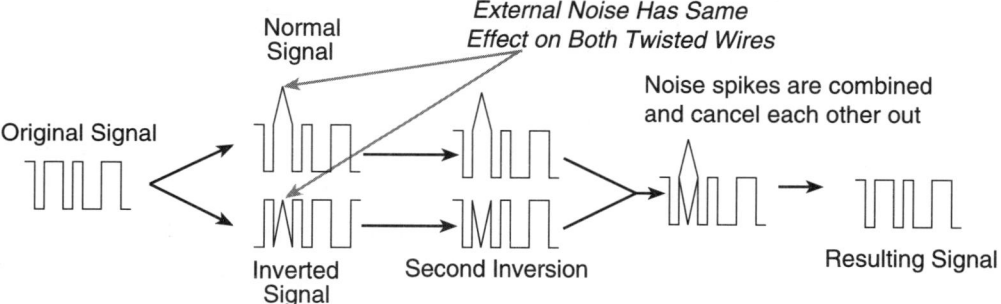

Figure 4–13 *Purpose of twisting.*

more twists per foot the twisted pair cable has, the better its resistance to interference.

The simplest example of twisted pair cable is a telephone wire. Almost all telephones use twisted pair that can run several miles without amplification.

There are two major classes of twisted pair:

- Unshielded twisted pair (UTP)
- Shielded twisted pair (STP)

Unshielded Twisted Pair

Unshielded twisted pair is the most popular type of twisted pair cable. Each pair consists of two insulated copper wires. As we said before, twisted pair can have a different number of twists per foot. Also, different types of twisted pair cable can have different signal attenuation levels. These and other electrical characteristics are described in the UTP standards, which are also known as *Electronic Industries Association and the Telecommunication Industry Association (EIA/TIA) 568 Commercial Building Wiring Standards*. These standards are needed to ensure product consistency. Without them, different products from different manufactures would not work in the same network.

The EIA/TIA 568 standards include several categories of twisted pairs. It is very important to be able to distinguish between the categories, since each has different characteristics and a different area of use:

- Category 1–refers to traditional UTP telephone cable, which can carry voice. Please note that this type of twisted pair is not able to carry digital signals, which means it was not designed to carry computer data.
- Category 2–certifies UTP cable for data transmissions up to 4 Mbps (Megabits per second). Usually it consists of four twisted pairs or eight wires.
- Category 3–certifies UTP cable for data transmission up to 10 Mbps. It consists of four twisted pairs. The standard also specifies the number of twists per foot.
- Category 4–specifies UTP cable for data transmissions up to 16 Mbps.
- Category 5–specifies UTP cable for data transmissions up to 100 Mbps.
- Category 6–became a standard in late 1998 and specifies UTP cable for data transmissions up to 1000 Mbps.

Shielded Twisted Pair

A significant problem with all cable types is *crosstalk*. Crosstalk occurs when signals from one line get mixed with signals from another line. Unshielded twisted pair is particularly sensitive to this phenomenon. To reduce crosstalk, as well as to protect the cable from external interference, shielding can be used. Another type of twisted pair, shielded twisted pair (STP), uses a woven copper braid jacket to provide this shielding. STP also uses a foil wrap between and around the wires. For additional protection double-foil shielding can be used.

Obviously shielded twisted pair is more expensive and more difficult to work with than UTP. For this reason, it is not as widely used as its unshielded counterpart.

Connecting Twisted Pair Cables

Twisted pair networks depend on a greater variety of hardware and equipment than that found in coaxial cable-based networks. If you decide to install a twisted pair network, be ready to deal with such components as RJ-45 connectors, distribution racks, rack shelves and even expandable patch panels. A good network designer is not only able to use each piece of equipment but can also combine them to achieve maximum network performance and scalability.

Connectors

The RJ-45 connector is a modular, plastic connector that is used in UTP cable installations. (See Figure 4–14.) The RJ-45 is called a keyed connector which means that you can plug it into a special RJ-45 port of the network adapter card only in one correct alignment.

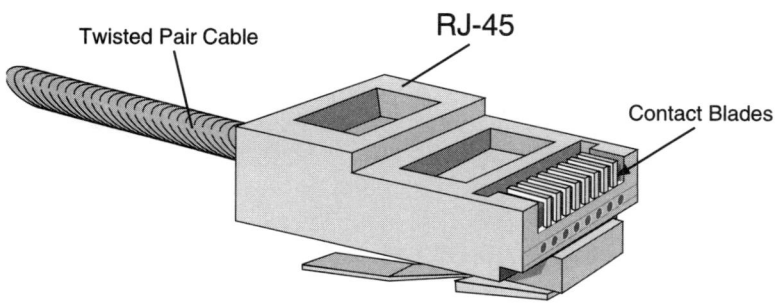

Figure 4–14 *RJ-45 Connector.*

The connector has a plastic body that is crimped onto a length of UTP cable using a special custom RJ-45 die tool. The connector body is often transparent and allows you to see how tight the twisted pair wires touch the contact blades or "pins."

RJ-45 connectors are available with many different modifications. Since the cabling industry is always improving and expanding their product lines, it is very hard to predict how connectors will appear in the future. Because of this, we will discuss only the two major classes of RJ-45 connectors. RJ-45 connectors for UTP cabling are available in two configurations: stranded and solid. (See Figure 4–15.) These names come from the type of wire to which they are designed to connect. You may remember that UTP cable can have solid or stranded copper wires. To provide better connection, the type blades in the RJ-45 connector should correspond the type of cabling being used.

As you may have deduced, the twisted pair cable is connected to an RJ-45 connector and the RJ-45 connector goes into the RJ-45 port on the network interface card. (See Figure 4–16.)

Typically, twisted pair cable has four twisted pairs or eight wires. This is convenient because RJ-45 connectors have eight blades! The question is: "In what order must you connect the wires to the blades to make it work?" Wiring order is important because certain wires in the twisted pair cable are used for sending data, while others are used for receiving it. You must be able to connect the RJ-45 connector properly or your computer will not be able to communicate.

To ensure consistency in wiring twisted pair connectors, several wiring standards have been developed. You will notice the wires that make up a length of UTP cable are color coded. The wiring standards specify which color must be connected to a particular RJ-45 pin.

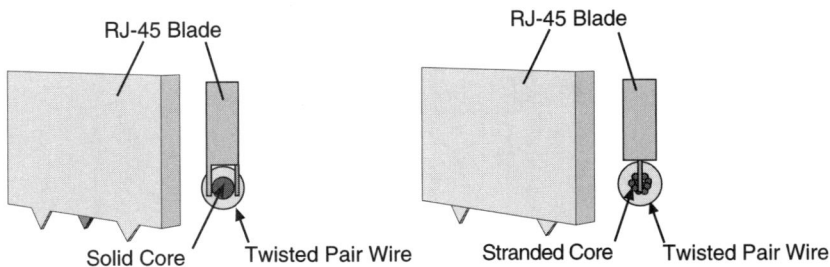

Figure 4–15   *RJ-45 blade types.*

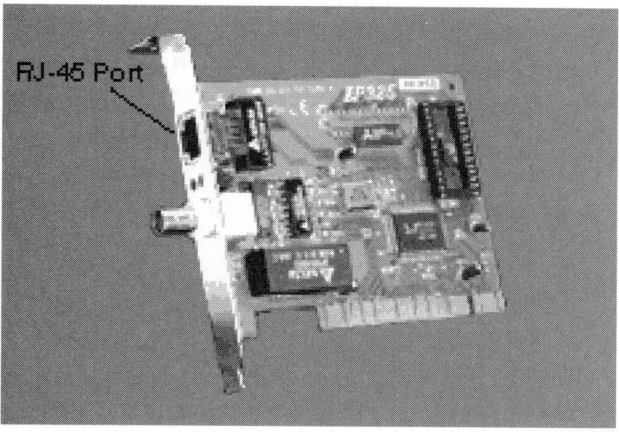

Figure 4–16 *Network adapter card with RJ-45 port.*

There are two main specifications in use around the world for the production of UTP cabling: EIA/TIA 568A and the EIA/TIA 568B. Every network administrator should know these two standards!

EIA/TIA 568A and the EIA/TIA 568B are mainly used in Ethernet-type networks. Other UTP wiring standards exist but they are not as popular as the two referenced previously.

If you plan to construct a twisted pair based network yourself, you should first select a wiring standard. Never use more than one wiring standard on the same network.

The wiring standard that is used in the 10-Mbps Ethernet type networks— EIA/TIA 568A— is shown in Figure 4–17.

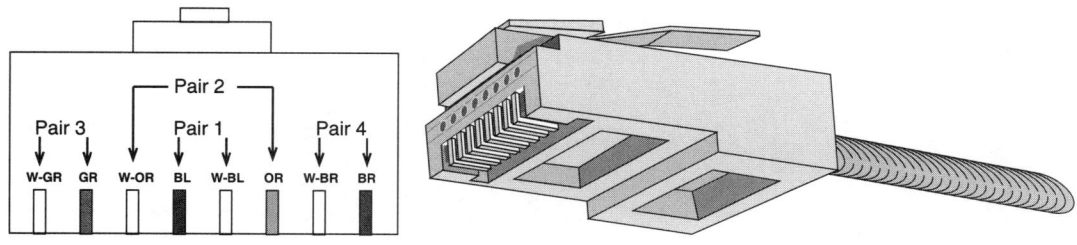

Figure 4–17 *RJ-45 connector pinout—EIA/TIA 568A.*

Carefully watch the orientation for the connector. On the diagram, the connector is pictured with the locking clip up. As you can see, the wire with the white and green insulation is connected to the first pin of the RJ-45 connector. The green wire is connected to the second pin, etc.

The wires with the white stripes are always connected to odd pins in the RJ-45 connector.

The EIA/TIA 568B specification exchanges Pair 1 and Pair 3, but does not change the association of pairs within the cable.

As the last comment regarding the RJ-45 connectors, we need to mention that they are often confused with the standard RJ-11 connectors (also known as modular telephone plugs). The RJ-11 connector that is used to connect your phone has only four pins, while the RJ-45 has eight. RJ-11 connectors are rarely used in computer networks. One of the few exceptions is the ArcNET network which uses the RJ-11 and is discussed later in this chapter.

Concentrators

Twisted pair networks are usually constructed according to the star topology. That means there is always a central component called a concentrator. You can use a hub, a switch, or even a router as a concentrator, but in spite of their functional differences, they all can bring multiple twisted pair segments together and all qualify as *concentrators*. (See Figure 4–18.)

Workstations and servers are connected to the concentrator using twisted pair segments. The concentrator connects all these segments together to permit communication between them.

Patch Panels

A patch panel is a piece of cable termination equipment, which connects raw facility cabling to standard ports or connectors. Generally speaking, cable

Figure 4–18 *Concentrator showing twisted pair ports.*

termination equipment provides points where facility cabling is connected to jumper cabling. Of course you can construct your network without this termination equipment, but such a network may be difficult to expand and change.

If you look at the patch panel from behind (see Figure 4–19), you will notice you must manually wire the twisted pair cables.

The back of the patch panel is made up of a number of connection points for facility cable. From the front, however (see Figure 4–20), patch panels provide a series of modular ports or connectors such as those for a standard RJ-45 interface.

These ports or connectors may then be used for simplified connections to jumper cabling, allowing a single, manageable point of access for several cables.

Wallplates

Although it is possible to connect a computer to a concentrator using a single twisted pair cable, it is not recommended. The reason is because network wires are usually hidden inside or below walls, making it very difficult to ensure that the cable will be of the required length, especially if you plan to move the computer in future. For the same reason you have wall outlets for electrical power, you should use wallplates for computer networks. (See Figure 4–21.)

Technically speaking, a wallplate is a small patch panel typically used at end user locations. The goal of the wallplate is to provide a connection and termination point for the facility cabling to which a user station may be connected with a length of jumper cabling. Wallplates may provide only one connector or may be capable of supporting eight or more separate connections.

Using modular wallplate construction options, you may have wallplates with a mix of RJ45, BNC, or fiber optic ST connectors—all based

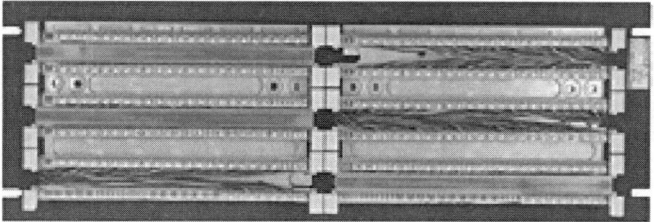

Figure 4–19   *Patch panel (rear view).*

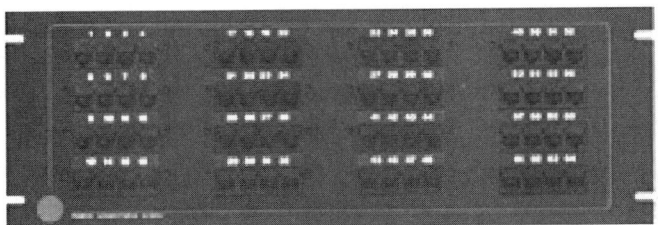

Figure 4–20   *Patch panel (front view).*

upon the needs of the location in question. The horizontal twisted pair cable, called a patch cable, is connected to the wall plate. The end user work-station (or other network device) is attached to the wall plate using a short piece of a twisted pair cable, called patch cord.

> Like cable, wallplates and nearly all other equipment have been assigned to categories. Make sure the category of the wallplate matches the category of your cabling system. Otherwise your network may suffer from performance degradations and even may stop functioning entirely.

Other Communication Equipment

Besides wallplates, hubs, and patch panels, other cable equipment may be used in building your network to make it more flexible and expandable. You can use punchdown blocks, distribution boxes, ty-wraps and adhesive

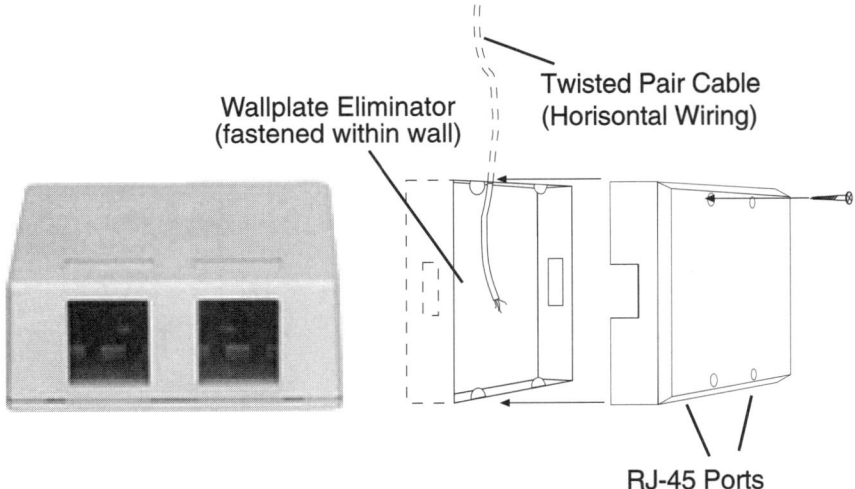

Twisted Pair Cable
(Horisontal Wiring)

Wallplate Eliminator
(fastened within wall)

RJ-45 Ports

Figure 4–21   *RJ-45 wallplate.*

anchors, and even relay racks and equipment cabinets. Whichever piece of equipment you use, you must carefully watch the standards. Never use equipment that follows different standards or your network may become nonoperational. If, for instance, you decide to use Category 3 wallplates in an otherwise Category 5 system, you will end up with a system that is only Category 3 capable.

Fiber Optic Cable

The third type of network media is fiber optic cable. Fiber optic cable is a high-performance medium constructed of glass or plastic. In contrast to the copper wires, where data is transferred as electric pulses, fiber optic cable uses pulses of light as a transmission method. Because of this, fiber optics is free of interference. The fact that fiber optic cable is not sensitive to external noise, combined with the extremely low rate of signal degradation and loss, makes fiber optics able to traverse extremely long distances without a need to be regenerated. The actual maximums are dependent upon the architecture being used, but distances of a mile or more are not uncommon. Additionally, visible light has a frequency of about 10^{12} MHz, so the bandwidth of an optical transmission system is enormous.

What makes fiber optic cable so remarkable? When we look inside, we find that glass optical fiber is made up of a glass strand, the core, which allows for the easy transmission of light; the cladding, a less transmissive glass layer around the core, which helps keep the light within the core; and a plastic buffer that protects the cable. (See Figure 4–22.)

You may think that fiber optic cables are all the same. Actually this is not completely true. There are two basic fiber optic cable types: multimode and single mode. The names come from the types of light used in the transmission process.

What keeps the light inside the internal glass core? The answer can be found in an interesting principal of physics: when light rays attempt to pass

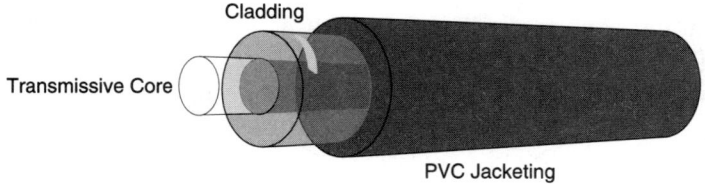

Figure 4–22 *Fiber optic cable construction (multimode).*

between media of different densities (in our case from the glass core to the cladding), they are refracted or bent at the boundary and routed back. The actual process is termed "total internal reflection" and can be described in terms of indices of refraction (you will be relieved to hear this lies outside the scope of this book). What you need to know is that the light *does* stay inside the glass core and can propagate many kilometers with little if any loss in intensity. This feature results in a reliable medium with far fewer transmission errors than we see when using wire.

The glass core itself has some thickness. To be more specific, some cables have a core that is about 50–60 microns thick. This permits several light rays (also called modes) to be bouncing around inside. This is exactly like a wide highway, which allows several cars to travel in one row and even allows them to change lanes. This type of fiber optic cable is called multimode. There is one significant drawback to multimode cable. Since the light rays (modes) can potentially travel along different paths within the core and may get bounced (reflected) a different number of times, they are likely to arrive at the other end of the cable at slightly different times. (Yes, light speed is finite!) This is called mode dispersion—another physics term. And again this plays an important role, because it limits the maximum bandwidth that we can put on a fiber optic cable.

If the diameter of the glass core is reduced to approximately 8–10 microns, only one ray (mode) of light can exist. This is similar to the situation when a narrow road can allow only one lane of traffic. This reduces the signal's bouncing options and allows higher transmission speeds over greater distances.

Multimode fiber uses inexpensive light emitting diodes (LEDs), and single mode fiber optics use lasers to achieve greater maximum distances. Since light from a laser consists of only a single wavelength and travels in a coherent ray, the resulting signal tends to be much clearer at the reception end than an LED signal under the same circumstances.

Fiber optics of both types are measured and identified by a variety of means. The usual means of referring to a fiber optic cable type is to identify if it is single mode or multimode and to describe the thickness of each strand. As we said before, fiber optic is very thin, and the diameter of each strand is measured in microns (μm). Two measurements are important in fiber optic identification: the diameter of the core, where signals travel, and the diameter of the cladding, which surrounds the core.

Thus, fiber optic measurements will usually provide two numbers separated by the "/" symbol. The first number is the diameter, in microns, of the core. The second is the diameter of the cladding.

Multimode fiber is usually marked as MM 62.5/125. MM stands for multimode, 62.5 is the diameter of the glass core in microns, and 125 is the diameter of the cladding. Single mode fiber is marked SM 8/125. S stands for single mode, the core diameter is 8 micron, and the diameter of the cladding is 125 micron.

Sometimes multiple cores of fiber optic cables are put in a single outer jacket. Additional metal central strength members and/or outside cording material can be added for durability. (See Figure 4–23.)

Connectors

Several connector types are available for fiber optic cables. However you have to keep in mind that most network architectures require you to use specific connector types. The Ethernet network standard defines the style of connector as being acceptable for both multimode and single mode fiber optic cabling. This is the straight-tip or ST connector.

ST connectors for single mode and multimode fiber optics are different in construction and are not to be used interchangeably.

As you can see in Figure 4–24, the ST connector is a keyed, locking connector that automatically aligns the center strands of the fiber optic cabling with the transmission or reception points of the network or cable management device to which it is connected.

Another type of connector that is used in fiber optic networks is the SC connector. It consists of two plastic housings: the outer and inner. The inner

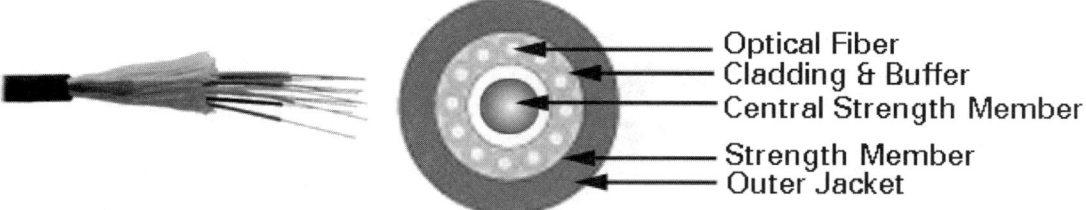

Figure 4–23 *Multimode breakout cable.*

Figure 4–24 *ST connector family.*

housing fits loosely into the outer and slides back and forth with a travel of 0.08 inches. This type of connector is typically used in 100 Mbps networks. The connector is designed this way because a very precise alignment of the fiber optic strands is required in order to make an acceptable connection in high-performance networks. In order to accomplish this, SC connectors and ports each incorporate "floating" ferrules to make the final connection between fibers. (See Figure 4–25.)

Other types of fiber optic connectors are available in the industry, but ST and SC are the most popular ones.

Choosing the Right Cable Type

Now that we have learned about the major cable types and their characteristics, we can summarize by making some recommendations concerning what cable types are suitable for particular networks. Before choosing a network type, you may want to answer the following questions:

- How heavy is the network traffic expected to be?
- What are the security requirements for the network?
- What territory must the cable cover?
- What is the budget for the project?

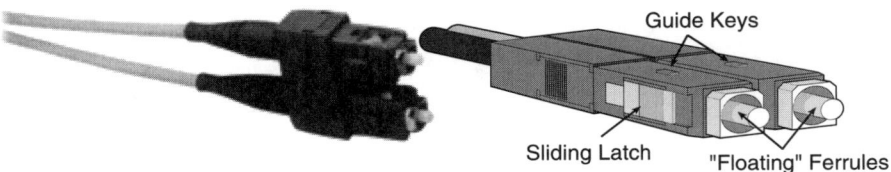

Figure 4–25 *SC connector family.*

Giving answers to these questions will help you to focus on the right things while planning your network. The problem of choosing a suitable cable type for your network is always a trade-off. You can initially save some money by using a sub-standard cable; but soon you may notice that your network suffers from low performance, high delays and inadequate security. It is best to keep the following considerations in mind when planning the cabling structure for your network:

- Installation logistics—it is always a good idea to consider how easy the cable is to install and work with. Sometimes the speed of installation is essential; sometimes it is not the issue. Obviously the cabling system for an office LAN will be different from that for a banking network. In smaller networks where distances are short, it does not make a lot of sense to choose cumbersome and expensive cable.

- Installation coverage—you may remember that different cables are able to carry signals over different distances. This means that you have to carefully measure the maximum distance your network will span. For example, if the most distant points are located 1,000 feet from each other, a single piece of the coax cable will not work. You may want to consider fiber optic cable that is able to carry the signal over the required distance.

 When we speak about maximum distances that a cable can carry a signal, we imply that we do not use any active equipment such as hubs, repeaters, or bridges. Using this equipment can overcome existing cable attenuation or access limitations. We will discuss usage of such equipment in the next chapters.

- Crosstalk—crosstalk as well as other external interference can cause significant problems, especially in the large networks where data security is critical. Some cables may have low resistance to outside electrical fields and other sources of electronic interference or "noise." To reduce or eliminate the influence of external noises and crosstalk, shielding can be used. The general rule is that the noisier the area in which the cable will be used, the more shielding will be required.

- Bandwidth (transmission speed)—as you may remember, transmission rates are measured by bits per second (bps). For high bandwidth networks we use megabits per second (Mbps). Do not confuse Megabits per second with megabytes per second (MBps)—you will err by a factor of eight! A standard LAN transmission speed is considered

Table 4.2 *Cable comparison summary*

Characteristics	Thinnet thin coaxial	Thicknet thick coaxial	Twisted pair	Fiber optics
Maximum cable length	607 ft (185 m)	1640 ft (500 m)	328 ft (100 m)	6562 ft (2 km)
Transmission rates	2–10 Mbps	10 Mbps	4–1000 Mbps	4–1000+ Mbps
Flexibility	Fairly flexible	Less flexible	Most flexible	Depends on the installation
Ease of installation	Easy to install	Easy to install	Moderately easy to install	Difficult to install
Resistance to external noise	Resistant	Resistant	Less resistant	Not affected
Connectors	BNC connectors	N series connectors	RJ-45	ST, SC connectors
Typical topology used	Bus	Bus	Star	Star

to be 10 Mbps. If you need higher speeds, you may want to consider using fiber optic cable, which is capable of transmitting data at speeds in excess of 1 Gigabit per second.

- Cost—sometimes choosing the best cable is not the best solution. Better cable, which transmits data over longer distances, is typically more expensive. Always keep in mind the cable costs and the installation costs, or you may run over of budget.

Table 4.2 summarizes what we have learned about different cable types.

Access Methods

Now that we understand different cable types, we turn our attention to how different network architectures function. In all networks, the data needs to be put on the wire and transmitted. This doesn't seem difficult, until we consider the situation where two computers transmit at the same moment in time. For simplicity, we will assume we have a bus network. If you think the data signals will meet in the wire, interfere with each other, and corrupt the data, you are right! This is called data collision. (See Figure 4–26.)

In order to provide reliable data communication, network architecture must be able to resolve these simultaneous transmissions. To do this, networks use one of several techniques, called *access methods*, to control access to the cable or other network media. Technically speaking, an access method is a set of rules defining how a computer puts data onto the network cable,

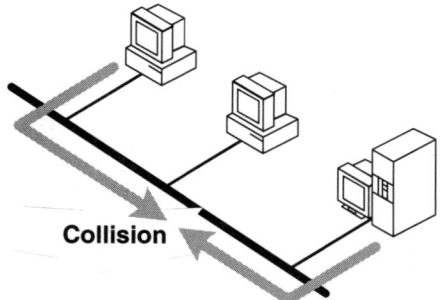

Figure 4–26 *Two computers that transmit simultaneously cause data collision.*

takes data from the network cable, and acts when the data becomes corrupted.

There are several methods to prevent simultaneous use of the cable. They are as follows:

- Carrier-sense multiple access with collision detection
- Carrier-sense multiple access with collision avoidance, which is a clone of the previous method
- A demand priority method
- A token passing method

Carrier-Sense Multiple Access with Collision Detection (CSMA/CD)

With this method each computer on the network, including clients and servers, can access the network at any time. In other words, the network is potentially accessible by several computers at once (multiple access). Before sending data, computers "listen" to the network to see if it is already in use (carrier-sense). If so, the station wishing to transmit, waits. If the network is not in use, the station transmits. Sometimes two stations listen for the network traffic; and when there is none, they transmit simultaneously. In this case, both transmissions are damaged. As we mentioned before, this is called a collision. The sending computers detect this collision and retransmit data at some later time (collision detection). Different network architectures use different algorithms to determine when the colliding stations should retransmit. For simplicity, assume that they retransmit after a random amount of time.

The CSMA/CD method has one significant drawback. When the number of computers increases, the method becomes less and less effective. As we discussed before, after each collision both computers involved in the collision must retransmit their data after a random time. If the network is busy, there is a good chance that the next attempt to retransmit will result in collisions with packets from other computers. If this happens, more computers must retransmit their data to recover from collisions, and so on. This proliferation of collisions and retransmissions can bring the entire network down. That is why most network architectures that use the CSMA/CD method recommend no more than a few hundred computers per network segment. To overcome this limitation, network devices, such as bridges, switches, and routers, may be used.

CSMA/CD is considered a *contention* method, because computers on the network complete (contend) for an opportunity to send data. This contention is, however, not normally noticeable to end users. Most CSMA/CD methods are fast enough to prevent users from experiencing performance degradations.

Carrier-Sense Multiple Access with Collision Avoidance (CSMA/CA)

This method is not as popular as its clone, CSMA/CD. In the carrier-sense multiple access with collision avoidance method, each computer signals its intent to send before it actually transmits data. Usually, this signaling is done by using broadcast messages that are received by all computers on the network. Having heard such an announcement, the other computers wait until the originator of the announcement sends its data, thus avoiding the dreaded transmission collisions.

As you may have determined, the CSMA/CA method increases the amount of network traffic on the cable because of the necessity to broadcast the transmission intent. CSMA/CA is generally considered a slower method than CSMA/CD, making it less popular in local area networks.

Token Passing

In the token passing method, a special type of packet, called a token, circulates around a cable. Token passing methods are usually implemented in ring topologies; however, token passing can be used in a bus topology as well.

When any computer wants to send data across the network, it must wait for a free token. No computer is permitted to transmit its own data without having a token. This method is noncontention based, which means that because only one station on the network can send data at a given time, stations do not have to compete for access to the transmission medium. The token is a unique set of bits that is recognized by each station on the ring. A station may initiate data transfer only when it holds the token. A special timer, called a *token holding timer,* controls the maximum time that a station can use the network before releasing the token. The token is passed from one station to another, providing each station in turn with an opportunity to transmit. A station obtains a token from its upstream neighbor and, when finished with the token, passes it to its downstream neighbor. A station will always pass the token to the next active station physically in line. To use the token, a sending station sets the token to busy and sends its data attached to the busy token.

Because there is only one token in the network, only one computer can transmit data. This means that the token-passing-based networks are completely collision free and no time is spent waiting for computers to retransmit collided data. While an environment devoid of collisions may seem like the solution to all the world's computing problems, it comes with a price. In large token ring, for instance, the time required for a computer to wait for the token may exceed the time required to make a retransmission or two. Generally speaking, contention systems out-perform token-ring systems in light, sporadic traffic environments.

Demand Priority

This access method is based on having a special central unit arbiter in the network hub. All computers and other devices are connected to this central hub according to the star topology. The arbiter is usually a special hub that manages network access by doing round-robin searches for requests on its ports. These requests are sent by the end nodes (e.g., computers) when they want to transmit data.

If two devices want to transmit data, the hub arbiter gives this right first to the device that has higher priority. Usually the priority is based on the type of application that requests data transfer. For example, multimedia applications are of higher priority than others.

The demand-priority method is generally more efficient that CSMA/CD. Unlike the CSMA/CD method, it broadcasts transmissions to the entire network. In demand priority, each hub knows about the nodes that are connected to it and will not propagate the signal to other nodes. Although the demand priority access method is considered faster, CSMA/CD was already in widespread use when demand-priority became available. Because of this and the fact that demand priority is more complex and, therefore, more expensive, CSMA/CD remains the dominant access method today.

Network Architecture

Now that we have seen the different cable types and access control methods, we are prepared to dive into network architectures. Network architectures combine standards, topologies, and protocols. Even more importantly, they delineate how all these things work together to produce a reliable network. We will discuss four of the most popular network architectures: Ethernet, token ring, FDDI and 100VG-AnyLAN. We will highlight the differences between them and describe advantages and disadvantages of each.

Ethernet

Ethernet, one of the oldest network architectures, was developed in the late 60s at the University of Hawaii. At that time only the basics of the technology were developed; and while there was a lot of theory, there was little implementation. One of the architecture's key features was the CSMA/CD access control method, which you will remember from the last section. The first Ethernet product that we would recognize today was actually created in 1975 in the laboratory at the Xerox Palo Alto Research Center. The first Ethernet network had less than 3-Mbps bandwidth, but the experiments were so successful that soon afterwards Xerox, Intel Corporation, and the Digital Equipment Corporation created a new standard for a 10-Mbps Ethernet.

As mentioned before, Ethernet is a carrier-sense multiple access/collision detection (CSMA/CD) technology. Nodes on an Ethernet segment can access the network at any time. Before sending data, Ethernet stations listen to the media to see if it is already in use. If the network is being used by another workstation, the station wishing to transmit waits. If the network is not in use, the station transmits. As we discussed before, when two stations "listen" for network traffic, "hear" none, and then transmit simultaneously, a collision occurs. In this case, both transmissions are damaged and the stations, sensing this collision, must retransmit at some later time.

Ethernet is a broadcast network. In other words, all stations see all frames, regardless of whether they represent an intended destination. Each station must examine received frames to determine if that station is the destination. If so, the frame is passed to a higher protocol layer for appropriate processing.

The typical Ethernet bandwidth is 10 megabits per second, although later developments have produced fast-Ethernet bandwidths of 100 megabits per second. There are drafts for 1 gigabit per second speeds.

Ethernet can transmit packets over a coaxial cable, fiber optic cable, or twisted pair cable. The topology is usually bus or star, where the coaxial or fiber optic cable typically represents the backbone, while twisted pair is used as a low-cost connection from the backbone to the desktop.

When Ethernet standards were created, the physical characteristics of the cables had to be considered. Originally, Ethernet standards enforced media restrictions primarily because of signal attenuation considerations. Ethernet specifies the following maximum cable lengths for cable runs without repeaters:

- 100 m for twisted pair cable
- 185 m for thin coaxial cable
- 500 m for thick coaxial cable
- 2,000 m for multimode fiber optic (10BASE-F) cable (5,000 m for single mode)

Even though the cabling industry has improved the cables' attenuation characteristics, Ethernet standards have remained the same. Some Ethernet products, such as network adapter cards and other equipment, are able to support longer cable runs. Typically, however, such networks will work reliably only if all components are from the same manufacturer. It is always recommended to follow the standards to the letter. Of course, this does not mean that if you exceed the maximum cable length by a foot, the network will stop working. But if your network does not comply with the standards, there is no guarantee of consistently reliable operation.

Study Break

Encoding Methods

Most computer networks require that information transmitted between two stations be divided into blocks called frames. In some networking books these frames are referred to as packets, but the correct technical term is frame. For these frames to be sent successfully to other computers, a certain algorithm must be used and some extra information must be added to the data. Additionally, the way this information is arranged inside the frame must conform to a specific format. Let's take a quick look at the way an Ethernet device places the bits of data into frames before the frame is sent across the wire. The algorithm that is used to place the data bits is called Manchester Encoding.

As you may already know, the information that has to be transmitted through the cable is converted to the form of a constantly changing voltage signal. This signal is effectively DC signal with a value of either 0 volts (v) or −1.2 volts. These electrical states are converted to the ones and zeroes the computer uses through a process called *Manchester encoding*. With Manchester encoding, the incoming digital signal is checked at specific time intervals for its change of state. In other words, the signal is checked to see if it is changing from 0 volts to −1.2 volts or from −1.2 volts to 0 volts. (See Figure 4–27.) Depending on its change of state over this specific time interval, also known as a *bit time*, the signal is assigned a logical value of "1" or "0." The result is a steady stream of bits with values of either logical "1" (corresponding to a change from −1.2 v to 0 v) or a logical "0" (corresponding to a change from 0 v to −1.2 v).

If there is no change of state during a certain bit time, that bit time is assigned a value corresponding to the value of the bit time preceding it.

10BASE-T Ethernet

In 1990, the IEEE committee published the standard for running Ethernet over twisted pair wiring. The abbreviation 10BASE-T stands for a 10 megabits-per-second network using the baseband transmission method over twisted pair cable (the letter "T" symbolizes twisted pair). Typically, this type of network uses unshielded twisted pair (UTP) category 3, 4, or 5 to connect computers and/or other network devices. Shielded twisted pair may also be used without changing any 10BASE-T characteristics.

A 10BASE-T network is configured in such a way that the resulting topology is a star. A multi-port repeater (also known as a hub) is used in a central location, such as a wiring closet, with twisted-pair segments going to workstation locations. Each segment can be a maximum of 328 feet (100 meters) in length, with no other taps or branches allowed. (The maximum number of 328 feet assumes the hub also functions as a repeater. For passive

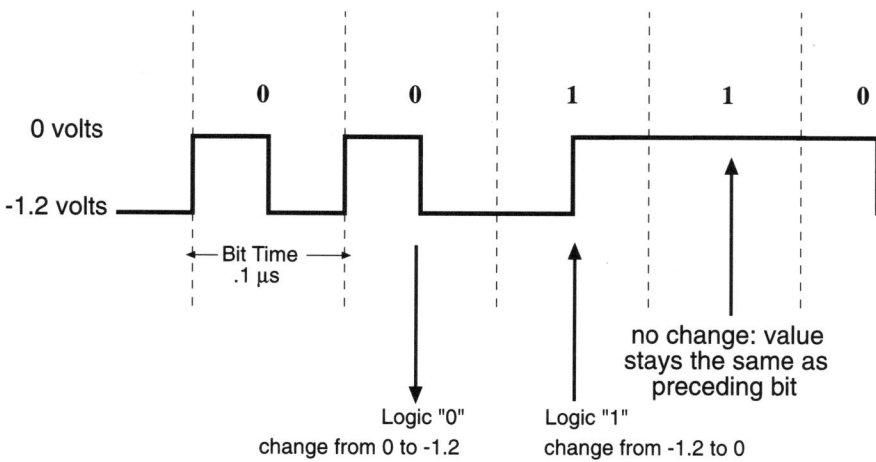

Figure 4–27 *Manchester encoding.*

hubs, each cable run should be not greater than half of this distance.) The 10BASE-T Ethernet standard also limits the minimum length of the cable between a hub and a computer — 8 feet (2.5 meters).

Since the number of ports in a hub is finite (usually limited to 8, 12, or 24), it is reasonable to ask: "How can I expand a 10BASE-T Ethernet network?" To get additional hubs, simply cascade multiple hubs to make the topology look like the picture on Figure 4–28.

Expanding 10BASE-T networks by adding extra hubs or other *active* devices overcomes the network's attenuation limitations (remember we mentioned that twisted pair wire is capable of transferring signals over a distance of 328 feet—100 meters). There are certain limitations, however, for the maximum number of hubs an Ethernet network will support. A rule of thumb is: the longest path a signal should travel between the most distant computers should not exceed four hubs and five cable segments. For example, the network pictured in Figure 4–29 will work since the longest path between the two most distant computers is five segments running through four hubs.

If you slightly redesign the network by connecting the fifth hub to the fourth one, this will make the longest path six segments through five hubs. Such a network may not work. (See Figure 4–30.)

These limitations are caused by the signal propagation delays in the wire (we will address how this is related to access methods later in the chapter). If you want to expand your 10BASE-T network further, you must use devices, such as bridges and routers, which operate at higher layers of the OSI model.

In addition to the hardware described above, a 10BASE-T network can use patch panels, wall plates, and other equipment. Whatever equipment you decide to use must be compliant with 10BASE-T Ethernet standards.

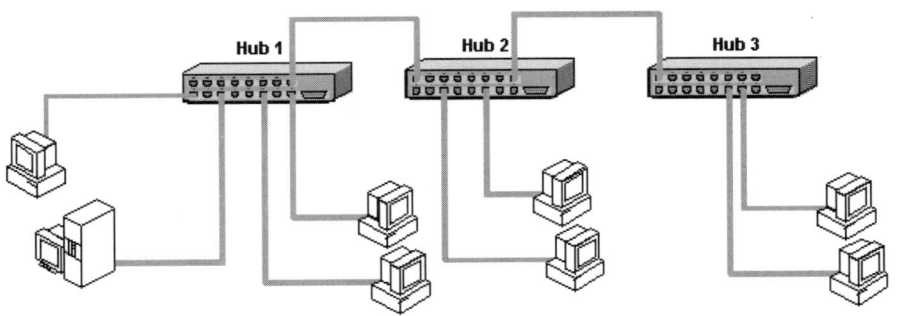

Figure 4–28 *You can cascade hubs to expand the 10BASE-T network.*

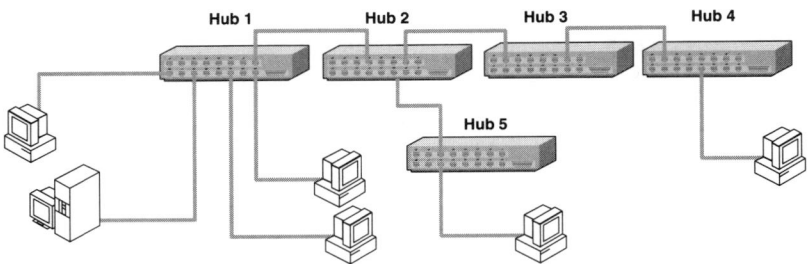

Figure 4–29 *10BASE-T network with 5 hubs.*

10BASE-5 Ethernet

10BASE-5 is also a 10-megabit per second network. Like 10BASE-T, it uses the baseband transmission method. The number five indicates that this type of network is capable of transferring data across a distance of 500 meters (five times greater than 10BASE-T). Also known as standard Ethernet, 10BASE-5 networks use thick coaxial cable.

The use of thick coaxial cable implies usage of equipment such as AUI cables and transceivers. The cable must be terminated at both ends with N-type connectors and 50-ohm N-type terminators. The cable used for this type of network should be marked with annular rings by the cable manufacturer every 2.5 m indicating potential transceiver tap points. The 10BASE-5 standard also limits the maximum number of network devices attached to the segment to 100 nodes (a node is a computer, repeater, bridge, etc.).

Since 10BASE-5 networks run over greater distances than 10BASE-T networks, they can be used as a backbone to connect several remote network segments. You can combine several 10BASE-5 networks using repeaters. Repeaters should be connected to the thicknet cable in the same

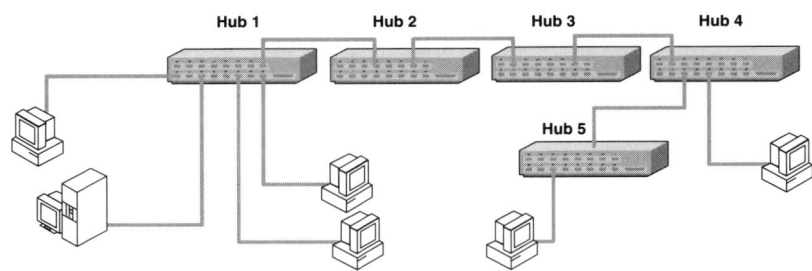

Figure 4–30 *10BASE-T network with 5 hubs.*

manner you would connect the regular workstations—using vampire taps. (See Figure 4–31.)

Repeaters can be used to connect up to three 10BASE-5 segments before special considerations need to be taken into account. If it is necessary to connect more than three coaxial segments together, then an inter-repeater link (IRL) must be used. An IRL is a segment that spans between two repeaters with no other devices attached to it. It can be made up of thin coaxial cable, thick coaxial cable, fiber optic cable, or twisted pair cable with the appropriate media limitations being observed. The 10BASE-5 standard allows only four repeaters connecting 5 thicknet segments. Only three of these segments may be populated by devices—if required, the other two may only be IRLs. This allows a total linear distance of 2,500 m when only 10BASE-5 thick coaxial cable is used.

Note

This concept "five segments connected with four repeaters and only three segments are populated" is also known as the 5–4–3 rule.

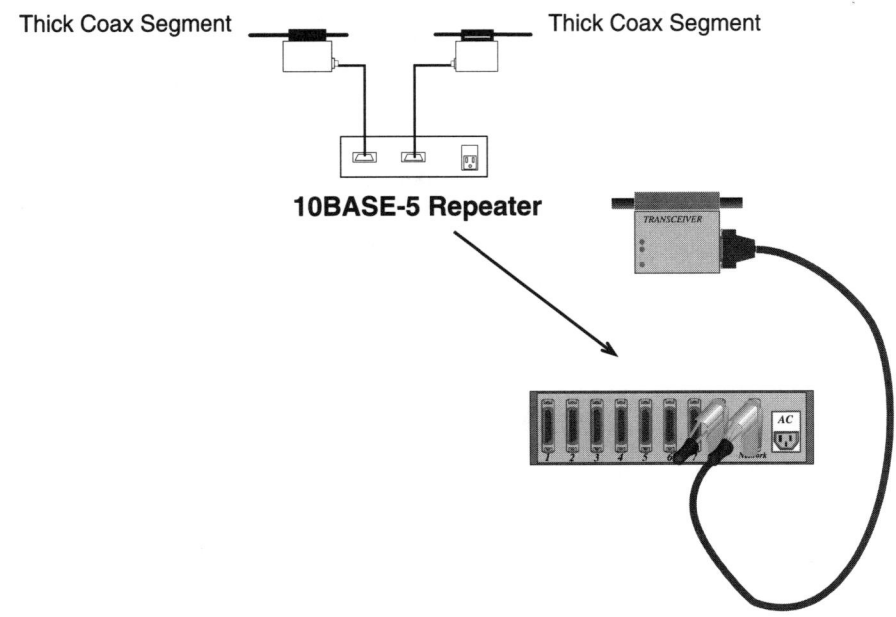

Figure 4–31 *Connecting thicknet segments in 10BASE-5.*

10BASE-2 Ethernet

10BASE-2 is another IEEE specification for Ethernet running on RG58 A/U or thin coaxial cable. As we discussed earlier in this chapter, 10BASE-2 coaxial cable is more flexible and less expensive than 10BASE-5 coaxial cable, while still maintaining the required 50-ohm nominal impedance. According to the 10BASE-2 standards, the maximum length of a 10BASE-2 cable segment is 185 m. The two in 10BASE-2 represents the 185 meters rounded up to 200. Only 30 taps are allowed on a 10BASE-2 segment, and the cable is connected using BNC T connectors and terminated using 50-ohm BNC terminators. The minimum cable length between two computers is 0.5 meters (20 inches).

Like 10BASE-5, 10BASE-2 must comply with the 5–4–3 rule. That is, you can use no more than 4 repeaters, only 3 segments can be populated with computers, and the other two are inter repeater links.

10BASE-FL Ethernet

The IEEE committee also published a specification for running Ethernet-type networks over fiber optic cable. This specification is known as 10BASE-FL, where F stands for fiber optics. Please note that this type of Ethernet network functions at the speed of 10 megabits per second even though the bandwidth provided by the fiber optics is greater. The limitation of 10 Mbps is due to compatibility issues with other Ethernet networks. The primary reason for using 10BASE-FL is to serve as a backbone between repeaters and to connect distant locations. The maximum distance for a 10BASE-FL Ethernet is 2,000 meters, and this limitation is caused by the attenuation characteristics of multimode fiber optic cable.

Study Break

Combining Different 10 Mbps Ethernet Networks

Today, networks that consist only of one cable type are rare. Sometimes you need to combine, for example, thick coaxial cable and thin coaxial cable. Or you need to connect two 10BASE-T networks that are separated by a kilometer, which requires a cable type that will support such a distance. You may combine cable types through the use of repeaters designed for such adaptations. There is one rule, however, that you never want to break—if you are using repeaters, you can only connect networks that are of the same architecture and speed. For example, it is possible to connect 10BASE-T and 10BASE-FL segments, but trying to connect segments of 10 and 100 megabits per second will not be successful. Additionally, repeaters cannot be used to connect networks of different architecture (for example Ethernet and token ring) because of differences in their frame types.

You may remember that we spoke about the 5–4–3 rule that prevented us from using an unlimited number of repeaters. You may be surprised to learn that this rule of thumb is actually *too* restrictive and is used only to avoid complex calculations.

Why couldn't we use, for example, 100 repeaters to connect thick coaxial cable segments. Obviously, attenuation is not a problem, since each repeater will regenerate the signal. There must, then, be some reason beyond attenuation. The answer to this rather complex question is hidden in the term *propagation delay*. Earlier in this chapter we mentioned that Ethernet, like any other network type, transmits data using small blocks called frames. IEEE defines both a minimum and a maximum frame size. The minimum frame size is 64 bytes (46 bytes for data and 18 bytes for system information). The maximum frame size is 1,518 bytes (same as mentioned before with a 1,500-byte data field). What happens when a workstation transmits a 64 byte (512 bit) frame? At 10 megabits per second, it takes 0.1 µs to send one bit or 51.2 µs to transfer 512 bits. This may not seem particularly important, until we remember what access control method is used by Ethernet. You may recall that Ethernet uses CSMA/CD; that means in order to function properly, a workstation must still be transmitting when it receives a collision signal. Otherwise the workstation will not recognize that the collision signal pertains to the transmission it just made and will be unable to tell that its transmission was corrupted before reaching the destination host.

Under the worst case scenario, it would make sense that within 25.6 µs (half of 51.2 µs), our transmitted signal should have reached the farthest point on the network. If a collision were to happen at the farthest point on the network, the collision signal will have the remaining 25.6 µs to travel back to the transmitting node to alert the node that its transmission needs to be re-sent. If it takes more than 25.6 µs for the signal to come back, the sending workstation may have stopped transmitting and would, therefore, miss the collision alert.

Now that we understand propagation delay, we can make a general rule for Ethernet networks that function at 10 Mbps. The network length (between the most distant nodes) should not exceed 25.6 µs.

Each device and each meter of cable adds its own propagation delay. For example, a typical multi-port repeater or hub has approximately 1.5 µs delay, one meter of twisted pair cable adds 0.0057 µs. If you add propagation delays from all devices in the network, this value should not exceed 25.6 µs.

The 5–4–3 rule is an approximation that is much more restrictive than the propagation delay rule. If the 5–4–3 rule is satisfied, the propagation delay rule is satisfied as well. If you want to overcome the limitation of these rules, you must use other network devices that operate above the *physical layer*, for example bridges, switches, and routers.

100-Megabits-per-Second Ethernet Standards

As networks grew larger, demand for higher bandwidth grew as well. In 1993, the IEEE committee introduced two competitive technologies that were capable of transferring data at a speed of 100 Mbps. One of them became what is now known as fast Ethernet. Fast Ethernet standards are also known as 802.3u standards.

Ethernet standards for 100 Mbps are divided into several categories depending on cable types and encoding methods. The types of 100-Mbps-Ethernet networks are as follows:

- 100BASE-TX
- 100BASE-T4
- 100BASE-FX

100BASE-TX • This standard describes the physical layer of the network. It specifies the Ethernet-type network that runs over the 2 twisted pairs (4 wires) of category 5 UTP. 100BASE-TX also allows the use of shielded twisted pair. The use of two twisted pairs permit the allocation of one pair for sending data and another pair for receiving data. Some network devices are able to send and receive data simultaneously—this is called full duplex. (We will discuss full duplex networks in greater detail later in this book.)

The biggest advantage of the 100BASE-TX network is that it is fully compatible with the 10BASE-T network at the cable level. This effectively means that if you have used category 5 to build your existing 10BASE-T network, upgrading may require only changing active equipment, such as network adapter cards and concentrators. The cabling system can remain untouched as long as its installation followed appropriate 100BASE-TX guidelines, such as the way it is attached to the wall.

Note

The category of cabling used in a network installation is dependent upon all the components that make up the cable run. If, for example, an installation utilizes category 5 cabling, but the wallplates and patch panels to which that cabling is connected are category 3 compliant, the cable does not meet the EIA/TIA end-to-end specifications for a category 5 installation.

100BASE-T4 • This standard specifies 100-megabits per second Ethernet over a twisted pair cable category 3, 4, or 5. At this point, you may be surprised that the category 3-twisted-pair cable can be used for 100-Mbps technologies. The answer is found in the number of twisted pairs employed and the encoding techniques used.

100BASE-T4 uses four twisted pairs or eight wires. Three twisted pairs are dedicated for sending and receiving data and the fourth twisted pair is used to sense collisions.

100BASE-FX · The 100BASE-FX specification defines the 100 Mbps Ethernet network over a fiber optic link using two strands of 62.5/125 multimode cable. One strand is used for sending data, another for receiving. As with 100BASE-TX, some devices support a full duplex connection, meaning that they can send and receive simultaneously.

FAST ETHERNET TOPOLOGY · Fast Ethernet uses a star topology. As a concentrator, fast Ethernet uses a multiport repeater (hub) just like 10BASE-T. Obviously because of the speed difference, you can not use your 10BASE-T hub on a fast Ethernet network unless it supports both technologies—a so-called 10/100 hub. (This is a completely new type of device that uses switching technologies).

While all concentrators for 10BASE-T are functionally identical, fast Ethernet prescribes two different types of concentrators (repeaters)—class I repeater and class II repeater.

The difference between the two classes is the method each uses to handle received signals for transmission. The different techniques result in different configuration rules for fast Ethernet networks.

Class I repeaters receive the 100BASE-TX electrical signal on one interface and translate that signal from its electrical form into a digital series, much in the same way that a fast Ethernet station receives a transmission. Then the new signal is generated on each of the repeater's interfaces using the translated digital series. This translation is necessary to reflect the differences in physical layer technologies that can be connected to class I repeaters (100BASE-TX and 100BASE-T4). Typically the class I repeater does not make any decisions based on the received signal, nor does it perform any error checking. The translation of the received signal is intended to improve the strength and validity of the repeated fast Ethernet frame. The fact that class I repeaters translate signals causes higher delays but allows combining technologies such as 100BASE-TX and 100BASE-T4.

The class II repeater receives and immediately repeats each received transmission without performing any translation. The repeating process is a simple electrical duplication and strengthening of the signal.

Study Break

Propagation Delay in Fast Ethernet

Earlier in this chapter, we discussed the propagation delay in 10 Mbps Ethernet networks. We discovered that 10-megabit Ethernet technologies are limited in length to 25.6 μs. Remember that this limitation is caused not because of the attenuation, but because of the collision discovery algorithms that are used in CDMA/CD. When the network radius becomes more that this critical value, collisions of the shortest frames cannot be properly discovered. If you think that 100 megabits per second Ethernet technologies inherit similar limitations, you are right! With 100 Mbps, however, the situation becomes even more critical. Now the maximum one-way propagation delay must be no more than 2.56 μs — 10 times smaller than in the 10 Mbps Ethernet. One might think that, because of this, the network radius for 100BASE Ethernet networks must be ten times smaller. Fortunately, 100 Mbps repeaters have smaller delays in signal propagation, and because of this, the twisted pair segments that connect end workstations to concentrators can still be as long as 100 meters.

The number of repeaters that can be used in an unbridged[2] fast Ethernet network is different from that found under 10 Mbps technologies. You can use only one class I repeater or two class II repeaters between any two workstations in fast Ethernet. There is a simple explanation to this limitation. Because the delays in signal propagation for class I repeaters are higher (approximately 0.7μs), adding the second class I repeater will exceed the maximum propagation delay for the network and will bring the entire segment down. In contrast, you can place two class II repeaters in a single Ethernet segment, due to their smaller propagation delay — 0.46 μs.

Sometimes you may see even more technical interpretation of the above rule. In fast Ethernet, there should be no more that one class I and no more than two class II repeaters in a single collision domain.

To increase the number of stations on a fast Ethernet segment, you can obtain stackable hubs. In this case a stack of hubs (repeaters) is considered as one device. (The increase, however, may not be "free," since, in most cases, the resulting "device" comes with additional propagation delays.)

100VG-ANYLAN: AN ALTERNATIVE 100 MBPS TECHNOLOGY • Both fast Ethernet and the network architecture called 100VG-AnyLAN are about 5 to 10 times faster than standard Ethernet. The "VG" in 100VG-AnyLAN stands for voice grade. This is an emerging network technology that combines elements from both Ethernet and token ring networks. It was developed by Hewlett-Packard and quickly became popular (of course not as popular as Ethernet).

[2]This is a network that doesn't use devices such as bridges or routers to extend its length.

Later, 100VG-AnyLAN was refined, and now it is described by the IEEE standard 802.12 as *Standard for Transmitting Ethernet Frames and Token Ring Packets.*

The specifications for 100VG-AnyLAN include, but are not limited to

- A minimum data rate of 100 Mbps
- Cascaded star topology over categories 3, 4, and 5 UTP
- *Demand priority* access method with two priority levels—high and low
- Filtering of frames based on the destination address to achieve a high level of security and privacy
- Support for both Ethernet (802.3) and token ring (802.5) packets

100VG-AnyLAN requires the use of special concentrators (hubs) and network adapter cards. The network can be expanded by adding child hubs and connecting end computers to them. The parent hub controls transmission of computers attached to its children.

100VG-AnyLAN concentrators have a special port dedicated for connections to parent concentrators. This port is called an uplink port. 100VG-AnyLAN concentrators also have several downlink ports for connecting end workstations.

Token Ring

The token ring architecture was suggested by IBM back in the 1980s. Its popularity quickly spread. The technology was adopted by IEEE in the 802.5 specification which is fully compatible with the native IBM token ring network. Although it has been around for a long time, the technology is still a core network architecture for IBM local area networks. The term "token ring" is used to reference IBM token ring networks using two different standards—4 and 16 Mbps.

General Considerations

You may have guessed that token ring networks use the token passing access control method. Token ring is, therefore, considered noncontention based, which means that because only one station on the network can send data at one time, stations do not have to compete for access to the transmission medium.

The token is nothing more than a unique set of bits that is recognized by each station on the ring. As we discussed before, a workstation may initiate data transfer only when it holds the token. The token is passed from one station to another, providing each station in turn with an opportunity to transmit. A station obtains a token from its upstream neighbor and, when finished with it, passes the token to its downstream neighbor. The next logical question is what if a workstation wants to send gigabytes of data? What prevents a workstation from holding the token unreasonably long and making other workstations wait? The secret is found in the token holding timer that controls the maximum amount of time a station can use the network before releasing the token.

A station will always pass the token to the next active station physically in line on the ring. After receiving the token, a sending station sets the token to busy and sends out a data message to the next workstation. The data is passed from station to station around the ring, being accepted by the station for which it is addressed. After being copied by the destination station, the data circulates until it arrives back at the source station, where it is deleted from the ring. Thus the sending workstation acts like a garbage collector, preventing data frames from endlessly looping in the ring. The station then releases the token onto the ring for the next station to claim.

Topology and Connectors

As it follows from the name, the token ring topology is a ring. As you may remember, the ring topology is a point-to-point network in which the network devices are connected, machine-to-machine, in an unbroken unidirectional circle. In Chapter One, we said that most ring topologies resemble a physical star, but careful examination will reveal a logical ring.

The ring is most typically constituted by sets of multistation access units (MSAUs) interconnected via their ring in/ring out (RI/RO) ports. The RI/RO ports allow multiple MSAUs to be connected to form a single ring. (See Figure 4–32.)

Each MSAU typically has eight to twenty-four trunk coupling units (TCU), or lobe ports, into which stations are connected via lobe cabling.

In token ring, adding or removing stations on the network is relatively simple. Although it seems unrealistic, you can even do this without powering down the network. Software included with the token ring adapter cards in each station on the ring automatically reconfigures the logical ring in response to the addition or removal of stations on the ring. Obviously to take advantage of this functionality, special connectors or ports must be used to maintain the integrity of the ring. For example, the medium interface connector (MIC) is made up of a plastic outer shell and four gold-plated contacts arranged in two rows of two each. (See Figure 4–33.) The design of the MIC connector allows it to internally self-short. When the connector is

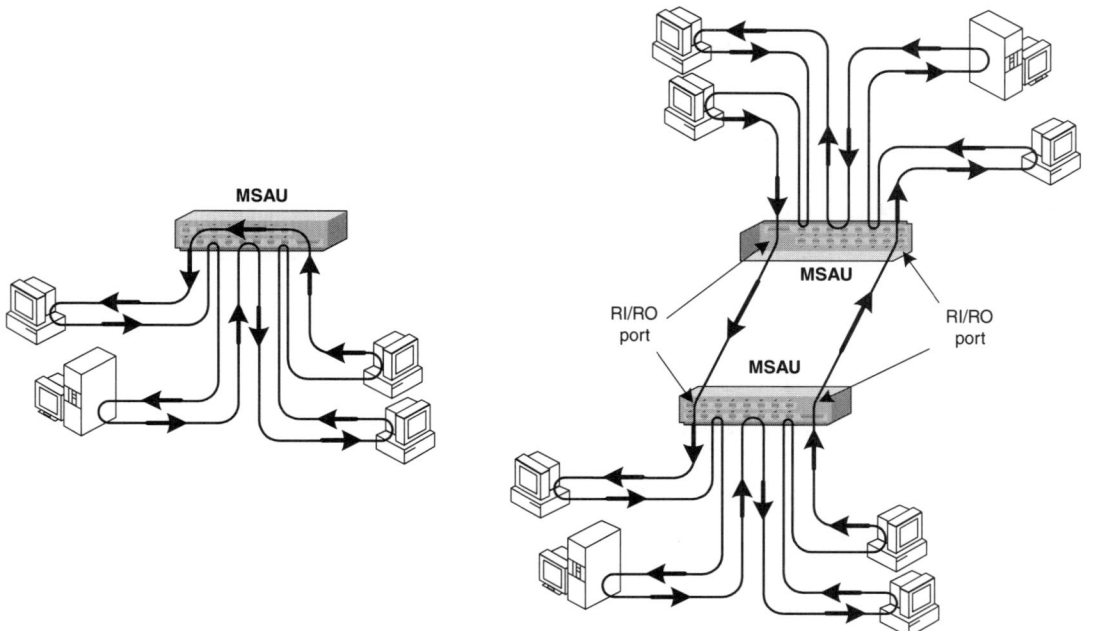

Figure 4–32 *Token ring MSAUs can be connected together to form a single ring.*

properly attached to another MIC connector, spring-release mechanisms open the transmit and receive paths. Once unplugged, the paths are looped back onto one another, allowing token ring signals to travel back through the cable and remain in the token ring network. This keeps the ring whole, when a connector is unplugged from a jack.

Study Break

Physical Layer Signaling Technique

Token ring networks use a signaling technique known as differential Manchester encoding. Differential Manchester encoding uses a signal transition at the *start and center* of the bit cell time to represent a 1, 0, J, or K bit. In the case of the two data symbols binary 1s and 0s, a signal element of one polarity is transmitted for one half of the bit cell time followed by the transmission of a signal element of the opposite polarity for the remainder of the bit cell time. With differential Manchester encoding (see Figure 4–34), the sequence of signal polarities is completely dependent on the polarity of the second half of the previous bit cell time.

If a bit to be transmitted during any given bit cell time is a 0 (zero), then the polarity of the first half of that bit cell time is opposite to that of the previous bit cell time. For a zero, then, polarity changes occur at the start of the bit cell time and at the midbit time.

If the bit to be transmitted is a 1 (one), the polarity of the first half of that bit cell time is the same as that of the previous bit cell time. In other words, for a one there is no polarity change at the start of the bit cell time, but there *is* a polarity change at the midbit time.

In order to transmit bit J, there is no polarity change at the start of the bit and no polarity change at the midbit time either.

Finally, bit K is transmitted with a polarity change at the start of the bit but no midbit polarity change.

Both J and K violate the differential Manchester encoding scheme since they have no midbit polarity transition. These bit types are used to construct frame delimiters (to recognize when the frame begins and ends) and serve other system functions such as token management.

In addition to MIC connectors, token ring networks can use DB9 and RJ-45 connectors, as well as ST connectors, for fiber optic cable.

Ring Management

Obviously, token ring networks must have some ring management functions. Each ring must have a master station known as the active monitor (AM). The active monitor plays a critical role in both the MAC/data link layer and the physical layer functions. All stations have the ability to be the active monitor, but only one active monitor is allowed per ring at any one

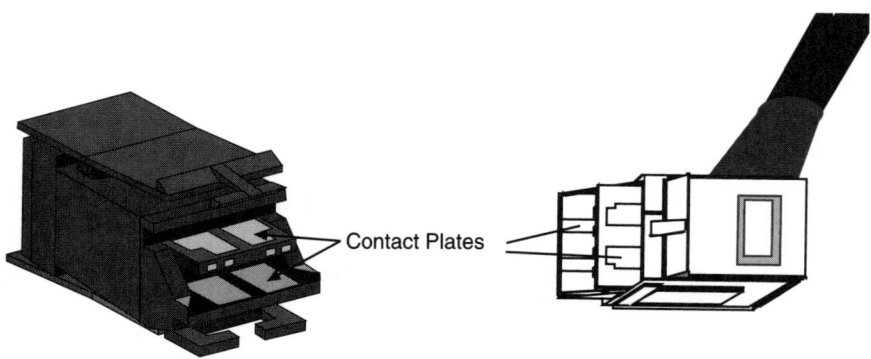

Contact Plates

Figure 4–33 *Token ring MIC connector.*

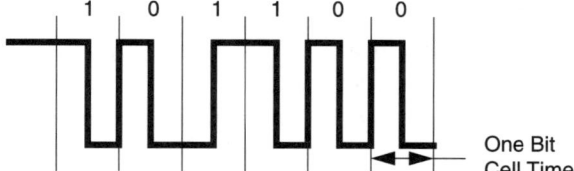

Bit = 0 if there are two polarity changes in a bit cell time
Bit = 1 if there is one polarity change in a bit cell time

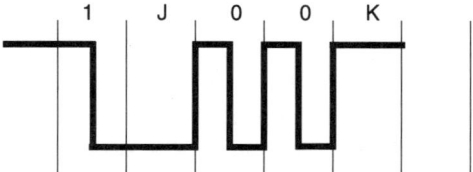

Bit = J if there is no polarity change at start of bit time
Bit = K if there is a polarity change at start of bit time

Figure 4–34 *Differential Manchester encoding.*

time. The AM is usually selected at initialization time and is usually the first station to access the ring.

In some situations, a new AM is required, for example, when the AM loses power. The process to select a new AM is known as *monitor contention.*

The act of powering up a station does not immediately enable it to become part of the ring. Certain tests are performed while the adapter is being initialized by the software drivers. The basic tests are known as insertion tests and include active monitor tests, duplicate address tests, ring poll tests, and request initialization.

Cable System

Computers on a token-ring network can be connected using standard STP, UTP, fiber optic cable, or special IBM-type cables. Depending on the cables used, there are certain limitations to the maximum cable length and the maximum number of workstations in the ring. For example, if shielded twisted pair (STP) is used in the 16 Mpbs token-ring network, the maximum distance between a MSAU and end computer is 100 meters. When the same STP cable is used in a 4 Mbps token-ring network, the maximum cable length limit becomes 200 meters.

The recommended maximum cable lengths and number of stations in the ring for different types of token-ring networks are presented in Table 4.3. The two values in each cell represent active and passive equipment accordingly.

ArcNet

ArcNet was originally classified as a local area network, or LAN, when it was originally introduced as an office automation network by Datapoint Corporation in the late 1970s. Datapoint envisioned a network with distributed computing power operating as one large computer. This system was referred to as ARC (attached resource computer), and the network that connected these resources, was called ArcNet.

Although ArcNet's use as an office automation network has diminished, it continues to find success in the industrial automation arena because its performance characteristics are well suited for control. ArcNet has proven itself to be very robust and fast. It provides deterministic performance and can span long distances making it a suitable *fieldbus* technology. The term fieldbus is used in the industrial automation discipline to signify a network consisting of computers, controllers, and devices mounted in the field. ArcNet is an ideal fieldbus. Unlike office automation networks, a fieldbus must deliver messages in a time-predictable fashion. ArcNet's token-passing protocol (token bus) provides this timeliness. Fieldbus messages are generally short. ArcNet packet lengths are variable up to 507 bytes with little overhead and are coupled with a comparatively high data rate, typically 2.5 Mbps. The successor of ArcNet, ArcNet Plus, supports transmission rates up to 20 Mbps.

In terms of the OSI reference model, ArcNet conforms to the physical and data link layers. In other words, ArcNet provides successful

Table 4.3 *Recommended Maximum Cable Lengths and Stations for Token Ring Networks*

Cable Type	Max Stations 4 Mbps	Max Cable length 4 Mbps	Max Stations 16 Mbps	Max Cable length 16 Mbps
STP Type 1,2	250/250	300 m/200 m	250/250	150 m/100 m
UTP Cat. 5	150/100	250 m/130 m	150/100	120 m/85 m
Multimode FO	250	2 km	250	2 km

transmission and reception of a data packet between two network nodes. Nodes are assigned addresses called MAC (media access control) Ids, and one ArcNet network can have up to 255 uniquely assigned nodes.

Topology

ArcNet is a very flexibly cabled network. It supports different topologies such as bus, star, and distributed star topologies. In a bus topology, all nodes are connected to the same cable as in 10BASE-2 Ethernet. The star topology requires a device called a hub (passive or active), which is used to concentrate the cables from each of the nodes.

ArcNET passive hubs require no power, and their sole purpose is to match line impedances, which they do with resistors. They are relatively inexpensive. These hubs usually have four ports to connect four coaxial star transceivers. The disadvantage of using these hubs is that they limit the network to 200 feet. Unused ports of an ArcNet passive hub must be terminated with a 93-ohm resistor for proper operation.

The distributed star (all nodes connect to an active hub with all hubs cascaded together) offers flexibility and allows the network to extend to greater than four miles (6.7 km). Media support includes coaxial, twisted-pair, and glass fiber optics.

ArcNET active hubs are essentially electronic repeaters. They require power, and support longer distances than passive hubs. They provide isolation and guard against cabling faults and reflections. Unused ports on an active hub need not be terminated. Unlike passive hubs, active hubs do not attenuate signals and can be cascaded.

Media Access Control Method

We have already said that ArcNet uses a token passing method. Similar to token ring, ArcNet uses a unique signaling sequence that is passed in an orderly fashion among all the active nodes in the network. As with token ring, when a particular ArcNet node receives the token, it has the sole right to initiate a transmission sequence or pass the token to its logical neighbor. This neighbor can be physically located anywhere on the network (in contrast to token ring, which passes the token to the next downstream neighbor only). The next logical neighbor has the next highest address to the node currently holding the token. Once the token is passed, the recipient has the right to initiate a transmission. This token-passing sequence continues in a logical ring fashion serving all nodes equally. Node addresses must be unique and can range from 1 to 255. Address 0 is reserved for broadcast messages.

Node assignments are independent of the physical location of the nodes on the network. Once the network is configured, the token is passed from one node to the node with the next highest node address even though another node may be physically closer. All nodes have a logical neighbor and will continue to pass the token to their neighbor in a logical ring fashion regardless of the physical topology of the network.

Cabling

ArcNet can use several cable types to support its topologies. Among the most commonly used are as follows:

- Coaxial cable—RG-62/u was the original choice for cabling ArcNet systems, and is recommended over RG-59/u if possible. RG-62/u (93 ohm) is a better impedance match to the coaxial transceiver and has less attenuation than RG-59/u (75 ohm), yielding greater distances. Standard BNC connectors and tees are used.

- Twisted-pair—Unshielded twisted-pair cabling can be used with several connectors such as RJ-45 and RJ-11. Twisted-pair cable is inexpensive, convenient to use, and easy to terminate. However, twisted-pair cable has much greater attenuation than coaxial cable and, therefore, has limited distance capability (244 meters or 800 feet).

- Fiber optics—Fiber offers the greatest distance, but requires more attention to its application. The use of 62.5/125 duplex cable for conventional installations and single mode for long distances is suggested. Fiber optics can span the greatest distance, but has a lower propagation factor than coaxial cable. It may be necessary to calculate the resulting signal delay to ensure it is within ArcNet limits.

Summary

In this chapter we discussed the physical and data link layers of the OSI model. We spoke about cable connections and cable types. We discussed the features of the most popular cables used in today's networks: twisted pair, coaxial cable, and fiber optic cable. You should now understand the difference between these groups of cables, and be able to determine what cable type is appropriate based on the network requirements.

We defined two types of coaxial cable: thin coaxial cable and thick coaxial cable and pointed out their limitations. We saw that, because of signal attenuation, the maximum recommended distance for running an unrepeated signal in thin coaxial cable is 185 meters and in thick coaxial cable, 500 meters. We saw what connection methods can be used to connect network nodes using coaxial cable. We studied vampire tap technology, which involves using external AUI transceivers and AUI cables. Thin coaxial cable uses a different connection scheme—BNC connectors. We saw how BNC connectors and BNC terminators look and discussed how they can be used.

The next type of cable described in this chapter was twisted pair. We divided twisted pairs into two broad categories—shielded twisted pair and unshielded twisted pair—based on the type of external shielding being used. We also pointed out different categories of twisted pairs, from category 1 to 5, based on transmission rate. We saw, for example, that category 5 twisted pair supports transmission rates up to 100 Mbps. We saw that twisted pair cables employ RJ-45 connectors, wall plates, patch panels, and concentrators.

Next, we turned our attention to fiber optic cable. We saw the differences between the multimode and single mode fiber and learned the distance limitations for both of them. You may have noticed that fiber optic cable has less attenuation and thus is capable of transferring signals over greater distances (2 km for a multimode fiber optic cable versus 100 meters for UTP). We also covered some of the fiber optic connectors, such as ST and SC.

We studied the access control methods that solve the problem of simultaneous access to the wire. We looked at the CSMA/CD, CSMA/CA, token passing, and demand priority methods and gave examples of networks where these methods are used.

Finally, we paid quite a bit of attention to network architectures such as Ethernet, token ring, 100VG-AnyLAN, and ArcNet. When we spoke about these architectures, we brought together what we already know about connectors, cables, and access control methods. Now you are familiar with such concepts as propagation delay, Manchester encoding (a technology to encode and send data across the wire). Class I and Class II repeaters (used in 100 Mbps Ethernet networks), active monitor (that controls and manages the ring in token passing architectures), and many others. We showed you how to overcome some limitations related to attenuation and signal loss by suggesting the use of repeaters and concentrators.

Your next logical step is to learn how to expand local area networks and overcome the limitations enforced by the technology itself (such as the propagation delay restriction). In the next chapter, we will speak about devices such as bridges and switches which can solve some of the problems repeaters and hubscan not.

▲ REVIEW QUESTIONS

1. *What is used to connect coaxial cable over long distances to strengthen the signal?*

    A. A barrel connector

    B. A long continuous cable

    C. A repeater

    D. A hub

    E. A terminator

2. *What is the maximum distance that thin coaxial cable is able to carry signal without noticeable attenuation?*

    A. 185 m

    B. 200 m

    C. 500 m

    D. 2 km

3. *What technology or connector type is used for thick coaxial cable?*

    A. BNC T connector

    B. RJ-45 connector

    C. RJ-11 connector

    D. AUI connector

    E. SC connector

    F. ST connector

4. *Both ends of an AUI cable should always be* _____

    A. Male-female

    B. Female-female

    C. Male-male

    D. Genderless

5. *Which of the following BNC connectors are used to connect devices to thin coaxial bus? (Refer to Figure 4–35.)*

A   B   C

Figure 4–35 *Cable connectors.*

    A. A

    B. B

    C. C

    D. A and B

    E. B and C

    F. A and C

6. *What is the transmission rate that twisted pair Cat. 4 is capable of?*

    A. 4 Mbps

    B. 10 Mbps

    C. 16 Mbps

    D. 20 Mbps

    E. 100 Mbps

7. *True or False. When wiring a twisted pair cable, it is not important to connect specific wires to specific pins in the RJ-45 connector. The only concern is that wires of the same colors are connected to the same pins on both ends of the cable.*

    A. True

    B. False

8. *What is the drawback of using multimode fiber?*

    A. Since modes can potentially travel along different paths, bouncing different numbers of times, they will arrive at the other end of the cable at different times. This is called mode dispersion, and this limits the maximum speed and lengths of the cable.

    B. The diameter of the glass is smaller than in a single-mode cable, making it difficult to work with.

    C. Multimode cables require using lasers, making the technology more expensive.

    D. Multimode fiber is more difficult to vampire tap, because you need to do this with each mode individually.

9. *What does MM 62.5/125 stand for?*

    A. The internal cylinder is 62.5 micron in diameter and the cladding diameter is 125 micron.

    B. The minimum allowed transmission speed allowed is 62.5 Mbps the maximum is 125 Mbps.

    C. The minimum distance between nodes is 62.5 meters, the maximum is 125 meters.

    D. The propagation delay for this network should be no more than 125 μs, and one-way propagation delay should be no more than 62.5 μs.

10. *You need to connect 10 computers in location A and 15 computers in location B. Locations A and B are separated by 130 meters. You do not want to use any active connectivity equipment in this area and want to minimize the costs of the project. What cable type would you use?*

    A. Twisted pair

    B. Fiber Optic Cable

    C. Thick coaxial cable

    D. Thin coaxial cable

11. *What term is not related to the other three?*

    A. CSMA/CD

    B. Token passing

    C. Demand priority

    D. BNC

12. *10Base-T uses only _____ for transmitting and receiving the signal.*

    A. Two fiber optic cables

    B. Two twisted pairs (4 wires)

    C. Four twisted pairs (8 wires)

    D. Ten twisted pairs (20 wires)

13. *100Base-T4 uses only _____ for transmitting and receiving the signal.*
    A. Four fiber optic cables
    B. Two twisted pairs (4 wires)
    C. Four twisted pairs (8 wires)
    D. Ten twisted pairs (20 wires)

14. *Will the Ethernet network displayed in Figure 4–36 work?*
    A. No
    B. Yes, but only if the network is 10Base-T
    C. Yes, but only if the network is 10Base-T or 100Base-TX
    D. Yes, in all cases

15. *Will the fast Ethernet network displayed in Figure 4–37 work?*
    A. No
    B. Yes, only if the concentrators are Class I repeaters
    C. Yes, only if the concentrators are Class II repeaters
    D. Yes, in all cases

16. *You want to expand a network, which was built with thick coaxial cable. You already have 3 segments, and you plan to add 3 more. You plan to use thicknet only. Is it possible to do this using 10Base-5 repeaters?*
    A. Yes
    B. No

17. *What is the maximum allowable propagation delay in fast Ethernet?*
    A. 25.6 µs
    B. 2.56 µs

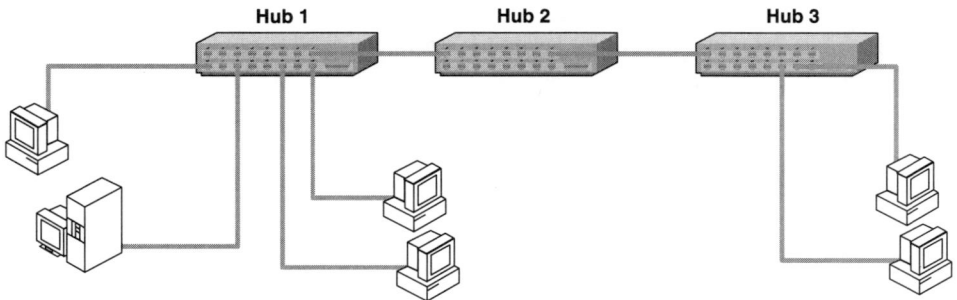

Figure 4–36 *Ethernet network.*

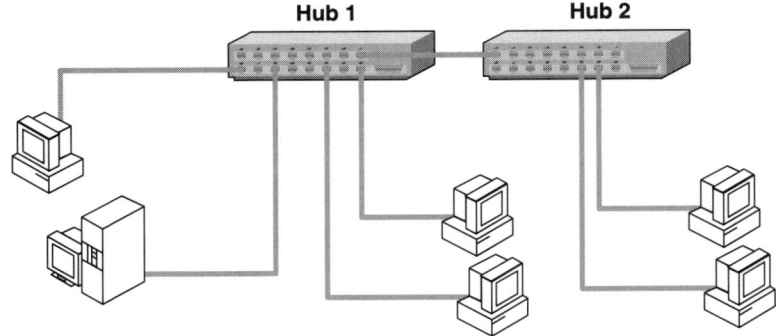

Figure 4–37 *Fast Ethernet network.*

    C. There is no propagation delay concept in Ethernet. Only token passing has this concept.

    D. Propagation delay depends on the class of repeater being used.

18. *A Token ring network is logically a ring but physically a*

    A. Star

    B. Bus

    C. Token bus

    D. MSAU

19. *The active monitor in token ring is*

    A. The first station that joins the ring

    B. MSAU

    C. A special device

    D. Active monitor concept does not exist in token ring.

20. *ARCNET uses _____ method as media access control.*

    A. Token passing

    B. CSMA/CD

    C. CSMA/CA

    D. Demand priority

Wide Area Networks

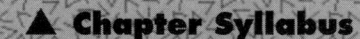
▲ **Chapter Syllabus**

Introduction to Wide Area Network Technologies

LAN Expansion Equipment

Wide Area Network Technologies

This chapter introduces the various technologies and mechanisms used in wide-area-network (WAN) environments. We will discuss point-to-point links, circuit switching, and packet switching. We will pay some attention to virtual circuits; define bridging, switching, and routing; and explain the most important technologies of internetworking.

After completing this chapter you will be able to do the following:

- Identify reasons for LAN expansion and discuss how to obtain the desired results
- Explain the use and operation of repeaters, hubs, bridges, switches, routers, brouters, and gateways
- Explain the technology associated with point-to-point links, circuit switching, packet switching, virtual circuits, and dial-up services.
- Discuss the salient features of T1, DDS, switched 56, frame relay, ATM, ISDN, and DSL technologies

141

Introduction to Wide-Area-Network Technologies

You will remember that we have already defined a wide area network (WAN) as a data communications network that covers a relatively broad geographic area and possibly uses transmission facilities provided by common carriers, such as telephone companies. Before we dive back into the world of WANs, however, let us discuss the evolution of our Local Area Network (LAN) to try to determine the point at which we need to expand to include WAN capability. There are three main reasons to expand your LAN:

- To connect two or more LANs
- To segment the existing LAN to overcome limitations of LAN technologies
- To connect your LAN to other foreign systems and environments

Connecting Two or More LANs

Suppose you have two or more individual LAN segments and the goal is to bring them together. It is relatively easy if these two segments are located on the same floor and use the same network architecture, for example, 10Base-2. In this case, connecting these separate segments together can be as simple as using a BNC barrel connector.

What if these segments use different network architecture? For example, one of them could be an Ethernet network and the other, token ring. In this case, simply connecting the segments together will not make the system work because of the different media access control methods used in the respective network architectures. The computers will not understand each other and will not be able to decide which transmits and which keeps silent. Even if the networks were all of the Ethernet type but some of them operated at 100 Mbps and others at 10 Mbps, the speed difference would still make it impossible to simply connect the wires together. We will need to use some intelligent devices to handle the differences in the media access control in the first example and the speed difference in the second.

The situation becomes even more complex when the LAN segments are distributed across distances greater than the maximum distance allowed by the local area network technology. For example, if two Ethernet networks are located in different cities, we cannot just use a single coaxial cable to connect them because of attenuation considerations. Someone could propose using repeaters to overcome the signal attenuation. This solution, however, will not work because of the propagation delay limitation discussed in Chapter 4 that limits the maximum number of repeaters in Ethernet-type networks. Similar restrictions exist for token ring, ArcNet, 100VG-AnyLAN, and other local area network architectures. You will need to use mechanisms such as point-to-point links or circuit switched solutions to connect these remote locations. We will discuss these mechanisms a bit later in the chapter.

Segmenting the Existing LAN

Sometimes, even if you have a single network segment that does not exceed the technology limitations, you may still want to modify your LAN. The most common candidate for modification is the Ethernet network with too many nodes in it. Let us see what problems arise in this scenario.

Notwithstanding the limitations imposed by the network standards, there are many practical reasons for limiting the number of nodes in Ethernet-type segments to not more than a few dozen. These practical reasons focus on shared use of the media among multiple workstations.

An example of this is a 10-Mbps Ethernet network. Each node utilizes the entire bandwidth—10 Mbps—during the very short time it transmits. The rest of the time, the node has to wait until other nodes finish their transmissions. Even if we accept the ideal situation where all nodes get an equal amount of time for transmission and there is no unproductive time loss, the average bandwidth available for each node is 10/N Mbps, where N is the total number of nodes in the segment. Obviously, when N grows, each node receives less and less time to transmit and the average bandwidth for each node decreases. At a certain point of network growth, end users can experience a significant performance drop. Too many nodes (too many Ns) can even stop some applications from functioning because delays in access to network resources can exceed the applications' time-outs.

The random nature of the media access algorithms used in the Ethernet networks makes the situation even worse. If nodes transmit at random times, the possibility of collisions grows as the number of nodes grows. As you know, collisions require retransmissions and this leads to the ineffective usage of the channel—the same data is transmitted more than once. That means the average amount of time given to a particular node to transmit is getting smaller. Figure 5–1 shows the exponential relationship between the number of delays in accessing the medium and the number of workstations in the Ethernet segment.

Other local area network technologies such as token ring, 100VG-Any-LAN, and ArcNet also experience media access delays as the number of nodes increases.

Until recently, multimedia applications (which can place a heavy load on all computing resources) were not heavily used on networks. The

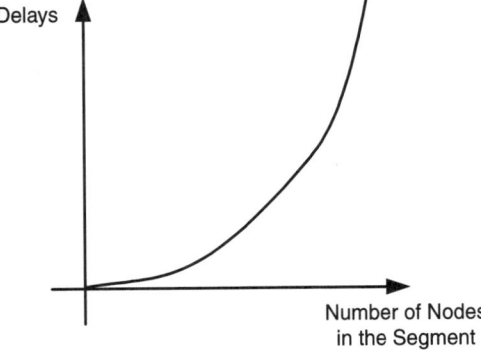

Figure 5–1 *Relationship of media access delays to the number of nodes in an Ethernet segment.*

heavy-use applications primarily dealt with text information and did not put a significant load on the network. That is why the empirical rule of "30 node maximum per shared Ethernet segment" existed for a long time. As information technology has matured, the situation has changed dramatically. Now even two or three computers that run multimedia applications can congest the entire bandwidth of a 10-Mbps network. We can see that the simple "30 nodes per shared segment" rule is not descriptive enough to characterize the required network performance and reserve capacity. The more universal criterion is *network utilization,* which is calculated as Σ_i $m_i/14880$. Here Σ_i m_i is the sum of all Ethernet frames that were transmitted by all nodes in the segment at a given second, and 14880 is the maximum number of frames that can be potentially transmitted in the 10-Mbps Ethernet. (A fundamental constant for 10-Mbps Ethernet networks is 14880. You may see this number in many Ethernet equipment manuals.)

We arrived at 14880 frames per second by dividing 10 Mbps by (512+ 96 + 64) bits, where 512 bits is the minimum Ethernet frame size, 64 is the preamble and 96 is the interframe gap.
For more information about number of frames per second for different network architectures, see RFC 1944.

Usage of the network utilization value is more accurate than using the number of nodes per segment and may be the only way to determine the optimum number of nodes on networks subject to extreme use. Empirical modeling of Ethernet-type networks shows that when the network utilization is 0.4–0.5, collisions and, consequently, media access delays result in a chain reaction that quickly limits the available bandwidth.

Many network administrators, therefore, use a network utilization value of 0.3 (30%) as an indicator that the network needs reconstruction. A reasonable question at this point is, "How can I measure my network utilization?" Fortunately, this value is usually displayed by network monitoring programs such as network sniffers and analyzers. Figure 5–2 shows the capability in the Microsoft Network Monitor, which is shipped with Microsoft Windows NT Server and Microsoft Systems Management Server.

Although we used Ethernet technology in the foregoing example, similar limitations exist for other LAN technologies with shared media access. The only difference is in the critical network utilization value. Token-passing network architectures, for example, use 0.6–0.7 as a maximum recommended network utilization value.

The last, and maybe the most important, question is what to do if your network grows and the network utilization grows as well. The typical solution to this problem is to segment your network utilizing smart devices such as bridges and routers, which we will discuss later in the chapter.

Connecting Your LAN to Other Foreign Systems and Environments

Sometimes the differences between two systems are so great that even when they are connected properly at the physical and data link levels without violating network architecture rules, they still cannot speak to each other. Consider, for example, two computers, one running Windows NT Server and

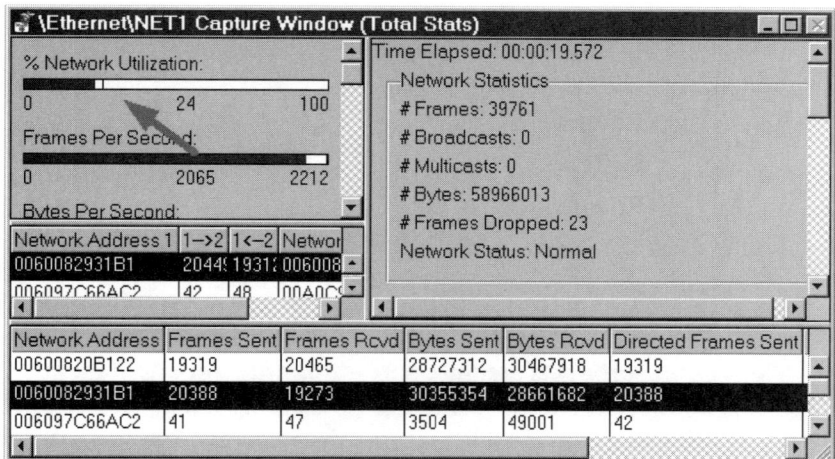

Figure 5–2 *Network utilization is displayed by most network monitoring software.*

another running UNIX. The question is how can we have UNIX users log on to the Windows NT server to gain access to files and folders residing on it?

Even connected to the same wire with no problems concerning propagation delay and media access method, these two computers are still not able to interoperate without the installation of additional software. The main problem is that these systems operate using different protocols; and even though they are able to send and receive packets, they are unable to understand what the packets contain because of differences in packet construction. Additional software must be installed on one or both machines to perform packet translation and permit the dissimilar systems to understand each other. A little later in this chapter we will see how this is done.

As we have seen, most networks have a tendency for expansion. Now that we are familiar with the problems inherent to that expansion and understand the reasons for network reconstruction, it is time to look at ways of solving expansion-related problems and how to facilitate the necessary reconstruction.

LAN Expansion Equipment

Technically speaking, some networks can be expanded using only a British Naval Connection (BNC) barrel connector. We will, however, focus on more active equipment. As you may remember from our previous discussion, active equipment must be connected to a power source in addition to its normal network connections. Several types of active equipment are available in the market. These types include, but are not limited to the following:

- Repeaters
- Hubs
- Bridges
- Switches
- Routers
- Gateways

You may find some products that use a combination of these technologies and have functionality of several of the base types previously listed. Some products are pure hardware while some contain quite a bit of software to make them more intelligent. We will look at each of these types individually and define their place in the network. We will also describe the basic concepts of these devices as they were originally designed. Keep in mind, however, particular products can differ from the description provided here due to manufacturers' enhancements.

Repeaters

You may remember from Chapter 4 that the signal (electrical or optical) attenuates when traveling across the medium. Different media types have different attenuation characteristics; but, sooner or later, the signal becomes too weak to be adequately received and decoded on the other side. You may remember that we mentioned *repeaters* are used to boost and regenerate a signal, so that it can travel greater distances.

On what layer of the (OSI) model do repeaters work? This question is essential, since by knowing the layer at which a particular device works, we are able to describe its functions and limitations.

Technically speaking, repeaters work at the physical layer of the OSI model. Their function is to provide bit synchronization between the segments they connect. We already know that information on the physical layer is presented using a raw stream of bits. This means, that at the physical layer, there is no way for a repeater to find out what *type* of data it is working with. If the repeater is connecting more than two segments, it is often referred to as a hub. Many sources define a *multiport* repeater as a hub. This terminology can create quite a bit of confusion; because the industry produces many different types of hubs, among which are switching hubs, which are a completely different type of device. It is more accurate to refer to a classical hub (multiport repeater) as a *repeater hub*. In this case we must make a very important statement: repeater hubs, as a type of repeater, propagate the incoming signal from one port to all other ports.

As you can see in Figure 5–3, if workstation 1 wants to send a packet to server 1, the repeater hub will duplicate the packet bits to all its ports. The same packet arrives at server 1, workstation 2, and workstation 3. Only the network adapter card of server 1 processes the packet and sends it up through the OSI model. Workstation 2 and workstation 3 discard the packet since it has a MAC address different from their own.

This example demonstrates one very important feature of the repeater or hub. Repeaters and hubs do not filter network traffic. In other words, they cannot make intelligent decisions such as, "the packet is not destined for workstation 2 so I won't, send it to the segment that services workstation 2." The main reason for this is the inability of the repeater to gain access to the data inside the packets, such as source and destination MAC addresses. Technically speaking, repeaters don't even understand the concept of packets, they operate with bits.

Repeaters cannot connect segments that use different media access control methods, such as Ethernet and token ring. They can, however, connect segments with different media such as coaxial and fiber optics.

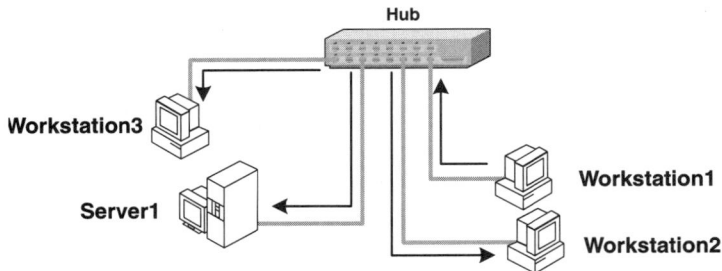

Figure 5–3   *Repeaters perform bit synchronization by propagating signals from one port to all other ports.*

Obviously, because repeaters perform bit synchronization between all connected segments, they cannot connect segments that operate at different speeds, for example, 10-Mbps Ethernet and 100-Mbps Ethernet.

In Ethernet networks, when a repeater senses a collision on one of its ports, it propagates a special *jam* signal to all of its ports to notify adjacent segments of the collision. Repeaters cannot sense corrupted packets such as those with invalid Cyclic Redundancy Check (CRC) data. Some repeaters can, however, improve network reliability. If a repeater, for example, connects two segments of coaxial cable and one of them becomes unterminated, the repeater may be able to isolate the second segment and prevent the entire network from going down. Additionally, most repeaters have LED indicators showing port activity, which can be used for network monitoring.

Repeaters and repeater hubs are the simplest active network devices. They are the most inexpensive way to expand your network when the issue is attenuation. A typical repeater hub has 5, 8, 12, 24, or more ports. This can provide an easy and cost-effective way of expansion in large environments. Repeaters, however, will not help when you have too many workstations connected to the network segment and the network performance is slow. Remember, different networking technologies allow different maximum numbers of repeaters to be connected in serial. For example, 10-Mbps Ethernet allows only 4 repeaters and 100-Mbps Ethernet allows no more that 2 repeaters. Other networking architectures have similar limitations. These limitations are derived from the propagation delay, which we explained in Chapter 4.

The following summarizes the repeater features we have just covered:

- They connect two cable segments by boosting and regenerating the signal.
- They function at the physical layer of the OSI model.

- They cause very small delays in propagating the packets.
- They pass incoming traffic to all connected ports. (They do not perform data filtering.)
- They cannot connect segments with different media access control methods.
- They have limits in cascading (the number you can connect serially).
- They can increase network reliability.

Study Break

Segments, Repeaters, and Collision Domains

When we discussed Ethernet technologies in the previous chapter, we often used the word *segment*. Most of the limitations for Ethernet-type networks apply to a single network segment. For example, the limitation of 25.6 μs applies to a network segment. But what is a network segment? Is it a piece of cable between computers or a part of the complete network? If a segment is a part of the network, then where do we draw the borders of the segment? It is more technically correct to use the term, *collision domain*. The term collision domain is very important to understand since most modern networking tutorials and white papers use it. A collision domain is formally defined as a single CSMA/CD network in which there will be a collision if two computers attached to the system transmit at the same time. Having already said that repeaters propagate collisions, we can state that an Ethernet system composed of multiple cable segments linked with repeaters is a network that functions as a single collision domain.

If you want to refer to a part of the network that consists of a single piece of cable, it is more accurate to call it an *unrepeated network segment*.

Study Break

Ethernet Data Frame Structures

Before diving into our discussion about bridges, we need to introduce another concept—the data link layer frame structure. We will use Ethernet as an example. Other network architectures construct data link frames similarly, with slight variations in field names and lengths.

We discussed in Chapter 4 how Ethernet-data signals are transformed into bits and have seen that before these bits are sent onto an Ethernet network, they must be formatted into specific groups called data frames. Data frames have dedicated parts, which contain addressing, timing, protocol, and error correction information as well as the actual data that is being sent. Table 5.1 shows the typical Ethernet frame structure. Please note that there are several Ethernet frame formatting algorithms that may result in slight differences. The frame structure used in Table 5.1 as an example is of IEEE 802.3 type.

To better understand how this whole thing works, the following discusses the purpose of each section of the frame:

- Preamble—effectively determines the beginning of frame transmission. The signal pattern of the preamble is a repeating pattern of ones and zeroes. The length of the preamble is 7 bytes.

- SFD—The start frame delimiter (SFD) consists of the following sequence of bits: 10101011. SFD follows the preamble; and its purpose is to indicate the start of information by the last two bits, which is 11. SFD is a total of 1 byte.

- Destination address—represents the address of the station, or stations (in case of a broadcast or multicast frames), that the data frame is intended for. It follows the SFD and is 6 bytes in length.

- Source address—indicates the address of the station initiating the transmission. The source address is 6 bytes in length.

- Length field—follows the source address and indicates the length of the data field. The length field is 2 bytes in length. In Ethernet version 1.0 or version 2.0, this field is called a type field. The main purpose of this field is to indicate the type of network layer protocol being used, for example, TCP/IP, Novell IPX, DECNet.

- Data field—has variable lengths from 46 bytes to 1500 bytes in length. This field contains the actual data being sent across the network along with some control information. If the computer needs to send less than 46 bytes of data, a special bit pattern called a PAD (Packet Assembler/Disassembler) is used to fill in up to the 46-byte minimum.

- Cyclic redundancy check (CRC)—follows the data field and is 4-bytes long. This field is used to check the integrity of the frame.

The standards of IEEE define both a minimum and a maximum frame size for Ethernet-type networks. The minimum frame size is 64 bytes (12 address bytes, 2 length bytes, 46 data bytes and 4 CRC bytes). The maximum frame size is 1,518 bytes.

Table 5.1 *802.3 Ethernet Frame Structure*

Frame Part	Size
Preamble	7 bytes
SFD	1 byte
Destination address	6 bytes
Source address	6 bytes
Length	2 bytes
Data	46–1500 bytes
CRC	4 bytes

Bridges

Besides using repeaters to expand your network, you can use more sophisticated devices such as bridges. Bridges are data communications devices that operate principally at layer 2 of the OSI model. As such, they are referred to as *data link layer devices*. The first commercially available bridges appeared in the early 1980s. At the time of their introduction, bridges connected and enabled packet forwarding between homogeneous networks, such as Ethernet to Ethernet. More recently, bridging between different networks has been defined and standardized.

A bridge is a device that connects two (or, in rare cases, more) network segments by first buffering and then propagating transmitted packets. In contrast to a repeater, a bridge does not have to support bit synchronization between joined segments. Instead of this, it acts like a competent node for each of the segments. When a bridge gets a packet from one of the segments, it buffers it, analyses the destination MAC address, and then propagates the packet if, and only if, the packet is destined to the second network segment.

> **Note**
>
> **You may be interested in why the bridge captures every packet whether or not it is destined for it. Previously, we mentioned that network adapter cards process only packets designated with their own MAC address. Why, then, do bridges operate in such a strange way? Bridge interfaces function in the so-called promiscuous mode, which means all packets are processed without regard to their MAC addresses. As we will soon see, this is a critical factor in the operation of a bridge.**

For example, if computer A sends a packet to computer B, (see upper portion of Figure 5–4), the bridge will get the packet and examine the destination MAC address. Since the destination computer is B and it has already received the packet, the bridge simply discards the packet. Please note that bridges do not send packets back to the port from which they came.

If computer A sends a packet to computer D (see lower portion of Figure 5–4), the bridge will propagate it because computer D is located in a segment other than the one from which the packet originated. If a bridge receives a broadcast message, it propagates it to all ports except the port from which the message came.

In order for a bridge to propagate a packet to the next segment, it must gain access to the media in that segment, using the media access control methods appropriate to that segment. For example, if the networks depicted in Figure 5.4 are Ethernet networks and the bridge wants to propagate

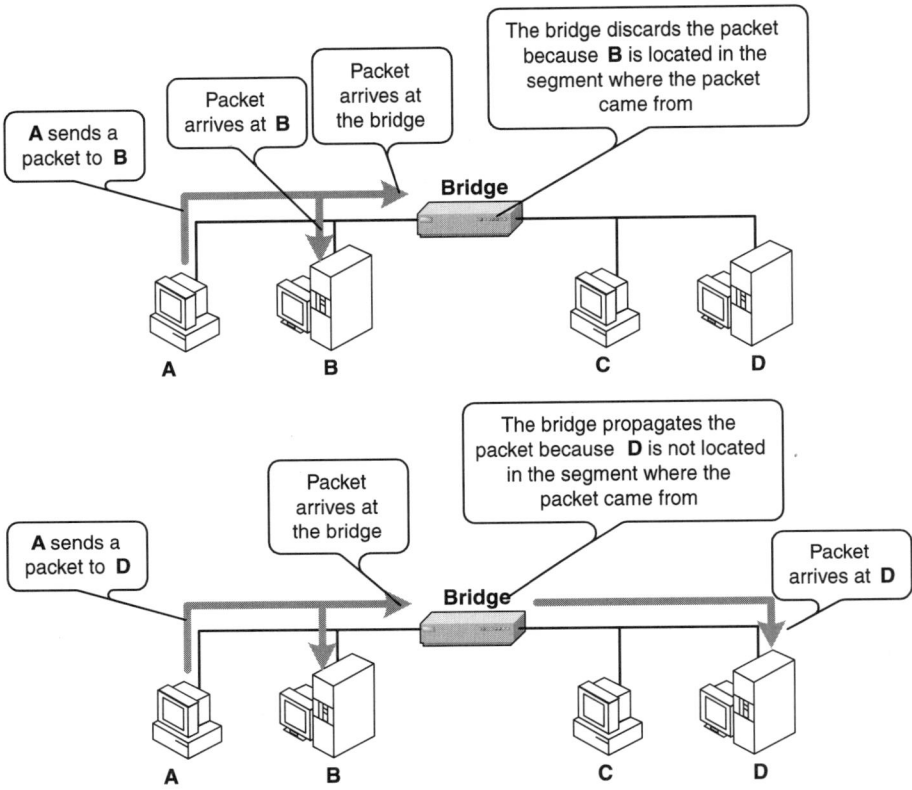

Figure 5–4   *Bridges can make decisions based on packets' MAC addresses.*

packets from network AB to network CD, it must wait until there are no transmissions in segment CD before it can transmit its packets (under the rules of CSMA/CD).

> Because bridges buffer packets and wait until they are able to gain access to the media in the destination segment, workstations in different segments connected by a bridge can transmit simultaneously without causing a collision. In other words, a bridge can divide the network into several collision domains.

Study Break

Types of Bridging

Now that you have a basic understanding of how bridging works, we can take a quick look at several of the types of bridging that exist in the industry today; such as

- Transparent bridging

- Source-route bridging

- Translational bridging

- Source-route transparent bridging

Transparent bridging is found primarily in Ethernet environments, while *source-route bridging* occurs primarily in token ring environments. *Translational bridging* provides translation between formats and transit principles of different media types (usually Ethernet and token ring). Finally, *source-route transparent bridging* combines the algorithms of transparent bridging and source-route bridging to enable communication in mixed Ethernet/token ring environments. Because it has become the base for currently popular switching technologies, this chapter focuses on transparent bridging.

Bridge Learning Process

To review, we have learned that bridges analyze incoming frames, make forwarding decisions based on information contained in the frames, and forward the frames toward the destination. In some cases, such as source-route bridging, the entire path to the destination is contained in each frame. In other cases, such as transparent bridging, frames are forwarded one hop at a time toward the destination. Upper-layer protocol transparency is a primary advantage of bridging. Because bridges operate at the link layer, they are not required to examine upper-layer information. This means that they can rapidly forward traffic representing any network-layer protocol without the significant overhead required to peel back and replace the lower layers to examine the layer 3 data. (This peeling back and replacing is typically referred to as "repackaging.") It is not uncommon for a bridge to move AppleTalk, DECnet, TCP/IP, and other traffic between two or more networks.

Note

Bridges are capable of filtering frames based on any layer 2 fields. A bridge, for example, can be programmed to reject (not forward) all frames sourced from a particular network. Bridges can also be programmed to discard the broadcast messages (this is more the exception than the rule). Because datalink layer information often includes a reference to an upper-layer protocol, bridges can usually filter on this parameter.

You may say, "OK, bridges analyze the destination MAC address of the packets, but how do they know which computer is connected to which network segment?" In terms of the network in Figure 5.4, if computer B is moved to another network segment, a packet sent from A to B will have to be propagated by the bridge. The secret of the bridge's intelligence is in its routing table. Each bridge has a table that simply maps the MAC addresses of devices to the bridge ports to which they are connected. More accurately, this table should be called a bridging table, since the term routing table properly belongs to routers.

In Figure 5–5, we see how bridges can use their tables to make bridging decisions using three port bridges. Initially, the bridge table is empty and the bridge has no knowledge of the network. In the figure, question marks in the MAC address fields show the bridge has no information about these nodes. When the bridge receives a packet from one of its ports (for example computer A sends a packet to computer B), the bridge examines the MAC address of the destination (the first address in the packet's header).

Since it doesn't know where the intended recipient is located, it has to propagate the packet to all ports except the port from which the packet came. (See Figure 5–6.) Before propagating the packet, however, the bridge examines the source MAC address (the second address in the packet header).

The purpose of this is to learn about the network. Having obtained the MAC address of computer A from the transmitted packet, the bridge updates its table by concluding that, because the packet came from port one, computer A must be connected to that port. The bridge has just learned about one node on the network!

Imagine that in the next couple of moments, network communications from D to E and from B to E occurr. The bridge consults its table to make

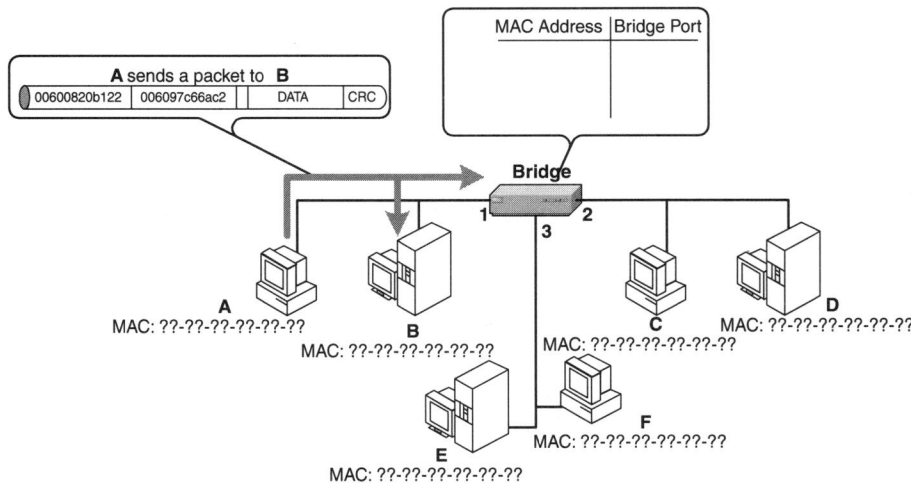

Figure 5–5 *Initially the bridge table is empty.*

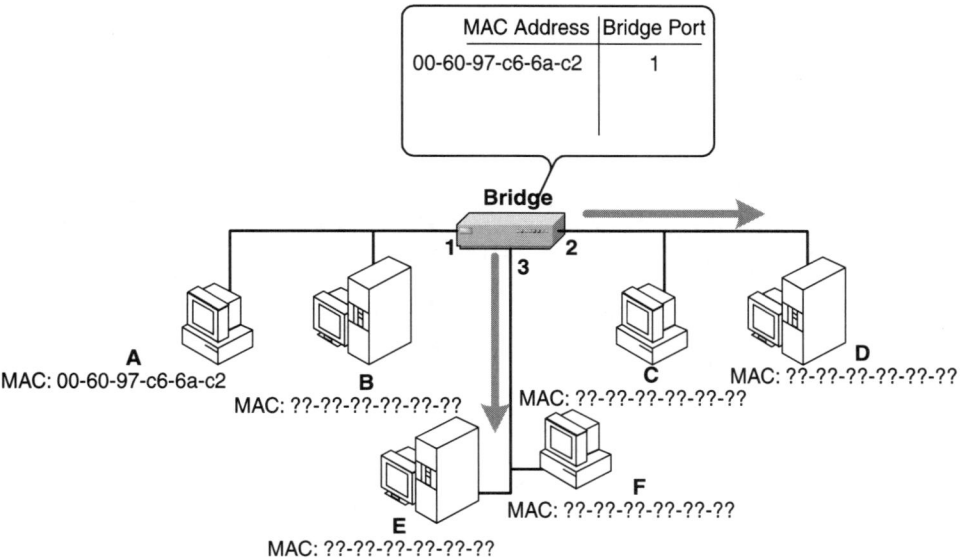

MAC Address	Bridge Port
00-60-97-c6-6a-c2	1

Bridge

A
MAC: 00-60-97-c6-6a-c2

B
MAC: ??-??-??-??-??-??

C
MAC: ??-??-??-??-??-??

D
MAC: ??-??-??-??-??-??

E
MAC: ??-??-??-??-??-??

F
MAC: ??-??-??-??-??-??

Figure 5–6 *The bridge propagates a packet with an unknown destination MAC address to all other ports.*

intelligent decisions, but the information contained there is not enough, so the bridge has to propagate both packets to all other ports. During these exchanges, however, the bridge also learns about two more nodes on the network, D and B, and updates its table accordingly. (See Figure 5–7.)

> **Note**
>
> The process of propagating a packet to all ports except the port from which the packet has come, is called *flooding*. Flooding occurs when the bridge table is empty, when the bridge table has no entry for the destination MAC address, or when the packet is a broadcast packet.

Finally, let us see what happens when a bridge receives a packet with a destination address that it is aware of. (See Figure 5–8.) When computer A sends a packet to computer B and computer's B MAC address is in the bridge's table, there is no need to propagate the packet to all ports. It is enough to send the packet only to the port to which computer B is connected. In this case, the bridge consults its table and determines that computer B is located on the segment at port 1. By knowing this, the bridge concludes that there is no need to propagate the packet at all, since computers A and B are located on the same segment.

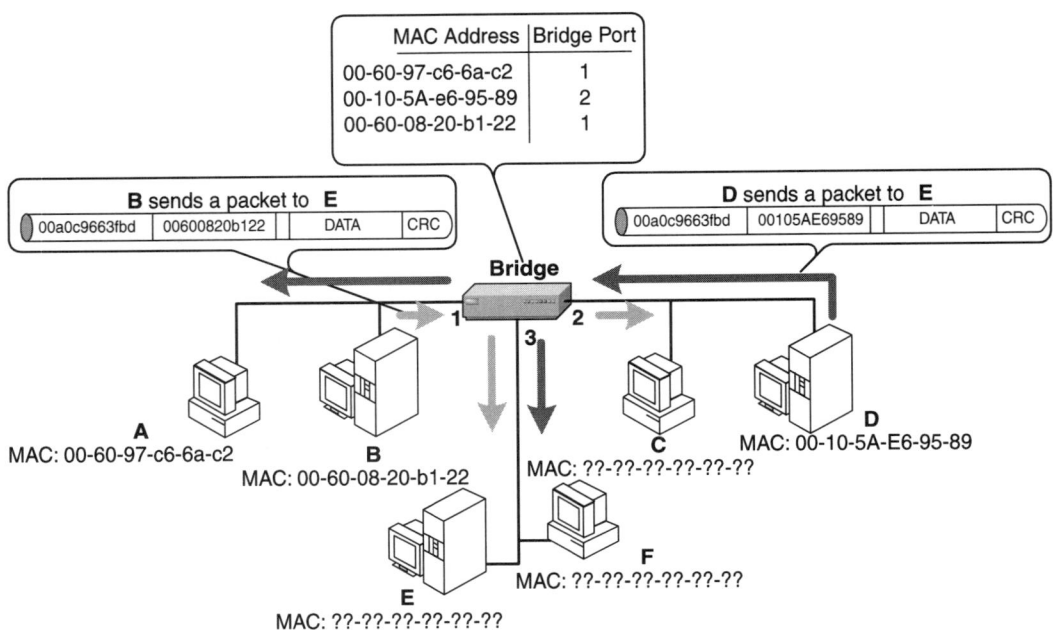

Figure 5–7 *Bridge is learning about the network structure automatically.*

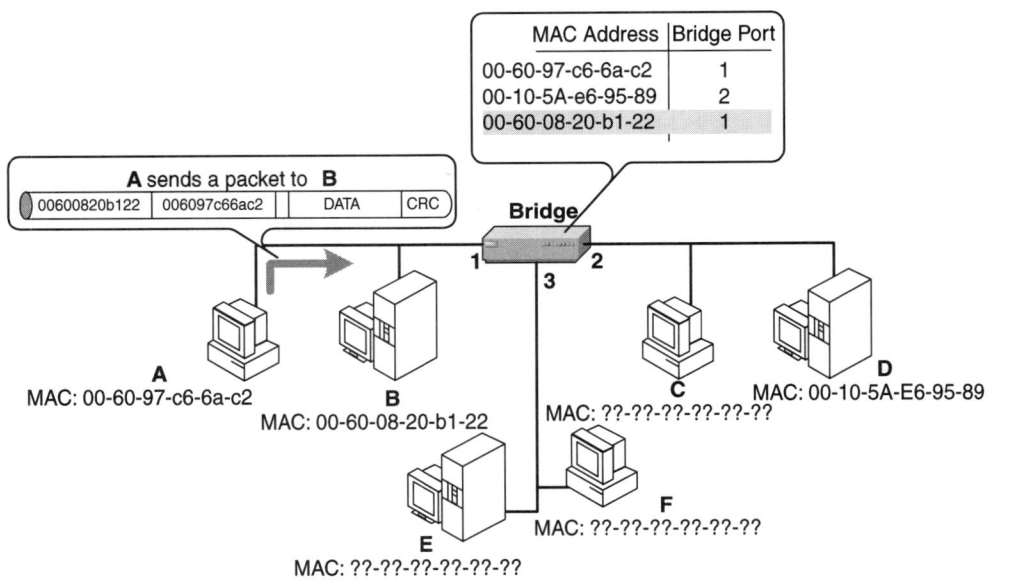

Figure 5–8 *Bridge performs packet filtering when it knows the destination MAC address.*

Similarly, when, for example, computer F sends a packet to computer D, the bridge propagates it to segment 2, but not segment 1. This is because it has information about computer D's location from its table. (During this exchange it will also learn computer F's location.) At this point, the bridge has learned quite a bit about the network structure; and if, for example, computers A and B decide to exchange large amounts of data, their traffic will not go beyond their segment to impact the performance of neighboring segments.

The concept that bridges are able to learn provides us with a very important bridging feature. When the network topology changes or you add or remove nodes, you do not have to reconfigure bridges—they will learn about the changes automatically. Another important consideration about bridges is that each entry in the bridge table is dynamic and has a time-to-live (TTL) value. If a bridge has not heard from a particular node for a long time, the entry in the table expires and gets deleted. This permits the removal of nodes without affecting the consistency of the bridge table. In addition to the dynamic bridge table entries, network administrators can configure static entries. Static entries never expire and can serve as filters to isolate undesired traffic and restrict access to certain resources.

As we have just seen, by dividing large networks into self-contained units, bridges provide several advantages. Because only a certain percentage of traffic is forwarded, a bridge diminishes the traffic experienced by devices on all connected segments. Additionally, because bridges buffer packets before forwarding them, propagation delay problems are no longer an issue. Bridges extend the effective length of a LAN, permitting the attachment of distant stations that could not be supported by repeaters.

Loops

The length to which bridges can extend a network can be quite long. It is not uncommon to use synchronous modems to connect LAN segments through bridges over digital telephone lines. Several LAN segments joined in this way will likely use several telephone lines for connection, which may provide multiple paths between bridges. Under these circumstances, it is possible for the bridges to actually form a loop where bridges ultimately connect back to themselves. This results in a serious problem since a single broadcast message could infinitely circulate inside the loop and, effectively, shut the entire network down.

To solve the looping problem, the spanning-tree algorithm (STA) was developed by Digital Equipment Corporation. Digital's algorithm was subsequently revised by the IEEE 802 committee and published in the IEEE 802.1d specification. STA will detect the existence of multiple routes, select the most efficient as the primary route, and disconnect the other routes from the bridge. Should the primary route become unavailable, one of the other routes will be activated. Bridges that support STA can operate properly even while forming loops.

Performance Considerations

So far we have assumed that using a bridge instead of a repeater to connect two network segments always increases performance. This was because the number of nodes in each segment decreases and the percentage of bandwidth for each node accordingly increases. This is correct if the bridge propagates the intersegment traffic without significant delays. When using bridging algorithms, however, a bridge can delay frames and, under certain circumstances, lose them.

The delay produced by a typical bridge is at least as large as the time required to put the incoming frame into the buffer. The greater the frame size, the greater the delay. Additionally, time is needed to consult the bridge table, especially if the bridge table is large. The total time required by a bridge to process a packet includes both the packet delays and the possibility the packet will be lost. If the time to process a packet is greater than the time until the arrival of the next packet, the incoming packet is put into the buffer where it will wait until the bridge finishes processing the previous packet. Obviously, if the average rate of incoming traffic exceeds the bridge's ability to process packets, the bridge's buffers will overflow and the bridge will drop incoming frames.

Discarding (or losing) a frame is very undesirable, since it cannot be recovered at the lower layers of the OSI model through the LAN protocols. This is because the lower layer protocols have only one method to control the consistency of packets—CRC. CRC travels inside the same packet as the data and, if the whole packet is lost, the CRC is lost as well. Packet loss is detected only at the higher layers of the OSI model by transport and application level protocols that enumerate packets and will sense data loss and request retransmission. But think about the processing overhead for such recovery. In the case of regular data link layer packet loss, network performance can decrease several times because timeouts for upper-layer protocols are much longer than the transmission time at the data-link layer. The retransmission of the lost packet may occur after dozens of seconds.

To prevent packet loss, a bridge must have an average productivity higher than the average intensity of the intersegment traffic. That is to say, it must be able, on average, to handle the traffic that needs to go through faster than the traffic that arrives for processing. In addition to speed, the bridge needs a large memory buffer for storing packets during peak load. In a local area network, an often-used rule of thumb is "80/20." This means that a bridge should divide the network so 80% of the traffic remains local and only 20% is intersegment. If this rule is applied for a 10-Mbps Ethernet network, a bridge must have a capacity to process $0.2 \times 14,880 = 3,000$ frames per second.

Bridges play a considerable role in network management. Processing all the network traffic from all connected segment bridges is an excellent way to monitor and collect statistical information. Gathered information can be displayed on the terminal connected to a bridge through its serial port, or a bridge can have an agent—a special program that works with a remote management program to provide the desired information (e.g., SNMP).

The following summarizes what we have learned about bridges:

- They operate at the Data-link layer of the OSI model.
- They have higher processing overhead than repeaters.
- They segment networks into collision domains.
- They propagate broadcast messages.
- They can connect segments with different media access control methods.
- They make intelligent decisions based on a bridging table.
- They can improve network performance by isolating intrasegment network traffic.
- They may overflow during excessive network traffic.

Switches

The concept of *switching* was initially introduced in the early 1990s by Kalpana in response to the growing demand for high-bandwidth links between high-end servers and end-user workstations. Switching technology takes us from simply sharing network segments to using special devices called switches that allow the transfer of packets between ports at great speed. Technically speaking, switching is a repackaging of multiport bridging technology with significant performance improvements and increased scalability. Just like bridges, switches forward frames based on the layer 2 Ethernet, token ring, Fiber Distributed Data Interface (FDDI), or other network architecture MAC addresses. Functionally, a switch works just like a multiport bridge: by analyzing the headers of the incoming frames, it builds a table and, based on the table, forwards each frame to one of its ports. The innovation found in switching technologies is parallel processing of incoming frames. A bridge can process only one frame at a time. Parallel processing is achieved by using several internal processors, each of which can perform bridging functions. You can think of a switch, therefore, as a multiport bridge that achieves high performance through internal parallel processing.

Like bridges, switches are completely transparent to the nodes they support. You do not have to set up users' workstations and other nodes in your network to accommodate the presence of a switch. Because switches can learn just as bridges do, you don't have to "show" a switch what network devices are connected to it. As with bridges, manual switch configuration is possible and may be used to enhance the existing network functionality.

Switching Algorithms

Usually a switch has six or more ports. Let us discuss a switching algorithm using a six-port Ethernet switch as an example.

Each port of a switch is serviced by a dedicated Ethernet packet processor (EPP). EPPs are usually of *reduced instruction set computer* (RISC) or *application specific integrated circuit* (ASIC) architecture. Additionally, each switch has a *system module* that coordinates the work of all EPPs. To transfer data between ports, the *switching matrix,* or simply, the *matrix* is used.

When a frame arrives at any of the switch's ports, the switch analyzes the destination MAC address, consults its table, and determines the port through which the frame should be forwarded. If the incoming frame is a MAC-level broadcast, it is forwarded to all ports.

> **Note**
> MAC-level broadcast is a term that is used to characterize frames that have a broadcast address in the data link (MAC) portion of a frame. For Ethernet-type networks, the MAC broadcast address is FF-FF-FF-FF-FF-FF.

Usually the process of consulting the switch's table is split into two stages: First the local port cache is reviewed, then, if the desired address is not found, the local processor goes to the system module and looks in the global address table. During the lookup time, the receiving module buffers the incoming frame. If the frame does not need to be propagated, the processor simply clears the buffer.

If the frame needs to be forwarded, the port processor refers to the switching matrix and tries to establish a path from the source port to the destination port. (See Figure 5–9.) The switching matrix can establish the path only if the destination port is free (not currently connected to any other ports).

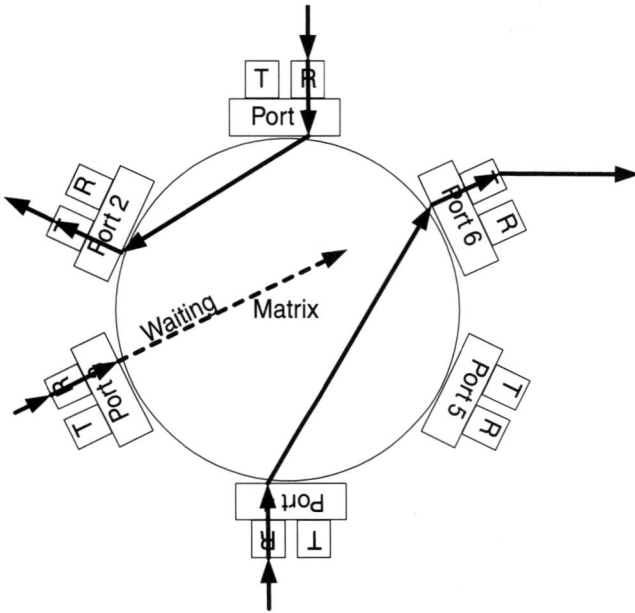

Figure 5–9 *Switching operation is done by the matrix.*

If the destination port is busy (it is already receiving a frame), the frame is buffered until the port is free.

If we compare a switch to a bridge, we will see that a switch is much faster than a bridge. The speed is gained because frames coming from different ports are processed simultaneously—delays occur only when the target ports are busy.

Study Break
_____

Types of Switches

There are two main types of switches, and they use different methods to process frames: *store and forward* and *cut through*. While neither is right or wrong, an understanding of the two will enable you to determine which is best for your particular application. The main differences between these two types are outlined as follows:

- A Store-and-forward approach results in a device design that works like a LAN bridge. The entire incoming frame is captured, an address lookup occurs to resolve the outgoing port, a cyclic redundancy check (CRC) is performed on the frame check sequence (FCS) to validate the frame, and the frame is sent to the proper port. Because of the full buffering, this technique provides higher levels of error detection since corrupt frames can be detected and discarded, while valid frames are processed, queued, and transmitted. Most software-based packet switches are of the store-and-forward variety.

- Cut-through switches start selection and frame transmission well before the entire frame is received. A cut-through switch will reduce the amount of introduced time latency, because the switch begins transmitting the frame to the receiving port as soon as the destination address is decoded (usually within the first 20–30 bytes of the frame). This will also include corrupt frames since the error checking of a cut-through switch is severely limited. Most of these switches are hardware-state machines that have a high level of sophistication at the electronics layer, resulting in a higher price per port. Since the frames are forwarded from the transmitting port to the receiving port immediately upon the decoding of the destination address, very little processing is required after opening the port.

Some switches utilize both processes. They begin with cut-through switching and, through CRCs, monitor the number of errors that occur. When that number reaches a certain point (a threshold) they become store-and-forward switches. They remain so until the number of errors declines; then, they change back to cut-through. This type of switching is called *threshold detection* or *adaptive switching*. Because they offer the best of both processes, these switches are the most popular.

Performance Considerations

You may think that using a switch gives better performance than using a hub or bridge. While this is generally the case, there are some exceptions.

Like a bridge, a switch divides a network into collision domains. In other words, each segment connected to a switch acts as a separate zone of collisions and does not affect other segments when excessive collisions occur. While this provides a clear performance advantage, you will remember that when we spoke about bridges, we said that they could lose frames when they receive an excessive amount of network traffic. We pointed out that the problem is because of the finite limit to the bridge's processing capabilities. With the enhanced performance of switches, processing performance is not an issue. The bottleneck for switches occurs because of the speed of the network. For example, a 10-Mbps network is not capable of transmitting more than 14,880 frames per second even if a switch is able to handle far more than that.

Let us consider the situation pictured in Figure 5–10. A multiport switch connects six Ethernet segments of 10 Mbps each.

If computers connected to segments 1 through 5 start transmitting simultaneously and do so for a significant amount of time, and if all their

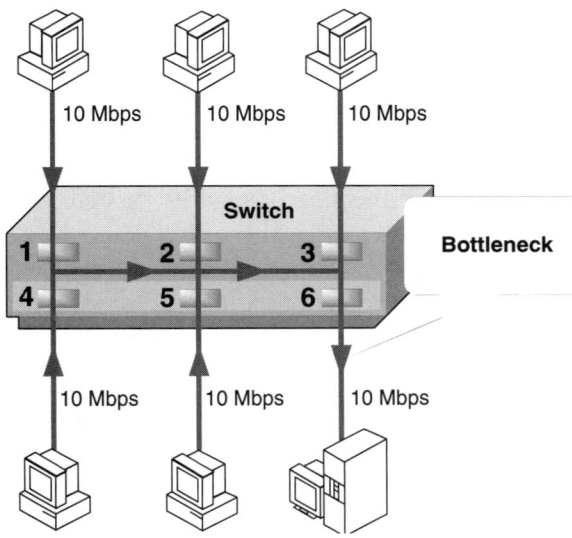

Figure 5–10 *Funneling.*

traffic is destined for the server, a so-called funnel problem is created. Because of the segment speed limitation (10 Mbps), segment 6 cannot accommodate such a large amount of data at one time. When this occurs, only one switch port (for example port 3) will be connected to port 6 directly. All other ports will be in a buffering state. It is very easy to perform the math and calculate when the switch starts losing frames. If the switch port buffer is 1MB and the segment speed is 10 Mbps, it will overflow in less than a second. You will recall, losing a frame results in a significant performance drop because the loss must be detected at the higher layers of the OSI model, with all its attendant overhead processing. In this particular scenario, we would have been better off with a hub. With a hub, collisions occur when workstations try to transmit simultaneously. Collisions, however, are processed at the data link layer, so less system overhead is required to recover from collisions than from packet loss.

You just saw how improper network design can reduce the advantage of using switches to zero and can even make the situation worse. A reasonable question at this point would be, "how can I *really* improve performance?"

The first thing is to determine the proper location for your switches. *The general 80/20 rule we used for bridges does not apply to switches.* In contrast to the scenario where we designed our network to allow only 20 percent of the traffic to cross the bridge, by its very nature, 100 percent of traffic must pass through the switch. The approach where all nodes must go through a switch to talk to each other is called *microsegmentation*. The main idea when you choose the location of the switch is to avoid the funnel effect. For example, it would not be a good idea to connect all ten corporate servers to the same 10-Mbps switch port and have all clients access them simultaneously. You can instead connect each server to its dedicated switch port and select 100-Mbps ports.

The second way to improve performance in the switching networks is to use higher speed links to resources that are consistently under high demand. For example, in the scenario where 5 computers wanted to talk to the server over the six-port switch, we could have upgraded the server link to 100-Mbps Ethernet (assuming the switch can allow this). (See Figure 5–11.) The extra bandwidth available to the server would more than handle any simultaneous traffic from the other computers.

Because switches can buffer frames and access connected network segments just like regular nodes, they can connect networks that function at different nominal speeds.

Another way to improve performance in the switching environment is to use *full duplex* links. Let us look at full duplex by examining its implementation in the Ethernet. Normally, Ethernet-type devices cannot transmit and

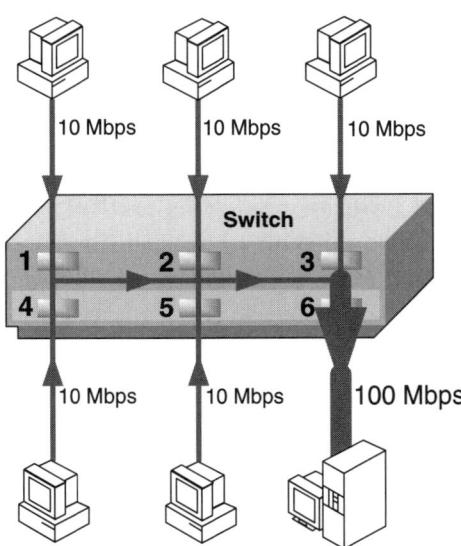

Figure 5–11 *Upgrading the link to the server to solve the funneling problem.*

receive simultaneously. This limitation likely stems from the fact that the first Ethernet products worked with coaxial cable (e.g., 10BASE-2, 10BASE-5), which provides only a single wire for transmission—the coax core. Today, most network communications are done over twisted pair and fiber optic cables, which offer separate media for transmitting and receiving. For example 10BASE-T and 100BASE-TX standards specify twisted pair 2 for transmission and twisted pair 3 for receiving. This means we can potentially transmit and receive simultaneously, and because signals are propagated through different wires, this will prevent collisions. This technology is called *full duplex*. Technology where a node can either transmit *or* receive (not both) is called *half duplex*.

Obviously, full duplex is a modification of the data link standards, and for this reason, both nodes that establish a full duplex transmission must understand and support it. Most modern network adapters support full duplex connections but can work in a half duplex mode as well. Switches, though, usually have one or a few full duplex ports. These ports are typically connected to high performance servers where high bandwidth becomes critical. With full duplex connections, the effective bandwidth doubles. (See Figure 5–12.)

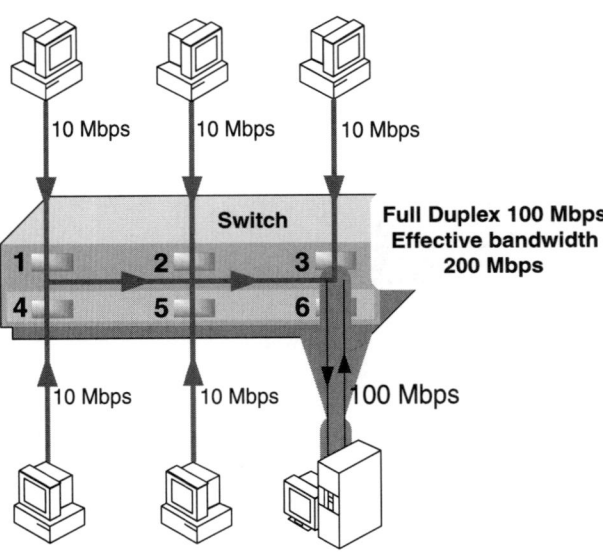

Figure 5–12 *Full duplex links double the effective bandwidth.*

Because typical LAN technologies do not natively support full duplex connections, such connections cannot simply be established among any given set of network nodes. When using a switch, however, we can have several full duplex connections, each of which consists of two nodes— the switch on one side and the end computer on the other.

Study Break

Using Switches with Repeater Hubs

When we discussed microsegmentation issues, we said we would connect our workstations to the switch ports. This can become very expensive because to use this approach, we must provide a dedicated switch port for each workstation. It would be more reasonable to connect concentrators, such as multiport repeaters or hubs, to the switch ports. (See Figure 5–13.)

Although this configuration seems effective, it will not necessarily work with all types of switches. You can connect a hub (or any other concentrator) to the switch only if the switch supports multiple MAC addresses per port (this is also called *shared port*). This feature is implemented mostly in enterprise-level switches. Workgroup switches usually have only one shared port that can be used for cascading and connecting to the rest of the network.

Some network products are called *switching hubs*. They are act as switches and have the same advantages and disadvantages as switches.

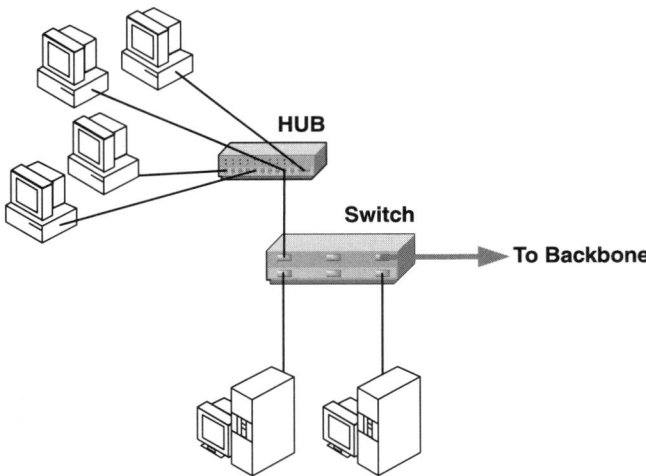

Figure 5–13 *Connecting a hub to a switch.*

The following summarizes what we have learned about switches:

- It operates at the data link layer of the OSI model.
- It functions very similarly to a bridge but has higher performance because of parallel processing.
- It has a higher processing overhead than a repeater.
- It segments networks into collision domains.
- It propagates broadcast messages.
- It can connect segments with different media access-control methods and speeds.
- It is transparent to end devices—meaning they require no special configuration to be aware of the switch.
- It improves network performance by implementing microsegmentation.
- It may support full duplex on some or all of its ports.
- It may overflow because of the funnel effect.

Routers

As you may already have noticed, this chapter moves from the bottom of the OSI model up. First we discussed repeaters that operate at the physical layer of the OSI model. Next we looked at bridges and switches, which operate at the data link layer. It is logical to assume that we will next be at the network layer. If this is what you thought, you are right! Routers operate at the network layer, and they will be the next milestone in our discussion.

Basics of Routing

Usually routing is defined as the act of moving information across an internetwork from a source to a destination. Along the way, at least one intermediate node is typically encountered. Routing is often contrasted with bridging, which might seem to accomplish precisely the same thing to the casual observer. As you may have already guessed, the primary difference between the two is that bridging occurs at layer 2 (the data link layer) of the OSI reference model, whereas routing occurs at layer 3 (the network layer). This fundamental difference provides routers with an ability to gain access to the network header of the packet (for example IP or IPX addresses). Because routers operate at layer 3, they are usually slower than bridges and switches. Because routers have access to additional information (layer 3 addresses), however, they are capable of making more intelligent decisions than bridges or switches. Routers can, for instance, choose the best paths to the destination from a group of paths available. The destination computer in this case may be located on the other site of the room or the other side of the world.

Today, the device we call a router usually works with a number of layer 3 protocols (such as IP or IPX). A router must have knowledge of these protocols to properly handle their addresses. That is why a router has some sophisticated software that must be configured by the administrator. This software enables a router to make the best decision for the delivery of the packet.

When a router gets a packet, it first examines it at the data link layer and passes it to the routing software only if it is not corrupt. This means that routers can *filter corrupted packets*. If the packet is not corrupt, it is examined to see if it is a broadcast packet. By default, routers do not propagate broadcast packets. This behavior is intended to lighten the load on the internetwork. Routers can, however, be configured to pass certain type of broadcasts. Thanks to routers, the broadcast packets that are generated by your computer when it boots are not forwarded to the other end of the world across the Internet. That means routers perform *broadcast traffic isolation*. Without such isolation, we would constantly run the risk of broadcast storms.

The part of the network that is located between routers is often called a subnetwork or a subnet. Some sources refer to it as a broadcast domain—giving a definition that it is a part of the network where a broadcast message generated by one node is propagated. In these terms, routers split the united network into broadcast domains. Please note that neither bridges nor switches do this because they forward broadcast messages.

You may ask how a router can make intelligent routing decisions. The key to this process is a special *routing table*. A routing table is somewhat similar to the bridge table, but there are a couple of differences. The routing table deals with Network (layer 3) addresses. Additionally, the routing table has more information on how to reach the destination and usually has the associated cost value associated with a particular path. The following listing shows a fragment of a routing table for an IP router:

Destination	Netmask	Gateway	Interface	Metric
207.22.36.0	255.255.255.0	195.209.225.1	195.209.225.50	1
207.22.36.0	255.255.255.0	195.209.225.10	195.209.225.50	2
194.0.0.0	255.0.0.0	193.11.17.44	193.11.117.1	8

The first two columns specify the destination network. You can think of the information there as the address of the node located somewhere on the internetwork. The only exception is that each line represents not a single node (like in a bridge table), but a group of nodes (called a subnet). The second and the third columns instruct the router how the packets can reach the target networks. For example, the gateway cell specifies the next downstream router that takes care of further delivery. The last column, *Metric*, represents the cost of the path. The packet will be sent along the path with a minimum metric. For example, the first and second lines in the routing table specify two different paths to the same network. The router will send packets along the second path only if the first becomes unavailable. This is because the first path has a lower metric and thus, is, preferable.

You may be wondering where routing tables come from. The network administrator must configure the routing tables before the router can function. Properly configuring a routing table requires a lot of knowledge concerning different network layer protocols and a strong theoretical background of networking. Methods of configuring routing tables for different routers are very vendor and protocol specific and lie outside the scope of this book. Routers that use routing tables that are entirely configured by the administrator and do not change as they "learn" about the network are referred to as *static routers*. Some routers, however, have a capability to exchange their knowledge about different network routes and conditions. Using routing protocols they perform link advertisements that contain information about their routing tables. This enables them to share information about network topology, avoid dead ends, handle topology loops, eliminate broken links, and route packets more efficiently. Such routers are called *dynamic routers*. Some routers allow both manual and automatic configuration. These routers are called *hybrid* routers: They can act as both static and dynamic routers at the same time.

Routable and Nonroutable Protocols

We just said that in order for a router to propagate packets, it must be able to gain access to the network layer address in the packet and, based on this, make a decision on how to send the packet. This implies that the packet contains the network layer information. What if it does not? Let us stop for a second and think whether all protocols use network layer addressing. We said that the OSI model is a recommendation but not a requirement and that certain protocols may not follow it to the letter to attain some specific goals.

For example, the TCP/IP protocol suite includes the IP protocol that provides network layer addressing to allow routers to route TCP/IP packets. (Consider the Internet, for example.) IPX/SPX (or its Microsoft implementation NWLink) also has network addresses that allow packets to be routed.

Such protocols are called *routable* protocols. Besides IP and IPX, routable protocols include DECnet, AppleTalk, XNS, and some others.

What price do we pay for the privilege of being routed? The answer is processing overhead for constructing layer 3 headers, management overhead for assigning network layer addresses (they are typically not built in but are assigned by an administrator), and packet-size overhead (the network layer header occupies some space and this data must be transmitted in each packet).

If you use TCP/IP in your network, the system overhead to create an IP packet is a minimum of 20 bytes. That means we pay an extra 20 bytes per packet for the privilege of routability.

Some protocols sacrifice routing capabilities in the name of speed. A typical example of such a protocol is NetBEUI. NetBEUI (or, as it is often called in various technical papers, NBF, or NetBIOS Frames) is *nonroutable*. This means, when a router receives a NetBEUI packet, it cannot locate any network layer information and consequently cannot route it. Another example of a nonroutable protocol is LAT (a protocol that is used by Digital Equipment Corporation).

To generalize this concept, nonroutable protocols cannot be used across routers. Their communication will be limited to the local subnet only.

We should mention that NetBEUI is often called a nonroutable, but *bridgeable* protocol, since it can cross bridges and switches.

Routable protocols are able to cross routers, but proper node and router configuration is required. Nodes have to be aware of a router presence. For example, in the TCP/IP world, a computer must be specifically set up to use the router by providing a *default gateway* address in its configuration settings. The very basic idea behind the default gateway is that it provides an address to route packets to when the computer is unable to determine another destination to which to send them. This is typically how computers reach the Internet.

In some implementations, routers are often referred to as gateways. This is for historical reasons. This term is not 100% technically correct from the network perspective. Later we will give a definition of a gateway and you will see that the term can refer to a completely different type of device.

Let us now summarize what we have learned about routers. A typical router

- Operates at the network layer of the OSI model
- Has higher processing overhead than bridges or switches
- Can make intelligent decisions about how to reach the remote computer more efficiently
- Does not propagate broadcast messages; rather, it segments networks into broadcast domains
- Can connect segments with different media access control methods and speeds
- Works only with routable protocols (for example, IPX and IP)
- Must be configured by the administrator before functioning
- Must have end notes that are specifically configured to use it

Brouters

To solve problems associated with the router's inability to route nonroutable packets, a new class of device was introduced. These devices are called *brouters*. The abbreviation brouter comes from bridge router. These devices can act like bridges or routers depending on the type of protocol being used. For example, if a brouter receives a packet, it will first try to route it. If it fails for some reason, for example the incoming frame has no network layer addresses, the brouter will bridge it using appropriate bridging algorithms. Most brouters can have their bridging or routing capabilities enabled or disabled, permitting them to operate as bridges, routers, or both.

Gateways

Now we climb to even higher layers of the OSI model: to the transport layer and above. You may say that we covered repeaters, bridges, routers and this seems enough to support even a very complex network. What problems can't we solve using the devices described previously?

In the beginning of this chapter we spoke about the necessity to connect dissimilar systems, for example, Novell NetWare and Windows NT. In this case, even if packets can get routed between the two systems, they will not be able to understand each other because of differences in architecture. Neither repeater, nor bridge, nor even a router can solve this problem. We need some other sort of device that does data translation between the two systems. Such devices are called *gateways*.

Gateways repackage and convert data going from one environment to another. They repackage the information to match the way the destination system can accept it. Gateways can change the actual data inside the packet so the application on the receiving end can accept it. They can also change the information in packet headers at different layers of the OSI model.

> Do not confuse *gateway* used in the current context with the *default gateway* setting in the TCP/IP world. The TCP/IP default gateway is effectively a router and its name is applied for historical reasons. We will speak about default gateways again in Chapter 6, when we discuss TCP/IP concepts.

Typically gateways are used to connect two systems that use different communication protocols or different data formatting procedures.

How Does It Work?

The first very important thing to mention is that gateways are *task specific*. That means a gateway that is used in one environment will not typically work in another. You can think of a gateway as an interpreter who translates from English to German. Obviously, the same interpreter will not be of help if you need a Chinese-to-Russian translation.

But how do gateways work? The principle behind nearly all gateways is basically the same. A gateway takes data from one environment, strips off its old protocol stack, and then repackages the extracted data using the protocol of the destination network. When the reply comes from the destination system, the gateway performs the same action but in the reverse order.

In order to perform their functions, gateways need to speak the native language of both systems. That means they must have software to perform the translation functions. This software, of course, varies from gateway to gateway. The beauty of the gateway is that both connected systems think that they are speaking to the gateway but not to each other. This makes a gateway a perfect point for monitoring and implementing security barriers.

You may wonder about the OSI level at which gates work. The answer varies depending on the type of gateway. Typically, gateways work at the application layer, but they can work at other layers as well. Some gateways, for example, operate at the transport layer while others even work down to the network layer.

Let us discuss some examples of commonly existing gateways. You may have already used some of the gateways we will cover and may look at them from a different perspective after our discussion.

Microsoft Windows NT Gateway Services for NetWare

With Gateway Services for NetWare (GSNW), you can create a gateway through which Microsoft client computers without NetWare client software can access NetWare file and print resources.

> **Note**
>
> Here we assume that Microsoft client computers do not have Novell NetWare connectivity software, such as Client for NetWare Networks, installed locally.

GSNW acts as an intermediate device between a Windows NT network and a NetWare network. What differences in these systems prevent them from directly talking to each other? First of all, Microsoft type networks use the server message block (SMB) protocol to exchange files and gain access to printers. Novell NetWare networks, on the other hand, use the NetWare core protocol (NCP) for the same purpose. When a gateway is enabled, network clients running Microsoft client software can access NetWare files and printers without having to run NetWare client software locally. All Microsoft clients speak only to the computer running GSNW.

Hotmail.com SMTP to HTTP Gateway

Another example of a gateway is the popular Internet server: `http://www.hotmail.com`. Users who do not have mailboxes can connect to this server and establish one. If you think about it from the technical perspective, Internet Mail works by using simple mail transfer protocol (SMTP), which is not supported by Web browsers such as Netscape Navigator and Microsoft Internet Explorer. Web browsers use hypertext transfer protocol (HTTP) to gain access to web pages. The hotmail.com gateway accesses an e-mail using the standard SMTP interface and translates it to the HTTP format to make it accessible through a web page.

TCP and IP-to-IP Gateways

Many Internet firewalls have built in gateways that function on the TCP (transport) layer and even the IP (network) layer. The purpose of these firewall-gateways is to provide translation of transport- and network-level addresses for security purposes. When the packet comes from the Internet, the gateway examines the contents of the packets, performs source validation or other security checks, and repackages the packet data with a new IP header. The new packet gets forwarded to the internal network, which is not directly accessible from the Internet. This results in a scenario where the internal network never speaks directly to the Internet and vice versa. This is similar to what happens in court when a person speaks to his or her lawyer and the lawyer speaks to the judge on his or her behalf.

> **Note**   Another name for the IP-to-IP gateway is network address translator (NAT).

Performance Considerations

Because gateways operate on the higher layers of the OSI model (usually transport and above) they incur extra overhead to process the low layer addressing, extract data, and then repackage the data into the new protocol stacks. Obviously, the speed of data communication through a gateway is much slower than it is through bridges or routers. You may want to avoid the excessive use of gateways where possible. For example, consider installing connectivity software on one of the communicating sides. In our example we used Gateway services for NetWare but could have come up with a similar solution by installing client services for NetWare on all Microsoft computers. This would significantly improve performance; but, using this approach, we would have to modify more systems, which would produce a greater administrative overhead.

To sum it up what we have learned about gateways, a gateway

- Operates at the higher layers of the OSI model (usually transport and above)
- Has a higher processing overhead than bridges or switches
- Is application specific, which means gateways will work only in the environments for which they were originally designed.
- Repackages protocol stacks
- Speaks to each end node but the end nodes do not speak to each other
- Must be configured by the administrator before operating

Wide Area Network Technologies

So far we have discussed different network expansion devices such as repeaters, bridges, hubs, and switches. What if we wanted to connect two branch offices, for instance one in California and one in New York City? Of course, we could put hundreds of repeaters and bridges and even some routers on our way from one place to the other, but you will likely agree that this sounds a bit unrealistic. Another question that may come to mind is, "What about the Internet?" You have not seen any routers connecting your house to the global networking systems, but you are still able to get your e-mail from half way around the world. To answer these questions, we need to introduce another concept: the wide area network (WAN).

The WAN was already mentioned in previous chapters but now we will expand the concept and review the most popular technologies used in conjunction with the WAN.

What is a WAN?

A WAN is a data communications network that covers a relatively broad geographic area and often uses transmission facilities provided by common carriers, such as public switched telephone networks (PSTN). WAN technologies function at the physical, data-link, and network layers of the OSI model.

WAN technologies can be logically divided into several classes:

- Point-to-point links
- Circuit switching
- Packet switching
- Virtual circuits
- Dialup services

Let us characterize each of these classes. A *point-to-point link* provides a single, preestablished WAN communications path from the customer premises through a carrier network, such as a telephone company, to a remote network. A point-to-point link is often called a leased line because its established path is permanent and fixed for each remote network reached through the carrier facilities. The main characteristic of the point-to-point link is that the carrier company reserves these links for the private use of the customer.

In *circuit switching,* a dedicated physical circuit is established, maintained, and terminated through a carrier network for each communication session. This method is used in telephone networks. You can think of circuit switching as a normal telephone call. The well-known technology, integrated services digital network (ISDN) is an example of a circuit-switched WAN technology.

Packet switching is also a WAN switching method. In comparison with circuit switching where the circuit is usually used by a single device or LAN, in packet switching, multiple network devices share a single point-to-point link to transport packets from a source to a destination across a carrier network. The technology that is used in packet switching is called statistical multiplexing. Examples of packet switching networks are asynchronous transfer mode (ATM), frame relay, and X.25.

A *virtual circuit* is a logical circuit created to ensure reliable communication between two network devices. This virtual circuit is established over the existing carrier. Some of these virtual circuits are dynamically established on demand and terminated when transmission is complete—they are called switched virtual circuits (SVC). Another type is a permanently established virtual circuit (PVC). PVCs are used in situations where transfer between devices is constant.

The last type of WAN technology is *dial-up services*. These services offer cost-effective methods for connectivity across WANs. There are two popular dial-up implementations: *dial-on-demand routing* (DDR) and *dial backup*.

Using the DDR technique, a router can dynamically initiate and close a circuit-switched session as transmitting end stations demand. Certain logic can be implemented on routers. For example, a router could be configured to consider certain traffic "interesting" (usually this is traffic from a particular protocol) and establish a connection when it senses it. Other traffic is considered "uninteresting" and does not lead to connection establishment. The only situation where uninteresting traffic is propagated is when the connection is already established. If the router receives no interesting traffic before a special idle timer expires, the circuit is terminated.

Dial backup is a service that activates a backup serial line under certain conditions—for example, when the primary link fails or when the load on the primary link reaches a certain level. Dial backup offers some protection against WAN performance degradation and downtime.

WAN Devices

In order to participate on a WAN and to build WANs, you need special equipment that supports the WAN technologies outlined above. WAN equipment is very task specific but we have already learned most of the principles that support it. Typical WAN equipment includes WAN switches, access servers, modems, channel service unit/data service unit (CSU/DSU) devices, ISDN terminal adapters, and others. You can even find devices like ATM switches and multiplexers on the WAN.

T1

T1 is a high-speed point-to-point digital network technology developed by AT&T in 1957 and implemented in the early 1960s. The primary innovation of T1 was to introduce "digitized" voice.

T1 standards are often referred to as a network that has a speed of 1.544 Mbps and was designed for voice circuits or "channels" (24 per each T1 line or "trunk"). Each channel is 64 Kbps. Combining or multiplexing different numbers of channels, we get the different speeds represented in Table 5.2

A couple of questions usually come to the mind while looking at this table. Why does a single channel occupy 64 Kbps? The answer for this question is found in the history of the technology. Originally T1 technology was designed to carry digitized voice. To provide an acceptable quality for digital transmissions of the human voice, it is necessary to sample the voice data at twice the rate of the voice's audio frequency. Since the high-frequency limit of a normal human voice is taken to be about 4 kHz, to digitize it with acceptable quality we must sample at twice the rate, or 8 kHz. As you know, 8 kHz means 8,000 times per second. Each sample is represented by 1 byte or 8 bits, which gives us 8,000 x 8 = 64 Kbps.

You may be wondering why table 5.2 shows a value of 1.544 Mbps when doing the math reveals that 24 x 64 Kbps = 1.536 Mbps. The trick is T1 technology sends data by continuously putting bytes from all 24 voice channels one by one into one physical channel. First comes the first byte from the first channel, then comes the first byte from the second channel, and so on. Finally the first byte from the 24th channel is sent. After a byte of data is sent from each voice channel, a special synchronization bit is sent. This special bit is also called a frame bit. This results in an 8000 x 1bit = 8 Kbps control channel. (1.536 Mbps + 8 Kbps = 1.544 Mbps)

Digital Data Service

Another point-to-point technology is the digital data service (DDS). DDS provides full duplex communication at 2.4, 4.8, 9.6, or 56 Kbps. Networks are connected to DDS through bridges that connect to a channel service unit/data service unit (CSU/DSU). The CSU/DSU accesses the DDS line and

Table 5.2 *Combining Voice Channels*

Number of Voice Channels	Data Rate	Carrier System	T1 Channels	Signal Level
1	64 Kbps	N/A	1/24 T1	DS0
24	1.544 Mbps	T1	1 T1	DS1
48	3.152 Mbps	T1C	2 T1	DS1C
96	6.312 Mbps	T2	4 T1	DS2
672	44.736 Mbps	T3	28 T1	DS3
1,344	89.472 Mbps	T3C	56 T1	DS3C
4,032	274.176 Mbps	T4	168 T1	DS4

converts the LAN's digital signals to digital signals compatible with the DDS synchronous environment.

Switched 56

Switched 56 is a dialup version of DDS. This 56-Kbps service is an on-demand service so there is no need to pay for a dedicated line. Although switched 56 provides the capability to access (dial up) more than one switched 56 site, all sites must be equipped with CSU/DSU equipment.

Frame Relay

At the end of the 1980s, several network trends were combined to create a need for a new form of wide area network switching. The new WAN switching technology required high speed, low delay, port sharing, and bandwidth sharing. While existing circuit switching technologies and X.25 packet switching[1] had some of these characteristics, only Frame Relay offered a full complement. This made frame relay an ideal solution for connecting busy networks in the LAN/WAN arena.

Frame relay is a high-performance WAN protocol that operates at the physical and data link layers of the OSI reference model. Frame relay originally was designed for use across integrated services digital network (ISDN) interfaces. Today, it is used over a variety of other network interfaces in hundreds of networks throughout the world to connect LAN, Internet and voice applications. Basically, frame relay is a way of sending information over a wide area network that divides the information into frames or packets. Each frame has an address that the network uses to determine the destination of the frame. The frames travel through a series of switches (frame relay switches) and arrive at their destination. Many of the error-checking functions that were present in X.25 networks were omitted to make frame relay much faster. Because these checking functions were striped away, frame relay requires reliable and error-free lines to function efficiently.

Note Although frame relay offers significant advantages, other wide area network switching technologies, such as X.25 packet switching, will remain important where line quality is not as good. In the case of earlier and slower packet switching technologies, the network itself guarantees error-free delivery through built-in control functions that are not implemented in frame relay.

---

[1]We will spend more time on X.25 in Chapter 8.

As mentioned above, frame relay is often referred to as a streamlined version of X.25, offering fewer of the robust capabilities, such as windowing and retransmission of last data, that are present in X.25. As mentioned earlier, frame relay is strictly a layer 2 protocol suite, where X.25 provides services at layer 3 (the network layer) as well. This enables frame relay to offer higher performance and greater transmission efficiency than X.25.

A frame relay network includes endpoints such as users' workstations, servers, host computers, and frame relay access equipment (frame relay bridges, routers, hosts, frame relay access devices). Additionally, a frame relay network would include some of the network equipment we already discussed, such as network routers and T1 multiplexers. Frame relay access equipment is responsible for delivering frames from the endpoints to the network in the prescribed format. Network devices switch or route frames through the network to the destination access equipment, which routes them to the destination user device (endpoint).

A frame relay network will often be depicted as a network cloud because the frame relay network is not a single physical connection between one endpoint and the other. Instead, a logical path is defined within the network. As we discussed previously, this logical path is called a virtual circuit.

Frame relay provides a number of benefits over alternative technologies:

- Lower cost of ownership
- Open architecture that is implemented through well-established and widely-adopted standards
- Integration and interworking with other new services and applications (such as ATM)
- Low overhead combined with high reliability
- Network scalability, flexibility, and disaster recovery

ATM

The next technology, Asynchronous Transfer Mode (ATM) is fundamentally different from the majority of LAN networking technologies and the most difficult to visualize. Unlike most existing LAN technologies, ATM uses a connection-oriented transmission strategy. Another very important difference of ATM is that it uses small, fixed-length blocks of data called cells. The format of these cells provides special characteristics to ATM networks. From one perspective, using cells offers advantages over traditional, variable- length, frame-based networking technologies. On the other hand, the use of cells could be considered a limitation.

Study Break

Why Variable Length Frames No Longer Satisfy Our Requirements

As you know from the previously discussed material, a frame-based network uses random-length frames that are generated by the source system. The only limitation is that these frames must fall between minimum and maximum lengths, specified by standards. The actual frames that are generated depend on the amount of data transmitted. For example, an Ethernet frame has a lower limit of 64 bytes and an upper limit of 1,518 bytes. In some token ring networks, the size of a frame can be as large as 18,000 bytes. At first glance these variable-sized frames are very efficient at moving large amounts of data. This is because a single frame could contain a large portion of the data and only a few frames are needed to perform large data transmissions. This concept makes frame-based technologies efficient in pure data networks.

On the other hand, variable-size frames are very difficult to predict. The delay between the frames is variable and depends on several factors including the size of the frame. Networking devices have to read and retransmit the frame. Some types of devices (for example bridges, switches, and routers) must read and examine a portion of the frame to determine how to respond to it. The necessity to process all incoming frames and to make individual decisions about each frame produces delays in moving through a forwarding device. This delay is often referred to as *latency*. Latency is usually not a problem for most data applications. Voice and video transmissions, however, are very sensitive to latency. (If latency is high but constant, it will result in low quality but consistent audio or video signals.) This makes variable-length, frame-based technologies difficult to implement in environments where low and predictable latency is required. This is where cell switching technologies such as ATM become very attractive.

Cell Switching

Let us now look at how cell switching technology works. A cell-based networking technology such as ATM uses fixed-length cells rather than variable length frames. Every cell on an ATM network, no matter what kind of data it contains, is 53 bytes in length. What advantages does the fixed length offer? Because an ATM cell is smaller than a variable-length frame, switching and sending the cell to the next device is much faster. The small cell size can also be a drawback since smaller cells hold less data. The 53-byte ATM cell is a compromise between short switch latencies and useful data capacity.

Another very significant advantage of having fixed length cells is that they are very predictable. This allows an ATM switch to greatly reduce the total latency and variations in latency. Additionally the small and fixed size of ATM cells and the standard arrangement of the cells' headers allows ATM switches to perform extremely fast switching operations using hardware logic instead of using software-based switching or routing algorithms. ATM speeds are nominally characterized as 155 Mbps and 622 Mbps. ATM is, however, capable of even higher speeds. The theoretical bandwidth is as high as 1.2 Gbps.

ATM transmits fixed-size 53 byte cells. Five of the 53 bytes are devoted to the cell header and the remaining 48 bytes are used for data. The header field of an ATM cell contains addressing and priority information and a CRC analog.

ATM functionality is much more complex than just using fixed-size cells and switching. ATM standards specify many service and management functions, such as cell preparation, cell handling, and traffic and call management. Describing these standards lies outside the scope of this book.

ISDN

Integrated services digital network (ISDN) is comprised of digital telephony and data-transport services offered by regional telephone carriers. ISDN digitizes signals to permit voice, data, text, graphics, music, video, and other source material to be transmitted over existing (digital-quality) telephone lines. One of the original goals of ISDN was to link businesses and homes using the existing copper wire infrastructure.

ISDN is available in two different implementations. The ISDN basic rate interface (BRI) service splits the existing twisted pair copper telephone wire into three separate channels—two B channels and one D channel (2B+D). BRI B-channel service operates at 64 Kbps and is meant to carry user data; BRI D-channel service operates at 16 Kbps and is meant to carry control and signaling information.

D channel also potentially supports data communications and in some special cases can support user data transmission.

A device attached to the ISDN network can use both of the B channels for a combined 128 Kbps data stream. At the same time, it is possible to use only one of the B channels for data and another B channel for voice communications.

The second implementation of ISDN, primary rate interface (PRI) service offers 23 B channels and one D channel in North America and Japan. This gives a combined bit rate of 1.544 Mbps (the PRI D channel runs at 64 Kbps).

ISDN PRI in Europe, Australia, and other parts of the world provides 30 B channels plus one 64-Kbps D channel and a total interface rate of 2.048 Mbps.

In order to use ISDN, special equipment, such as ISDN modems and network adapter cards, must be used. We will look into ISDN further in Chapter 8.

Digital Subscriber Line

You may have already heard about the digital subscriber line (DSL), a network access technology with a unique advantage: it can provide high-speed digital transmission over the 750 million ordinary phone lines that make up the existing global telecommunications infrastructure.

DSL technology enables today's users to gain continuous access to the Internet or corporate LANs at speeds up to 100 times faster than 56.6-Kbps modems. It is expected that in the next several years, top transmission speeds will grow to 53 Mbps or higher. Such speeds are achieved by using the special DSL modems. DSL modems use sophisticated digital coding techniques to get as much bandwidth from an ordinary copper phone line as possible. DSL technology is a modem technology that uses existing twisted-pair telephone lines to transport high-bandwidth data, such as multimedia and video, to service subscribers.

DSL services are dedicated, point-to-point, public network access over twisted-pair copper wire on the local loop between a network service provider's central office and the customer site or on intrabuilding or intra-campus local loops.

Sometimes you may hear the term *xDSL* that covers a number of similar forms of DSL, including ADSL, SDSL, HDSL, RADSL, and VDSL. The main reason for such a wide number of technologies is because DSL services come in a variety of types, each designed to suit different functions.

ADSL

Asymmetric or asynchronous digital subscriber line (ADSL) technology is asymmetric. That means it allows more bandwidth downstream from a service provider office to the customer site than upstream from the subscriber to the central office. The reason behind this approach is that ordinary users typically download much more information than they send. This is true for Internet/intranet surfing, video-on-demand, and remote LAN access.

With ADSL, an ADSL modem is connected to each end of a twisted-pair telephone line, creating three information channels—a high-speed downstream channel, a medium-speed duplex channel, and a basic telephone service channel. The purpose of the basic telephone channel is to guarantee uninterrupted basic telephone service, even if ADSL fails. The high-speed channel varies from 1.5 to 6.1 Mbps, and the duplex channel speed runs from 16 to 640 Kbps. Each channel can be submultiplexed to form multiple lower-rate channels.

SDSL

Symmetric Digital Subscriber Line service provides up to 768Kbps of bandwidth in both directions. SDSL's affordable cost and its ability to support high-speed transfers of information in both directions makes SDSL ideal for most business applications, including Internet access, telecommuting, or connecting remote offices of large corporations.

Other types of DSL are also available, such as ISDN digital subscriber line (IDSL), that provides ISDN signaling over the DSL circuit, high-speed digital subscriber line (HDSL) that provides high speed access and runs at approximately 6 Mbps, and very high speed digital subscriber line (VDSL) which provides very high-speed access at a rate from 8 Mbps to 53 Mbps.

■ Summary

This chapter concentrated on devices, concerns, and techniques involved with expanding and optimizing a network. We looked at a LAN with an eye to upsizing it to a WAN. We found three reasons to want to expand a LAN: to connect two or more LANs, to segment an existing LAN to overcome attendant LAN limitations, and to connect the LAN to foreign systems and environments.

We reviewed the factors involved in connecting LANs and saw issues including that differing LAN speed and propagation delay would require the use of additional equipment. We looked at how the number of nodes on a network impacts available bandwidth and saw the value of LAN segmentation to limit the number of nodes per network. We also introduced the *network utilization value* to give a more accurate picture of the number of nodes a network segment could support. When we considered connecting our LAN to foreign systems and environments, we quickly decided we would need more equipment and technology since, even if dissimilar networks could exchange packets, they might not understand the packets' contents without something to translate between the dissimilar environments.

We continued our quest for LAN expansion by reviewing some common networking devices. We found *repeaters* could do an admirable job of beating signal attenuation, but since they work at the physical layer at the bit level, they weren't particularly useful in the expansion scenarios we had previously identified.

We then turned our attention to *bridges*. We saw bridges could connect networks with different architecture or could expand networks with similar architectures because they buffer and propagate transmitted packets.

Next, we examined switches. We saw that switches go a step beyond normal hubs by sending packets only to the port(s) they need to go to. We found switches to be like multiport bridges but much faster because of the use of parallel processing. When we analyzed switch performance, we discovered that, while the switch is a very high performance device, when traffic exceeds the bandwidth capabilities of the network, the switch must buffer the traffic attempting to pass through it. When the switch buffers overflow, packets are lost. (We called this a *funneling* problem.)

Moving up through the layers of the OSI model, we next examined *routers*. Routing, we saw, is like bridging, except under routing, we are concerned with the packet's network address and not its physical address. Because routing works at a higher OSI layer, it is slower than bridging or switching.

Going still higher through the OSI layers, we looked at *gateways*. These devices were good for connecting dissimilar networks (e.g. Windows NT and NetWare) by tearing down and rebuilding packets in accordance with the structure expected by the target network. Gateways, we found, are sophisticated but task specific, that is they will only act as gateways for the particular systems they are designed to link. Clients of the gateway think they are talking only to the gateway and not to each other. Gateways operate at the highest levels of the OSI model and, therefore, incur much more network overhead and are slower than switches, bridges, and routers.

With a firm understanding of network devices, we continued our discussion of actual WAN technologies. These technologies operate at the physical, data link, and network layers and are divided into several classes. We looked at *point-to-point links*, *circuit switching*, *packet switching*, *virtual circuits*, and *dialup services*.

We reviewed the *T1/T2/T3/T4* point-to-point network technology, which dates back to the late 1950s and is capable of data speeds from 64 Kbps to 274.176 Mbps through addition of multiple data channels. Another point-to-point technology was the *digital data service* (DDS). DDS also features a circuit-switched version, *Switched 56*. Both variants required the use of bridges and *channel service unit/data service unit* equipment to access the service.

We saw that *frame relay* technologies depend on highly reliable lines to allow them to reduce the degree of error checking used in older packet switching technologies such as X.25. *Asynchronous transfer mode* (ATM) systems use a standard length (53 byte) cell to simplify data routing and switching and increase data speeds to 155 to 622 Mbps with theoretical speeds as high as 1.2 Gbps.

We looked at the *integrated services digital network* (ISDN) and saw a digital service available from the telephone company with an available bandwidth of up to 1.544 Mbps (2.048 Mbps in Europe and Australia). Finally, we saw the many variants of digital subscriber line (DSL) technology. DSL can provide exceptionally high-speed data transmission over ordinary telephone lines.

▲ REVIEW QUESTIONS

1. *You might want to expand your LAN to (select all that apply)*

    A. Connect two or more LANs.

    B. Make use of repeaters, routers, and gateways.

    C. Segment the existing LAN to overcome limitations of LAN technologies.

    D. Connect it to other foreign systems and environments.

2. *The rule that states that there may be a maximum of 30 nodes per Ethernet segment is*

    A. A firm rule that is true and which must be followed in all cases

    B. Incorrect.

    C. An empirical rule that provides a good guideline, but which is not as accurate as determining the network utilization value.

    D. Only applicable in networks using coaxial cable (10BASE-2; 10BASE-5).

3. *Repeaters*

    A. Operate at the physical layer and provide packet synchronization.

    B. Operate at the data link layer and provide frame synchronization.

    C. Operate at the data link layer and provide bit synchronization.

    D. Operate at the Physical layer and provide bit synchronization.

4. *A multiport repeater*

    A. Functions as a bridge.

    B. Can work as a bridge or a router.

C. Is really a repeater hub.

D. Uses parallel processing to speed up data transfer.

5. *Select all that apply to classical bridges*

A. Operate at the data link layer of OSI model.

B. Can overflow due to excessive traffic.

C. Can make intelligent decisions to propagate frames more efficiently when multiple paths to the destination exist.

D. Have higher processing overhead than routers.

6. *The process called flooding occurs*

A. When repeater receives a broadcast packet.

B. When repeater gets a packet with an unknown MAC address.

C. When the protocol being used is nonroutable.

D. Flooding is not defined for repeaters.

7. *What happens when a bridge receives a packet with a destination MAC address that is not present in the bridge table?*

A. Bridge discards the packet.

B. Bridge propagates the packet to all its ports.

C. Bridge propagates the packet to all its ports except the port from which the packet came.

D. Bridge does not examine MAC addresses of incoming frames and cannot make decisions based on that criterion.

8. *Why is it so undesirable when a switch drops frames due to excessive traffic on its ports?*

A. Because packet loss cannot be recovered at the lower layers of the OSI model and can be detected only at the higher layers by transport- and application-level protocols, with all the overhead associated with this process

B. Because switches request the frame retransmission and stop further operations until they receive the requested packet.

C. Because a lost frame means that the file or message this frame is part of will become corrupt.

D. This is not a problem at all. Switches do not drop frames because of their high performance. Only bridges do that.

9. *You install network monitoring software on one of the computers connected to a dedicated port of a 3COM switch. The other 100 computers in your network are connected to the same switch. You read in the documentation that this monitoring software allows you to capture all packets by switching the network adapter to the promiscuous mode allowing it to process all the packets it sees. Will you be able to monitor network traffic from all computers in your network?*

    A. No.

    B. Yes.

10. *Which type of switching technology can detect corrupted frames?*

    A. Cut through.

    B. Store and forward.

    C. Full duplex.

    D. Half duplex.

11. *A Network consists of 40 workstations and 1 server, as pictured in Figure 5–14. Users often use multimedia applications that are run from the server and consume a large amount of bandwidth, causing delays to other computers. Through the use of network monitoring software, you discover your network experiences a high level of collisions because users access the server simultaneously to download large multimedia files. You decide to substitute a 10BASE-T hub with a 10BASE-T switch. How will this affect the situation?*

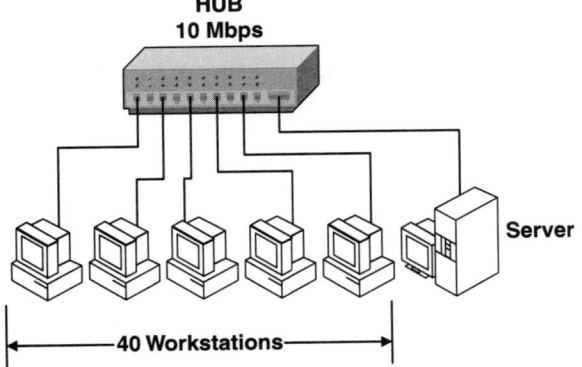

Figure 5–14 *Client/server network.*

    A. The performance will dramatically increase and delays will be illiminated.

    B. There will be a slight performance improvement, delays become less frequent.

    C. This will not change the situation. Performance will stay on the same level.

    D. Performance will decrease. Delays will become even longer.

12. *You have a large 10BASE-5 network that consists of four segments connected by three repeaters. You decide to substitute two repeaters with one router and one bridge. How many collision domains will your network have?*

    A. 1.

    B. 2.

    C. 3.

    D. Collision domains are not defined for 10BASE-5 networks, since they use token passing technology, which prevents collisions.

13. *At what layer of the OSI model do routers work?*

    A. Physical.

    B. Data link.

    C. Network.

    D. Transport.

    E. Network and transport.

    F. data link and network.

    G. All of the above.

14. *How does a router propagate the packets it receives?*

    A. By examining the destination MAC address and consulting its routing table.

    B. By examining the network ID portion of the network address and consulting its routing table.

    C. By propagating packets to all its ports.

    D. By examining the network address and, if no decision can be made based on this, examining the MAC address.

15. *Will the fast Ethernet type network pictured in Figure 5–15 work? (Assume that the network uses classical hubs.)*

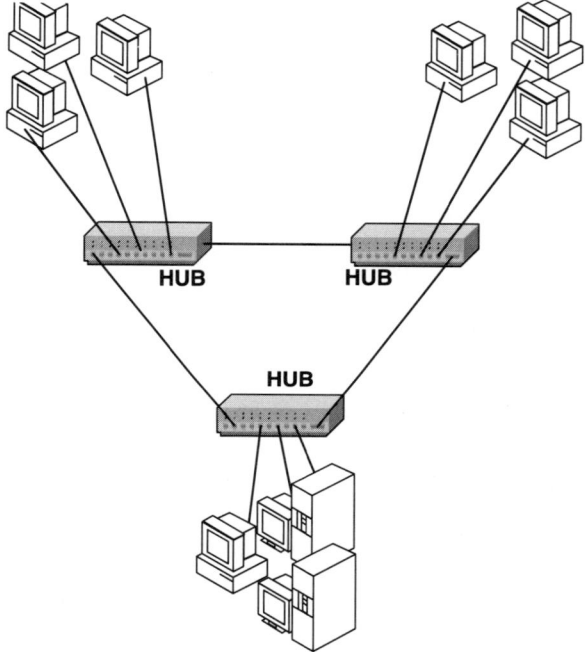

Figure 5–15 *Fast ethernet network.*

    A. No.

    B. Yes.

    C. Yes, if this is 100BASE-T4 network.

    D. Yes, if this is 100BASE-TX network.

16. *The 10-Mbps network with a classic hub pictured in Figure 5–16 has low performance due to the high network utilization level. Client computers constantly access the corporate server to download large CAD files, thus producing network delays. To improve performance, but to keep the migration costs as low as possible, you*

    A. Upgrade the link from the hub to the server to 100-Mbps.

    B. Implement a full-duplex connection between the hub and the Server.

    C. Substitute a switch for the hub.

    D. Replace the hub with a switch and implement a 100-Mbps, full-duplex connection to the server.

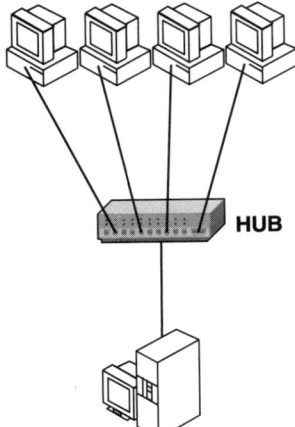

Figure 5-16   *10-Mbps network.*

17. *Your Ethernet bus-type network running only the NetBEUI protocol experiences a large number of broadcast messages. You want to segment the network by using two routers to reduce broadcast messages. How will this affect your network?*

   A. The entire network will stop functioning.

   B. The network will continue to operate and the level of broadcast messages will be reduced.

   C. The network will continue to operate but the level of broadcast messages will not be reduced, since routers are transparent for broadcasts.

   D. The network will be broken into three segments that are not able to communicate with each other.

18. *You have two networks: one is an SNA-type network and one is Microsoft based. What type of device would you use to connect these networks to let them talk to each other?*

   A. Repeater.

   B. Bridge.

   C. Router.

   D. Gateway.

19. *You need to connect a Microsoft network and a Novell NetWare network. Two solutions have been suggested: either install a gateway or install client software on all Microsoft-based computers. Which solution offers better performance?*

A. Gateway solution.

B. Client software on each Microsoft-based computer.

C. Both solutions have the same performance.

D. Microsoft and Novell NetWare networks cannot talk to each other since they use completely different sets of protocols.

20. *At what speed does T1 operate?*

A. 1.544 Mbps.

B. 128 Kbps.

C. 64 Kbps.

D. 10 Mbps.

21. *What is the size of the ATM cell?*

A. From 64 to 1,542 bytes.

B. 53 bytes.

C. 1 KB.

D. 64 bytes.

22. *What ISDN channel is capable of data transmissions?*

A. A channel.

B. B channel.

C. C channel.

D. D channel.

TCP/IP Fundamentals and Configuration

▲ **Chapter Syllabus**

TCP/IP Basic Information

TCP/IP Architecture

IP Addressing Basics

Automating IP Address Assignment Using DHCP

NetBIOS over TCP/IP

Host Name Resolution

In this chapter, we will look at the history of transmission control protocol/Internet protocol (TCP/IP) and discuss its terminology and perspectives. We will look at TCP/IP standards and major utilities. We will also discuss the protocols that comprise the TCP/IP protocol suite and look at some TCP/IP configuration and troubleshooting information.

This chapter provides a broad overview of IP addressing. You will learn the differences between the three main address classes (class A, class B, and class C), as well and the ins and outs of network and host IDs. We will also examine subnet masks and their default values for various IP address classes.

We will look at the dynamic host configuration protocol (DHCP), a service that greatly simplifies the process of assigning IP addresses and reduces the possibility of costly configuration errors.

We will introduce NetBIOS over TCP/IP concepts. We will see how computers communicate

193

with each other using computer names. We will define the term *NetBIOS name* and will devote significant attention to how to communicate with computers possessing NetBIOS names. Much of our interest will center on how to resolve a NetBIOS name to an IP address and, ultimately, to a MAC address.

In addition to the Windows-dependent NetBIOS name resolution, we will discuss a computer naming system that can be used with any computer running TCP/IP: *host names*. We will see how host-name resolution works, discuss industry standard methods of host-name resolution, and mention the Microsoft-specific methods.

This chapter will familiarize you with a number of configuration files such as LMHOSTS and HOSTS. You will learn about NetBIOS node types and Windows Internet naming service (WINS) and domain name system (DNS) functions. You will also see how complex TCP/IP networks function. After completing this chapter, you will be able to do the following:

- Describe TCP/IP
- Identify major TCP/IP utilities
- Identify valid and invalid IP addresses
- Discuss the classes of IP addresses
- Identify the network ID and host ID for a particular IP address
- Define DHCP
- Explain the steps of the DHCP process
- Describe the DHCP lease duration and renewal process
- Install DHCP on a Windows NT computer
- Explain the function of a DHCP relay agent
- Define NetBIOS and identify the services it provides
- Define NetBIOS names
- Explain the NetBIOS name registration, discovery, and release processes
- Identify and explain NetBIOS name resolution methods
- Define a host name and explain the difference between a host name and a NetBIOS name
- Describe the methods of host name resolution
- Outline the Microsoft host name resolution process
- Understand the purpose of HOSTS and LMHOTS files

TCP/IP Basic Information

TCP/IP stands for *transmission control protocol/Internet protocol* and it is an industry standard suite of protocols designed for wide area networks (WANs). Since the Internet is an example of a WAN, we can say that TCP/IP is the protocol suite for the Internet. The most common mistake is to think that TCP/IP is one protocol or two protocols (TCP and IP). As we will see, the TCP/IP abbreviation represents several protocols. Among them are some you might already have heard about: HTTP (hypertext transfer protocol) which is used to navigate the World Wide Web, FTP (file transfer protocol) that provides reliable file transfer over the Internet, and SMTP (simple mail transfer protocol) which supports e-mail communications. Some of the protocols that are included in the TCP/IP suite are quite exotic, for example, Internet control message protocol (ICMP), simple network management protocol (SNMP), and trivial file transfer protocol (TFTP) (we will discuss these a bit later in the chapter.)

Standards and How They Appear

Today, TCP/IP is often associated with the Internet. Its architecture and design are closely bound with Internet advances and growth. Since, however, there is no organization that owns the Internet, you might ask how this whole system is controlled. There are organizations responsible for setting up standards and controlling the advance of TCP/IP technologies. Some examples include The Internet Society and The Internet Architecture Board.

You may wonder how these organizations' decisions are documented. *Requests for Comments* (RFCs) are a series of notes, started in 1969, about the Internet (originally the ARPANET). The notes discuss many aspects of computing and computer communication and focus on networking protocols, procedures, programs, and concepts. RFCs also include meeting notes, opinion, and an occasional bit of humor. TCP/IP standards are always published as RFCs.

Warning Although TCP/IP standards are always published as RFCs, not all RFCs specify standards. Some of them have *limited use* or even *not recommended* status.

When a document is published, it is assigned an RFC number. The original RFC number is never updated; but when changes are required, a new RFC is issued with a new number. Therefore, when you are looking for information in the RFCs, be sure you have the most recent one. You can find some of the TCP/IP-related RFCs at *http://www.alidatrain.com/rfc*. You can also find links to RFC sites as well as a wealth of Internet information at www.networksolutions.com.

Advantages of TCP/IP

Modern networks are large and complex. They are connected with routers and need reliable protocols with which to communicate. Implementing TCP/IP in a corporate network gives you a standard, routable environment. Since TCP/IP offers robust, scalable architecture, you can easily expand your network. This is why most of today's large networks rely on TCP/IP.

Imagine a large enterprise network with hundreds of computers, many of which work under different operating systems such as Microsoft Windows NT, UNIX and Novell NetWare. A reasonable goal would be to connect all these computers so users could exchange information seamlessly. Obviously, this will require common protocols as well as connectivity utilities and tools to access and transfer data. Since TCP/IP is supported by all modern operating systems, it has become the logical choice when connecting dissimilar systems. In addition to a common network protocol, however, compatible applications are needed on both ends. Typically, every TCP/IP implementation includes various useful utilities that provide access to hosts running dissimilar network operating systems (NOS) for data transfer, monitoring, and remote control. For example: file transfer protocol (FTP), tracert, and telnet.

Remember, also, that the Internet is based on TCP/IP. Adding TCP/IP to a computer will allow it to gain Internet access (assuming, of course, it has physical connectivity to the Internet.)

Finally, TCP/IP offers the sockets interface, which can be used for developing client/server applications that can run on sockets-compliant stacks from various vendors. By using sockets, TCP/IP provides a robust, scalable, cross-platform client/server framework.

Study Break

What are Sockets?

The term sockets, (in Microsoft's implementation, Windows sockets or WINSOCK) may seem a little foreign. Sockets refers to a connection-oriented interprocess communication protocol. An interprocess communication is the way programs communicate with each other. A connection-oriented protocol is distinct from a connectionless protocol because in connection-oriented communications, the transmitter gets a positive response from the receiver when it sends a communication. (We use a telephone call analogy for a connection-oriented protocol and a letter for a connectionless one.) In sockets, each participant in the communication agrees on a logical data location — the socket — at each end of the communication channel. Communications are sent to these sockets, which are kept open for the duration of the communication session.

To summarize;

- TCP/IP is an industry standard suite of networking protocols.
- TCP/IP is a routable transport for many computer networks.
- TCP/IP provides the ability to share information between hosts using different network operating systems.
- TCP/IP provides the ability to log onto remote TCP/IP-based hosts from a workstation.
- TCP/IP adheres to Internet community standards, providing access to thousands of networks worldwide.

TCP/IP Utilities and Services

TCP/IP provides a way to access hosts running various NOS, tune its configuration, and troubleshoot connectivity problems. This is achieved through a number of tools and utilities. Knowing how to use the utilities often helps you to solve network-related problems. To get started, we will identify the purpose of the most important utilities. TCP/IP utilities can be logically divided into several groups based on their purpose: configuration utilities, data transfer utilities, remote execution utilities, printing utilities, and diagnostic utilities.

TCP/IP configuration utilities are used for configuring TCP/IP properties for network interfaces and setting parameters for them. These utilities allow an administrator to assign such parameters as the IP address, the subnet mask, type of interface, etc.

Different operating systems have different implementations of these utilities. On UNIX-like hosts the chief configuration utility is `ifconfig` (interface CONFIGuration), which allows you to assign and view IP parameters for the network interfaces. There are no built-in configuration utilities in Windows-based network operating systems. All configuration and administration is performed using the graphical user interface (GUI). Novell implementations rely on a set of utilities which load, activate, and configure parameters for the host's network interfaces. These utilities are called LOAD and BIND.

Data Transfer Utilities

Table 6.1 lists the tools that allow you to transfer data between two computers. The computers can be located anywhere as long as there is a TCP/IP connection between them.

Remote Execution Utilities

The utilities (listed in Table 6.2) allow you to launch applications and processes on remote hosts.

Printing Utilities

TCP/IP printing utilities provide a way to submit, receive, and manage print jobs in a TCP/IP environment. (See Table 6.3.) TCP/IP printing utilities allow TCP/IP based clients to submit print jobs for printers connected to UNIX computers or any other computers running TCP/IP printing services.

Diagnostic Utilities

In addition to the data transfer utilities we have already discussed, many operating systems provide tools for diagnosing TCP/IP-related problems. Table 6.4 describes the major diagnostic utilities that are included in the most TCP/IP implementations.

Using the LOAD and BIND Utility

To load and activate the TCP/IP protocol stack on the Novell servers, the LOAD and BIND utilities can be used. One of them, LOAD, is designed to load and link a loadable module into the operating system. To effect TCP/IP configuration, the LOAD utility loads and activates the TCP/IP stack, which is implemented as a module. Once the protocol stack is loaded, the BIND

Table 6.1 *TCP/IP Data Transfer Utilities*

Utility	Function
File transfer protocol (FTP)	Provides bi-directional file transfers between two TCP/IP hosts. One host is acting as an FTP server, while another is acting as a client.
Trivial file transfer protocol (TFTP)	Provides bi-directional file transfers between two TCP/IP hosts where one is running TFTP server software
Remote copy protocol (RCP)	This connectivity command copies files between a remote computer and a computer running the remote shell server service or daemon (rshd). (A service is called a daemon in UNIX.)

Table 6.2 *TCP/IP Remote Execution Utilities*

Utility	Function
Telnet	Provides terminal emulation to a TCP/IP host running Telnet server software. When you connect, your computer acts as if your keyboard is attached to the remote computer. This means that you can run programs on a computer on the other side of the world, just as if you were sitting in front of it.
Remote shell (RSH)	Runs commands on a UNIX host.
Remote execution (REXEC)	This connectivity command runs commands on remote hosts running the rexec service. Rexec authenticates the user name on the remote host by using a password before executing the specified command.

utility allows the administrator to bind it to network interfaces as needed. For example, the following syntax loads the appropriate driver for a particular NIC, loads TCP/IP stack, and binds the stack with the network interface, assigning an IP address:

```
LOAD NE2000 INT = 3 PORT = 320 FRAME = ETHERNET_II
LOAD TCPIP
BIND IP NE2000 FRAME = ETHERNET_II ADDR = 192.44.7.2
```

Using the IFCONFIG Utility

The IFCONFIG utility can be used to view, change and assign configuration parameters that apply on all or some interfaces of an IP host. As described

Table 6.3 *TCP/IP Printing Utilities*

Utility	Function
Line printer remote (LPR)	LPR lets a client application on one computer send a document to a print spooler service on another computer. The client application is usually named LPR and the service (or daemon) is usually named LPD.
Line printer queue (LPQ)	This diagnostic utility is used to obtain the status of a print queue on a host running the LPD server.
Line printer remove (LPRM)	This client side utility provides a way to remove the print jobs from remote print spooler service on another computer. This utility is implemented in UNIX environments only.
Line printer daemon (LPD)	A line printer daemon (LPD) service on the print server receives documents from line printer remote (LPR) utilities running on client systems. For example, with LPD installed, a Windows NT server can receive print jobs from UNIX-based computers.

Table 6.4 *TCP/IP Diagnostic Utilities*

Utility	Function
Finger	Retrieves system information from a remote computer that supports the finger service.
Address resolution protocol (ARP)	Displays and modifies the cache of locally resolved IP addresses to media access control (MAC) addresses.
NBTSTAT	This utility (or analogue) exists on NetBIOS-enabled hosts only. It displays protocol statistics and current TCP/IP connections using NetBIOS over TCP/IP. This utility is also used to determine the registered NetBIOS name and to view the local name cache. Some functions of the Microsoft NBTSTAT utility are included in the nmblookup utility that comes with SAMBA package for UNIX. SAMBA is a famous implementation of NetBIOS over TCP/IP for the UNIX environment.
Packet Internet groper (PING)	Verifies the availability of the remote host by sending the echo request and analyzing replies.
TRACEROUTE	Traces the route for packets from local hosts to the specified remote host. The TRACEROUTE utility is know as TRACERT in the Microsoft world. IPCONFIG displays current TCP/IP configuration including IP address(es), DNS and WINS addresses. This utility is primarily used in Microsoft operating systems
IFCONFIG	Displays current IP configuration parameters for given interface. Can be used like a configuration utility to assign and change these parameters. This utility is used in UNIX-like operating systems.
HOSTNAME	Returns the local computer's host name. You can use it in log-on scripts for identification. (In some network operating systems this utility, when used with the –s switch, will also set the host name.)
NSLOOKUP	Displays information from domain name system (DNS) name servers about a particular host or domain. You can also use this utility to check the availability of the domain name.
NETSTAT	Displays protocol statistics and current TCP/IP network connections.
ARCHIE	A utility that allows a user to search anonymous FTP sites for files on a specified topic.
ROUTE	Views and modifies the local routing table

above, this utility is used primarily on UNIX hosts, and therefore is implemented as a command-line utility. Different versions of UNIX-like operating systems may use slightly different syntax to execute the command. Differences are, however, relatively minor.

If you use this utility with a single parameter specifying the name of the network interface, it will display configuration information for the specified interface, as in

```
$ ifconfig lan0
lan0: flags = 63< UP,BROADCAST,NOTRAILERS,RUNNING >
        inet 194.226.192.51 netmask fffffe0 broadcast
194.226.192.63
```

> Different implementations of the **ifconfig** utility have different syntax and different command output. You can use the **-h** switch with **ifconfig** for a quick reference on a command's parameters.

Using the IPCONFIG Utility

To verify the TCP/IP configuration parameters (including the IP address) subnet mask, and default gateway in Microsoft TCP/IP implementations, use the IPCONFIG utility (or equivalents as discussed further on). The IP-CONFIG utility is provided as a part of the Microsoft TCP/IP installation in Microsoft Windows NT. In Windows 95/98 the utility is called WINIPCFG. Some UNIX implementations use /sbin/ifconfig. The IPCONFIG family utilities are useful in determining whether your parameters have been initialized or what values these parameters received.

In Windows NT, for example, ipconfig is a command line utility, and the simplest way to use it is to type the following at the command prompt:

```
ipconfig
```

If the TCP/IP configuration is initialized, the assigned IP address, subnet mask, and default gateway (if configured) appear. For example, consider the following statement:

```
C:\WINNT>ipconfig
Windows NT IP Configuration
Ethernet adapter Elnk31:
        IP Address. . . . . . . . . : 137.200.0.10
        Subnet Mask . . . . . . . . : 255.255.255.0
        Default Gateway . . . . . . : 137.200.0.1
```

Using the PING Utility

While the IPCONFIG utility is used to test the configuration parameters on a local computer, the PING utility will test connectivity with other computers. A PING implementation is included in almost all network operating systems. PING is a diagnostic tool that can report basic TCP/IP problems such as connection failures or router problems. For example, you can use the PING utility to verify that contact can be established between the client and server.

The work of the PING utility is based on the Internet control message protocol (ICMP). PING sends ICMP echo packets to the host and listens for echo reply packets. PING waits up to one second for each packet sent and displays the number of packets transmitted and received. Each packet is validated against the transmitted message.

PING is a command line utility. In most TCP/IP implementations, its syntax is as follows:

```
ping IP_address
```

Where *IP_address* is the IP address of the destination host

The successful PING returns a sequence of replies similar to the following:

```
C:\WINNT>ping 137.200.0.1
Pinging 137.200.0.1 with 32 bytes of data:
Reply from 137.200.0.1: bytes=32 time<10ms TTL=128
Reply from 137.200.0.1: bytes=32 time<10ms TTL=128
Reply from 137.200.0.1: bytes=32 time<10ms TTL=128
Reply from 137.200.0.1: bytes=32 time<10ms TTL=128
```

If communication problems exist (e.g., the destination node is powered down) the PING output may look like this:

```
C:\WINNT>ping 137.200.0.2
Pinging 137.200.0.2 with 32 bytes of data:
Request timed out.
Request timed out.
Request timed out.
Request timed out.
```

This listing indicates a problem with a router:

```
C:\WINNT>ping 137.200.3.1
Pinging 137.200.3.1 with 32 bytes of data:
Destination host unreachable.
Destination host unreachable.
Destination host unreachable.
Destination host unreachable.
```

The IP address 127.0.0.1 is called the loopback address—it will actually make your machine call itself. You can use `ping 127.0.0.1` to check if TCP/IP is loaded correctly on your computer.

You may notice, for example, the Windows NT PING command sends four 32-byte packets and waits for four replies by default. The following syntax will cause PING to continuously send packets until interrupted with a Control-C:

```
ping -t IP_address
```

You may notice several differences for the PING utility in UNIX environments. By default, PING will continuously ping the specified host. To interrupt the sequence of pings, press Ctrl-C. In contrast to the Windows-based PING, UNIX implementations usually send 64- (vice 32-) byte packets.

In the Novell implementation, you must type LOAD PING in order to load and run the utility. This is a console tool and it allows an administrator to specify parameters in special fields for display. To select an IP node, enter its host name or IP address in the Host Name field. You can also specify the number of seconds between each packet transmission and the size of the packet, in bytes.

To start sending packets, press Esc. The sending node continues to send request packets and collect response time statistics until you press Esc again to exit PING.

To select additional IP nodes, press Insert. Enter the hostname or IP address of the node in the Host Name field and press Esc to start sending packets.

The Novell command line utility is called TPING and uses only three command line parameters: host address, packet size, and retry count. It pings the specified host by sending packets of the specified size. The default retry count value is equal to 5.

Note In some implementations of the PING utility, the syntax and the command output may vary. You can try an argument of `-?` or `-h` with both PING and IPCONFIG for a quick reminder of all applicable options for the given utility implementation. (i.e. `ping -?` or `ipconfig -?`)

TCP/IP Architecture

As you already know, the way information is handled under the open systems interconnect (OSI) or Department of Defense (DoD) models is often referred to as *encapsulation*. You will remember that encapsulation is the process of adding a header to the data accepted from a higher-level protocol. When the application *originates* the data or sends a request to *get* data, the data or request moves down through the protocol stack, and at each level a new header is added. This increases the total size of the information until it reaches the wire. The individual zeros and ones are sent via the wire to the remote computer where each of the headers is opened and peeled off, much like peeling the skin and layers off an onion. The header information is stripped off at each layer and the information is finally sent upward to reach the intended application.

Now that we have seen the theoretical models that make up the network standards defining the elements of the TCP/IP protocol suite, we will take a look at the *functionality* of the TCP/IP protocols.

Address Resolution Protocol

When one computer wants to send an IP packet to another computer in the TCP/IP network, it knows only the IP address on the destination computer. In order to send a packet successfully, we must specify the hardware address of the recipient in the header of the packet. The purpose of the address resolution protocol (ARP) is to permit the successful mapping of an IP address to a hardware address. The process starts where one host sends a local broadcast to obtain a hardware address and puts the resulting information into a cache for future reference.

The exact ARP sequence varies with the network operating system and configuration. The following example from Windows NT is representative of the general sequence. Let us suppose you try to ping a particular IP address. The first action in this procedure is a query to the existing ARP cache. If no match for the IP address is found in the cache, an ARP broadcast is sent.

The target machine answers the broadcast with its hardware address, and the calling machine stores the information in its cache. Once the calling machine has the target's hardware address, it can use directed communications from that point on. (When we say *directed communications*, we are talking about a communication to a particular machine vice a *broadcast* to all machines on the local network.).

The concept described previously works on a broadcast-based network, such as Ethernet or token ring. Network architectures that do not support broadcast messages may have different IP address resolution methods. Point-to-point networks (such as modem links), for example, do not use ARP for IP-to-hardware address resolution.

Resolving a Remote IP Address

If a computer tries to resolve a remote host's address to the remote host's hardware address, there is a need to traverse a router. To minimize network and Internet traffic, IP routers do not typically permit ARP broadcasts to go from one subnet to another. How then does a remote IP address get resolved? The following outlines what happens when a computer—we will call host 1—initiates communication with a computer for which it does not have a hardware address (host X):

1. Host 1 initiates a command using an IP address for host X.
2. TCP/IP determines the destination host is on a remote network.
3. Host 1 checks its internal route table for a route to the destination network via an available gateway. (If no entry is found for the remote host network, host 1 the uses the IP address of its properly configured default gateway.)
4. Host 1 broadcasts an ARP request to resolve the gateway's IP address.
5. The gateway sends an ARP reply to host 1's request, which updates the ARP cache on both machines.
6. Now that it knows the gateway's hardware address, host 1 sends a request for the destination host to the gateway.
7. At this point the delivery of the packet is the responsibility of the gateway. The gateway starts with step 2, and the process is repeated until a router on host X's local network is able to deliver the packet to the recipient computer.

Overview of the ARP Cache

The ARP cache on each host consists of static and dynamic entries that map IP addresses to hardware addresses. The static entries remain in the ARP cache until the computer is restarted or until they are manually deleted. An entry will be dynamically changed if the host receives an ARP broadcast for an IP address that is already in the cache but with a different hardware address than the existing entry. In many implementations of TCP/IP (for example Microsoft TCP/IP and most UNIX versions), an address can be added manually to the ARP cache by typing `arp -s IP_address hardware_address`. (e.g., `arp -s 172.13.3.1 00-10-4B-86-76-3D`). To delete an entry, type `arp -d IP_address` (e.g., `arp -d 172.13.3.1`). To view the information in the ARP cache, type `arp -a`.

The dynamic entries are added and deleted from the ARP cache based on the exchange of information between local and destination hosts. If a dynamic entry is not used within a certain time, it is deleted from the cache.

The expiration time for an arp cache entry usually depends on the NOS implementation and is, in most cases, on-the-fly tunable. Two minutes is the default expiration time for both Windows and UNIX implementations.

Internet Control Message Protocol

Internet control message protocol (ICMP) is responsible for handling the errors that occur when data packets are transmitted across a network. PING, as well as other utilities, uses ICMP to operate. If a host fails to respond to a `ping` request, ICMP notifies the originator that the transmission was unsuccessful.

ICMP Source Quench Messages

Sometimes during normal communications, hosts will send information faster than the routers, gateways, and links between them can handle it. Some routers can send an ICMP source quench message to request that a host transmit at a slower rate. A TCP/IP host will accept source quench messages and comply by reducing its rate. Some software routers, for example, a multihomed Windows NT computer configured for packet forwarding, will simply drop datagrams that cannot be buffered because they are not able to send source quench messages to the sending host. Generally speaking, the flow control obtained through source quench messages is a difficult and complex feature to implement and is not found in most of today's network operating systems. However, operating systems designed to specifically support routers (Cisco IOS and some UNIX implementations, for example) do provide good flow control support.

Internet Group Management Protocol

The Internet group management protocol (IGMP) is used to inform routers that a host or group of hosts, designated as members of a specific multicast group, are available on a given network. A multicast group is a set of hosts identified by a single destination address. Using IGMP, each router that supports multicasting is made aware of which host groups are on which networks. IGMP packets are sent as user datagram protocol (UDP) datagrams, which makes the IGMP packets unreliable.

Internet Protocol

The Internet protocol (IP) provides several necessary functions such as the addressing and routing of packets to and from destination hosts. If the packets need to be fragmented and reassembled, the Internet protocol provides for this.

The Internet protocol is considered connectionless, which means that it does not expect nor need to be connected to the other side in order to do its job. There is no session established when IP is used by itself. Because there is no positive response from the target computer when it receives a communication, there is no *guarantee* that the communication will take place and a "best effort" is used to get the information to the other side. Because of this, data can sometimes be lost or received out of sequence and neither the sending nor receiving host know about it. In this case, acknowledgement for the receipt of packets and the sequencing of the received packets to place them in the correct order is the responsibility of a higher-layer transport protocol, such as TCP.

IP on the Router

When it traverses a router, the following happens to an IP packet:

1. The packet's time to live (TTL) is decremented for each second inside the router (a minimum decrement of 1 is always required). If TTL becomes 0, the IP packet is discarded. This prevents IP packets from endlessly looping in the internetwork. (In this example, we decrement based on time; in some implementations, packets are decremented based on the number of hops—routers through which they pass.)
2. Packets that are too large to be pushed onto the next network segment (due, for instance, to differing network standards) get broken into smaller fragments and are numbered.
   - A new header for each new packet along with a packet flag to indicate its sequence is created along with a fragment ID and fragment offset.
3. A new checksum is calculated and applied.
4. The hardware address of the next router is determined.
5. The packet is forwarded.

Transmission Control Protocol

Transmission control protocol (TCP) is *connection oriented*, meaning the remote computer is expected to be *connected to* the remote host before exchange of data takes place. TCP guarantees a more reliable method of delivery of information through use of sequence numbers, acknowledgements, and a three-way handshake.

TCP uses byte stream communications, which is where the data elements are handled as a sequence of bytes without any boundaries. Each segment of data is assigned its own sequence number so the data can be reassembled at the receiving end. To ensure that the data is received as transmitted, the receiving host must send an acknowledgement, or ACK, within a specific period of time. If the ACK is not received, the segment is retransmitted. If a segment is received in a corrupt or unusable condition, the host on the receiving end simply sends it to the bit bucket without sending an ACK. In the absence of an ACK, the sending station knows to resend the information.

TCP functions through numbered ports to provide specific delivery locations. Any port with a number of less than 1,024 is considered a *well-known port*. Table 6.5 shows some of TCP's well-known ports.

Study Break

What is a Three-Way Handshake?

A three-way handshake is simply the way two hosts ensure they have exchanged accurate and complete data. To do so, they must make sure they are properly synchronized to send and receive portions of the data, that they each know how much data the other can receive at one time, and that they have established a virtual connection. The handshake takes place in the following three steps:

1. The machine that wishes to start the communication sends a data segment with the synchronization (SYN) flag set to on.

2. The target machine sends a segment with SYN on, with a sequence number to indicate the starting byte for the next segment (if any) it will send, and an acknowledgment (ACK) that includes the sequence number of the next segment it expects to receive.

3. The first machine returns a segment that contains the acknowledged sequence number and an acknowledgement number.

Table 6.5 *TCP Ports*

Port	Description
21	FTP
23	Telnet
53	Domain name server (DNS)
139	NetBIOS session service

User Datagram Protocol

The *user datagram protocol* (UDP) is a connectionless protocol that does not establish a session nor provide for guaranteed delivery. By connectionless, we mean the UDP packets are sent out over the network very much like a telegram—the receiving computer does not send an acknowledgement. The message is sent and we must assume it has been received. This is distinct from a telephone call where we are able to establish two-way communication to ensure the person on the other end of the line has received and understood our message. Much like IP, UDP neither guarantees delivery nor the proper sequencing of delivered packets. If these are important to the application using UDP, the application or a higher-level protocol must supply an additional level of checking. While UDP does utilize a checksum for error checking, this is an optional field and not enforced by the protocol.

UDP is most often used in one-to-many communications of small amounts of data. Later in this chapter, we will discuss broadcast messages, especially in relation to the resolution of NetBIOS names to IP addresses. Normally when we talk of broadcasts in the context of TCP/IP, we are referring to UDP traffic.

UDP operates through distinct UDP ports. Although TCP and UDP may use the same port number in some instances, these numbers do not represent the same port. A UDP port is a 16-bit address that exists only to transmit datagram information to the correct location above the transport layer of the protocol stack—simply a location for sending messages. UDP ports can receive more than one message at a time and are identified by "well-known" port numbers. Before it can use UDP, an application must supply an IP address and port number for the target of its message. Table 6.6 defines the well-known UDP port numbers.

Table 6.6 *UDP Ports*

Port	Keyword	Description
15	NETSTAT	Network status
53	DOMAIN	Domain name server
69	TFTP	Trivial file transfer protocol
137	NETBIOS-NS	NetBIOS name service
138	NETBIOS-DGM	NetBIOS datagram service
161	SNMP	SNMP network monitor

Ports and Sockets

Our protocol discussion has, thus far, taken us from the wire, through the network interface card, all the way up to the transport layer of the DoD model. The only remaining step is to see how the data flows to and from the applications that use and create it. The vehicles to accomplish this last step are *ports and sockets*. Figure 6–1 provides an overall view of where they fit into the data transmission picture.

A port provides a location for sending messages. It functions as a multiplexed message queue, which means that it can receive more than one message at a time. Ports are identified by a numerical value between 0 and 65,536. The port numbers for client-side TCP/IP applications are assigned dynamically by the operating system when a request for service is received. The port numbers for well-known server-side applications are assigned by a

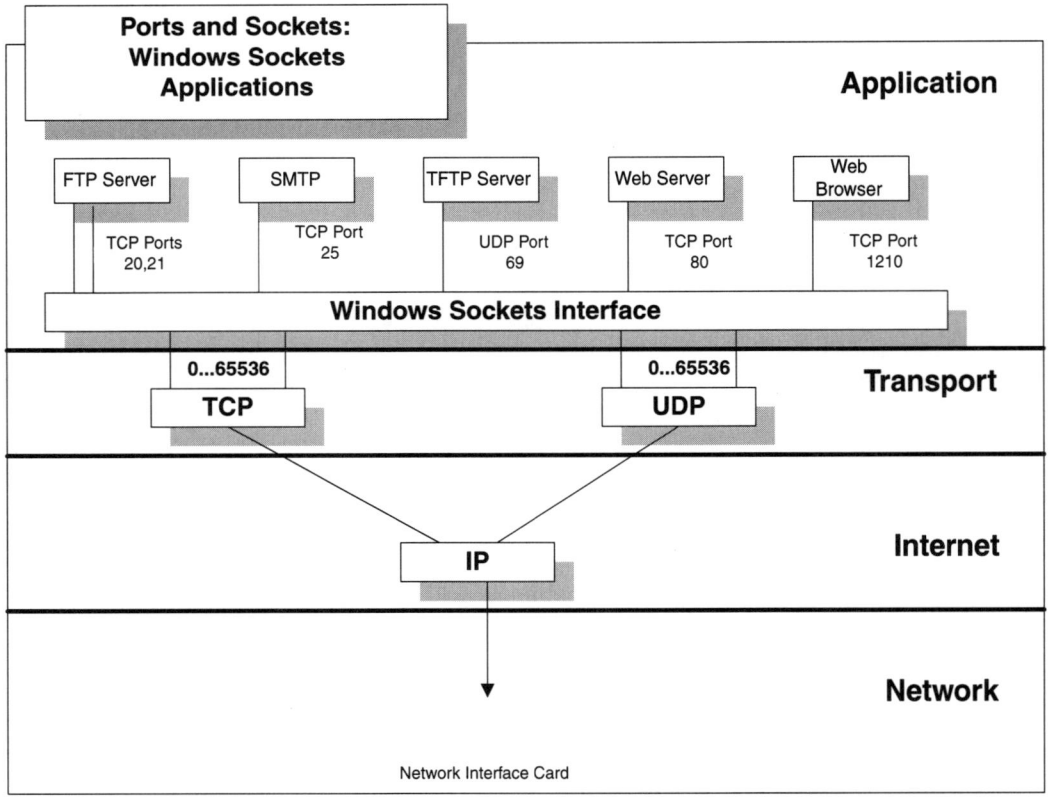

Figure 6–1 *Ports and sockets.*

group called the Internet Assigned Numbers Authority (IANA) and do not change. These well-known port numbers are documented in RFCs 1060 and 1700. If your system is running Windows NT, you can find the port numbers in the following ASCII text file: `\winnt\system32\drivers\etc\services` and in most UNIX implementations in a file called `/etc/services`.

We already discussed that a socket is a bidirectional *pipe* for exchanging data between networked computers. The sockets' API (application program interface) is a networking API used by programmers in building applications that will communicate over a network. The API consists of a set of calls which perform defined functions and pass information back and forth to the lower protocol layers. An application creates a socket when it specifies the IP address of an intended host, the type of service requested (TCP for connection-based requests, UDP for connectionless based requests), and the port that the particular application will use. Sockets are identified within a host through the use of unique protocol port numbers.

IP Addressing Basics

Each system attached to an IP-based network must be assigned a unique, 32-bit IP address value. As you already know, the administrator assigns the IP address to the computer. IP addresses are neither built into the operating system, nor are they part of the network adapter interface. Configured by the administrator, the IP address provides the logical identification number of a computer connected to an IP-based network.

To gain a basic understanding of what an IP address is, it is convenient to draw an analogy between the IP address and a street address. Just as the street address uniquely identifies a house on a particular street, the IP address points to a computer on a network.

Dotted Decimal Notation

We have already discussed that IP addresses are 32-bit binary numbers; but for your convenience, the 32-bit value is divided into four 8-bit fields called octets. (See Figure 6–2.) Octets are written in the decimal form and separated with periods. This style of writing the IP addresses is called *dotted decimal notation*.

Although you will normally work with IP addresses written in dotted decimal form, you should be able to convert the binary form to decimal. This is essential for planning and troubleshooting.

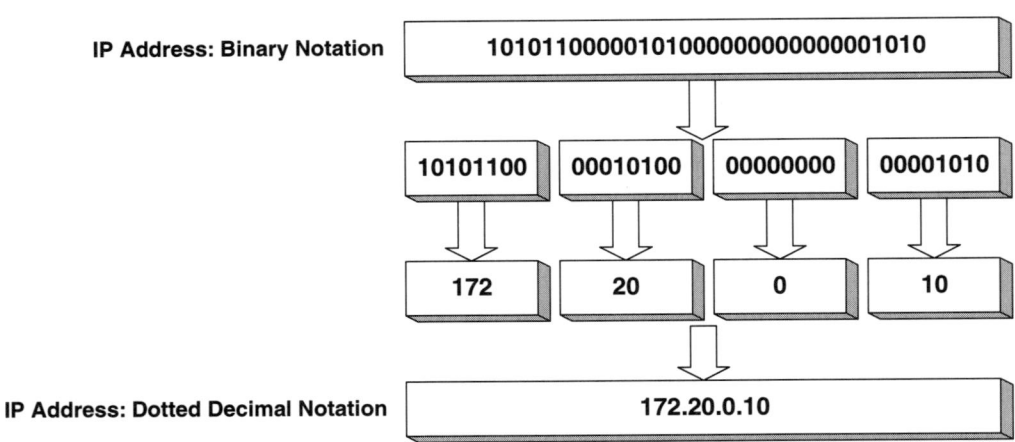

Figure 6–2 *Binary and dotted decimal notation of the IP address.*

You may already know that in binary notation each bit that is set to 1 has an assigned decimal value. The bit that is set to 0 has a zero value. In an octet, the rightmost bit represents the decimal value of one, the next bit represents two, the next one four, up to the leftmost bit which represents the decimal value of 128. To get the decimal result, sum all the bit values. (See Figure 6–3.)

Note that each octet represents a decimal number ranging from 0 (00000000 binary) to 255 (11111111 binary). Thus the IP address 172.315.16.3 is invalid by inspection because the second octet is greater than 255 (all bits are set to 1).

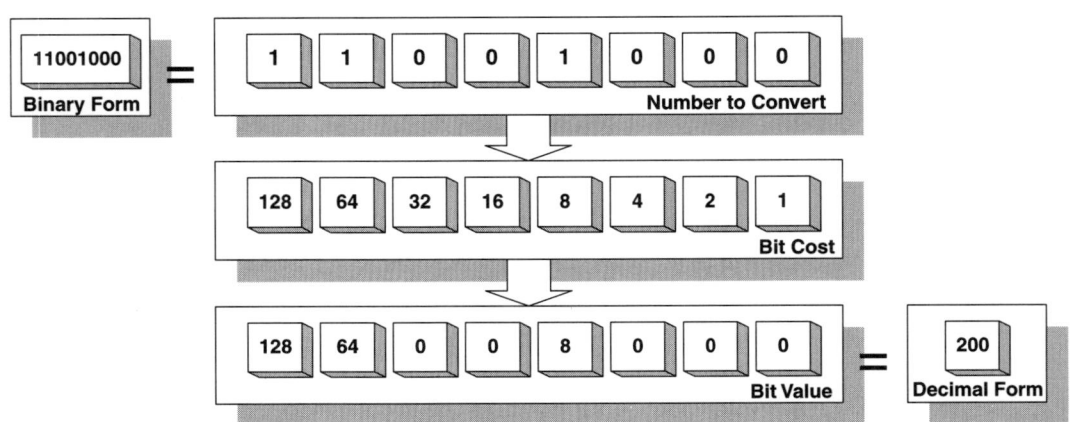

Figure 6–3 *Converting an IP address octet from binary to decimal.*

Table 6.7 illustrates some examples of how the numbers in one octet are converted from binary form into a decimal value.

Study Break

Now You Do It

1. Convert the following binary numbers to decimal format:
   10000001 _____
   11100000 _____
   00011111 _____
   00100000 _____
   10101010 _____

2. Convert the following decimal values to binary format:
   255 _____
   21 _____
   192 _____
   240 _____
   150 _____

Table 6.7 *Examples of Converting One Octet From Binary to Decimal*

Binary Code	Bit values	Decimal value
00000000	0	0
00000001	1	1
00000011	2+1	3
00000111	4+2+1	7
00001111	8+4+2+1	15
00011111	16+8+4+2+1	31
00111111	32+16+8+4+2+1	63
01111111	64+32+16+8+4+2+1	127
11111111	128+64+32+16+8+4+2+1	255
11111110	128+64+32+16+8+4+2	254
11111100	128+64+32+16+8+4	252
11111000	128+64+32+16+8	248
11110000	128+64+32+16	240
11100000	128+64+32	224
11000000	128+64	192
10000000	128	128

Two Parts of an IP Address: Network ID and Host ID

Let us consider another example. IP addressing can be compared to the telephone numbering system, for example, 722–151–1936. In this example it is obvious that 722 is the area code, 151 the local telephone exchange and 1936 is the telephone number within the particular exchange. Things become less obvious if we omit the parentheses and hyphen and write the same telephone number as 7221511936. Now you have to take some time to distinguish the area code from the exchange and number. The same applies to the IP addresses.

Just as the telephone number contains two parts—the area code and the telephone number within the area—the IP address is composed of two parts as well. These parts of an IP address are called *network ID* and *host ID*. The border between the network ID and the host ID lies somewhere in the middle. Note that there is no visual boundary between the network ID and the host ID. It is like writing a telephone number with no hyphens and spaces.

Note	In recent years, the network ID field has been often referred to as "network prefix".

When we look at the IP address 172.20.0.10, we see that the network ID and the host ID are both there but not easily distinguishable. (See Figure 6–4.) In this case we may assume that the border is between the second and third octet. (Later we will learn how to determine its exact position.) In this example, the network ID is like an area code and the host ID is like a local telephone number.

The network ID identifies the systems that are located on the same physical segment just as the area code identifies telephone subscribers located in a particular area. All systems on the same physical segment must have the same network ID. The host ID identifies a workstation, server, router, or other TCP/IP device within the network segment. The host ID must be unique within the given network ID just as the local telephone number must be unique within the area code. Figure 6–5 shows three computers with different IP addresses.

Computer 2 and computer 3 must be located in the same physical network, because the Network ID of their IP addresses is the same. On the other hand, it is apparent that computer 1 and computer 2 are located in different network segments since *their* network IDs are different. Although, computer 1 and computer 2 both have identical host IDs, there are no network problems because these computers are located in different networks. This latter case is analogous to two people with the same telephone number but in different area codes.

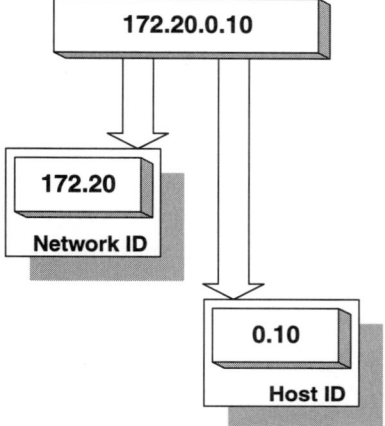

Figure 6–4 *Network ID and host ID.*

Address Classes

Earlier, we said all TCP/IP hosts within a particular network segment must have the same network ID, but different host IDs. It is reasonable to ask how many host IDs are available within a specific network. To answer this question, we must determine where the border between the network and host portions of the IP address lies. Knowing this, we can determine how many bits are devoted to the network ID and host ID and thus calculate the maximum number of hosts in the network segment.

Different networks require different amounts of available host IDs. Large companies need to set up thousands of computers while smaller

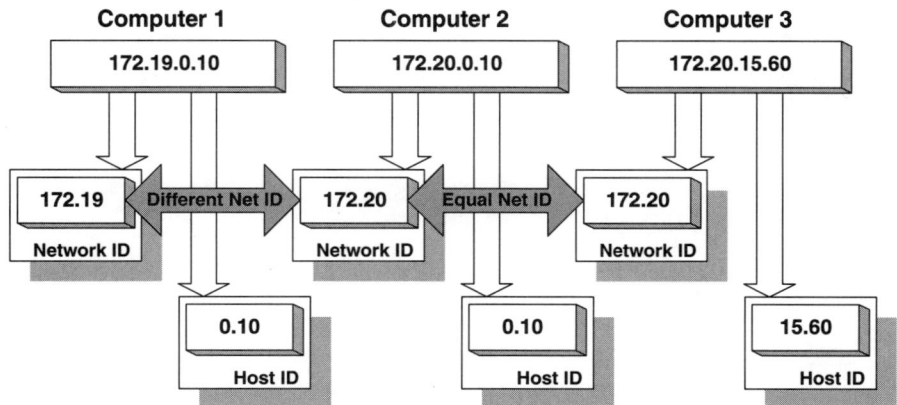

Figure 6–5 *Computers with similar but unique addresses.*

companies may require only a few computers on their network segment. In order to provide the flexibility required to support different sized networks, the designers of the TCP/IP protocol have decided that the IP address space should be divided into several different address classes. The address classes that are available for use are *class A*, *class B*, and *class C*. This approach is often referred to as *classful* addressing.

Each class fixes the boundary between the network ID and the host ID. In other words, the class of address defines how many bits are devoted to the network ID and how many bits are used for host ID. This indirectly defines the possible number of networks in the given class and the number of hosts per network.

Class A

Class A addresses are useful for organizations with an extremely large number of hosts. The first octet (first eight bits) is devoted to the network ID. Accordingly, the last tree octets (24 bits) are host ID bits.

One of the fundamental features of classful IP addressing is that each address contains a self-encoding key that identifies the dividing point between the network ID and the host ID.

The high order bit of the class A address is set to zero. This serves as the self-encoding key by which class A addresses can be identified from other address classes. The next seven bits in the first octet complete the network ID. If the IP address is written in dotted decimal notation, you can distinguish a class A address by looking at the first octet. If the first octet of the IP address is between 1 (**00000001** binary) and 126 (**01111110** binary), this is a class A IP address.

You may ask what happened to 127 since it also has the leading bit set to zero. Remember all IP addresses beginning with 127 are special case IP addresses. They represent the loopback address and thus cannot be assigned to a real host.

Other examples of class A IP addresses would be 30.24.5.0, 15.0.0.1, and 120.6.0.3.

Class B

Class B addresses are assigned to medium-sized organizations. The network ID occupies two octets. This time the first two bits of the IP address are fixed to be 10 binary. These two bits are the self-encoding key for class B addresses. The remaining fourteen bits complete the network ID. The host ID is 16 bits in length.

You can also identify a class B address by the decimal value of the first octet. If the first octet is between 128 (**10000000** binary) and 191 (**10**111111 binary), you have a class B address. The total number of class B networks is 16384—which is how much the 14 available bits in the network ID allow. The remaining two octets allow approximately 65,000 hosts per network.

Class C

Class C addresses are used by small organizations. This standard defines three octets for the network ID and one octet for the host ID. The three high-order bits in class C IP addresses are set to binary 110. The next 21 bits complete the network ID. This allows 2^{21} class C networks with 254 hosts per network.

Written in dotted decimal notation, the first octet of the class C address ranges from 192 (**11000000** binary) to 223 (**110**11111 binary). Some examples of class C IP addresses are 207.46.130.139 and 194.226.192.23.

Class D

Class D is a special class of IP address. Class D addresses are used for multicast group usage. The multicast group may contain several hosts. The four high-order bits in class D are set to binary 1110. No network and host IDs are defined in class D addresses. Class D IP addresses can be recognized by the first octet which is between 224 (**1110**0000 binary) and 239 (**1110**1111 binary).

Class E

The rest of the IP address space is class E. Class E is used for experimental addresses and is not available for general use. The four high-order bits in the class E IP address are set to binary 1111. In decimal form the first octet of the class E IP address is greater than 240 (**11110000** binary).

Note

If you plan to directly connect to the Internet, you must obtain the network ID portion of the IP address from the InterNIC (www.networksolutions.com). This guaranties the uniqueness of your IP addresses across the Internet. If, of course, you will never connect to an outside network, you may select virtually any IP address you wish (except, of course, special addresses like the loopback address).

To summarize, IP addressing space has been divided into several address classes. Some of the classes (class A, class B, and class C) are available for assignment while others (class D and class E) are special addresses that cannot be used to configure a computer. Figure 6–6 displays the address class summary.

Study Break

Now You Do It

1. Write the address class to each IP address:
   10.0.0.1 _____
   9.255.255.0 _____
   200.0.56.1 _____
   192.15.67.3 _____
   127.0.0.1 _____
   191.233.42.3 _____

2. Which of the following IP address pairs have the same network ID?
   10.0.0.1 and 10.45.2.6 _____
   192.56.2.6 and 192.56.1.6 _____

Number of Networks	Number of Hosts per Network	First Octet (Binary)	Range of the First Octet (Decimal)	
126	16 777 214	0 * * * * * * *	1 - 126	Class A
16 384	65 534	1 0 * * * * * *	128 - 191	Class B
2 097 152	254	1 1 0 * * * * *	192 - 223	Class C

Figure 6–6 *Classful IP addressing summary.*

131.107.2.1 and 131.107.3.1   _____

200.0.0.1 and 200.0.0.254   _____

191.18.3.9 and 191.18.44.3   _____

3. Your network consists of 5,000 computers. Which network classes satisfy your needs?

_____ and _____

Study Break

IP-The Next Generation (IPng)

The structure of the IP packet has not been changed since the 1970s. This is, of course, a tribute to its original design. Over the past few years, however, the Internet has experienced an unprecedented growth heralding the eventual exhaustion of available IP address space. The current version of IP, also known as IP version 4 (IPv4), defines a 32-bit host address which means that there are only 2^{32} (approximately 4 million) addresses available. Remember not all IP addresses are available for assignment—the finite number of IP addresses will eventually be exhausted and a new version of IP needed. *IPng* is a *proposed* new Internet protocol to replace IPv4. The formal name for IPng is *IPv6* (6 being the new version number). IPv6 is defined in RFCs 1883, 1884, 1885, 2147, 2373, and others.

What's new in IPv6? IPng is not just an IPv4 upgrade. You may consider IPv6 a whole new protocol. Its addresses and headers are different. It provides more options and supports autoconfiguration. Some of the new features of IPv6 are as follows:

- Extended address space

  IPv6 addresses are 128 bits long. They can identify individual nodes and sets of nodes. IPng addresses can be unicast (single node), anycast (a group of nodes where the packet is delivered to one of the nodes—typically the nearest one), or multicast (group of nodes where the packet will be delivered to all nodes in the group) addresses. 128 bits can express over 3 x 10^{38} possible combinations. Unlike IPv4, IPv6 addresses are written in hexadecimal form such as:

  `3A3F:BE67:F890:56CD:3412:AE52:9011:FA03`

- Simplified header

  In Ipv6, the header has been greatly simplified. Many of the current IPv4 fields have been omitted, while many others have been made optional. The cost of processing packets has become as low as possible. In spite of a greatly increased address size, the headers are only twice as big as those in IPv4. Anything that is not included in the IPv6 header can be added through IPv6 extension headers.

- Ipv6's automatic network configuration

  This feature is one of the key changes in IPv6. Its aim is to ease the creation of new networks. This will allow network devices find and claim their own network address as soon as they are installed on the network.

- Flow control

  In order to support applications which require some degree of consistent throughput, a new field, delay and jitter, was added in the IPv6.

  Although IPv6 will make life in the TCP/IP world much easier, it is time to return to current reality. All the concepts discussed in the rest of the text correspond to the IP version 4 and should not be directly applied to IPv6.

Valid and Invalid Host IDs and Network IDs

Some of the network and host IDs are reserved for special use and should not be assigned to real hosts. Follow these guidelines when assigning host and network IDs:

1. The network ID cannot be 127. This ID is called the loopback address and is not for general use. For example, the IP address of 127.0.15.32 is invalid for use on the network.

2. Neither the network ID nor the host ID may be all 0's. If all bits in either are set to zero, it is interpreted as this network only. For example, the IP addresses 0.15.6.8 (network ID is all 0's), 10.0.0.0 (host ID is all 0's), and 195.209.225.0 (Host ID is all 0's) are invalid.

3. The network ID and the host ID cannot be all 1's. If all bits within the network ID or host ID are set to 1, the address is interpreted as a broadcast message. For example, the IP addresses 255.255.255.255 (network ID is all 1's) 10.255.255.255 (host ID is all 1's), 172.20.255.255 (host ID is all 1's), and 195.209.225.255 (host ID is all 1's) are invalid.

Study Break

Now You Do It

Which of the following IP addresses are invalid for host assignment?

172.0.0.1 _____

200.200.200.200 _____

123.350.2.18 _____

195.209.225.255 _____

172.18.2.255 _____

255.255.255.255 _____

127.12.3.4 _____

190.56.3.0 _____

Explain why they are invalid.

Subnet Mask

We already know how to determine the network ID and the host ID with the help of the IP address class. Based on this information we can ascertain whether two computers are located in the same or different network segments. When you set TCP/IP on your computer, however, you have no ability to explicitly specify the IP address class. Instead of the IP address class, you specify the *subnet mask*.

The subnet mask is also a 32-bit value; but, unlike the IP address, it doesn't identify any host in the network. It is used for blocking out a portion of the IP address to distinguish the network ID from the host ID. (See Figure 6–7.) In other words, the subnet mask specifies where the border between network ID and host ID lies.

The basic subnet mask is generated in the following way: Bits that correspond to the network ID in the IP address are set to 1 in the subnet mask, all others are set to zero. (See Figure 6–8.) Like IP addresses subnet masks are often written in dotted decimal notation.

When you configure TCP/IP on your computer, you have to specify the subnet mask, even if you have a single segment network. The subnet mask can be either a default subnet mask, when your network is not divided into subnets, or a custom subnet mask, when your network is subnetted.

Figure 6–7 *Subnet mask.*

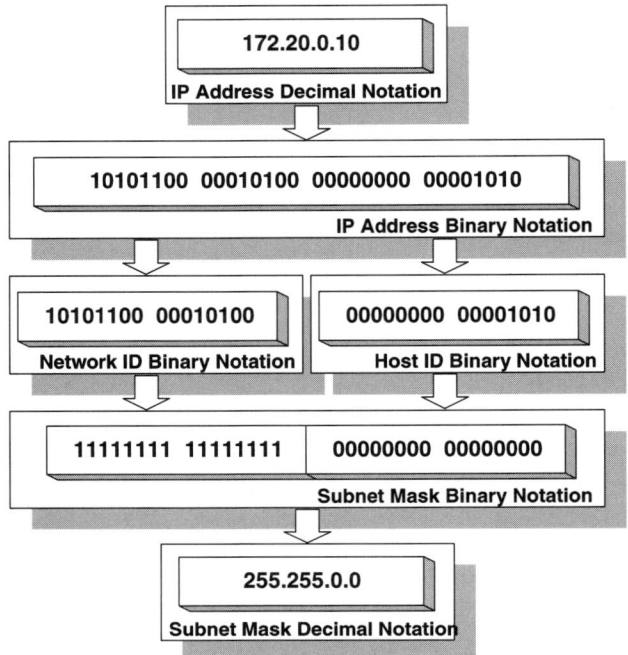

Figure 6–8   *Subnet mask.*

Default Subnet Masks

If you have assigned your network a network ID and your network is not divided into segments by routers, you can use the default subnet mask. The default subnet mask depends on the address class because different address classes have different numbers of bits dedicated for network and host IDs. Figure 6–9 shows the default subnet masks for class A, class B, and class C subnets.

How Does the Computer Use the Subnet Mask?

When the computer sends a packet to another computer, it determines if the destination host is located in the same or a remote network. If the destination computer is in the same network, a broadcast address resolution protocol (ARP) request is sent to obtain the hardware (MAC) address. If the destination computer is located on a remote network, a broadcast ARP request will not work, because broadcast messages will not pass through the router to the remote network. When the destination host is not on the local network, the packet is sent to the IP address of the router; and the router takes care of delivery.

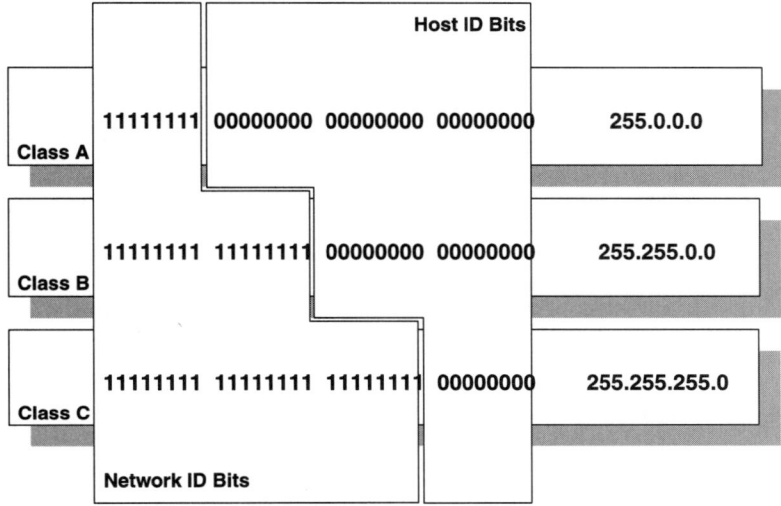

Figure 6–9 *Default subnet masks.*

The subnet mask is used to determine whether the destination computer is local (in the same network segment) or remote (in another network segment). When TCP/IP is initialized, the computer performs a logical AND mathematical operation on its IP address with the configured subnet mask.

ANDing extracts the network ID from the local computer IP address. (See Figure 6–10.)

Before the packet is sent, the IP address of the destination computer is ANDed with the same subnet mask and compared to the network ID extracted earlier. If both results match, the destination computer has the same network ID and, thus, is located in the same network segment.

Study Break

Now You Do It

What is the default subnet mask for each of the following IP addresses?

131.127.3.4	_____
201.200.20.1	_____
191.58.2.9	_____
192.17.24.6	_____
10.16.0.0	_____

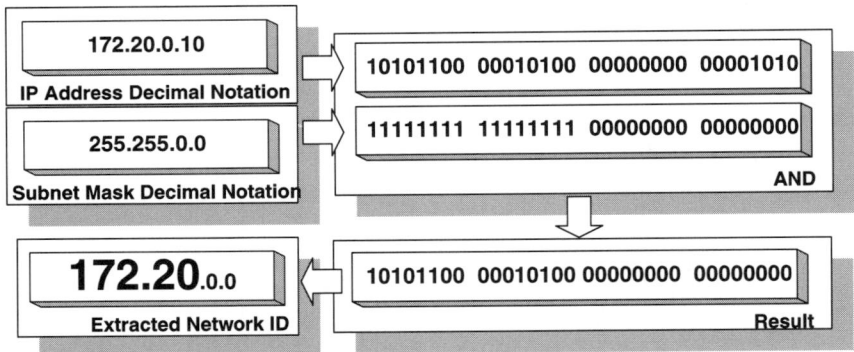

Figure 6–10 *Using the subnet mask to extract the network ID.*

Alternative Designation of Subnet Masks

We have already gotten used to the fact that subnet masks are expressed in dotted decimal notation. With the assumption that subnet IDs are contiguous and derived from high-order bits, we can simply define the number of bits that are allocated for the extended network prefix (network ID plus subnet ID) to uniquely identify the position where the host number begins. For example, there is an agreement to refer to class A networks as /8s (pronounced "slash eight" or just "eights") since they have the 8-bit network ID. Accordingly, class B networks are called /16s and class C networks are called /24s.

Although you might think that using slashes is easier, operating systems like Windows NT and most versions of UNIX have no ability to manipulate the masks written in this form. You should, therefore, always convert your masks to dotted decimal notation before using them.

Automating IP Address Assignment Using DHCP

While configuring a few machines with IP addresses can be a moderately tedious task, the management of the IP configuration of a large number of client and server computers can quickly become a nightmare. Even minor errors in IP addresses and subnet masks can cause the machine to become unavailable to the network. Duplicate IP addresses can bring down every machine with the duplicate address or possibly the entire network.

In addition to duplicate IP addresses problems, the physical movement of computers can cause other inconsistencies. Simply connecting a computer to a new wire can place it on a subnet it is not configured for—once again causing its network functions to cease.

When configuring a computer to use TCP/IP, we also need to configure a number of other features. Incorrect settings for *Windows Internet naming service* (WINS), *domain name system* (DNS), and *default gateway* can occur through machine movement or reconfiguration and can result in disastrous network consequences. Keeping track of all these factors on a large number of computers could quickly take all the network administrator's time. Even a relatively minor network change (such as the introduction of a new WINS server) could require the reconfiguration of a large number of workstations with the attendant possibility of mis-configuration and network paralysis.

Before you head for the Internet to find another line of work, take heart! *The dynamic host configuration protocol* (DHCP) can be installed on one or more machines in your network to permit the automatic and centralized administration and configuration of a number of critical TCP/IP factors (including all those mentioned previously). DHCP was developed as a cooperative effort between vendors and the *Internet Engineering Task Force*. It is covered under the following *Requests for Comment* (RFCs): 1533, 1534, 1541, and 1542. DHCP works by leasing an IP address to a client for a specified period of time. When the client signs the lease, the DHCP server can throw in a number of options, such as WINS and DNS addresses and default gateways, at no additional charge!

The DHCP Process

The choreography between a DHCP client and a DHCP server is a four-step process that permits the allocation and confirmation of important TCP/IP configuration information:

1. During the start-up process, the client computer initializes with a NULL IP address and broadcasts a DHCPDISCOVER message containing its hardware address and computer name and requesting an IP address from any DHCP server.

2. Any DHCP server that receives the DHCPDISCOVER broadcast and that has available valid configuration information for the client will respond with a DHCPOFFER message. Since the client still doesn't have an IP address at this point, the DHCPOFFER is sent via broadcast. The message contains the client's hardware address, an IP address offer, an appropriate subnet mask, the IP address of the server making the offer, and the lease duration. When the offer is made, the DHCP server marks the

offered IP address as unavailable to prevent it from being offered to another client pending the original client's decision to take the lease.

3. The client selects one of the DHCP offers (normally the first one it receives) and responds with a DHCPREQUEST message. This message contains the IP address of the selected DHCP server as well as a request for additional configuration information (e.g., WINS server address, DNS server address, etc.). Because the client's TCP/IP protocol is still not fully initialized, this message is also sent via broadcast. Since the DHCPREQUEST broadcast is received by all the DHCP servers who originally responded to the DHCPDISCOVER broadcast, the unselected servers are able to determine that their offers were rejected (by examining the message for the IP address of the *selected* server). Rejected servers then mark the IP addresses they offered as available.

4. The selected DHCP server responds with a DHCPACK (acknowledgment) message containing a lease for the accepted IP address and any other configuration parameters that might be available. This message is also sent via broadcast; but once it is received, the TCP/IP initialization is completed on the client. With initialization complete, the client machine is considered a *bound DHCP client,* which will be able to use TCP/IP for network communications.

Although the steps outlined here may seem fairly complex, they can be reduced to four short lines:
IP Lease request
IP Lease offer
IP Lease selection
IP Lease acknowledgement

DHCP Lease Duration

DHCP leases may be assigned for a duration as short as one minute; as long as 999 Days, 23 Hours, and 59 Minutes; or may be assigned for an unlimited duration. Times given are for Windows NT implementations. Other operating systems may have different times. According to the DHCP standard, the lease duration is stored as a 32-bit unsigned integer and is expressed in seconds, which gives us a maximum lease duration up to 136 years.

When half of the client's lease period has elapsed, the client will attempt to renew the lease with the original DHCP server. If the server responds with a DHCPACK message, the lease is renewed and the client continues to use the originally assigned parameters. If the server responds with a DHCPNACK (negative acknowledgment) message, the client is forced to send a DHCPDISCOVER broadcast and seek a new lease. If the DHCP client's lease expires and no renewal is obtained, it will cease to function on the network (using TCP/IP) until a new lease can be obtained. If this occurs during the machine's operation, it will continue to seek a DHCP server until one responds with a lease or until the machine is shut down or reconfigured.

When a DHCP client is shut down, it retains its lease. When the machine is restarted, it attempts to renew the lease. If it receives a DHCPACK, the lease is renewed.

All this discussion of DHCP won't do anyone any good unless a DHCP server is actually installed, configured, and available on the network. DHCP server software is available for most operating systems; for example, any Windows NT server version 3.5 or later can be configured as a DHCP server by installing a separate network service—Microsoft DHCP server. UNIX provides DHCP implementations for both home and commercial use, and Novell features DNS/DHCP services in its NetWare version 5 release.

Machines configured as DHCP servers MUST have a static IP address, and subnet mask. Additionally, if DHCP is running on a network with no DHCP relay agents and with routers that do not support RFC 1542, a DHCP server is required on each subnet.

DHCP Scopes and Options

Once we have installed DHCP, we still need to configure a *scope* and options for it to do us any good. The Windows NT 4.0 DHCP server configuration is accomplished through the *DHCP Manager* program, accessible through *Administrative Tools (Common)* in the *Start Menu*. This opens the DHCP Manager console. (See Figure 6–11.) In most UNIX implementations, DHCP services are configured by editing the associated special initialization files. Different versions of the operating system have different initialization files for the DHCP daemon and these files may have different syntax. The most popular DHCP server and client implementations for UNIX environments are supplied by the Internet Software Consortium (ISC). The name of the configuration file for the ISC DHCP server software (according to the UNIX traditions of names and locations for configuration files) is/etc/dhcpd.conf.

The basic service unit for DHCP is called a *scope*. A scope is simply a range (or pool) of IP addresses and a subnet mask the DHCP server can lease to its clients. The scope also includes the lease duration and an optional name and comment. Each DHCP server must have at least one scope. Each scope on the server can represent a pool of IP addresses for one and only one

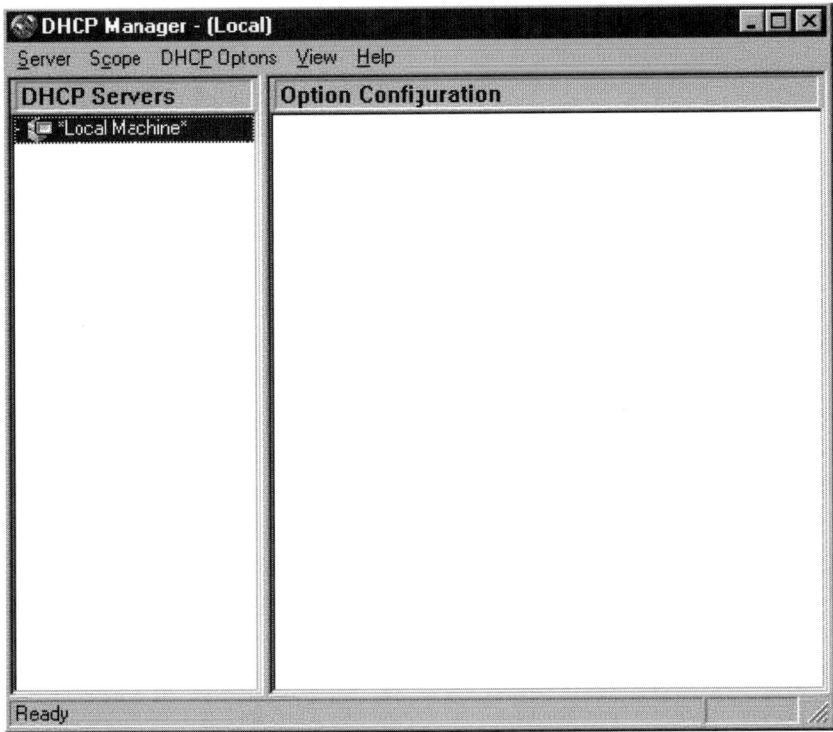

Figure 6–11 *Windows NT 4.0 DHCP manager.*

subnet (although the server may be configured with scopes for several different subnets).

With only one scope configured, the server will be available to provide IP addresses and subnet masks to any DHCP client that asks for an IP address on the subnet covered by the scope. Although DHCP servers would be quite useful if they provided only IP addresses, their capability to provide additional TCP/IP information further reduces the burden of TCP/IP administration. To configure this additional information, we must set DHCP options. Although the number of DHCP options that can be set is limited only by your ability to create them, the most common scenario is to set options only for a default gateway and WINS and DNS servers.

DHCP Relay Agents

Now that your DHCP server is up and running with a single scope, what if you wanted to add another scope? You could give out IP addresses for machines on other subnets; but since they must use non-routable broadcast traffic to reach your DHCP server, how will they communicate with the DHCP server? The answer is the *DHCP relay agent!* A router that conforms to RFC 1542 will perform as a DHCP relay agent. When an IP request packet reaches a DHCP relay agent, the relay agent will forward the request to the next network but will tag the packet with the requestor's home network to ensure the DHCP server will return an address for the appropriate subnet.

IPCONFIG and IP Parameters

The Windows NT IPCONFIG utility permits the viewing of client configuration information as well as the release and renewal of IP address leases. IPCONFIG is executed from the Windows NT command line with the following syntax:

```
Ipconfig [/? | /all | /release [adapter] | /renew [adapter]]
```

By typing IPCONFIG you can view the machine's IP address, subnet mask, and default gateway. If the IP address is shown as 0.0.0.0, you can conclude that the DHCP client was unable to obtain an IP address from the DHCP server. You can use IPCONFIG /RENEW to force an IP address renewal for the adapter specified or IPCONFIG /RELEASE to force the release of a DHCP supplied address for a particular adapter. If no adapter names are supplied, the release or renew will be for all adapters bound to TCP/IP on the machine. By typing IPCONFIG /ALL, you can view the detailed parameter list displayed in Figure 6.16. In addition to the basic information provided by IPCONFIG, the /ALL option provides other important information such as WINS and DNS server addresses, the default gateway address, and the computer's MAC address (physical address). If any DHCP supplied data is shown as zeroes or is not available, suspect a problem with the DHCP lease.

Here is the output from a typical ipconfig /all command:

```
C:\WINNT\system32>ipconfig /all
Windows NT IP Configuration
        Host Name . . . . . . . . . : exchange.alidatrain.com
        DNS Servers . . . . . . . . : 199.125.85.1
                                      199.125.85.2
        Node Type . . . . . . . . . : Hybrid
        NetBIOS Scope ID. . . . . . :
        IP Routing Enabled. . . . . : No
        WINS Proxy Enabled. . . . . : No
```

```
        NetBIOS Resolution Uses DNS : No

Ethernet adapter E100B1:

        Description . . . . . . . . : Intel EtherExpress PRO/100B PCI
                                       LAN Adapter
        Physical Address. . . . . . : 00-A0-C9-66-3F-BD
        DHCP Enabled. . . . . . . . : Yes
        IP Address. . . . . . . . . : 192.168.36.137
        Subnet Mask . . . . . . . . : 255.255.255.0        Default
Gateway . . . . . . : 192.168.36.150
        Primary WINS Server . . . . : 192.168.36.140
        Secondary WINS Server . . . : 192.168.36.140
```

Note There are differences between the IPCONFIG utility in the Microsoft Windows environment and the IFCONFIG in the UNIX world. IPCONFIG can display all configured parameters, such as DNS server addresses, WINS server addresses, default gateway, etc. The IFCONFIG utility in UNIX, displays the interface configuration information only and its output is limited to IP address, subnet mask, and a few other parameters. IFCONFIG can be used by an administrator to change the network interface parameters, while IPCONFIG is not able to actually change TCP/IP configuration information.

NetBIOS over TCP/IP

So far we have discussed a lot of operations accomplished by, through, and for the TCP/IP protocol. All these operations have at least one thing in common: they involve communication between computers. Do computers actually speak TCP/IP? Well... not exactly. The native language of computers (or more accurately, applications running on the computers) is *the network basic input/output system* or *NetBIOS*. In the TCP/IP arena, NetBIOS is transmitted over the network by TCP/IP as a protocol within a protocol.

Sytek Corporation developed NetBIOS in the early 80s for IBM to permit applications to communicate over a network. Because the NetBIOS interface and all related network components were natively created for IBM and Microsoft operating systems, they have limited support in other operating systems. Nevertheless, there are some packages on the market that add NetBIOS support to UNIX and Novell NetWare. Since NetBIOS functions are well documented and standardized, the implementation of the NetBIOS concepts is similar in all operating systems.

NetBIOS operates at the application level and the session/transport level. At the application level, NetBIOS is a standard *application programming interface* (API) that permits user applications to communicate with network protocol software. Any protocol (such as TCP/IP) that supports the NetBIOS interface will support programs using the NetBIOS API. At the session/transport level, NetBIOS functions through underlying protocol software such as the *NetBIOS frames protocol* (NBFP), *NetBIOS extended user interface* (NetBEUI), or *NetBIOS over TCP/IP (NetBT)* to accomplish the network I/O required for the NetBIOS API to function on the network.

NetBIOS supports the following network services:

- Network name registration and verification
- Session establishment and termination
- Connection-oriented session data transfer
- Connectionless datagram data transfer
- Support protocol (driver) and adapter monitoring and management

Of all the services provided by NetBIOS, the one we have most control over is its network-naming feature. Because of this, we will now turn out attention to names and how we can find a particular computer (host) through the use of those names and the NetBIOS services.

NetBIOS Names

What, you may ask, is a NetBIOS name? NetBIOS names are simply the names we give computers and other NetBIOS resources within a network. These names make it easy for us to identify a resource (it is far easier to remember the name *server 1*, for instance, than trying to remember an IP address or a MAC address). NetBIOS names allow us to identify particular resources (such as an exchange server or a structural query language (SQL) server) without regard to a particular transport protocol. An exchange server could, for instance, function on multiple protocols using the NetBIOS name as long as there was a way to associate that name with a particular address (much more on this later).

A NetBIOS name is a unique 16-byte address. NetBIOS names may be unique (to identify a single resource) or group (to communicate with several computers simultaneously). As we will see, unique names are used not merely to communicate with a single computer but with a particular process running on that computer. NetBIOS names consist of a 15-character computer name plus a 16th character that identifies the particular process. Table 6.8 shows the 16th character associated with some common processes. Most of the Windows NT network services register a NetBIOS name, and each Windows NT network command uses these services through their NetBIOS names.

Special software packages for UNIX clients permit them to access Net-BIOS-based servers and take advantage of these names as well.

NetBIOS Name Registration, Discovery, and Release

NetBIOS names are only useful if they are recognized by the machines on the network. To make this happen, the names must be registered, machines must be able to determine what name corresponds to a particular machine, and when the machine owning the name leaves the network, the name should be removed from the list of valid names.

Name Registration

When a computer boots up and initializes its services, it registers its Net-BIOS name with a NetBIOS *name registration request*. The request is made either through a direct message to a NetBIOS name server (NBNS) or through a broadcast. If the name was previously registered by another host, a *negative name registration response* is returned. For example, if registration was attempted through broadcast, the negative response comes from the computer that previously registered the name. If a message to a name server was used, the response comes from the name server. If a negative name registration response is received, the computer suffers an initialization error. If *no* negative name registration response is received, the machine continues its initialization with the knowledge that it has successfully registered its name with the network.

Table 6.8 *Common NetBIOS Names*

Registered Name	Description
\\computer_name[00h]	Name registered for workstation service
\\computer_name[03h]	Name registered for messenger service
\\computer_name[20h]	Name registered for server service
\\username[03h]	Current user name. This name is registered by the messenger service and permits the user to receive messages sent through net send. If the user is logged onto several computers, the first computer the user logs on to receives the message.
\\domain_name[1Bh]	The domain name registered by the primary domain controller that is also the domain master browser.

Name Discovery

When a machine on a local network wishes to find a machine by a NetBIOS name, it either uses a broadcast or queries the local NetBIOS name server. If the designated name is found on the network, a *positive name query response* is sent by the name server or (if a broadcast was used) by the host possessing the name.

Name Release

When a NetBIOS application or service stops, the host sends a *name release* message to the name server (if a name server was used) or simply stops sending negative name resolution responses when another machine attempts to register the same name (if a broadcast was used). This releases the NetBIOS name and makes it available to other hosts.

NetBIOS Name Scopes

The NetBIOS name space can be segmented by appending a scope ID to the NetBIOS name. In Figure 6–12 WORKSTN1.ENG and WORKSTN2.ENG can communicate with SERVER1.ENG but not SERVER1.ACTG and WORKSTN1.ACTG; and WORKSTN2.ACTG can communicate with SERVER1.ACTG but not SERVER1.ENG.

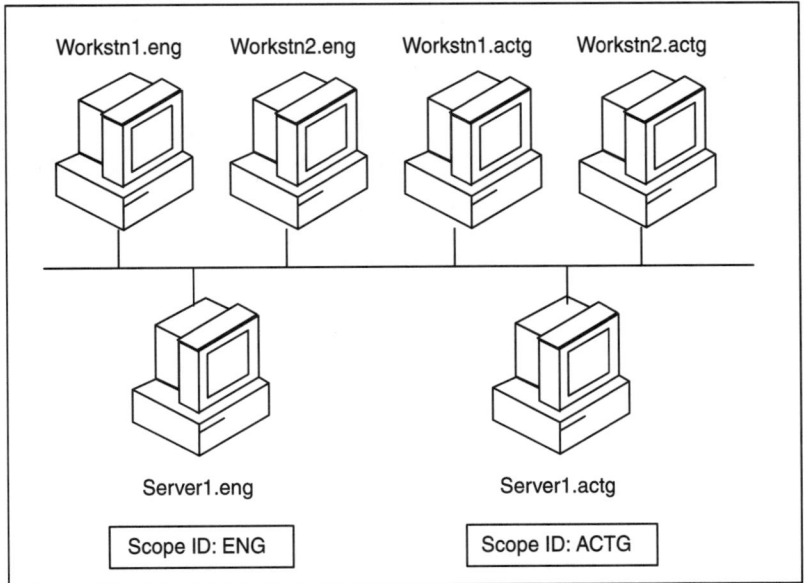

Figure 6–12 *NetBIOS scopes.*

When scope IDs are not used, NetBIOS names must be unique throughout the entire network; with scope IDs, names must be unique only within the scope. NetBIOS resources within the scope, however, are not able to communicate with resources outside their own scope using NetBIOS over TCP/IP. The NetBIOS scope becomes part of the NetBIOS name, resulting in a unique NetBIOS name. In Figure 6–12, even though the two servers have the same NetBIOS name, the different scope IDs make them unique. In the Windows NT operating system, you configure the `Scope ID` from the `WINS Address` tab of the `TCP/IP Properties` dialog box as shown in Figure 6–13.

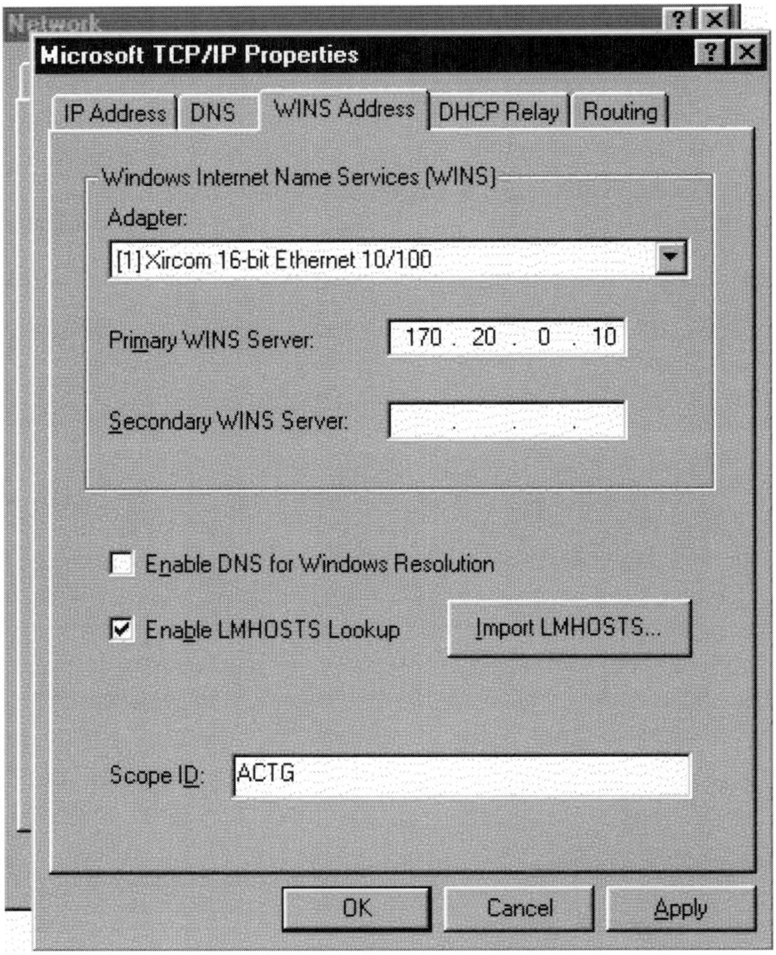

Figure 6–13 *Setting scope ID.*

The most popular implementation of NetBIOS over TCP/IP for UNIX environments is called the Samba suite. The Samba suite was developed by team of developers at the Australian National University (*http://samba.anu. edu.au*) and is freely distributed software. Scope IDs are fully supported by the Samba suite. The UNIX configuration procedure is a bit different from that of the NT world. Typically in UNIX environments, configuration is done by editing a configuration file or through command line switches. For example, to configure the Samba server daemon with a scope ID, you should use the –i <Scope ID> parameter in the command line to the smbd daemon.

NetBIOS Name Resolution

TCP/IP does NOT use NetBIOS names! Why, then, are we even discussing NetBIOS names in a TCP/IP chapter? As we said before, NetBIOS names permit us to identify resources in a protocol-independent fashion. They also make it easier for humans to remember and identify resources. How then do we resolve the issue of using NetBIOS names with TCP/IP? The key to this question is name *resolution*. In order for TCP/IP to function when presented with a NetBIOS name, it must have a way to determine the IP address that goes with the name. This determination is called mapping or name resolution. There are several methods to accomplish this name resolution.

Standard Name Resolution Methods

When a computer needs to resolve a NetBIOS name, it follows a procedure, using several methods until one yields the desired information or the process fails. The following are the standard steps used to find an IP address when the NetBIOS name is known.

NetBIOS Name Cache

Every time a machine resolves a name, it places it into its local name cache. When it needs to find the IP address for a NetBIOS resource, it checks its own cache first.

NetBIOS Name Server

A NetBIOS name server (NBNS) is any server implemented under RFC 1001/1002 to provide NetBIOS name resolution. A computer trying to locate a NetBIOS resource can query the NBNS for a name/IP address mapping. Microsoft's implementation is called the *Windows Internet Name Service* (WINS). In the UNIX world, NBNS server support is implemented through installing third-party software. The Samba server, for example, can act as an NBNS server and as a NetBIOS proxy agent. The Samba WINS function is configured through two configuration parameters stored in the /etc/smb.conf configuration file; such as

```
wins server = 137.102.2.100
name resolve order = wins bcast lmhosts hosts
```

The `wins server` parameter specifies the IP address or the domain name of the WINS server. (Remember that Windows platforms provide the ability to specify only the IP address of the WINS server, and you cannot use domain names.) The second parameter `name resolve order` specifies the sequence of methods that can be used for NetBIOS name resolution. Some of the values of the `name resolve order parameter`, called node types, will be discussed shortly.

Local Broadcast

If a computer cannot find a mapping in its cache or from a name server, it can send a broadcast over the local network. If the target computer receives the broadcast, it will respond with its IP address to permit full TCP/IP communication.

Name Resolution Methods Specific to Microscoft

In addition to the standard resolution methods, Microsoft uses some additional ways to map NetBIOS names and IP addresses:

LMHOSTS File

An LMHOSTS file is a text file on the local computer that contains both the NetBIOS name and IP address of Windows-based computers on remote networks. As we will see later in this chapter, an LMHOSTS file requires manual entry and maintenance.

HOSTS File

Like the LMHOSTS file, the HOSTS file is a text file on the local computer that requires manual entry and maintenance. Unlike the LMHOSTS file, the HOSTS file maps IP addresses to hostnames or fully qualified domain names (e.g., www.alidatrain.com) rather than NetBIOS names. For this reason, HOSTS files may be used to resolve IP addresses for both Windows and non-Windows networks. This file is frequently used in name resolution for TCP/IP utilities.

Domain Name System

The domain name system (DNS) is a server that maintains a database of IP addresses and fully qualified domain names. Like the HOSTS file, DNS requires manual entry and maintenance and can be used for resolution in Windows and non-Windows networks. When a client needs an IP address mapping, it can query the DNS server in much the same way as it would query a NetBIOS name server.

Name Resolution Nodes

Are you wondering how a computer knows when to broadcast and when to query a NetBIOS name server? Well, the answer is through use of NetBIOS over TCP/IP resolution nodes. In Window NT these node types are simply registry values that tell the computer how to go about name resolution.

B-node

This is a *broadcast* node and it tells the system to use broadcast (actually a UDP datagram) resolution. If broadcast resolution fails, the computer will not attempt to find a NetBIOS name server. Microsoft systems use the *Microsoft enhanced B-node*. With the enhanced B-node, computers use the LMHOSTS file in addition to broadcasts. Microsoft systems default to the enhanced B-node unless they are configured to use a WINS server.

> **Note** Remember that broadcast name resolution typically works only within the local network and can increase the network load because of the attendant increase in broadcast message traffic.

P-node

The P-node is called a *peer-to-peer* node. Computers using the P-node will accomplish name resolution through use of a NetBIOS name server. If the name server is down or if the name server cannot provide the appropriate mapping, the P-node computer will NOT resort to broadcast name resolution. While this can curtail local broadcast traffic, when the name server goes down, it will bring communications, even on the local network, to a halt.

M-node

The M-node is a *mixed* node. M-node systems use B-node resolution first and resort to P-node resolution if the B-node attempt fails. While this is the most complete resolution plan we have seen so far, it does little to limit network broadcast traffic.

H-node

This is a *hybrid* node. Under an H-node, a system first attempts P-node resolution. Should that fail, the system seeks resolution through B-node broadcasts. The H-node not only provides a comprehensive resolution plan, it limits network traffic by ensuring broadcasts are used only as a last resort. Microsoft systems configured to use at least one WINS server are configured to use the H-node by default.

The LMHOSTS File

Previously we said one of the Microsoft-specific name resolution methods is the LMHOSTS file. LMHOSTS is a static text file that is stored on the local machine. The LMHOSTS file is named *LMHOSTS* (with no extension), and in Windows NT it resides in the `\systemroot\system32\drivers\etc` directory.

The file contains NetBIOS names and IP address mappings for computers on the network. You can create an LMHOSTS file with any text editor, or you can use the sample LMHOSTS file (LMHOSTS.SAM) found in `\systemroot\system32\drivers\etc` as a template. Figure 6–14 shows a simple LMHOSTS file.

You should use the following guidelines when creating an LMHOSTS file:

• Entries are not case sensitive.

• Place each entry on a separate line.

```
205.10.12.10    Wkstn1
205.10.12.11    Wkstn2
200.18.22.10    Server1    #PRE    # SQL Server
200.18.22.12    Server2    #PRE    # Print Server
210.22.18.10    Server3    #PRE    # Exchange Server
```

Figure 6–14 *Sample LMHOSTS file.*

- Enter the IP address in the first column and type its corresponding computer name immediately after it.
- Separate the address and the computer name by at least one space or tab.
- The # character usually marks the start of a comment. It is also used to designate special keywords, as described below.

In the UNIX world, the Samba server can use the /etc/lmhosts file for NetBIOS name to IP address mapping. It is very similar to the `/etc/hosts` file format, except that the hostname component must correspond to the NetBIOS naming format. The UNIX format is that used by Windows NT, except that it does not use the special keywords described next.

Each line of this file contains a single IP-to-NetBIOS name mapping. The two fields on each line are separated from each other by white space. Any entry beginning with the "#" character is ignored. Each IP-to-NetBIOS name mapping entry contains an IP address in dotted decimal format and a NetBIOS name. The NetBIOS name may be a maximum of fifteen characters with an optional trailing "#" character followed by the NetBIOS service type as two hexadecimal digits. If the trailing "#" is omitted, the same IP address will be returned for any name lookup, whatever the service type is requested.

LMHOSTS Keywords

Windows LMHOSTS files use a number of predefined keywords to make the list more useful and easier to create and maintain. Some of the more useful keywords are detailed in Table 6.9, while Figure 6–15 provides an example of how to employ them.

> **Keywords listed in this section can be used in LMHOSTS files using Microsoft TCP/IP. LAN Manager 2.x, however, will treat these keywords as comments.**

Of all the LMHOSTS keywords, the one used most frequently is #PRE. When using this entry, it is important to remember that the NetBIOS name cache and LMHOSTS file are read sequentially. To increase efficiency, it is best to put the computers you access most frequently at the top of the list and entries tagged with #PRE at the bottom. Since #PRE tagged entries are cached at TCP/IP initialization, they will be read from the list only once (at initialization).

Table 6.9 *LMHOSTS Keywords*

Keyword	Meaning
#PRE	Causes an entry to be preloaded into the NetBIOS name cache. #PRE entries in LMHOSTS are looked up and cached prior to WINS lookup.
#DOM:*domain_name*	Associates an entry with the domain specified by *domain*. This affects how the browser and log-on services behave in routed TCP/IP environments. It ensures datagram requests are forwarded to remote subnets and will permit machines to obtain logon validation by browsing domain controllers (for their domains) located in other subnets.
#INCLUDE *filename*	Causes the system to seek the LMHOSTS-formatted file called *filename* and parse it as if it were local. If you use a universal naming convention (UNC) *filename*, you can use a centralized LMHOSTS file on a server.[1]
#BEGIN_ALTERNATE	Groups multiple #INCLUDE statements. The success of any #INCLUDE statement causes the group to succeed.
#END_ALTERNATE	Marks the end of an #INCLUDE grouping.
#NOFNR	Prevents the use of NetBIOS directed name queries on LAN manager UNIX systems.
#MH	Permits multiple entries for multihomed computers.
\0x*nn*	Allows the entry of nonprinting characters in NetBIOS names. Enclose the NetBIOS name in quotation marks and use \0x*nn* hexadecimal notation to specify a hexadecimal value for the character.

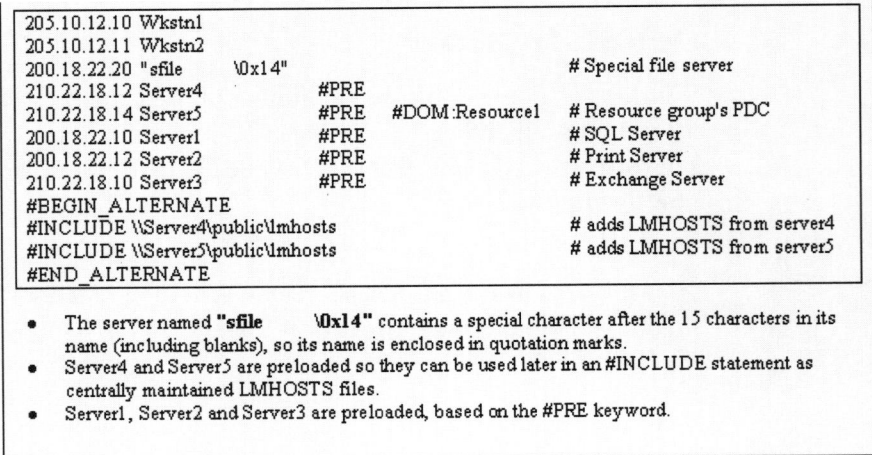

Figure 6–15 *LMHOSTS file showing keyword use.*

[1]You must place an IP address mapping in your LMHOSTS file for the server and identify it with the #PRE keyword before the #INCLUDE section (otherwise, the #INCLUDE will be ignored).

 LMHOSTS files are static and must be maintained on each computer (except for those portions that are #INCLUDEd from another server). Make sure you update all LMHOSTS files each time a computer is added, removed, or renamed in your networking environment.

Using NBTSTAT

The NBTSTAT command line utility enables us to check the state of current NetBIOS over TCP/IP connections. It will also allow you to determine your registered name and scope ID and permits you to update the LMHOSTS cache. NBTSTAT is particularly useful for troubleshooting the NetBIOS name cache. NBTSTAT features are described in Table 6.10.

 The Samba implementation of NetBIOS features the NMBLOOKUP utility that is only used to lookup NetBIOS names registered on the local host and any remote NetBIOS hosts.

Host Name Resolution

You may be excited about NetBIOS names and the fact that you won't need to memorize all those IP addresses since you can just use the NetBIOS name and let the computer do the work of determining the IP address for you. Unfortu-

Table 6.10 *NBTSTAT Parameters*

Parameter	Description
-a	Returns the remote computer's name table giving its host name.
-A	Lists the remote computer's name table giving its IP address.
-c	Displays the NetBIOS name cache.
-n	Lists the NetBIOS names registered by the client, either by b-node broadcast or by a WINS server.
-R	Manually purges and reloads the NetBIOS name cache using LMHOSTS entries tagged with #PRE. Ensure you use this after changing entries tagged by #PRE to update their new values in the current cache.
-r	Lists name resolution statistics for Windows networking.
-S	Displays workstation and server sessions, listing the remote hosts by IP address only.
-s	Displays workstation and server sessions. It attempts to convert the remote host IP address to a name using the HOSTS file.
Interval	Redisplays selected statistics, pausing *interval* seconds between each display. Press CTRL+C to stop redisplaying statistics. If this parameter is omitted, **nbtstat** prints the current configuration information once.

nately, NetBIOS names are natively available only in the Windows environment (or on other systems that have third party NetBIOS helper programs).

The good news is: computers that don't support NetBIOS names can use a *host name* that can be related to an IP address just like a NetBIOS name. The better news is that Windows computers can also have and work with host names, making this a very robust method of computer naming!

In the UNIX environment, all network communication can be accomplished through the use of an IP address (which, of course, is translated to a MAC address). To relieve the tedium of always using IP addresses, however, you may also use a *host name* or *fully qualified domain name*. A fully qualified domain name (FQDN) is a combination of the host and domain names.

Windows systems can also communicate through host names and fully qualified domain names. Originally, Windows computers using Microsoft network commands, such as `net use`, could use only NetBIOS names in those commands. Current Windows operating systems, such as Windows NT 4.0 and Windows 2000, permit the use of IP addresses, host names, and fully qualified domain names in most network commands.

What Is a Host Name?

A *Host Name* is any alias that can be assigned to a computer to identify a TCP/IP host. By default, in a Windows environment, the host name is the NetBIOS name. This, however, is not required—a host name can be *any* 256-character string. A single computer can even have multiple host names.

Like the NetBIOS name, a host name can be used in place of an IP address in TCP/IP utilities. The host name will always correspond to an IP address stored in the machine's HOSTS file or in a DNS database. If the host name is the same as the NetBIOS name, it will also correspond to an IP address stored on a NetBIOS name server or LMHOSTS file.

Unlike NetBIOS names, host names are created when they are placed in a HOSTS file or loaded on a DNS server. To assign a host name to a Windows NT 4.0 computer, select the DNS tab of the TCP/IP properties dialog (in the network dialog) and set the name as shown in Figure 6–16. In the figure, the computer's host name is `MyComputer` and the fully qualified domain name is `MyComputer.mydomain.com`. Typing `HOSTNAME` at the command prompt will reveal the hostname of the local computer.

As with NetBIOS names, a host name does not do much good if we can not resolve it to an IP address. The methods of name resolution listed below should look familiar since they are essentially the same methods we discussed for NetBIOS name resolution. The perceptive student will, however, notice that they are listed in a different order.

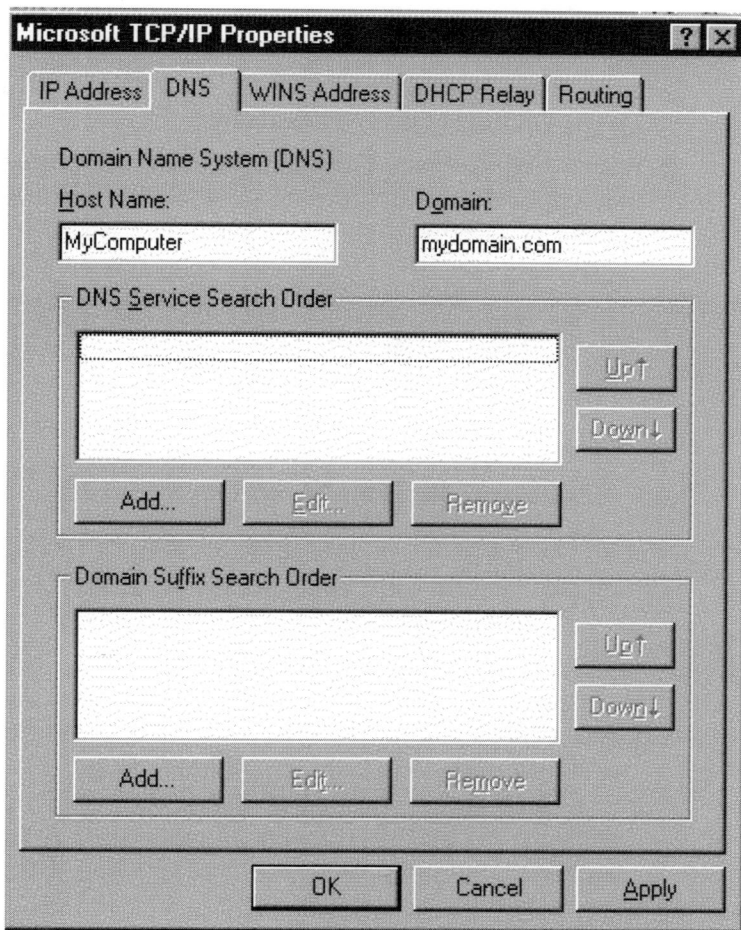

Figure 6–16 *Setting the host name of a Windows NT 4.0 computer.*

Standard Name Resolution Methods

The following methods are standard throughout TCP/IP networks:

- Local host name—The first step in host name resolution occurs when the local machine checks its own host name. If it discovers the destination host name is the same as its configured host name, it doesn't need to perform any further resolution.

- HOSTS file—The HOSTS file is a text file on the local computer that requires manual entry and maintenance. Checking this file is always the second host name resolution step (after checking the local host name). The HOSTS file maps IP addresses to host names or fully qualified domain names. (HOSTS files use the same format as the 4.3 Berkeley Software Distribution UNIX\etc\hosts file.) We will look at HOSTS files in some detail later in this chapter.

- Domain name system (DNS)—The domain name system is a server that maintains a database of IP addresses and fully qualified domain names. Like the HOSTS file, DNS requires manual entry and maintenance.

Note On NetBIOS enabled systems, host name resolution may be configured to use NetBIOS resolution methods if the above steps fail. This assumes the NetBIOS and host names are the same—usually a safe assumption.

Name Resolution Methods Specific to Microsoft

In addition to the standard resolution methods, if the host name and the NetBIOS name are the same, some Microsoft methods can be used to map host names to IP addresses on Windows systems:

- NetBIOS name server (NBNS): An NBNS is any server implemented under RFC 1001/1002 to provide NetBIOS name resolution. A computer trying to contact a machine with a particular host name can query the NBNS for a name/IP address mapping. If the host name is equivalent to a NetBIOS name found in the NBNS database, the NBNS will return the IP address mapped to the NetBIOS name. (As we have seen, the Microsoft implementation of an NBNS is WINS.)

- Local broadcast: If a computer can not find a mapping from a name server, it can send a broadcast over the local network. If the target computer receives the broadcast and recognizes the host name as its NetBIOS name, it will respond with its IP address to permit full TCP/IP communication.

- LMHOSTS file: An LMHOSTS file is a text file on the local computer that contains both the NetBIOS name and IP address of Windows networking computers on remote networks. If the host name is equivalent to a NetBIOS name found in the LMHOSTS file, the computer will use the IP address mapped to the NetBIOS name.

Name Resolution Using a HOSTS File

If you remember what you learned about name resolution using the LMHOSTS file, you already have a good idea about the function of the

HOSTS file. Like the LMHOSTS file, the HOSTS file resides on the local machine and requires manual update and maintenance. Unlike the LMHOSTS file, which is used to find only remote machines, the HOSTS file contains mappings for both local and remote hosts.

When a computer needs to resolve a host name, it first checks to see if the host name is the same as the local host name (in other words, it checks to see if the name it is looking for is its own.). If the host name being sought is not the local host name, the computer checks its HOSTS file for an appropriate mapping. If the HOSTS file does not contain the required information, the computer will attempt name resolution using the alternate methods described in the previous section (DNS, NBNS, etc.). If none of the host name resolution methods yield an IP address mapping, the network communication fails and the user receives an error message.

Once an IP address mapping is obtained (through the HOSTS file or other name resolution method), the computer will use the address resolution protocol (ARP) to resolve the host name to a hardware address. If the host is on the local network, ARP will return the host's hardware address (ARP first checks its cache to see if it has already obtained a mapping; if none is found, it uses a broadcast to resolve the IP address to a MAC address). If the host is on a remote network, ARP returns the hardware address of a router that can lead to the destination host and the communication is routed to it.

Name Resolution Using a DNS Server

Like the HOSTS file, a *domain name system* (DNS) server maintains IP address mappings in a manually maintained and updated list. As you might expect, however, the DNS does not need to reside on the local computer. Another distinction between the HOSTS file and a DNS server is, while a HOSTS file can contain host names and fully qualified domain names (FQDNs), the DNS server contains only FQDNs (host name resolution using fully qualified domain names is no problem since the host name is found within the FQDN).

DNS name resolution is very similar to resolution using the HOSTS file. Assuming the calling computer is configured to use DNS name resolution, when it is unable to locate a mapping in its HOSTS file, it queries the configured DNS server. If the DNS server has a mapping, it returns the information and the computer will use ARP to resolve the host name to a hardware address. If the host is on the local network, ARP will return the host's hardware address. If the host is on a remote network, ARP returns the hardware address of a router that can lead to the destination host, and the communication is routed to it.

If the server does not respond, the client makes several additional attempts at varying intervals. If the server fails to respond after the additional attempts or if it responds but has no mapping for the desired target host, the client tries other methods. If the client isn't configured to use additional resolution methods, or if they fail, communication cannot be established with the target host and an error message is returned.

Summary

In this chapter we covered a very difficult networking concept—TCP/IP. We walked though the various TCP/IP standards and utilities. We saw that utilities could be classified as configuration utilities, data transfer utilities, remote execution utilities, printing utilities, and diagnostic utilities. You learned how to use different configuration utilities, such as `ifconfig`, which allows you to assign and view IP parameters for network interfaces on UNIX hosts. You also learned how to use the `ipconfig` utility to verify the TCP/IP configuration parameters, including the IP address, subnet mask and default gateway in Microsoft TCP/IP implementations.

We saw how the PING utility can be used to check the accessibility of the remote hosts and examined how PING is implemented in Windows NT, UNIX, and Novell NetWare environments.

We discussed TCP/IP architecture and the methods used for IP address to MAC address resolution. We looked into ARP requests and the ARP cache that exists on each host. We saw that the ARP cache consists of static and dynamic entries that map IP addresses to hardware addresses. We discussed ports and sockets and saw that the port number identifies an application on a particular computer.

We also examined IP addressing and subnet masking. We saw how an IP address is formed and how to determine its host ID and the network ID. We discussed IP address classes and specifically reviewed class A, B, and C addresses.

We also introduced the dynamic host configuration protocol (DHCP). DHCP can be installed on one or more machines in your network to permit the automatic and centralized administration and configuration of TCP/IP parameters. We reviewed the dynamic IP address assignment process that includes sending four DHCP packets over the network and saw how the IPCONFIG utility can be used to renew and release IP parameters.

The fundamental concepts of NetBIOS and host name resolution were also covered in this chapter. We learned that NetBIOS support is built into Microsoft operating systems but must be installed manually on UNIX as a third-party add-on. We also saw that different applications use different name resolution methods. For example, a sockets-based application uses host names, whereas applications written using the NetBIOS API use Net-BIOS names. Finally, we saw how different methods are available to resolve host and NetBIOS names into the IP addresses. The Broadcast-based method, LMHOSTS file method, WINS/NBNS method, HOSTS files method, and DNS method were all introduced and covered.

▲ REVIEW QUESTIONS

1. *Which of the following utilities is used to capture network traffic for analysis?*

    A. IPCONFIG.

    B. PING.

    C. Network monitor.

    D. Performance monitor.

    E. LPD.

2. *Select all that apply: Which utility (utilities) is (are) NOT used for TCP/IP printing?*

    A. LPR.

    B. PING.

    C. LPQ.

    D. telnet.

3. *Which of the following function as both client and server applications on Windows NT 4.0?*

    A. PING.

    B. IPCONFIG.

    C. FTP.

    D. REXEC.

4. *Select all that apply: Why is it important to obtain the most recent RFC on a particular topic?*

    A. RFC numbers are not replaced.

    B. RFC numbers are reviewed and changed weekly.

    C. New RFC are created with new numbers.

    D. RFC number corresponds to its publishing date.

5. *TCP/IP is really*

    A. One protocol.

    B. Two protocols: TCP and IP.

    C. More than two protocols.

    D. A set of rules published in RFCs.

6. *Which of the following is used to connect to other hosts in TCP/IP networks? (Choose two.)*

    A. IPCONFIG.

    B. FTP.

    C. PING.

    D. telnet.

7. *What parameters are used to configure Microsoft TCP/IP on windows NT 4.0? (Choose all that apply.)*

    A. IP address.

    B. Subnet mask.

    C. Internal network number.

    D. The maximum speed of the WAN link.

8. *What protocol handles the resolution of IP addresses to media access control addresses on your network?*

    A. Ping.

    B. ARP.

    C. IP.

    D. ICMP.

9. *What protocol reports errors associated with IP traffic?*

    A. IGMP.

    B. ICMP.

    C. ARP.

    D. TCP.

10. *What is the class of address 194.226.192.52?*

    A. Class A.

    B. Class B.

    C. Class C.

D. Class D.

E. Class E.

11. *How many bits does the IP address occupy?*

  A. 8 bits.

  B. 16 bits.

  C. 32 bits.

  D. 64 bits.

12. *What class of network has 254 hosts per network?*

  A. Class A.

  B. Class B.

  C. Class C.

  D. None of the above.

13. *Which of the following are invalid for network ID?*

  A. All 0's.

  B. 127.

  C. All 1's.

  D. 100.

  E. 195.

14. *What class network is 10.0.0.0?*

  A. Class A.

  B. Class B.

  C. Class C.

  D. Class D.

15. *What is the network ID for 200.0.0.1?*

  A. 200.

  B. 200.0.

  C. 200.0.0.

  D. 200.0.0.1.

16. *You are setting up TCP/IP on a computer in a small company. Can you assign this computer the IP address of 127.56.10.45?*

  A. Yes.

    B. No, because this is a special purpose IP address.

    C. No, because the network ID is all 1's.

    D. No, because this is a class A IP address and is suitable for large enterprises only.

17. *You physically move a DHCP client computer to a new subnet but it fails to function on the network. What might account for this?*

    _____

18. *What can you use to determine the current DHCP client configuration?*

    _____

19. *Linda wants to view the NetBIOS name cache on her computer. What should she type on the command line?*

    A. arp –a.

    B. nbtstat –c.

    C. ping.

    D. netstat –c.

    E. nbtstat –r.

20. *Lynn manages a large network that relies on LMHOSTS files for name resolution. One of her users complains that the time required to connect to remote hosts has become excessive. Lynn examines the user's LMHOSTS file and discovers a large number of #PRE and #DOM tagged entries in the file. What can Lynn do to increase the speed with which the LMHOSTS file is read?*

    A. Move all the #PRE and #DOM tagged entries to the top of the file.

    B. Remove the "#" character from the #PRE tags. "B" reads "Delete the # PRE tage from every #DOM tagged entry in Appendix Q + A.

    C. Move the #PRE and #DOM tagged entries to the bottom of the file.

    D. Delete all the #PRE and #DOM entries.

21. *Your network uses a DHCP server to assign IP addresses and WINS information. You want to ensure your computers use WINS before resorting to broadcast name resolution. What node should you specify in the DHCP options?*

    A. P-node.

    B. B-node.

    C. H-node.

    D. M-node.

22. *Mike changed the NetBIOS scope value on the WINS address tab for several of his computers. What effect did this have on those machines?*

    A. Forced them to use the WINS database.

    B. Permitted their names to preload into the group's NetBIOS cache.

    C. Preloaded their names into the corresponding HOSTS file.

    D. Prevented them from communicating with machines not configured with that scope value.

23. *Sandy will use FTP to retrieve files from a UNIX server. Her computer is not a DNS client. What can she use to connect to the UNIX machine? (Select all that apply.)*

    A. WINS.

    B. LMHOSTS.

    C. DHCP.

    D. HOSTS.

24. *When Vicky uses the command "ftp FileSrv" she connects to a UNIX server on a remote network. When she types "ftp 122.36.5.22," however, the operation fails. What is the likely cause of the problem?*

    A. The UNIX server's LMHOSTS file has entries that conflict with Vicky's HOSTS file.

    B. Vicky does not have IP permissions on the UNIX server.

    C. 122.35.5.22 is not the IP address of an FTP server.

    D. FTP will not work with IP addresses.

Troubleshooting TCP/IP

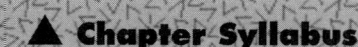
▲ Chapter Syllabus

General Considerations

Testing IP Communications

Testing TCP/IP Name Resolution

Troubleshooting Tools

In the previous chapter we discussed transmission control protocol/Internet protocol (TCP/IP) fundamentals and configurations. By now you should have a basic understanding of how TCP/IP networks function. You should also have discovered that TCP/IP services and parameters can be very complex. This chapter will help you determine what to do if something goes wrong. We will combine a review of the most important TCP/IP topics with some helpful troubleshooting guidelines. We will cover the major TCP/IP troubleshooting utilities and discuss how to use them most efficiently. Topics covered in this chapter summarize common TCP/IP-related problems, symptoms, and possible causes, as well as the concrete steps required to troubleshoot them.

After completing this chapter you will be able to do the following:

- Describe major TCP/IP-related problems
- Choose utilities to diagnose the TCP/IP problem
- Search for problem sources

General Considerations

When something goes wrong, we often try to choose a tool that can immediately solve our problem. Before deciding which utility to use, however, you should determine the source of the problem. A number of problems turn out not to be TCP/IP-related (for example, a network interface card malfunction) and need to be solved by other methods. In this chapter, however, we will speak only of TCP/IP related problems.

TCP/IP Problems can be grouped by category as shown in Table 7.1.

When a problem occurs, you might want to ask yourself these simple questions:

- What should work?
- What does work?
- What does not work?
- What has changed since it last worked?

Answering these questions will help you choose the right tool to isolate the problem. For example, suppose that Kim complains that when she is using her Windows NT workstation computer, she is unable to connect to remote NetBIOS hosts by their computer name. After speaking with her you find out that recently she has accidentally deleted some files from the `%systemroot%\drivers\etc\` folder on her computer. Knowing what set of actions caused this problem you will not waste time in low-level connectivity checks but can go directly to the folder to check for an LMHOSTS file.

Diagnostic Tools Overview

Microsoft Windows NT server and workstation have many useful utilities to diagnose and troubleshoot TCP/IP. Many powerful utilities are included in

Table 7.1 *Major TCP/IP Related Problems*

Problem source	Symptoms
TCP/IP configuration	Host initialization fails, services fail to start, communication to all (some) other hosts is impossible.
Address resolution	Although you can ping your workstation, you cannot access some local or remote hosts.
NetBIOS name resolution	You can access a host by its IP address but cannot connect to it by its *computer name.*
Host name resolution	You can access a host by its IP address but can not connect to it by its *host name.*

the Windows NT Resource Kit. (For example, *Browstat* [a command line utility that can be used to force the browser elections for a specified domain], *Browmon* [a graphical utility that can be used to view browsers for selected domains], *Wntipcfg* [a graphical utility with the same functionality as IPCONFIG].) In addition, as you may already have heard, Microsoft Systems Management Server includes an advanced version of Network Monitor—a great program to trace and monitor your network at the packet level. Table 7.2 lists common diagnostic utilities that are included in TCP/IP implementation on Microsoft Windows NT 4.0.

Now we can look at the suite of diagnostic utilities available in UNIX-like systems. (See Table 7.3.)

Finally let us take a look at the diagnostic and troubleshooting utilities available in Novell NetWare systems. (See Table 7.4.)

Each utility may be used to diagnose only one part of the problem. Typically, none will solve the entire problem alone. Later in this chapter you will be introduced to how to use these utilities together to troubleshoot your network.

Table 7.2 *Microsoft TCP/IP Diagnostic Utilities*

Utility	Function
Address resolution protocol (ARP)	Displays and modifies the cache of locally resolved IP addresses to MAC addresses.
PING	Verifies the availability of the remote host by sending the echo request and analyzing replies.
TRACERT	Traces the route for packets from local hosts to the specified remote host.
IPCONFIG	Displays current TCP/IP configuration including IP address(es), DNS and WINS addresses.
ROUTE	Views and modifies the local routing table.
NBTSTAT	Displays protocol statistics and current TCP/IP connections using NetBIOS over TCP/IP. This utility is also used to determine the registered NetBIOS name and to view the local name cache.
NSLOOKUP	Displays information from DNS name servers about a particular host or domain. You can also use this utility to check the availability of the domain name across the Internet.
NETSTAT	Displays protocol statistics and current TCP/IP network connections.
Event Log	Standard Windows NT tool used to track events, warnings, and errors. (While the event log can be used for TCP/IP troubleshooting, its primary function is to track overall health of the system.)
Network monitor	Captures and displays packets.
Performance monitor	Displays performance counters
Microsoft SNMP service	Supplies information to SNMP management systems.

Table 7.3 *UNIX TCP/IP Diagnostic Utilities*

Utility	Function
Address resolution protocol (ARP)	Displays and modifies the cache of locally resolved IP addresses to MAC addresses.
PING	Verifies the availability of the remote host by sending the echo request and analyzing replies.
TRACEROUTE	Traces the route for packets from local hosts to the specified remote host.
IFCONFIG	Displays current IP configuration for the specified networks interfaces including IP address(es), netmasks, and so on.
ROUTE	Views and modifies the local routing table.
NMBLOOKUP	Displays protocol statistics and current TCP/IP connections using NetBIOS over TCP/IP. This utility is also used to determine the registered NetBIOS name and to view the local name cache. This utility is not included in the standard versions of UNIX. You must install third-party NetBIOS helper software to have it.
NSLOOKUP	Displays information from DNS name servers about a particular host or domain. You can also use this utility to check the availability of the domain name across the Internet.
NETSTAT	Displays protocol statistics and current TCP/IP network connections.
System Log Files	Special files are used to track events, warnings and errors. These files can be located in different places of file system, depending on the version of operating system. Usually located in /var/log/* or /var/adm/*.
TCPDUMP	This utility allows you to capture and display TCP/IP packets.
System Activity Reporter (SAR)	Displays system activity information.
SNMP service	Supplies information to SNMP management systems.

TCP/IP Troubleshooting Guidelines

There is no fixed sequence of steps to troubleshoot TCP/IP-related problems—everything depends on the particular scenario. There are, however, some basic guidelines that fit most situations.

The first thing you should do is to ensure that the physical connection is functioning (i.e. check the cable). It is useless to employ a host of troubleshooting utilities if the office hub is malfunctioning. When link reliability is in question (for example when the WAN link is malfunctioning), you may want to try a large number of *pings* to various remote hosts to check connectivity. (Some remote hosts, such as those protected by a firewall or proxy server may not respond to *ping* even though connectivity is working properly. Ensure you are pinging a host known to be able to respond to this diagnostic.)

Table 7.4 *Novell TCP/IP Diagnostic Utilities*

Utility	Function
PING and TPING	Verifies the availability of the remote host by sending the echo request and analyzing replies.
IPTRACE	Verifies the routing of packets to and from the server.
TCPCON	Utility that provides access to statistics and information about the status of various components of the TCP/IP protocol suite. It uses SNMP to access this information from any local or remote system on the network. You can use TCPCON to perform the following tasks: 1. Monitor activity in the TCP/IP network segments of your internetwork 2. Display configuration information and statistics about the following TCP/IP protocols: IP, ICMP, UDP, TCP, OSPF, and EGP 3. Display the IP routes currently known to a TCP/IP node 4. Display the network interfaces supported by a TCP/IP node 5. Access the trap log maintained by SNMPLOG (for local systems only) 6. Access TCP/IP information in any remote protocol stack supporting the TCP/IP Management Information Base (MIB)
Novell SNMP agent	Supplies information to SNMP management systems.

Once you are sure the links are functioning properly, you should start testing the local host's configuration parameters, then examine routing configurations, and finally check name resolution issues. The direction of troubleshooting steps is illustrated in Figure 7–1. Note that you test the lower layers of the TCP/IP stack first. Once the low-level TCP/IP functions are working correctly, you pass to the higher levels.

Identifying the TCP/IP Configuration

Checking the TCP/IP configuration is the most basic troubleshooting step. You might want to ensure the TCP/IP parameters have been entered without mistakes or that DHCP has set them correctly. You should begin by checking the TCP/IP configuration on the computer that appears to be experiencing problems.

A good starting point is the IPCONFIG, IFCONFIG, or TCPCON command line utilities. IPCONFIG displays the IP address, subnet mask, and default gateway, as well as other advanced TCP/IP parameters, such as WINS server, IP address, and node type on Windows NT systems. In UNIX environments, the `ifconfig` utility can be used for the same purposes. And as described earlier, you have to use console utility TCPCON in Novell's world.

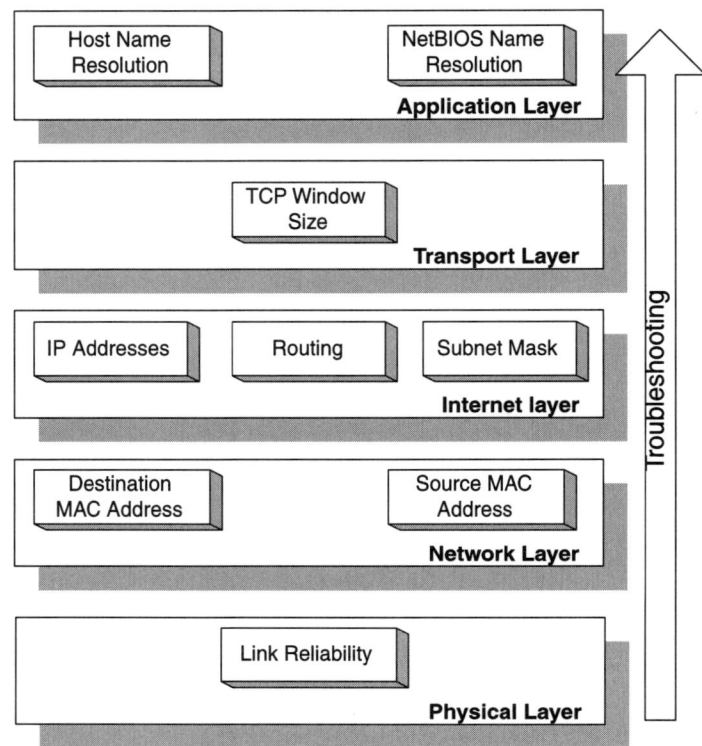

Figure 7–1 *TCP/IP troubleshooting guidelines.*

When using IPCONFIG, you should use the */all* switch because it produces a detailed report concerning the current TCP/IP configuration. The following is an example of the output from IPCONFIG:

```
C:\WINNT>ipconfig /all
Windows NT IP Configuration
        Host Name . . . . . . . . . : mcse.traincert.com
        DNS Servers . . . . . . . . : 172.20.0.10
        Node Type . . . . . . . . . : Hybrid
        NetBIOS Scope ID. . . . . . :
        IP Routing Enabled. . . . . : No
        WINS Proxy Enabled. . . . . : No
        NetBIOS Resolution Uses DNS : Yes
Ethernet adapter Elnk31:
        Description . . . . . . . . : ELNK3 Ethernet
Adapter.
        Physical Address. . . . . . : 00-20-AF-AC-3A-76
```

```
DHCP Enabled. . . . . . . . : No
IP Address. . . . . . . . . : 172.20.0.10
Subnet Mask . . . . . . . . : 255.255.255.0
Default Gateway . . . . . . : 172.20.0.1
Primary WINS Server . . . . : 172.20.0.10
```

In a UNIX environment, you can use IFCONFIG to get configuration information. IFCONFIG will provide the following output:

```
$ ifconfig lan0
lan0: flags=63<UP,BROADCAST,NOTRAILERS,RUNNING>
        inet 194.226.192.51 netmask ffffffe0 broadcast
194.226.192.63
```

In some cases just reviewing this report can locate the problem. For example, if the Windows NT-based DHCP client could not obtain an IP address, running IPCONFIG returns an IP address and subnet mask of 0.0.0.0. In some other operating systems, such as UNIX, you will get a 0.0.0.0 output if the interface was not configured by a network administrator, as in

```
C:\WINNT>ipconfig
Windows NT IP Configuration
Ethernet adapter Elnk31:
        IP Address. . . . . . . . . : 0.0.0.0
        Subnet Mask . . . . . . . . : 0.0.0.0
        Default Gateway . . . . . . :
```

This listing could indicate the DHCP server is down or there are no free IP addresses in the DHCP server's scope.

Incorrect IP Address Assignment

To determine if the computer has been assigned a valid IP address, you can use the following guidelines:

- Check that the IP address is from the correct subnet.
- Check that the IP address is not duplicated.
- Check that the IP address is not a broadcast address for the given subnet (Host ID is all 1's).
- Check that the IP address is not the subnet address (Host ID is all 0's).

Figure 7–2 shows a network where computers have IP addressing problems. Computer 1 and computer 3 have duplicate IP addresses. Computer 2 has the IP address that is the broadcast address for subnet 172.20.0.0, mask 255.255.255.0. Computer 4 has an IP address from another subnet.

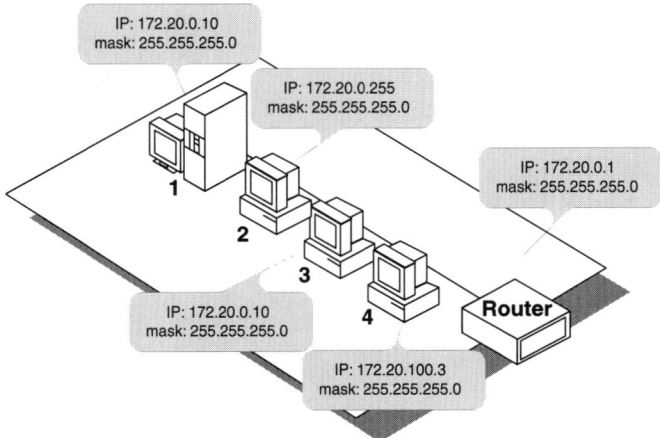

Figure 7–2 *IP addressing problems.*

Subnet Mask Problems

Subnet mask problems are very hard to diagnose and isolate. This is mainly because, depending on the actual numbers, an invalid subnet mask can have no negative impact or can make the entire network unreachable for a particular computer. In some cases an incorrect subnet mask could cause some computers to become unreachable, while the rest of network remains operational. In Figure 7–3, `computer 2` has an incorrect subnet mask (displayed in bold). Although it can successfully establish a connection with `computer`

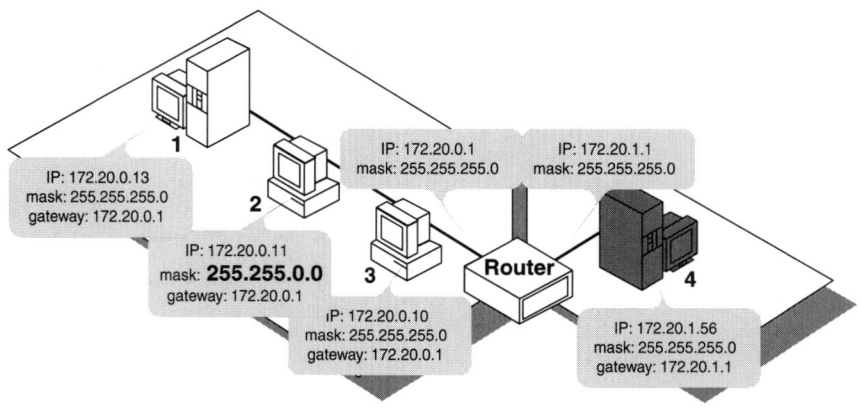

Figure 7–3 *An incorrect subnet mask may prevent your computer from communicating with one or more other machines.*

1, computer 3 and the default gateway, it fails to communicate with computer 4.

There are two common problems with subnet masks:

- The configured subnet mask is shorter than needed (too many bits are reserved for network and subnet ID)
- The configured subnet mask is longer than needed (too few bits are reserved for network and subnet ID)

Improper subnet mask configuration is often the result of inaccurate planning or by mistyping the subnet mask during manual TCP/IP parameter assignment. These problems are particularly prevalent when we implement custom subnet masking. (You might have experienced the tediousness of counting ones and zeroes in custom subnet masks and can appreciate how easy it is to make a mistake in doing so.)

If you suspect a subnet mask problem, you may want to verify the computer configuration with a manually completed network planning sheet (ask your network administrator for one). When you troubleshoot your IP network, it is also highly recommended to have a copy of your subnetting plan close by. This enables you to lookup broadcast addresses and subnet masks and check that they are not assigned to hosts.

Testing IP Communications

Once your computer has obtained an IP address and subnet mask, you should test the IP communications. PING is the utility that can be used for verifying IP-level connectivity. As you may remember, PING sends the ICMP echo request to the destination host and analyses ICMP echo replies.

The recommended sequence of pings is as follows:

1. Ping the loopback address (127.0.0.1). (If you are unable to ping the loopback address, it may indicate the computer has not been restarted after TCP/IP was installed and configured—accomplish a restart and try again.)
2. Ping the IP address of the local computer. (If you cannot ping the local IP address, check to ensure your computer has a valid IP address that is not duplicated elsewhere on the network.)
3. Ping the IP address of the default gateway. (If this step is unsuccessful, check the subnet mask on your computer.)
4. Ping the IP address of the remote host. (If this step is unsuccessful, check the default gateway address configured on the local computer,

the functionality of the link between routers, and remote computer availability.)

5. Ping the remote host by name. (If this step fails, check host name resolution.)

The PING utility has many switches that can be used to expand its functionality. To view the available command-line options, type PING -? or PING -h (for UNIX implementations).

Following is a sample of the ping -? command for Windows NT:

```
C:\WINNT>ping -?
Usage: ping [-t] [-a] [-n count] [-l size] [-f] [-i TTL] [-v TOS]
            [-r count] [-s count] [[-j host-list] | [-k host-list]]
            [-w timeout] destination-list
Options:
    -t              Ping the specified host until interrupted.
    -a              Resolve addresses to hostnames.
    -n count        Number of echo requests to send.
    -l size         Send buffer size.
    -f              Set Don't Fragment flag in packet.
    -i TTL          Time To Live.
    -v TOS          Type Of Service.
    -r count        Record route for count hops.
    -s count        Timestamp for count hops.
    -j host-list    Loose source route along host-list.
    -k host-list    Strict source route along host-list.
    -w timeout      Timeout in milliseconds to wait for each reply.
```

Options revealed by the UNIX PING –h command are as follows:

```
$ ping -h
Usage:  ping [-drvo] host [packet size] [npackets]
```

You can use the UNIX man command to get extended information about PING usage. Here is what the man ping command displays.:

```
-r          Bypass the normal routing tables and send directly to
            a host on an attached network. If the host is not on
            a directly attached network, an error is returned.
            This option can be used to ping a local host through
            an interface that has no route through it (such as
            after the interface was dropped by gated (see
            gated(1M)).
-v          Verbose output. ICMP packets other than
```

ECHO_RESPONSE that are received are listed.
-o   Insert ``record route'' IP option in outgoing
packets, summarizing routes taken when the program
exits. It may not be possible to get the round-trip
path if all hosts on the route taken do not implement
the ``record route'' IP option. A maximum of nine
Internet addresses can be displayed due to the maximum
length of the IP option area.

Novell's implementation of PING does not have any parameters and the TPING utility has the following syntax:

```
TPING host [packet size [retry count]]
```

You can specify the size of the packets to use, how many packets to send, and how much time to wait for a response.

Here is an example of the use of some advanced options of the Windows NT PING utility. We will specify the type of service (TOS), the initial TTL value, and the source route. These options directly affect the header of the IP packet in which the ICMP message is encapsulated. For example, the command

```
PING -v 12 -j 194.226.192.33 194.85.165.169 194.85.36.30
www.runnet.ru
```

will cause the following ICMP packets to be sent (note that by specifying the ping options -v and -j, we set the values of some fields in the IP header—printed in bold type):

```
+ FRAME: Base frame properties
+ ETHERNET: ETYPE = 0x0800 : Protocol = IP:  DOD Internet Protocol
  IP: ID = 0x2155; Proto = ICMP; Len: 76
      IP: Version = 4 (0x4)
      IP: Header Length = 36 (0x24)
      IP: Service Type = 12 (0xC)
          IP: Precedence = 0x0C
          IP: ...0.... = Normal Delay
          IP: ....1... = High Throughput
          IP: .....1.. = High Reliability
      IP: Total Length = 76 (0x4C)
      IP: Identification = 8533 (0x2155)
    + IP: Flags Summary = 0 (0x0)
      IP: Fragment Offset = 0 (0x0) bytes
      IP: Time to Live = 252 (0xFC)
```

```
IP: Protocol = ICMP - Internet Control Message
IP: Checksum = 0xF92C
IP: Source Address = 193.232.80.66
IP: Destination Address = 194.226.192.52
IP: Option Fields = 131 (0x83)
    IP: Loose Source Routing Option = 131 (0x83)
        IP: Option Length = 15 (0xF)
        IP: Routing Pointer = 16 (0x10)
        IP: Route Traveled = 194 (0xC2)
            IP: Gateway = 194.85.36.30
            IP: Gateway = 194.85.165.169
            IP: Gateway = 194.226.192.33
    IP: End of Options = 0 (0x0)
    IP: Data: Number of data bytes remaining = 40 (0x0028)
+ ICMP: Echo Reply, To 194.226.192.52 From 193.232.80.66
```

By using the previous PING command we have checked whether the target host is available by specific type of service (high throughput and high reliability) and the selected route (194.226.192.33, 194.85.165.169, 194.85.36.30).

Routing Problems

Even when your computer is properly configured, a malfunctioning router can cause difficulties. An improperly configured route typically causes the problem (in this case *improperly configured* could also mean *not configured*). If you are implementing a router on a Windows NT-based computer, re-member, if it does not have an interface on a given subnet, it will need a route to get there. You can do this by adding a static route or by using a multi protocol router (MPR). If a router is implemented on a Windows NT computer, you can check the existing routes by using the ROUTE utility. If in-consistencies are found in the routing table, you can correct them by using the ROUTE ADD and ROUTE DELETE commands. If you use another soft-ware/hardware platform for your router, you may want to consult the prod-uct manual for specific commands.

Note Having multiple network adapters on a Windows NT computer allows you to add a default route for each network card. Although it will create several 0.0.0.0 routes, only one default route will actually be used. You should configure only one card to have a default gateway—this will re-duce confusion and ensure the results you intended.

Problems in the routing tables can be solved by examining the output, provided by ROUTE or NETSTAT utilities. Some examples of UNIX output are shown here:

```
$ netstat -rn
Routing tables
Destination          Gateway              Flags    Refs      Use  Interface
127.0.0.1            127.0.0.1            UH        0       4268  lo0
default              194.226.192.33      UG        2     794337  lan0
194.226.192.32       194.226.192.51      U         1    4051607  lan0
$ route -n
Routing tables
Destination          Gateway              Flags    Refs      Use  Interface
127.0.0.1            127.0.0.1            UH        0       4268  lo0
default              194.226.192.33      UG        2     794337  lan0
194.226.192.32       194.226.192.51      U         1    4051607  lan0
```

In the Novell operating systems, you should use the TCPCON console utility for this purpose. If you examined the routing table and found errors, you can use the `route` command to make changes and correct the problem.

Route Trace Utilities

Network route tracing utilities can be used to determine where a packet stopped on the network because of an improper router configuration or a link failure

In Windows NT, the command is called TRACERT. In the example that follows, the second router has determined that there is no valid path for host 172.21.1.55. There is probably a router configuration problem, or the 172.21.1.0 network does not exist (a bad IP address):

```
C:\>tracert 172.21.1.55
Tracing route to 172.21.1.55 over a maximum of 30 hops
1. <10 ms    <10 ms    <10 ms    172.19.0.1
2. 172.18.6.54    reports: Destination net unreachable.
   Trace complete.
```

TRACERT is useful for troubleshooting large networks where several paths can be taken to arrive at the same point or where many intermediate systems (routers or bridges) are involved.

In the standard UNIX environment, the utility is named TRACER-OUTE and provides the following output:

```
$ traceroute -n 199.183.24.133
traceroute to 199.183.24.133, 30 hops max, 40 byte packets
```

```
 1   194.226.192.129   98.145 ms   33.704 ms   15.032 ms
 2   194.85.165.169   29.375 ms   12.617 ms   8.525 ms
 3   194.85.36.30   13.002 ms   14.519 ms   23.442 ms
 4   193.232.80.105   34.903 ms   227.156 ms   85.412 ms
 5   128.214.250.5   58.390 ms   111.828 ms   191.366 ms
 6   * 193.10.252.49   173.986 ms *
 7   193.10.252.158   258.395 ms   261.579 ms *
 8   207.45.202.25   308.080 ms * *
 9   207.45.223.170   357.716 ms *   238.679 ms
10   * 157.130.4.165   263.546 ms   343.603 ms
11   * 146.188.178.150   315.103 ms *
12   146.188.178.194   297.201 ms   325.079 ms *
13   146.188.178.194   328.756 ms 146.188.136.217   276.199 ms   304.495 ms
14   146.188.161.149   341.581 ms   295.059 ms   284.386 ms
15   146.188.163.173   368.164 ms   343.680 ms   255.367 ms
16   * * *
199.183.24.133      292.857 ms *   346.571 ms
```

To examine route information for the Novell environments, you should use the TCPCON utility.

If you can ping across the router but cannot establish a session or send other network traffic, check to see if the router is able to pass large packets. The PING utility sends its data in 74-byte blocks, but network packets can be significantly larger. You can use PING –l command to use a larger packet size. In Windows NT you need to edit the registry to specify a smaller packet size. This must be done on every problem computer.

Note Although we said PING sends its data in 74-byte blocks, you will see PING indicate it is using only 32 bytes of data. This is because Ping reports only its data block length. The actual ICMP packet is 74 bytes: 32-byte data block + 14 bytes for the Ethernet header + 20 bytes for the IP header + 8 bytes for the ICMP header. (i.e. 32 + 14 + 20 + 8 = 74)

Study Break

Editing the Registry to Specify a Smaller Packet Size in Windows NT

It is easy to say, "edit the registry to specify a smaller packet size," but how do we actually accomplish this?

All of the TCP/IP parameters are registry values located under HKEY_LOCAL_MACHINE\SYSTEM\CurrentControlSet\Services   \Tcpip\Parameters   or   HKEY_LOCAL_MACHINE\SYSTEM\

CurrentControlSet\Services\<Adapter Name>\Parameters\tcpip. In this case, <Adapter Name> refers to the subkey for a network adapter that is bound to the TCP/IP protocol.

There are two registry entries that can effect the TCP/IP packet size. The first one is found in the Tcpip\Parameters subkey and is called EnablePMTUDiscovery (REG_DWORD). This entry can be set to 0 (false) or 1 (true); its default is 1. When set to 1, it directs TCP/IP to attempt to discover the maximum transmission unit (MTU) — largest packet size — over the path to a remote host. This permits TCP/IP to eliminate fragmentation at routers along the path that connect networks with different MTUs. If you set this value to 0, an MTU of 576 will be used for connections to all machines that are not on the local subnet.

The other registry entry is found in the <Adapter Name>\Parameters\Tcpip subkey and is called MTU (REG_DWORD). MTU can be set anywhere between 68 and the actual MTU of the underlying network. (The 68 minimum is required to provide space for the transport header — using a value less than this will result in an MTU of 68.) Setting this parameter overrides the default MTU for the network interface.

Testing TCP/IP Name Resolution

Once IP-level connectivity has been checked, you should examine name resolution. Most name resolution problems occur because the computer cannot resolve the hostname or NetBIOS name to the IP address.

NetBIOS Name Resolution Problems

If you can ping the computer by its IP address but are unable to connect to it using its NetBIOS name (for example when using a NetBIOS-based application), you may want to check that the source and the target hosts are NetBIOS enabled. Most UNIX hosts are not NetBIOS enabled unless they have some third-party software (e.g. Samba server) installed. If hosts are NetBIOS enabled, make sure the scope ID on the source and target computers is the same. If scope IDs do match but you still cannot connect, you probably have a NetBIOS name resolution problem.

Verify that the NetBIOS name-to-address mapping is available through broadcast, WINS, or the LMHOSTS file. If you have a WINS server, check that it is operational and that the local computer has been assigned the proper WINS server address.

If you have a Windows-based computer and suspect trouble with the LMHOSTS file, check that it is located in `%systemroot%/system32/drivers/etc`.

On UNIX hosts with special NetBIOS connectivity software packages installed, you can use the LMHOSTS file if the installed software supports this option (it is supported by Samba). Remember the syntax of Samba-based LMHOSTS file is somewhat different from the Windows implementation.

Check that the file format matches the sample format originally installed with TCP/IP. Check for spelling errors and invalid addresses and identifiers. (Remember, the LMHOSTS file is parsed from the beginning; so if duplicate entries exist, only the first one is considered.) Check for capitalization errors (although the NetBIOS names in the LMHOSTS file are not case sensitive, entries like #PRE and #DOM are). Finally, ensure that the LMHOSTS file has no extension. In Windows NT and Windows 95/98, it is easy to edit and save the LMHOSTS file with the default .txt extension (especially when using an editor like Notepad). If you do this, the file will *not* be recognized as an LMHOSTS file. (When using Microsoft NotePad, you can avoid inadvertently saving a file with the .txt extension by enclosing the file name in quotes prior to saving.)

The LMHOSTS file does not support aliases for NetBIOS names. You must provide the actual NetBIOS name of each computer.

In some cases NetBIOS name resolution works but is extremely slow. This could be caused by the large number of #INCLUDE tags and other entries in the LMHOSTS file. To correct the problem, place the most commonly used names closer to the beginning of the LMHOSTS file. Optionally, you can use the #PRE tag to force entries to be precached.

You can use the Windows or UNIX NBTSTAT utility to check the state of current NetBIOS over TCP/IP connections, update the LMHOSTS cache, and determine the registered name and scope ID.

The NBTSTAT utility has many switches, which can be viewed by typing NBTSTAT without arguments:

```
C:\WINNT>nbtstat
NBTSTAT [-a RemoteName] [-A IP address] [-c] [-n] [-r] [-R] [-RR] [-s]
[-S] [interval]]
-a      (adapter status)   Lists the remote machine's name table given
                           its name
-A (Adapter status)        Lists the remote machine's name table given
                           its IP address
-c (cache)                 Lists the remote name cache including the IP
                           addresses
```

```
-n (names)              Lists local NetBIOS names
-r (resolved)           Lists names resolved by broadcast and via WINS
-R (Reload)             Purges and reloads the remote cache name table
-S (Sessions)           Lists sessions table with the destination IP
                        addresses
-s (sessions)           Lists sessions table converting destination IP
                        addresses to host names via the hosts file
-RR (ReleaseRefresh)    Sends Name Release packets to WINs and then,
                        starts Refresh
RemoteName              Remote host machine name
IP address              Dotted decimal representation of the IP address
Interval                Redisplays selected statistics, pausing interval
                        seconds between each display. Press Ctrl+C to stop
                        redisplaying statistics.
```

For example, you can use NBTSTAT -n to display the names that were registered locally on the system by applications, such as the server and redirector. NBTSTAT -c shows the NetBIOS name cache, which contains name-to-address mappings for other computers. NBTSTAT -R purges the name cache and reloads it from the LMHOSTS file.

On the UNIX hosts, we can use the nmblookup utility in order to look up NetBIOS names on local and remote hosts. This utility only provides a subset of functionality of Windows NT NBTSTAT utility. The arguments and parameters for this utility are shown here:

```
$ nmblookup
Usage: nmblookup [-M] [-B bcast address] [-d debuglevel] name
Version 2.0.0
        -d debuglevel           set the debuglevel
        -B broadcast address    the address to use for broadcasts
        -U unicast    address   the address to use for unicast
        -M                      searches for a master browser
        -R                      set recursion desired in packet
        -S                      look up node status as well
        -r                      Use root port 137 (Win95 only replies to
                                this)
        -A                      Do a node status on <name> as an IP
                                Address
        -i NetBIOS scope        Use the given NetBIOS scope for name
                                queries
        -s smb.conf file        Use the given path to the smb.conf file
        -h                      Print this help message.
```

Host Name Resolution Problems

If you can ping a computer by its IP address but are not able to connect by its host name (for example when using a sockets-based application), you have a host name resolution problem. In this case you, should check that host name-to-address resolution is possible by means of a DNS server or HOSTS file or through NetBIOS methods if they are used.

If a HOSTS file is your primary method of host name resolution, check that the entries use the proper sequence and delimiters. If you use DNS, verify that the DNS server is operational.

Note Even if other methods of host name resolution are available, you should check that the DNS server is on line and functioning. A DNS client (resolver) has a certain timeout before passing control to other methods. If the client is configured to use DNS, but the DNS server is unreachable, the client may experience long delays in host name resolution.

You can use NSLOOKUP to check records, domain host aliases, domain host services, and operating system information by querying the Internet domain name servers.

Another problem can occur when a TCP/IP connection to a remote system appears to be "hung." In this case, you can use the Windows NT NETSTAT -a command to see the status of all activity on TCP and UDP ports on the local system. Good TCP connections usually appear with 0 bytes in queues. Large data blocks in either send or receive queues may indicate a connection problem or network delay. NETSTAT has several command line switches:

```
C:\>netstat -?
Displays protocol statistics and current TCP/IP network connections.
NETSTAT [-a] [-e] [-n] [-s] [-p proto] [-r] [interval]
  -a         Displays all connections and listening ports. (Server-side
             connections are normally not shown.)  (SP 3 only)
  -e         Displays Ethernet statistics. This may be combined with
             the -s option.
  -n         Displays addresses and port numbers in numerical form.
  -p proto   Shows connections for the protocol specified by proto;
             proto may be tcp or udp. If used with the -s option to
             display per-protocol statistics, proto may be tcp, udp, or
             ip.
  -r         Displays the contents of the routing table.
```

```
-s              Displays per-protocol statistics. By default, statistics
                are shown for TCP, UDP and IP; the -p option may be used
                to specify a subset of the default.
Interval redisplays selected statistics, pausing interval seconds be-
tween each display. Press CTRL+C to stop redisplaying statistics. If
omitted, netstat will print the current configuration information once.
```

The following command list displays the IP protocol statistics:

```
C:\WINNT\>netstat -s -p ip
IP Statistics
  Packets Received                    = 4383117
  Received Header Errors              = 4154
  Received Address Errors             = 311
  Datagrams Forwarded                 = 0
  Unknown Protocols Received          = 0
  Received Packets Discarded          = 0
  Received Packets Delivered          = 4378963
  Output Requests                     = 4865242
  Routing Discards                    = 0
  Discarded Output Packets            = 0
  Output Packet No Route              = 0
  Reassembly Required                 = 0
  Reassembly Successful               = 0
  Reassembly Failures                 = 0
  Datagrams Successfully Fragmented   = 0
  Datagrams Failing Fragmentation     = 0
```

While the preceding example is from a Windows NT implementation, the NETSTAT utility was developed by the University of California, Berkeley, and is a native UNIX utility for examination of the state of network connections. It is based on the sockets API. The utility has been ported to most UNIX implementations and has a slightly different set of parameters in each operating system. By default, netstat without any parameters will display network connection statistics as shown here:

```
$ netstat
Active Internet connections
Proto Recv-Q Send-Q Local Address        Foreign Address         (state)
tcp      0      0   194.226.192.51.23    195.209.229.227.4310    ESTABLISHED
tcp      0      0   194.226.192.51.7     128.197.177.78.41367    CLOSE_WAIT
udp      0      0   194.226.192.51.53    *.*
udp      0      0   127.0.0.1.53         *.*
```

```
Active UNIX domain sockets
Address  Type  Recv-Q Send-Q  Inode  Conn   Refs  Nextref Addr
215b200 stream  0      0       0      211c400 0     0 /usr/spool/sock-
ets/X11/0
```

Session Communications Problems

Sometimes you can ping the target computer by an IP address and by name but still be unable to establish a session. For example, you may not be able to FTP the target host. If this is the case, you probably have a session problem. You may want to check that the correct services are running on the target computer and that you have the proper permissions to access it.

If, for example, when trying to connect to a remote host with a command line FTP client you get the following error message:

```
C:\WINNT>ftp 168.20.0.100
-> ftp: connect:Connection refused
ftp>
```

The most likely cause is that the target computer does not have the FTP service installed or the FTP service is stopped.

Sometimes you are unable to connect because the maximum number of licenses is reached on the target computer. For example, if you are trying to connect to the Microsoft Internet Information Server FTP service you may get the following error:

```
C:\WINNT>ftp 168.20.0.100
Connected to 168.20.0.100.
421
User (none): jvacca
Connection closed by remote host.
```

In this particular situation, the target computer had a maximum connections limit.

If the remote host is a UNIX-based machine, check that the appropriate daemon (service) is configured and running.

Troubleshooting Tools

Before you let the plethora of network problems we have just highlighted overwhelm you, take heart. There are some very useful troubleshooting tools available to help you isolate problems and identify trends. Three very good ones, *Event Viewer, Performance Monitor, and Network Monitor,* are outlined next.

Event Viewer

If you are using a Windows NT computer, you can use the Event Viewer application to browse system information about TCP/IP. Important TCP/IP events, such as duplicate IP address, are recorded to the Event Log. (See Figure 7–4.)

Performance Monitor

The Windows NT Performance Monitor has many TCP/IP-related counters, which can be used to troubleshoot TCP/IP networks. Since it accesses

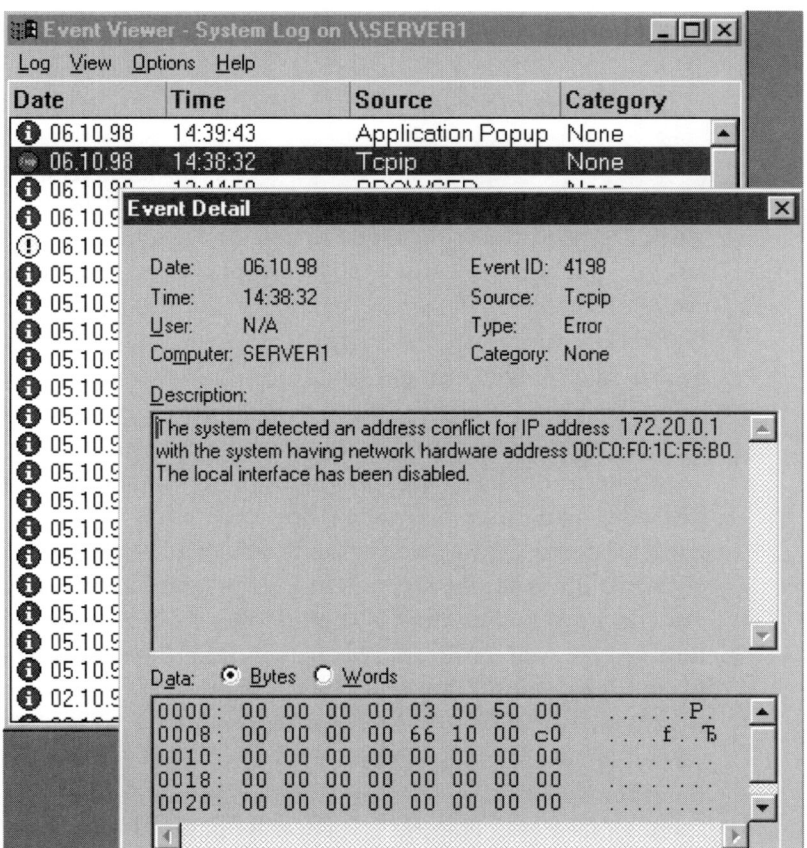

Figure 7–4 *The Windows NT Event Viewer can reveal a duplicate IP address.*

statistics that have been gathered by the SNMP agent, the SNMP service must be installed on computers that are to be monitored. Performance counters are available for IP, Internet control message protocol (ICMP), user datagram protocol (UDP), TCP, and other protocols of the TCP/IP suite. You can observe TCP/IP counters and thereby monitor the overall health of your system. One of the features of Performance Monitor is that it allows counters from various systems to be monitored from a single management window. It also permits you to set alerts for the counters being monitored. For example, you can set an alert when the number of TCP connection failures exceeds a predefined value.

In the UNIX environment, there are special daemons for logging. These daemons are known as `syslogd` and `klogd`. They are used for the application and kernel logging purposes. They use /etc/syslog.conf as their initialization and configuration file; and in most cases, all events from applications and the kernel will be logged to destinations specified in /etc/syslog.conf. Usually the log files are found in the /var/log/ and /var/adm/ directories.

Using Microsoft Network Monitor

Sometimes network problems become too complex to solve by means of simple diagnostic tools such as IPCONFIG and PING. In this case, Microsoft Network Monitor, the tool that is capable of capturing network traffic, may be helpful. Network Monitor is able to capture and display frames (also called packets) in order to detect and troubleshoot problems on local area networks. Network Monitor is particularly useful in diagnosing hardware and software problems when two or more computers cannot communicate. If the problem is too complex, you can capture network activity and send the capture file to a technical support group or network analyst for assistance.

Microsoft Network Monitor configures the network card to capture all incoming and outgoing frames. You can define capture filters and capture triggers so they capture only specific data. The version of Microsoft Network Monitor that is shipped with Windows NT Server 4.0 is limited to capturing only data originating from or destined to the computer that is run network monitor, as well as broadcast and multicast messages. The packets to and from other computers are invisible to the standard version of Microsoft Network Monitor. Microsoft Systems Management Server (SMS) includes a version of Network Monitor that can capture frames sent to or from any computer on the network, edit and transmit frames on the network, and capture frames remotely. The SMS version achieves this by setting the network adapter card to the so-called *promiscuous* mode.

Note You can use the SMS version of Network Monitor to capture frames remotely from Network Agents installed on Windows NT workstations and Windows 95 computers.

UNIX also features applications which monitor network traffic. The most popular one is TCPDUMP, which allows an administrator to capture and analyze TCP/IP traffic. TCPDUMP switches your network interfaces into promiscuous mode. This mode is used to capture all packets that come through your NIC. TCPDUMP includes filter and parser ability to enhance its functionality. Unfortunately, this utility has only a command line interface, making it somewhat more difficult to work with than the Windows product.

Installing Microsoft Network Monitor

You must be the member of the Administrators group to install Microsoft Network Monitor on Windows NT Server 4.0.

To install Network Monitor, you

1. Log on as Administrator.
2. Launch `Control Panel`. Double click the `Network` icon and select the `Services` tab.
3. Click `Add`. The Select Network Services dialog box appears. (See Figure 7–5.)
4. Select `Network Monitor Tools` and `Agent` from the `Network Service` list. Click OK.
5. You may be asked to provide the path to the Windows NT Setup files. Type the full path to the Windows NT distribution point and click `Continue`.
6. Click `Close` to exit the `Network dialog` box.
7. Click Yes to restart the computer.

After the computer restarts, you will be able to use Microsoft Network Monitor.

Using Microsoft Network Monitor

When the Microsoft Network Monitor is installed, you can access it in the Administrative Tools (Common) folder in Start menu. Figure 7–6 illustrates the layout of the Microsoft Network Monitor Window.

The typical procedure for using Network Monitor is as follows:

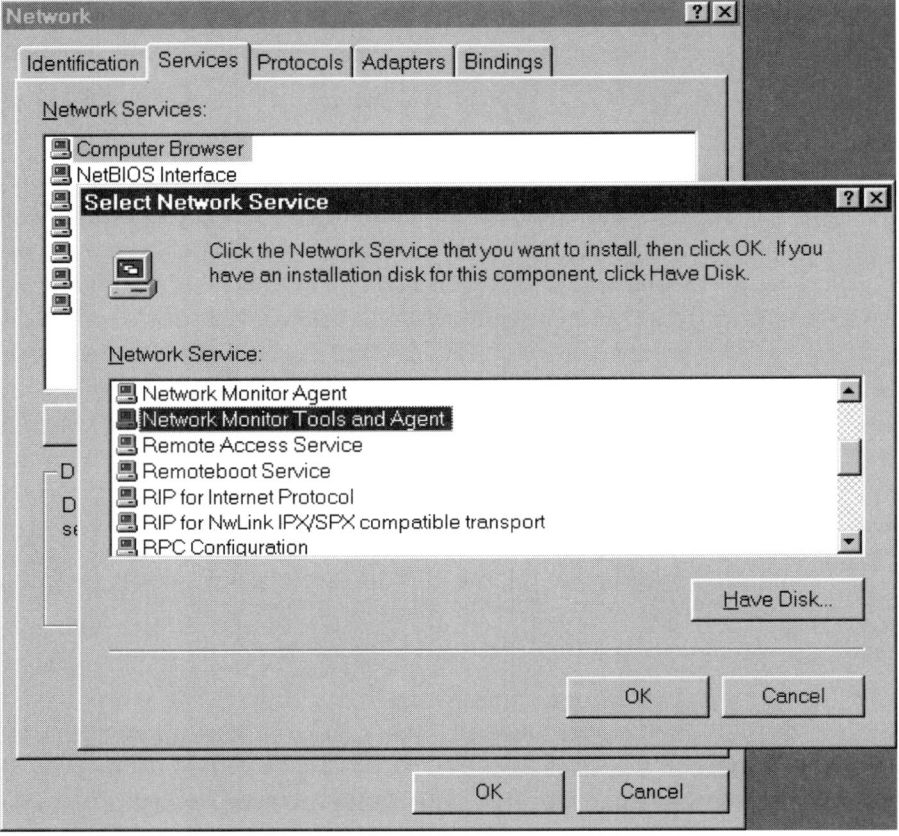

Figure 7–5   *Installing Microsoft Network Monitor on Windows NT Server 4.0.*

1. Start capturing
2. Generate network traffic to capture
3. Stop capturing
4. View captured data

STARTING A CAPTURE • To start capturing network traffic, use the **Start Capture** button on the toolbar. (You can also use the **Start** command from the **Capture** menu or press **F10.**) Captured frames are stored in the capture buffer. When the buffer overflows, new frames replace the oldest ones. You can control the buffer size with the `Buffer Settings` option in the `Capture` menu. When you are capturing the information, panes display capture statistics. The meaning of the panes is described in Table 7.3.

Table 7.3 *Microsoft Network Monitor panes: Capture view*

Pane	Displays
Graph	A graphical representation of the activity currently taking place on the network, including network utilization and broadcast level
Session Statistics	Statistics about individual sessions currently taking place on the network
Station Statistics	Statistics about the sessions in which the computer running Network Monitor participates. They include bytes and frames sent and received
Total Statistics	Summary statistics about network activity detected since the capture began

GENERATING NETWORK TRAFFIC • To generate network traffic you wish to analyze, use any network-based application such as Microsoft Internet Explorer or the PING command.

STOPPING AND VIEWING THE CAPTURED DATA • To stop the capture, use the `Stop Capture` button (see Figure 7–6), `Stop` command the `Capture` menu, or press `F11`.

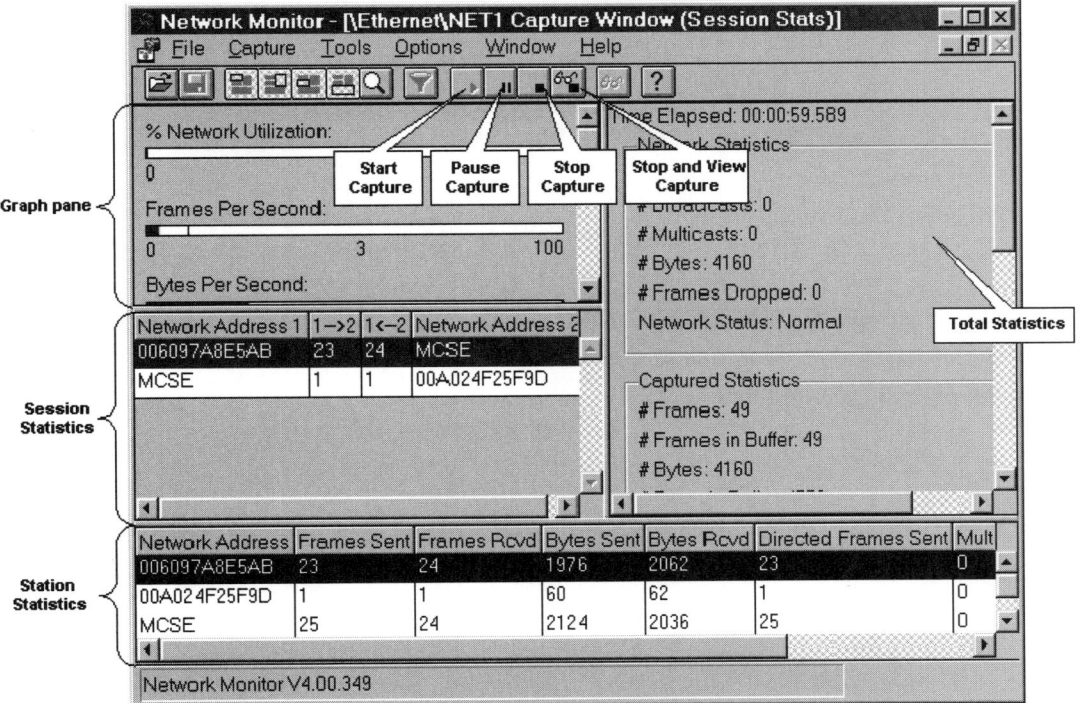

Figure 7–6 *Microsoft Network Monitor window.*

To view the captured data, use the `Stop and View` command from the `Capture` menu if you are currently capturing, or the `View` command from the `Capture` menu if the capture has already been stopped.

When opening a capture window, a `Frame Viewer` window appears. See Figure 7–7. The Frame Viewer window shows each captured frame. It contains a frame number, the time the frame was received, source and destination addresses, protocols contained in the frame, and other information. To get more detailed information about the particular frame, double click the frame.

The Frame Viewer window includes the panes listed in Table 7.4.

You can save the capture to hard disk for later analysis. To do this, choose `Save As` from the `File` menu. If the problem is beyond your capability, you can send the capture to a network analyst or support organization.

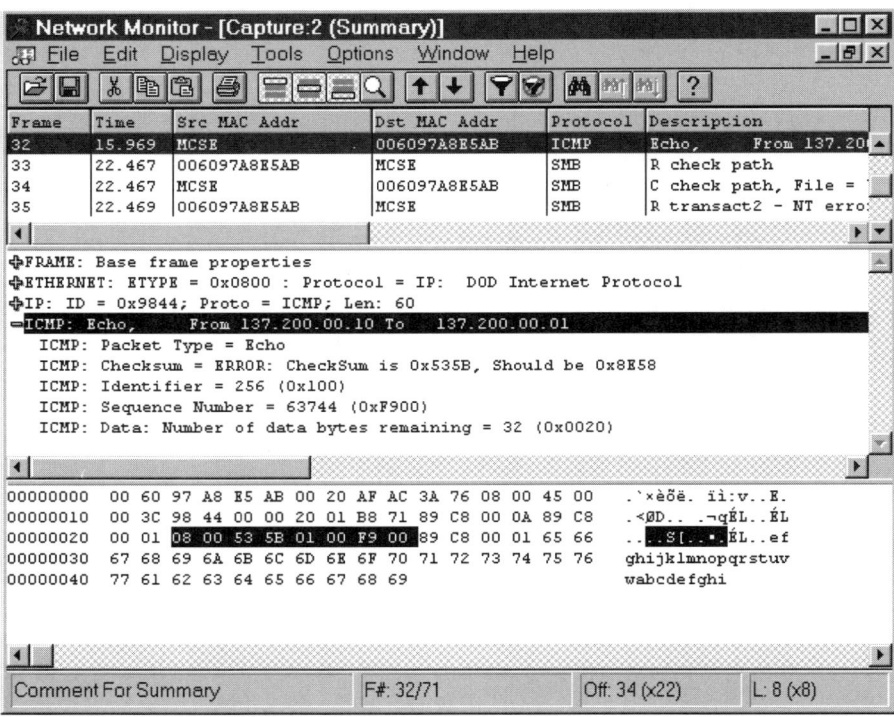

Figure 7–7 *Microsoft Network Monitor Capture view.*

Table 7.4 *Microsoft Network Monitor panes: Frame view*

Pane	Displays
Detail	The frame's contents, including the protocols used to send it
Hex	A hexadecimal and ASCII representation of the captured data
Summary	General information about captured frames in the order in which they were captured

Summary

This chapter summarized common TCP/IP-related problems. We learned quite a bit about major TCP/IP faults and methods of correcting them. You learned to troubleshoot a TCP/IP network by checking lower-level functions such as link reliability first and then progressing to IP connectivity checks and routing and name resolution tests. We discussed the typical symptoms of some TCP/IP-related problems. When you understand the symptoms, you can frequently solve network problems without even touching a machine. Finally, we introduced some powerful troubleshooting and monitoring tools: Microsoft Event Viewer and Performance Monitor, UNIX SYSLOGD and KLOGD, Microsoft Network Monitor, and the UNIX TCPDUMP program.

This chapter and Chapter 6 have provided a good overview of TCP/IP. This protocol is important to your Network+ study because it is, among other things, the "cost of admission" to the Internet. While the treatment of TCP/IP in this book is sufficient to master the Network+ course of study, it only scratches the surface of the subject. For a more in-depth look at TCP/IP, refer to the Prentice Hall MCSE Study Guide: *Internetworking with Microsoft TCP/IP on Microsoft Windows NT 4.0.* (Prentice Hall, ISBN 0-13-011251-8)

▲ REVIEW QUESTIONS

1. *You run IPCONFIG on your Windows NT Server computer and get the following output:*

```
C:\WINNT>ipconfig
Windows NT IP Configuration
Ethernet adapter Elnk31:
        IP Address. . . . . . . . . : 0.0.0.0
        Subnet Mask . . . . . . . . : 0.0.0.0
        Default Gateway . . . . . . :
```

What is the most likely cause of this?

 A. Duplicate subnet mask.

 B. TCP/IP is not installed on this computer.

 C. Default gateway is missing.

 D. This computer was unable to get the IP address from the DHCP server.

2. *Which utility is used to identify the subnet mask?*

 A. Network Monitor.

 B. IPCONFIG.

 C. PING.

 D. Event Log.

3. *Which address symbolizes the loopback address?*

 A. 127.0.0.1.

 B. 255.255.255.255.

 C. 255.255.0.0.

 D. 0.0.0.0.

 E. 176.20.0.10.

4. *Your computer is configured to use WINS, DNS, HOSTS, and LMHOSTS files for name resolution. You launch a command prompt and try to ping your neighbor's computer (located in the same subnet) by using its Net-BIOS name (PING MCTCOMP). The ping command hangs for about a minute and then gives you four successful pings. What is the most likely reason on such a delay?*

 A. DNS server is unreachable.

 B. WINS server is unreachable.

 C. The broadcast name resolution is a very slow method.

 D. PING cannot use NetBIOS names.

5. *You are the administrator of the network that is illustrated in Figure 7–8.*

 Using FTP client software, your workstation cannot connect to the FTP server in the remote subnet. You can, however, connect to the FTP server by using Windows NT Explorer. What is the most likely reason for this behavior?

 A. The computer running FTP server is down.

 B. Your workstation does not have the default gateway.

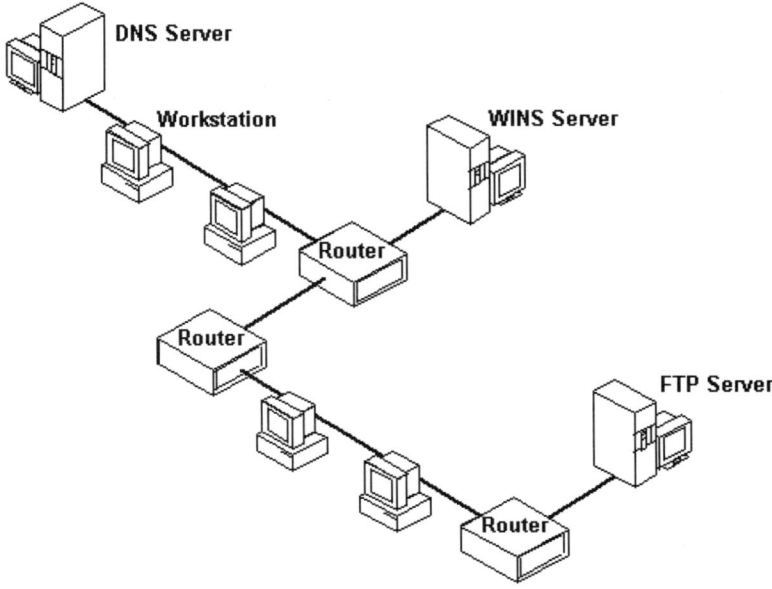

Figure 7–8 *Network example.*

    C. Your workstation is not configured to use DNS.

    D. Your workstation has a duplicate IP address.

6. *You can successfully ping all workstations in your subnet and most remote subnets in your Intranet. You cannot, however, ping all remote subnets in your Intranet. All other computers are able to ping each other. What is the most likely reason for this problem?*

    A. You computer has an invalid subnet mask.

    B. You computer has a duplicate IP address.

    C. The router is down.

    D. Your computer is not using WINS.

7. *Which utility would you use to check how your computer registers its Net-BIOS name?*

    A. NBTSTAT.

    B. NETSTAT.

    C. NSLOOKUP.

    D. IPCONFIG.

8. *You use Microsoft Network Monitor and you discover that your computer sends an ARP request for the default gateway address every time it attempts to contact another machine. What could be the problem?*

    A. Your workstation is not TCP/IP enabled.

    B. Your workstation does not use DNS.

    C. Your workstation has an invalid subnet mask.

    D. There is no problem, this is normal.

9. *Your computer has an invalid subnet mask. Which statement(s) is (are) true?*

    A. Your computer cannot communicate with all other computers.

    B. Your computer can only communicate with remote computers.

    C. Your computer can only communicate with local computers.

    D. Your computer possibly cannot communicate with some or all computers.

10. *You try to map a network drive to the computer named RED, that is located on the remote subnet, but you fail. Your computer is not WINS enabled, but it uses an LMHOSTS file. You check the TCP/IP configuration and discover that your computer has received valid TCP/IP parameters from the DHCP server. What should you check next?*

    A. Check that the DHCP server is turned on and functional.

    B. Check that an entry for computer RED is present and has the correct mapping in the LMHOSTS file.

    C. Check that your computer is NOT using broadcasts for name resolution.

    D. Check if computer RED is WINS enabled.

11. *A user is complaining that she is not able to connect to the corporate file server with Windows NT Explorer. From her computer you check that you are able to ping the corporate file server's IP address. What else should you check? (Select all that apply)*

    A. Check that the route to the corporate file server is configured.

    B. Check that the user's computer is configured to use WINS.

    C. Check that the user's computer has a valid LMHOSTS file.

    D. Check that the user's computer has a valid subnet mask.

12. *You are the administrator of the network shown in Figure 7–9. You are sitting at the computer named WKS1. You are able to access all computers in your Intranet, but you are not able to access server RED. What is the most likely reason for this?*

    A. DHCP Server is in another network segment.

    B. WINS Server is in another network segment.

    C. No route is configured to the subnet with server RED.

    D. File LMHOSTS is corrupted.

13. *You can successfully ping Mary's computer; but when you use the **net use** command to connect to it, you fail. You check that you are able to FTP her computer by name. What should you check next? (Select all that apply)*

    A. Check that Mary's computer is NetBIOS enabled.

    B. Check that your computer uses DNS.

    C. Check that both computers are using the same scope ID.

    D. Check that the link between these two computers is not broken.

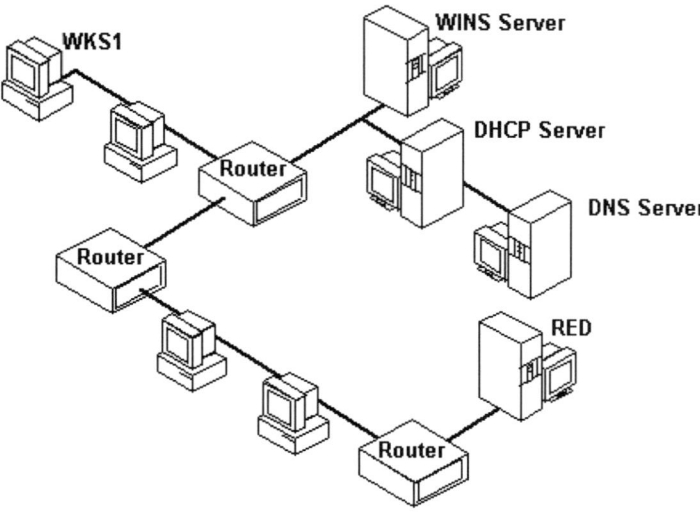

Figure 7–9 *Network example.*

14. *You suspect that your computer has a duplicate IP address. Which utility can you use to check it?*

    A. Network Monitor

    B. Performance Monitor

    C. Event Viewer

    D. Server Manager

15. *When you type the command, net use z: \\SRV\Public on your Windows NT computer, you connect to computer named SRV. But when you use FTP SRV, you connect to computer named RED. What is the most likely reason for this problem?*

    A. LMHOSTS file is missing.

    B. HOSTS file has an invalid entry.

    C. LMHOSTS file has duplicate entries.

    D. Server SRV is not a WINS client.

16. *Sandy's TCP/IP network has grown significantly in recent months, and the job of managing the TCP/IP configuration on all the network computers has taken valuable time from her other network management duties. What should Sandy install to reduce her workload?*

    A. Netmon.

    B. DHCP.

    C. SNMP.

    D. WINS.

    E. A Default Gateway.

Remote Connectivity

▲ Chapter Syllabus

Hardware and Software

Media

Protocols

Most of us have become so dependant on not only our computers but on our computer networks, that we couldn't imagine going "on the road" without taking our network connectivity with us. The need to check e-mail or have access to server based files drives us to find ways to stay "close" to the network. Since carrying miles of UTP in our suitcase would seem a bit impractical, we will explore the factors involved with remote connectivity.

After completing this chapter you will be able to do the following:

- List hardware and software requirements for remote connectivity
- Explain how to install and configure a modem
- Describe the telephone-based connectivity systems: public switched telephone network (PSTN) and integrated services digital network (ISDN)

- Explain the difference between the point-to-point protocol (PPP) and serial line Internet protocol (SLIP)
- Discuss the purpose and operation of the point-to-point tunneling protocol (PPTP)

Remote connectivity requires the use of the appropriate hardware and software: typically modems, dial-in terminal, or remote server software; a connectivity medium, usually a telephone line; and a protocol to get our communication over the line. As we are about to see, remote networking is analogous to networking in the LAN. Remote connectivity software functions in a fashion similar to the LAN's servers and redirectors. The telephone company provides the physical medium as a counterpart to the UTP, switches, and hubs we studied earlier. Finally, SLIP and PPP function in a manner akin to the LAN's Ethernet and token ring protocols.

Hardware and Software

First and foremost, to be able to engage in any sort of remote access, our computers must be running the appropriate software and be equipped with the right hardware to connect to the remote line.

Remote access software includes a host of terminal and modem programs as well as remote server software. The *Dial-Up Networking* software that comes with Microsoft Windows operating systems, for instance, allows you to connect to remote networks through a modem or ISDN adapter and provides support for both SLIP and PPP. The Windows NT *Remote Access Server* and *Routing and Remote Access Server* software will allow a Windows NT computer to act as a gateway between a network and a remote machine or even an entire remote network. The Novell *NetWare Connect* package provides a similar capability through a NetWare server.

The most common remote access hardware is the modem. A modem is simply a device that converts the computer's logical output (ones and zeroes) to an analog signal (typically, audio tones) that can be sent across a telephone connection. The term "modem," in fact, is a combination of the terms MOdulate and DEModulate, to indicate a device that is capable of modulating digital signals to transmit and demodulating analog signals to receive. This process of modulating and demodulating digital signals is slower than transmitting pure digital signals but it does result in a reliable means of communicating over long distances at a relatively low cost.

Modem Types

Modems are available in either the synchronous or asynchronous variety. Because of its simplicity and relatively low cost, asynchronous modems are the most common today, but their synchronous counterparts offer much better performance. You will find, for instance, relatively inexpensive multi-port asynchronous modems such as *Digiboards, Chiliports,* and *SHIVA Lan Rovers* at Internet service providers. More expensive synchronous modems, such as the *AT&T Paradigm 3160/3610 Channel Bank,* on the other hand, would be found on both sides of a high-speed communications link such as T-1/T-3. You may want to refer to Figure 8.1 during the following discussion to help you to better visualize the two types of modem communication.

Asynchronous Modems

As its name implies, asynchronous communications requires no synchronization between the sending and receiving computers. Because of this, the transmission must have something to divide up the communication so it makes sense. In written communication, we use spaces to mark the beginning and ending of words. If I were to write "Thequickbrownfoxjumpedoverthelazydog," you would have a hard time making sense out of it. If, on the other hand, I introduce some spaces to help you determine where the words start and stop, you can see that I wrote "The quick brown fox jumped over the lazy dog." In a similar manner, asynchronous communications make use of *Start* and *Stop* bits to signal the start and end of each transmitted byte.

While this method is a fairly simple and inexpensive way to transmit data, you can see that each 8-bit byte is accompanied by two additional bits to show where it stops and starts. This means that in asynchronous communication, 25% of the transmitted data is overhead and conveys no information. As we will see a little later in this chapter, stop bits may actually take up to two bits worth of space, increasing the overhead to almost 40%. Asynchronous communications can transmit data over normal telephone lines at up to 28,800 bps and, with the compression techniques we will discuss a little later, this can be boosted, theoretically, to as fast as 115,200 bps.

Synchronous Modems

Synchronous modems were developed to make better use of the transmitted data by eliminating the start and stop bits. To accomplish this, it is necessary to synchronize both the sending and receiving modem. Because each modem knows the exact time, relative to the other modem, start and stop bits are not required. Instead of looking for a bit to signal the start of a byte, the receiving modem simply checks its time base and recognizes the start of the byte based on the time its first bit is received. To keep the modems synchronized, the data transmission may imbed periodic synchronization pulses as depicted in Figure 8–1, or synchronization may be accomplished through an additional connection.

The extra equipment required to keep the modems synchronized increases the cost and level of complexity associated with synchronous modems. Although not typically used in the home market or by laptop carriers calling their office networks from their hotels, synchronous communication is found in most digital and network communications.

Modem Installation and Configuration

In today's plug-and-play computing environment, modem installation and configuration is frequently automated to the point that the only installation required is to connect the modem and click on the appropriate icon. Still, there are some configuration parameters you should know to permit you to optimize and troubleshoot your modem.

Serial Ports, IRQs, and I/O Addresses

Perhaps the most critical modem configuration is to ensure the modem is properly connected both physically and logically to the computer. To do this, you will need to be aware of the appropriate serial port, IRQ, and I/O

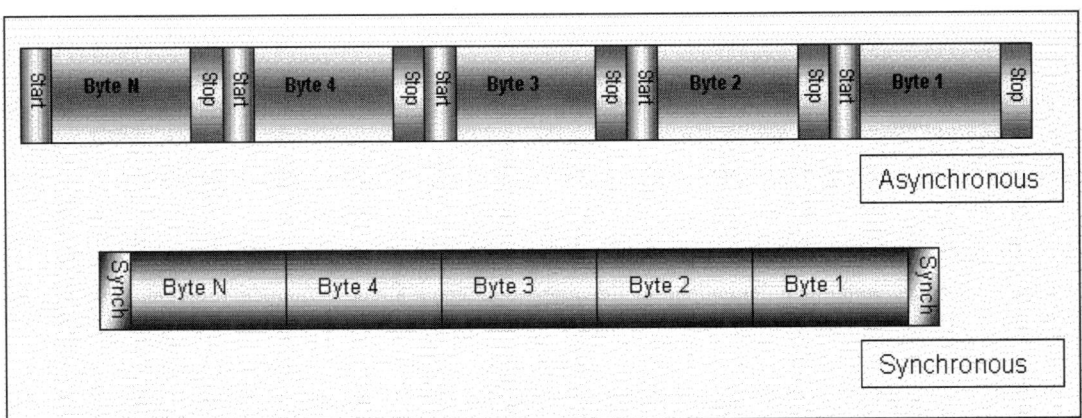

Figure 8–1 *Synchronous and asynchronous modem communication.*

address for the device. When configuring an external modem, this step is typically quite easy. You simply plug the modem into an available serial port (COM1 or COM2) and ensure the installed modem software knows to which physical port the device is connected (it may be able to figure this out on its own).

When using an *internal* modem, the operation becomes a bit more challenging. While a computer can have two *physical* serial ports, it can have a total of *four* logical serial ports (COM1, COM2, COM3, and COM4). When installing an internal modem, you will need to determine a *virtual* serial port through which the modem will function. To select the appropriate virtual port, you must first determine which serial ports are available. If, for instance, COM1 is in use to support a serial mouse and you assign COM1 to the modem, it is likely that neither device will operate. When selecting a port, you must pay attention to the port's associated parameters. Be mindful of the assigned interrupt request query line (IRQ) and Base I/O port address. The IRQ represents the hardware line through which the modem will send requests for service to the CPU, and the Base I/O port address specifies the channel used by the device to exchange information with the CPU. It is vital that these parameters be unique for each connected device. If you look at the default values shown in Table 8.1, you will notice that COM1 and COM3 share an IRQ, as do COM2 and COM4. When you select your virtual port, you need to ensure that both the port and IRQ are available for use. If, for instance, you have a serial mouse plugged into COM1, you might wish to use the COM2 or COM4 virtual port. This is because COM3 shares an IRQ with COM1.

Port parameters are typically configured on the modem through DIP switches or jumpers or through a software interface. In the latter case, and if your operating system supports it, you may be able to change the IRQ and I/O port settings from those defined as defaults. This could permit you to use all of your COM ports. Exercise great caution when doing this, however. Setting your modem to use an IRQ or I/O address currently in use by another device may render both devices inoperative or result in erratic operation.

Table 8.1 *Default values for serial ports*

Port	Base I/O Address	IRQ
COM1	3F8	4
COM2	2F8	3
COM3	3E8	4
COM4	2E8	3

S-Registers

Now that our modem is properly connected to, and interfaced with, the computer, let us discuss how the modem itself is programmed to function. Most modems (those known as *Hayes compatible*) know how to perform based on information stored in their *S-Registers*. S-Registers are memory locations (*registers*) in the modem that contain parameters to govern their operation. In most Hayes-compatible modems, register S0, for instance, governs whether the modem will automatically answer a call, S6 determines how long a modem will wait to detect a carrier signal, and S10 determines how long the modem will wait to hang up after it loses the carrier signal. There are, of course, many more register settings. Most settings are dependent on the capabilities of a particular modem and many have been expanded by manufacturers to make their products more flexible and robust.

AT Command

How do you suppose the values get into the S-Registers? If you are thinking there must be factory set defaults, you're right; but these values are also user settable. The command used to perform modem configuration or to get the modem to perform a function is the AT (*Attention*) command. In most of the applications we deal with today, AT commands are issued for us by the software. If you have communications software that allows you to set it to a *command mode* (a mode where the software lets you communicate directly with the modem), you may issue your own AT commands.

AT commands are used for telling the modem to dial a number, hang up, set an S-Register, and to perform many other functions. ATD 555–1234, for instance would tell the modem to dial the number 555–1234. To this you could add a 'T' for tone dialing or a 'P' for pulse dialing. ATDT 555–1234, will call the same number but will also ensure the modem uses tone dialing. ATH tells the modem to hang up.

To use the AT command to set an S-Register, use the syntax ATSr = n where *r* represents the number of the S-Register and *n* the value you wish to set. The command ATS0=3, for instance, tells the modem to automatically answer on the third ring while ATS0=0 would disable the auto-answer feature. If you wish to return your modem to its factory defaults, use the syntax AT&Fn where *n* represents the number of the factory default set. Factory default sets vary with modem and manufacturer so you will need to consult your modem documentation for the appropriate number to enter here.

Modem Transmission Rates

How fast your modem will transmit and receive is likely something of concern to you. If you wish to "feel" like part of the network, you will want a fast and reliable modem connection. Notwithstanding the speed of the line itself, modem speed is based on how fast the data can get from the computer to the modem through the serial port (maximum port speed), and how fast the modem can transmit the data (modem speed).

Maximum Port Speed

The port speed is governed by a chip called a universal asynchronous receiver-transmitter (UART). Internal modems contain their own high speed UART which is compatible with the modem, so there is no need to consider port speed in their case. For an external modem connected to the computer's serial port, however, the UART can have a significant impact.

There are currently two varieties of UART chip: 8250 and 16550 series. The 8250 chip is an 8-bit chip typically found on PCs built prior to the IBM AT (circa 1986). This chip will deliver a maximum of 9,600bps—obviously buying a 56k modem to operate on such a port would be a waste of money! The 16550 series chips are 16-bit devices and can support a port speed of 115,200bps.

Modem Speed

In the early days of modems when a transmission rate of 300 bits per second was considered blisteringly fast, modem speeds were rated in *baud*. The term baud is in honor of Jean Maurice Emile Baudot, a French signal corps officer and refers to the oscillation of the sound wave that carries the data bit over the telephone lines. Without data compression, 300 baud would represent 300 bits per second.

Modern modems employ data compression techniques, which means they may be rated at a higher rate of bits per second (bps) than their baud rate. Because of this, baud is rarely used when referring to today's modems. Specifications for modem speeds were developed by the International Telecommunications Union in the late 1980s. Because they are identified by a 'V' in their designation, they are sometimes known as *V Series* standards. Some of the standards contain the words *bis* or *terbo*. These French words mean second and third respectively and indicate a second or third version of a particular standard. Table 8.2 shows some of today's V Series standards.

Table 8.2 *V Series standards*

Standard	bps
V.22bis	2,400
V.32	9,600
V.32bis	14,400
V.32terbo	19,200
V.34	28,800
V.42	57,600
V.90	57,600

Study Break

Asymmetric Data Rates

If V.90 can achieve a 56 Kbps data rate, I can get a 56k connection between two computers using V.90 modems, right?

Unfortunately, this isn't true, because the V.90 standard (just as the proprietary K56Flex and X2 standards before it) calls for an *asymmetric data rate*. The standard assumes that one end of the session (the one going through the service provider) is a pure digital connection. The link *to* your modem is then digitally encoded to provide the higher speed. The upstream data (sent *from* your modem) is still analog data, sent at the slower conventional rate which is closer to the V.34 standard. This, of course, works well for Internet surfing since we are interested in downloading large amounts of data (graphics, audio, video, etc.) *from* the Web but, typically, send only a few mouse clicks *to* the Web.

Modem Connection Requirements

Now that our modem is properly installed and configured, is it ready to connect to another modem at the other end of the phone line? Maybe. It is important to ensure our modem and the one on the other end are speaking the same language at the right speed. We need to concern ourselves with the *transmission rate*, number of *data bits*, *parity*, and number of *stop bits* the modem is configured to use.

Modem Speed

Fortunately, most of today's modems are capable of multiple transmission speeds and will be able to automatically detect the calling speed and adjust to it (if the modem is capable of that transmission speed). Modems are frequently able to negotiate a data transfer rate based on the fastest speed available to both devices. Some older modems are not quite so agile. In the early days of computing, the modem at the other end of the line was expecting to operate at one particular rate and you had to configure your modem to operate at the same rate or no communication would take place. If you are working with older equipment, ensure both devices are set to the same transmission rate.

Stop Bits

As we saw earlier in the chapter, when we use an asynchronous modem, there needs to be a signal to indicate the start and end of the transmitted byte. Although these signals are called *start* and *stop bits*, they are not really bits in the sense that they are part of the transmitted byte. The start and stop bits do, however, consume a measure of transmission time proportional to that of a transmitted bit. While the start bit always consumes exactly one bit time, stop bits may consume one, one-and-a-half, or two bit times. Settings for stop bits are, therefore, 1, 1½, or 2, and must be consistent on each modem that will participate in the communication.

Parity and Data Bits

Parity is a method of determining if errors exist in the transmission. If parity is used, there will be only seven *data bits;* with no parity we have eight *data bits*. (Although it *is* possible to configure the modems to use no parity and only seven data bits and have everything work properly, doing so would unnecessarily limit the amount and type of data you could transmit.)

When parity is used, the eighth bit is set to make the total number of ones in the byte either odd or even. When *odd parity* is set, if there are an even number of ones among the seven data bits, the parity bit will be a one to make the total number of ones odd. If, on the other hand, there are already an odd number of ones, the parity bit will be zero. This, of course, works just the opposite for *even parity*. You may also set *mark parity*, where the parity bit is always set to one, or *space parity*, where the parity bit is always set to zero. This latter method will only detect data corruption when the parity bit itself is corrupted and may not be as effective as odd or even parity. Regardless of the parity method or number of data bits used, it is critical that both modems used in the communication be configured to the same values.

As with data transmission rate, many of today's modems and communication software packages are able to automatically detect the values for data bits, stop bits, and parity and configure themselves accordingly. Still, it is important to understand how these parameters work, because reviewing the modem's communication settings can be an important troubleshooting step when you find your modems won't talk to each other.

Media

Now that your modem is installed and configured, you will need to find something that will connect it with the outside world. Most of us start looking for a telephone line whenever we see a modem so we will devote most of this discussion to how the telephone company can support our remote computer needs.

Public-Switched Telephone Network

When you pick up the telephone or plug your computer into the telephone jack in your house, you are using the public switched telephone network (PSTN). Also known as the *plain old telephone system* (POTS), PSTN is the most widely used remote access medium today.

When considering PSTN, it is important to understand the meaning of *public* and *switched*. The first term seems pretty obvious but it is related to the main advantage of PSTN as a remote-computing medium. Because this is a public service, for the cost of admission to the telephone network, anyone can use the service from anywhere they can find a telephone jack. There is no need to run cables or lease permanent lines. If you don't know at breakfast where you will be at lunch, you can still be fairly sure you will find PSTN access there and will, therefore, be able to access your network.

The second term, *switched*, is a bit less obvious but still an important factor in remote computing. When you called Aunt Edna in Chicago at Christmas, and then again on her birthday, the only piece of telephone wire you can be absolutely sure you used both times is the run between your house and the "switch" at the local telephone company. Much like a router, a telephone switch connects your telephones through other switches to the telephone you are trying to call. There may be multiple lines to reach the same destination or calls may be routed to the same destination through different switches, depending on the load on a particular network segment. When you called Aunt Edna on Christmas, the lines were fairly busy and your call may have been routed from Boston, through Atlanta and Dallas to Chicago. Once you made it through all those switches, you essentially set up a "session" with Aunt Edna's telephone and you "owned" the lines until you terminated the session by hanging up. When you made the call on Edna's birthday, traffic was quite a bit lighter and your call went more directly through New York and Cleveland. You may remember that the first time you tried to call on Christmas, you got a message that "all circuits are busy." This is another feature of the *switched* network. If everyone who owns a telephone wants to make a call at the same time, we quickly discover there aren't enough lines to go around.

Switched, therefore, does two things to us: 1) Our calls may travel a different path each time we dial, and 2) we may not always be able to get through. The impact of the second is fairly obvious, but why should we care about the route our calls take? The answer is *speed and reliability*. Remember, the PSTN was not originally designed to permit computers to talk to each other. Lines designed for voice communication will, at best, support 64k bps, and that feat is rarely achieved. The transmission speed is dependent on many factors, such as line quality, distance to the local switch, and the condition of the switching equipment. When your computer connection is routed through good switches that are connected by fairly new, robust telephone lines you will likely be able to approach the upper bandwidth limit for voice lines—in fact, your 56k modem may actually get a connection close to its capabilities! If you had tried to connect to a computer at Aunt Edna's on Christmas, you may have discovered that your call was routed through *Hooterville*, between Atlanta and Dallas. Since the Hooterville switch was installed in 1952, you find the best connection you can obtain is 9,600!

Note Current Federal Communications Commission rulings on maximum permissible transmit power levels limit actual transmission speeds to 54 Kbps or less.

The public switched telephone network can be a very practical and convenient medium for computer communications. The advantages of PSTN are as follows:

- Inexpensive—setup costs only as much as it costs for a telephone connection; can use asynchronous modems.
- No special cabling required.
- Connections available almost anywhere in the world.

PSTN, in fact, has few disadvantages:

- Limited bandwidth—64k maximum and only when switched route will support it.
- May not be available during periods of high traffic.

Integrated Services Digital Network

Let us say that you just can't live with the relatively low bandwidth of PSTN and want to ensure you have a communication line available 100% of the time. A *relatively* inexpensive alternative to PSTN is the *integrated services digital network* (ISDN). ISDN is a *digital* service available from the same company that brings you POTS. Although ISDN uses copper wire, just like PSTN, the lines are capable of high bandwidth digital transmission. Most major telephone switches in the United States and many switches worldwide are already connected by digital-quality lines. In fact, the only non-digital link is most likely the line that runs from your home or office to the local telephone switch. Assuming the local switch is ISDN capable, your ISDN access can start as soon as the telephone company can provide you with a digital-quality line to the switch. (Typically, the telephone company will perform a "line qualification" on your current line to determine if it is, in fact, ISDN-capable.) If your local switch does not support ISDN, the telephone company may be able to provide a line extension to the nearest ISDN-capable switch (which will likely raise the rate you will pay for ISDN). The advertised maximum distance between your computer and the servicing switch is 18,000 feet. Many telephone companies offer a service called *ISDN Anywhere*, which means they will try to find a way to get you the connection if you are outside this distance. Although its availability continues to grow, ease of access to IDSN varies by location.

To use the ISDN connection, your computer will need to be equipped with an ISDN adapter. (ISDN adapters are sometimes referred to as ISDN *modems*. This term is inaccurate. Since ISDN is a digital service, neither modulation nor demodulation takes place within the ISDN adapter.)

ISDN can provide up to 23 64Kbps B channels and one 64Kbps D channel. The B channels are also known as *bearer* channels. It is these channels that are designated to carry the information, which can be voice, data, or imaging. Each B channel can carry its own session. It is possible, for instance, to make a voice call on one channel while simultaneously transferring data on one or more additional channels. The D channel (sometimes called the *delta* channel) is used for call setup and link management, although it can also be used for data. The ISDN B channels can be combined to increase the bandwidth.

The ISDN service we described previously is known as *primary rate* ISDN. You are not likely to need the entire available bandwidth. Fortunately ISDN is also available in a smaller measure. Basic rate ISDN consists of two 64Kbps B channels and a single 16Kbps D channel. Also referred to as 2B+D, basic rate ISDN can provide a reliable 128K (by combining the B channels) connection.

Although we indicated that ISDN was *relatively* inexpensive, its price tag does exceed that of PSTN. Since the tariff varies by state and telephone carrier, rates can vary widely. ISDN charges typically include the cost of installation, a monthly fee, and a per-minute usage charge. When considering ISDN, don't forget to include the cost of the ISDN adapter.

Like PSTN, ISDN is a dial-up service—it is not a dedicated line, designed for 24-hour operation. It is a good *digital* alternative to PSTN. Connections through ISDN are typically faster, but special equipment is required at the computer and at the phone company. When determining whether to upgrade to ISDN, consider the following advantages and disadvantages. ISDN advantages are as follows:

- Conversion from analog to digital not required—speeds throughput
- Better bandwidth than PSTN—can combine D channels to increase beyond 64k
- Reliable digital service—advertised bandwidth is what you get
- Fast connection speeds

    ISDN disadvantages are as follows:

- More costly than PSTN
- Requires special adapters
- Not available in all areas

Other Connection Options

Although we have spent a great deal of time detailing PSTN and ISDN, there are other options you may wish to consider for remote computing. The X.25 *packet switching network* has been available for many years. X.25 has used standard telephone lines as well as dedicated data lines to provide routed networks for data transmission. Computers accessing X.25 service must do so through a device known as an X.25 Packet Assembler/Disassembler (PAD). Today's X.25 networks can provide bandwidth of up to 56k (64k in Europe). Microsoft recommends the use of ISDN, where available, over X.25 because ISDN can provide greater bandwidth at higher reliability.

Other services include T-1, T-3, and frame relay. T-1 offers a bandwidth of 1.544Mbps (about the same as primary rate ISDN), while the T-3 bandwidth is 45 Mbps. Like ISDN, both of these services can be separated into channels of lower bandwidth. Like X.25, frame relay is a packet-switching network. Advances in cabling and network equipment permit frame relay to provide bandwidths from 56k to 1.544Mbps. Frame relay bandwidth may be purchased in 64k blocks. (T-1/T-3, frame relay, and other WAN network services are discussed in greater detail in Chapter 5.)

Protocols

Now that we have our modem installed and have selected the appropriate connectivity method, we will still be unable to communicate over the network without a protocol to get us through the wire. Remote access protocols are analogous to LAN protocols (e.g., Ethernet) in that they govern the transmission of information over the wire. Unlike LAN protocols, however, remote access protocols are designed to support one or more transport protocols (e.g., TCP/IP or IPX/SPX) over the WAN link to a remote access gateway (e.g., Microsoft *Remote Access Server* or Novell *NetWare Connect*). The gateway accepts the information and places it on the LAN (under the LAN protocol and the supported transport protocol). We will discuss the two major remote access protocols, *serial line Internet protocol* and *point-to-point protocol*, as well as the *point-to-point tunneling protocol*—an option that can provide a *virtual private network* (VPN) over the Internet.

Serial Line Internet Protocol

The serial line Internet protocol (SLIP) is an industry standard that dates back to 1984. SLIP was originally developed by students at the University of California, Berkeley, as a protocol for transmitting TCP/IP packets between UNIX computers over serial lines (e.g., PSTN). SLIP is a small, efficient protocol; but it offers no advanced features such as error checking or data compression (there is a separate version of the protocol called CSLIP that does provide some compression[1]). SLIP supports only TCP/IP and cannot make automatic connections to the receiving host. SLIP network connections are typically automated by running a logon script once the client has accessed the remote server. (Without a script the only option is to open a terminal window and perform the logon manually.) Limitations in the protocol prevent the use of encrypted authentication—all logons are conducted using clear text, a very insecure practice.

In addition to its other limitations, SLIP will not permit the client to receive any automatic protocol configuration information from the remote

---

[1]CSLIP utilizes VanJacobsen compression. In some Microsoft implementations of SLIP, CSLIP is invoked through the VJ compression check box. For this to work properly, both sides of the communication must select compression.

server. Figure 8–2 shows the SLIP TCP/IP settings dialog from the Windows NT Dial Up Networking feature. You will notice there are no options for automatic configuration of IP address or DNS or WINS addresses. This information must be entered prior to attempting to access the server. The IP address and other information selected must be consistent with the LAN being accessed through SLIP. If an IP address that won't work on the LAN is used, communication will likely be impossible. This is a serious limitation in remote access, because it means every remote called must be assigned a valid IP address whether they will use the network continuously or will only dial in periodically. There is rarely an excess of IP addresses in modern networks, and this requirement can put an even greater constraint on that commodity.

Point-to-Point Protocol

The point-to-point protocol (PPP) provides all the support found lacking under SLIP. Not constrained to serial lines like SLIP, PPP operates over a variety of media and can support a number of transport protocols. PPP-supported protocols include AppleTalk, DECnet, NetBEUI, TCP/IP, and IPX.

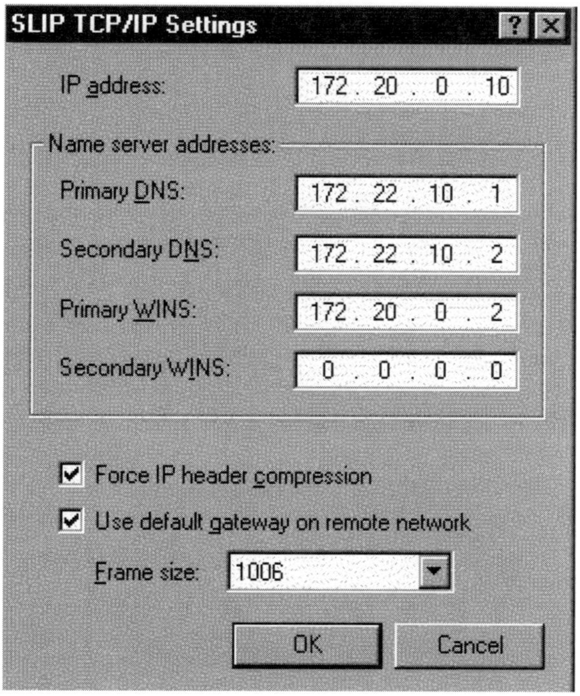

Figure 8–2 *SLIP TCP/IP settings (Windows NT Dial Up Networking).*

PPP uses the link control protocol (LCP) to manage and monitor the connection. LCP provides error checking and automatic configuration support between the client and server. PPP permits automated connection (no need to use a script) and encrypted authentication and features very sophisticated data compression.

Automatic protocol configuration can solve many of the problems associated with SLIP. Figure 8–3 shows the PPP TCP/IP settings dialog from the Windows NT Dial Up Networking feature. Notice that the dialog permits entry of specific information or allows it to be assigned by the server. The server may assign an IP address from a given pool of addresses or may use a DHCP server to provide the information.

The only down side to PPP is that it is more complex and larger than SLIP, and not all platforms and applications are designed to support it. (Of course,

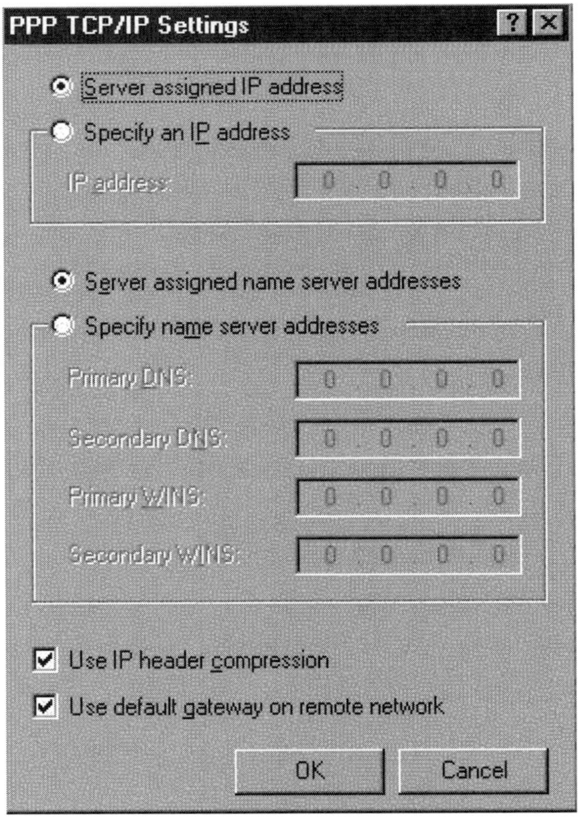

Figure 8.3 *PPP TCP/IP Settings (Windows NT Dial Up Networking).*

many of the newer applications, such as the server side of the Windows NT Remote Access Server package, support only PPP.) PPP is a recommended standard of the Internet Advisory Board (IAB). It is also detailed in a number of RFCs from the point-to-point protocol working group. When you make a connection through the Microsoft Network, CompuServe, America Online, or Prodigy, you are using PPP and likely receive your IP address from one of their DHCP servers.

Point-to-Point Tunneling Protocol

Today, many companies utilize the Internet not only for the purpose of gaining access to the information it contains, but also to provide network connections to employees who are out of the office or on the road. It has always been the case that utilizing the public Internet is a much cheaper form of connecting remote locations than using dedicated direct links or long distance telephone lines. However, there have always been concerns about transferring confidential or secret information though the public Internet. The solution to this problem is to create a virtual private network (VPN) based on encrypted tunnels provided by the point-to-point tunneling protocol (PPTP). PPTP is a network protocol that provides a secure way to transfer data from a remote client to a private server or network across TCP/IP-based data networks.

The idea behind PPTP is based on the encapsulation and encryption of IP packets into a secured tunnel. A tunnel is nothing more that a process of sending streams of encapsulated packets in secured envelopes that cannot easily be decrypted. Even if somebody captures such an envelope during its travel through the Internet, its contents will not make sense.

The networking technology of PPTP was created as an extension of the point-to-point protocol. While PPTP encapsulates PPP packets into IP datagrams for transmission over the Internet or other public TCP/IP-based networks, it can also be used in private LAN-to-LAN networking. The PPTP encapsulation technique is based on the Internet standard generic routing encapsulation (GRE) which allows tunneling of protocols over the Internet.

A typical PPTP scenario assumes the remote client already has an Internet connection from its local Internet service provider (ISP). Once connected to the Internet, the client makes a second dial-up networking call over the same Internet connection. Data sent using this second connection is in the form of IP datagrams that contain PPP packets. This second call actually creates a VPN connection to a PPTP server on the private enterprise LAN—this VPN connection is referred to as a *tunnel*.

Let us see how the PPTP client creates a packet to send to the PPTP server. For the purpose of our discussion, let's assume that the PPTP client is connected to the Internet using a LAN adapter.

The process of encapsulating the data in the PPTP datagrams is illustrated in Figure 8–4.

As you can see, when the application on the PPTP client computer sends a packet to the PPTP server, the data is first encapsulated in the IP datagram using the private IP address—the one that was assigned when the PPTP connection was established. The IP packet then gets encapsulated into the PPP packet and is encrypted through the PPTP and GRE modules. Next, the encrypted data is again inserted into the IP datagram—in this case, the real, globally routable, IP address. The packet is then transmitted over the Internet. On the receiving end, the PPTP server reverses the procedure. It receives the packet from the routing network and sends it across the private network to the destination computer. The PPTP server does this by processing the PPTP packet to obtain the private network computer name or address information in the encapsulated PPP packet.

The key point of this is that packets travel through the Internet in the PPTP tunnel. Even if a third party computer in the Internet captures the packet, it will not be able to use the data inside it. Through PPTP, you can create a virtual private network (VPN) over the Internet. The resulting secure connection will provide an excellent private communications path at a fraction of the cost of other secure options.

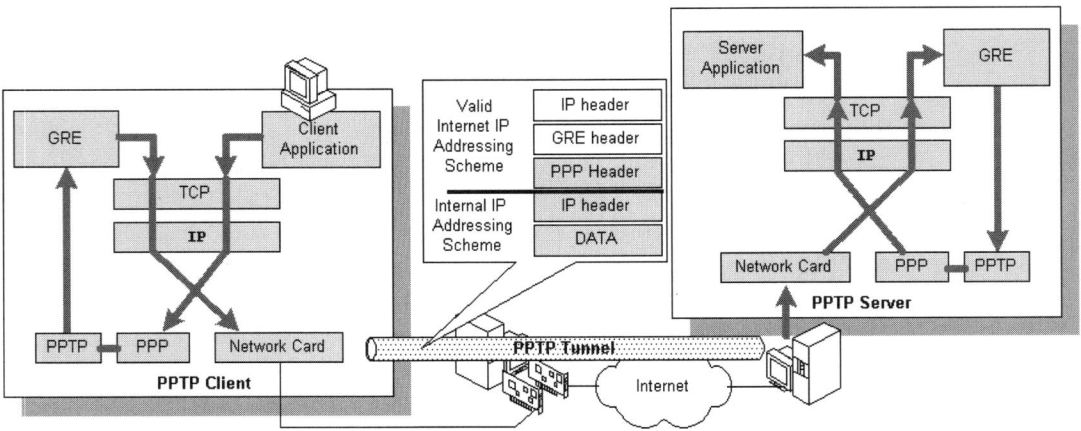

Figure 8–4 *PPTP concepts.*

Summary

This chapter provided an end-to-end overview of remote networking. Remote networking allows a user to connect to a network over a wide area network link and participate in network activities much as if he/she were directly connected to the LAN.

We first reviewed the hardware and software required to make the remote connection. Software such as Microsoft's Dial-Up Networking and Remote Access Server or Novell's NetWare Connect could get us on line, but we found a modem might be helpful in accessing the WAN. We saw that modems simply convert our digital signals to analog signals that can be transmitted over telephone lines. We looked at asynchronous modems which transmit start and stop signals to delimit transmitted words and synchronous modems which didn't need start and stop signals since both the sending and receiving modems were time synchronized. While the asynchronous modems were less complex, less expensive, and easier to use than their synchronous counterparts, the start and stop signals took up 25 to 40% of the transmitted information.

We looked at a number of factors concerning modem installation and configuration. When installing a modem, it is important to pay attention to the serial port, IRQ, and I/O addresses used. When using an external modem, these values may be preordained by the serial port to which the modem is connected. When using an internal modem, you must ensure the information is properly set. (Pay particular attention to the IRQ and serial ports selected since COM1 shares an IRQ with COM3 and COM2 shares an IRQ with COM4.)

We saw that the modem itself can be programmed to function in a particular way by setting values in the modem's S-Registers and that S-Registers are altered through a set of AT commands.

Looking at modem performance, we discovered that transmission rates were dependant on the maximum port speed of the serial port and the speed at which the modem could transmit data. Maximum port speed is governed by the universal asynchronous receiver-transmitter (UART) chip found in the computer for external modems or on the modem card for internal modems. Late model computers typically use a 16550 series UART chip capable of 115,200bps. The speed a modem can transmit data depends on both its speed of oscillation (baud rate) and how it compresses the data. Modems with a rate of 57,600bps are not uncommon today.

We looked at modem speed, number of stop bits, type of parity checking, and number of data bits and saw that these values had to be consistent between modems that were expected to communicate with each other.

With the modem installed and configured, we then turned our attention to media used to reach the remote network. We concentrated on the public switched telephone network (PSTN) and the integrated services digital network (ISDN). We saw PSTN (or the plain old telephone system) was an inexpensive medium that was widely available requiring no special equipment. Drawbacks to PSTN were the relatively limited bandwidth available (64k) and the switched nature of the system. The latter factor meant that we couldn't be sure our data would travel over the same path on each session (resulting in possibly different bandwidth capabilities from session to session) or if a path would be available under high traffic situations.

ISDN, on the other hand, provided a guaranteed digital quality dial-up line. Available bandwidth is as high as twenty-four 64k channels (which can be combined for greater capacity) although the typical basic rate service consists of two 64k data ("B") channels and one 16k control ("D") channel. ISDN offers a faster service that does not require conversion to analog signaling. It provides better bandwidth than PSTN with faster connection speeds. The service costs more than PSTN; however, it requires special adapters and may not be available in all areas.

We also took a quick look at some other connection options such as X.25, T-1, T-3, and frame relay.

Once our modem was connected to the wire, we still had to ensure the proper networking protocols were in place. We decided it was important to ensure our computer used a transport protocol (e.g. TCP/IP, IPX/SPX) that was in use on the remote network but then saw we also needed a remote access protocol. We took a close look at the serial line Internet protocol (SLIP) and the point-to-point protocol (PPP). We found SLIP a small efficient protocol that functioned only over serial lines. SLIP is dependant on TCP/IP, requires clear text authentication, and lacks the detail of support most users need. SLIP does not support automatic logon, nor will it permit automatic TCP/IP configuration. If you use SLIP, you must provide an IP address that will permit you to function on the remote network.

In contrast to SLIP, PPP is larger and more complex. It is not tied just to serial lines and supports a multitude of transport protocols. Encrypted logons are supported, as is automatic protocol configuration. Under PPP, for instance, you can automatically receive a valid IP address and WINS and DNS server addresses from the dial-in server.

We completed our remote networking discussion with a look at the point-to-point tunneling protocol (PPTP). PPTP permits us to create a virtual private network (VPN) on the Internet by encapsulating and encrypting packets during a second trip through the protocol. PPP packets ride on

PPTP packets through the Internet and are decrypted when they arrive at their destinations.

▲ REVIEW QUESTIONS

1. *The most common remote access hardware is*
    A. A remote access server.
    B. X.25 PAD.
    C. Modem.
    D. NIC.

2. *An asynchronous modem is as follows (Select all that apply):*
    A. Less expensive than a synchronous modem.
    B. Faster than a synchronous modem.
    C. More expensive than a synchronous modem.
    D. Slower than a synchronous modem.

3. *Sandy installs an asynchronous internal modem and configures it to use the COM3 port. After the installation, her mouse operates erratically. What could account for this?*
    A. The modem is using too much power.
    B. The mouse is plugged into the COM3 external port.
    C. The mouse uses COM1 which shares an IRQ with COM3.
    D. The mouse has failed coincidentally with the modem installation since there is no way a mouse and modem would conflict.

4. *Modems can be configured through*
    A. The Windows NT MODEMCONFIG.EXE utility.
    B. Returning them to the factory for resetting.
    C. The AT command, which alters information in the modem's S-registers.
    D. The AT command which alters information in the system registry.

5. *Modem transmission rates depend primarily on the following (Select all that apply):*

A. The system's maximum port speed.

B. The CPU speed.

C. The modem's baud rate.

D. Modem data compression.

6. *Internal and external modems will always have the same maximum port speed when installed on the same system.*

A. True.

B. False.

7. *Parity*

A. Is used to determine if a transmitted word was received correctly.

B. Is used to alter the transmission rate.

C. Is used to determine where a word starts and stops.

D. Is not used in asynchronous modem transmissions.

8. *PSTN connections are as follows (Select all that apply):*

A. Always provide a digital connection.

B. Are available almost anywhere in the world.

C. Provide a guaranteed path from source to destination.

D. May not be available during peak traffic periods.

9. *ISDN connections are as follows (Select all that apply):*

A. Always provide a digital connection.

B. Are available almost anywhere in the world.

C. Provide a maximum bandwidth of 128Kbps.

D. Should be used for dedicated, around-the-clock connections.

10. *Linda wants to dial into a Novell Network NetWare connect server. The Novell LAN uses IPX/SPX only. What remote access protocol should Linda use?*

A. NWLink.

B. SLIP.

C. PPP.

D. DLC.

11. *PPP is superior to SLIP because the following (Select all that apply):*
    A. It is smaller and simpler.
    B. Provides automatic configuration and encrypted authentication.
    C. Is universally supported by platforms and applications.
    D. Provides data compression and automated logon.

12. *If you needed to set up a VPN, which protocol would you use?*
    A. SLIP.
    B. PPTP.
    C. DLC.
    D. Ethernet Snap.

Network Administration

▲ **Chapter Syllabus**

Installation

Administration

Security

This chapter provides information on how to install, configure, administer, and secure a network. Network administration is a big job with far reaching impact on the enterprise. Do it well and you will collect a handsome paycheck; do it poorly and you may cause irreparable damage to your company. To help you with the broad range of responsibilities, we cover how to create and test standards for network administration and give you some valuable tips. We discuss the concepts of users, groups, password account policies, and general network administration. Finally, we move into the security arena—an area of prime importance to any administrator.

After completing this chapter, you will be able to do the following:

- Plan and implement the installation of a network
- Explain why administrative and test accounts, passwords, IP addresses, IP configuration, and relevant standard operating procedures must be obtained prior to network implementation.
- Identify good practices to ensure network security

Installation

When considering any type of network installation there will be a corresponding set or sets of information that must be collected, refined, and digested so that the end product meets or exceeds the goals established. The purpose of network installations is to support the need to exchange or share data. The users' needs are the starting point. Proper data collection precedes planning and provides an understanding of what type of information is necessary to begin an installation. There are many types of data that need to be gathered and considered because the prime directive is that the existing functionality cannot decrease in any way. Some of the things that you will want to be certain to address are as follows:

- Hardware—We must understand whether or not the computer(s) will do the intended job, so investigate the capabilities required and any known issues with hardware. Take time to determine if you absolutely must have the latest features that the hardware offers. Who established the requirement? How was the requirement formulated? In order to select hardware, you must understand what the hardware has to support, which comes from refining the user needs. You must know how many users will connect, what type of connection, what length or duration of connection, and what type of sustained operations to expect. Although most hardware is comparable, not all hardware has advanced features. Be sure to check about features you may need, such as pager boards, integrated secondary power supply, support for RAID (redundant array of inexpensive disks), and server fault tolerance capabilities.

- Operating Systems—What operating systems are in place now? Why are they there? What functional purpose do they serve? Will the installation of new equipment harm, reduce, remove, or otherwise adversely affect existing functionality?

- Applications—What applications are on the network and what purpose do they serve? What applications are needed and what functionality is required of them? Do any new applications need to be added? Have the new applications been tested with the existing application set? Have all issues been eliminated, reduced, or mitigated in some way?

- Administrative Accounts—Before removing any administrative accounts, has the system been tested with the account disabled? An example of the impact of this would be where an administrative-level account or service account is created for access to a database. The users might not know that this account is being used to logon because all users accessing the database would be connected via a batch file that sends the account and password on the user's behalf. If the account were removed, the database connectivity would no longer be available. If you need more administrative-level accounts, how should they be created? Remember not to use the known administrator accounts such as administrator, admin, supervisor, and superuser and keep the number limited to only what is needed.

- Test Accounts—It is usually a good idea to use an account that does not have administrative rights to test. Sometimes these accounts are removed when upgrading or installing with the result that the administrator would continue using an administrative logon to test BETA applications, hardware, or applications. Because the use of administrative accounts should be limited to actual administration, it is best to retain test accounts. To create test accounts, follow the guidelines mentioned previously and do not use the known test accounts such as test, tester, and testuser because they will be easier for unauthorized users to guess.

- Passwords—When installing, upgrading, or migrating, the passwords should remain intact to avoid user confusion. It is best to change passwords after the changes to the network have been made and the users are able to do their work. Injecting more variables than necessary is a formula for failure. There are some rather simple guidelines on creating passwords listed later in the chapter that make a lot of sense. Some of these guidelines include *not* using blank passwords, requiring a minimum password length of seven characters, and enabling auditing of system accounts.

- IP Addresses—Although the Internet protocol (IP) address information is spelled out in an earlier chapter, we believe it essential to document the IP address information if you are upgrading or migrating an environment. Keep in mind that the difference of one number makes communication impossible.

- IP Configuration—Again, the IP configuration information is supplied in an earlier chapter, but we are certain that any changes made to the IP configuration of your environment could cause the environment to fail. A review or check is always in order prior to commencing with the changes.

- Standard Operating Procedures (SOP)—Another area that must be consulted before spinning up for the installation is the required reading of the company SOPs. These may cover everything from vacation days to what types of configurations are permissible at the desktop of each or any particular user. The network administrator should be thoroughly familiar with topics such as electronic mail usage policy, Internet access, printing and department charge backs, disk quotas or storage space, and user administration. If there are no SOPs, it follows that the administrator would want to provide suggestions for their creation. This may be one of the most daunting tasks if you are not a writer. The process is to collect information by researching company policies and draft the recommended SOPs for approval and implementation.

Planning

As mentioned earlier, you now know more about the overall network requirement. As the network administrator, you will have to understand a multitude of items to properly conduct the business of administering the network.

Let's begin with an imaginary scenario. You have just taken over the Alida Connection corporate network. It is a small, fragmented network; and you have been given the latitude to implement just about anything that will make life easier for the users, one of whom is your boss. You don't have a very large budget but new computers have been ordered for a network upgrade. The network will have both Windows NT and Novell Netware servers, so integration of the two is important. Also, a UNIX-based web server is being considered. What should have been done *before* those computers were ordered? What do you need to know *before* you start a rollout? What should you be considering to make the network perform better? We have identified a few of the practices that are considered essential to good network planning in the preceding paragraphs. In order to deliver the required functionality, we will consider an upgrade of the existing servers. Don't lose sight of the fact that this is only one part of the picture. The implementation needs to be conducted with surgical precision. Remember, there are ongoing day-to-day network operations and upkeep that will need to continue throughout this process. Also, discuss user training before the rollout, otherwise you will have a great new network without users that can use the functionality.

The first, and most critical, step in network planning is to determine who will actually do it. Do you have a project large enough to create a project team to work on the various aspects of the network plan? If you are working with fewer than 50 users, it is likely that you will be able to do it yourself. If, on the other hand, you have thousands of users, you will need help. In large organizations, you should define responsibilities very early with one person designated to act as the project architect and another to provide analysis and reporting of existing information. Of course, in all cases, you will create a timeline for all aspects of the project and assign completion dates. Keep aware of costs and any changes to costs throughout the plan.

Whether you will work with a planning group or manage the implementation yourself, the list that follows is a good starting point. It is not meant to be all-inclusive or in-depth, but rather provides a good starting point to accomplish the tasks with understanding and enthusiasm.

Study Break

Network Planner

1. Perform an assessment of the user needs. Gather and quantify information so everyone on the team, whether contractor or in-house staff, is able to understand the applications and services the end users will require. Be sure to review and determine exact needs for:

   a. Office requirements—applications such as Word, Excel, SQL, and possibly, a gateway such as SNA or any other gateway functionality.

   b. Groupware requirements such as calendar, scheduling, E-mail, and contact management. What is being used presently? Do you keep and upgrade them or is there a compelling reason for a new system?

   c. Internet connectivity—browser, server, news, mail, FTP, and applications.

   d. Back up plan—How often has data been lost? Determine if there is a backup plan in place and how often backups are done and check the test restore schedule.

   e. Antivirus plans—Is there an antivirus plan in place? Does it scan E-mail and attachments? How often are updates received? Who applies the update and who tests it?

2. Determine the organization's geographic profile and discuss the potential for geographical growth. Ensure outlying sites and offices are adequately considered. Is this a single site or are there multiple locations? Will you need to consider wide area network links or can your entire network use a single wire?

3. Examine the existing network closely. What items affect the operation, security, and environment of the network? Concentrate on the following factors:

   a. What equipment and software are in place?

   b. What security model and policies are in place?

   c. What existing documentation is available?

d. What organizational standard operating procedures (SOPs) must be followed?

e. What is the existing transmission control protocol/Internet protocol (TCP/IP) addressing and what will change?

f. What applications require hard coded IP addresses (if any)?

g. What test accounts are used and must remain?

h. What is the existing password policy?

i. What administrative accounts already exist?

j. Is there sufficient power?

k. Has a uninterruptible power supply (UPS) been planned?

l. What is the current space allocation?

m. Is the ventilation sufficient for the existing equipment/new equipment?

n. What types of temperature control and humidity checks are done?

o. Is there some form of climate control already in the designated space?

p. What is the existing backup format?

q. What are the costs associated with failure of network upgrade?

r. How are the existing servers physically placed, and what needs to change?

s. What services (file, print, application) are being used?

t. What type of storage exists?

u. How large a storage capacity is required?

v. What foreign systems are interconnected?

w. What links exist to the outside world and to other company locations?

x. What other protocols are in use?

y. What applications are in use and by whom?

z. What applications will remain in their current configuration and what applications require porting? (Who will manage the application development for the ported applications?)

aa. What is the network bandwidth (total, available, and required)?

bb. What bandwidth usage patterns have been established?

cc. What trend analysis has been performed? (Review it.)

4. Evaluate the available security models of the network operating system and determine if they will meet corporate security needs. What system is used to provide the current level of security and is it adequate? What types of security are available? Is there a need for an additional security provider that is external to the network? Is there a need to two-key encryption mechanisms?

5. Define operational boundaries and ensure everyone knows what he or she may do and what he or she must do to make the network run.

6. Establish naming conventions for users, networks, workstations, servers, and other resources. If naming conventions are already in effect, determine if they will still be valid after the upgrade. Ensure naming conventions are properly implemented and enforced.

7. Plan server hardware, software, and functionality. Address the following issues:

   a. What do users need based on the existing network and required/or desired improvements.

   b. How is server use going to differ after the upgrade?

   c. What applications require additional memory, hard-drive space, or fault tolerance?

   d. If a disk quota is in place, is it realistic? Are users satisfied? How much additional space is required for any new applications or for the files that they use or create?

8. Plan connections to other systems. How many other systems must be interconnected? How is this connectivity to occur? Who is responsible for this?

9. Verify the overall design: plan, install servers, and test a prototype network.

10. Once the concept is proven and you receive authorization to move ahead, begin the installation according to a published calendar. Yes, be certain to let the users know ahead of time that there will be changes and that the training for the new system has been planned and is being executed in tandem with the rollout.

Performing the Installation

Wizards and other vendor-supplied enhancements continue to make network operating system installations easier and easier. In this section, we will provide information about a typical installation that might take place in the network environment described earlier. It is not possible to write each step of every operating system installation, so we will list the items that you should know before performing the installation. If we assume nothing, you will need to collect quite a bit of information and be certain that you have the answers to the setup questions that happen during the installation.

Assume a Novell NetWare server version 4.11 is in place and you would like to add a Microsoft Windows NT 4.0 server as an application server. As a minimum, you should consider the following installation and configuration issues:

1. Determine the goals of the network. Are we trying to provide for the integration of several computers, a subnet, a small additional network segment, or simply a single-use application server that will provide a new function on the network? (Examples of the latter would be database, mail, and group collaboration servers such as Lotus Notes, GroupWise, or Microsoft Exchange Server.)
2. Identify user needs:

   - Integrated file and print (size of storage)
   - Dial-in using RAS, NRN, or RRAS
   - Macintosh integration
   - Mail
   - Databases
   - Security model (e.g., NTDS, NIS, NDS)
   - Other connectivity requirements (ATM, Fiber)

3. Identify the server speed, central processing unit (CPU) sizing requirements, security requirements, disk size and partitioning issues, and file system requirements.
4. Identify the installation parameters. Collect information about the machine name; licensing mode; server role; setup options, such as Internet Information Server (for Web services); and protocol settings, such as frame type and network number.
5. Define the backup requirements and identify the backup program that will be installed to support the user needs stated earlier.
6. Define and implement user login/logon requirements after server installation, along with a security policy and an accounts policy. Also, review security documentation to ensure you haven't missed something.

Administration

This installation went well because of the effort we put into planning and data collection to get the answers to setup questions before beginning our project. We must now turn our attention to the proper configuration, day-to-day operations, and performance tuning and optimization of the network. There is much more about this in the next chapter. For now, you should follow up and test the network before signing off on the final documentation. Configuration normally includes many things. In our environment, we may see peer-to-peer UNIX machines, Windows NT domain elements, and/or perhaps an NDS tree. The security providers are responsible for the validation of users' logon/login for the purpose of resource access. Centralizing security and administration at a single location saves time and money. Consider the long-term impact of your work and be certain that you are thinking about the planning elements mentioned earlier while doing the chores such as adding users and changing security permissions on resources, etc. Whether you are using NDS, NIS or NTDS, your security provider will need to be backup protected in two ways. The first is a regular tape back up, which we discuss in the next chapter. The second type of backup is an online server function such as a Windows NT back-up domain controller (BDC) or NetWare server. In the event of a primary failure, this backup holds distributed partition information so that you don't lose the ability to validate users as they try to access the network. The backup should exist and be available at all times in the event of a catastrophic or network system crash.

The administrator of a UNIX network will create an account by modifying the /etc/passwd file, but this may vary with the specific versions of UNIX. For example, Linux has a utility called the User Configurator that can be used to create user accounts. An account is added in Windows NT through the use of a tool called the User Manager for Domains, while the NetWare Administrator (NWADMIN) is used in NetWare. Creating an account requires the user logon as an administrator, supervisor, or root. Accounts can be renamed or moved in some systems. Consideration should be given to renaming an account before deleting. Example: if you have a user that departs the company and another person takes his/her place, it makes more sense to rename the account and change the password than to create a new user and establish all of the required rights and permissions. Adding users on the different systems may be a bit difficult, but availability of the server at all times and the security of the system is critical. Usually it is beneficial to have the users grouped together for resource access. This way, instead of going to each resource and adding each user, as you would in a peer-to-peer environment, you could simply use the built-in groups or create a group that fits your needs and establish permissions on the resource for the group.

Some guidelines on account creation are in order. Only one account should be created for each user, and each user should use only his/her account. Create only the absolutely required number of administrative accounts. Usually, only one is required. Do not permit nonadministrators to use the account or know the password. The user account of an employee on an extended vacation or sabbatical should be temporarily disabled. Accounts for users that have left the company should be disabled and/or deleted regularly. No accounts should exist for anyone who does not need an account. Also, all accounts should have passwords. Generally speaking, no use of common names, dictionary words, or names of family relatives or pets should be used as the password for a user or resource because they are easy to guess. It is best to keep the passwords to a minimum of six or seven letters and have a combination of upper case and special characters to make your network security more difficult to crack. Why do we need to discuss risk of security loss and server protection? The value of the network is directly related to the types of information that it contains. In some cases, the value of the network data may be well into the millions of dollars.

Security

Computer networks typically contain information sensitive to the operation of your company and the proper operation of the network itself. Obviously, we don't want to allow just anyone to read or manipulate this information. Network security, therefore, is an important aspect of network administration. While we have extensive experience with risk, threat, and some of the utilities for advanced security, we restrict our discussion to the basics. Much more information on the topic of risk management, measurement tools and services can be found on the web at most of the search engines by looking for the following topics: Los Alamos Vulnerability and Risk Assessment (LAVA), Livermore Risk Analysis Methodology (LRAM), MicroSecure Self Assessment, MINIRISK, Risk Analysis System (RA/SYS), RISKPAC, RiskWatch, and SATAN. This is nowhere near a full listing, but gives you some direction if you decide to go further.

Good security depends on two factors: physical security and logical security. Unfortunately, when we speak of security, people normally forget about the physical kind.

Physical Security

The concept behind physical security is pretty simple: "keep your resources locked up." Good physical security, however, requires a fair amount of planning and education. Servers, for instance, should be secured in a server room. The only people who should have access to such a facility should be administrators and people with a genuine need to come into close contact with the equipment. The server room should be locked with a key or cipher lock, and only authorized individuals should have the key or code.

Although harder to secure, workstations provide a conduit to your network and its servers. Although workstations may be protected by good logical security, the lack of physical security may give an unauthorized individual the opportunity to hack into the network when no one is looking. Frequently, workstations contain data that is every bit as sensitive as that on the network's servers. An unsecured workstation (along with the sensitive data on it) is vulnerable to theft. Offices equipped with workstations should be equipped with locks, and users should be trained to secure their offices when no one is around. Users should also be reminded of the need to be alert and aware of unauthorized or suspicious activity.

Much of your network's information may be garnered from materials such as backup tapes, emergency repair disks, logs, floppy disk files, and documentation. Ensure everyone is aware of the need to properly safeguard these materials and make sure backup tapes are properly stored and secured.

Logical Security

Our networks would be pretty safe if we kept everything locked up and prevented access by anyone at any time. Unfortunately, this much security would also render the network useless. We must have a logical (computer-based) method to keep the network safe. Such a method would ensure only authorized users are able to access the network and would allow different levels of access to different levels of authorized user.

Logical security depends on a number of factors. We need to have a way to authenticate a user (usually through a user name and password). We need to develop or select a security model that governs how we apply the authentication to various resources to protect them. We may want to encrypt data to protect it during transmission, and we may want to install a firewall or other protective device to prevent intrusion into our network from outside networks (such as over the Internet). Finally, and most importantly, we must ensure our users are trained on how to best employ these security techniques. It does no good, for instance, to have the best security and the hardest to crack passwords if users commonly log onto their workstations and leave them unattended or give out their passwords to other users.

User Authentication

To be authenticated on a network, users will need a user account. Although user accounts are associated with a user name, the actual account is usually encrypted and identified by an encrypted numeric identifier (UNIX calls this the user identifier (UID), while Windows NT uses a security identifier (SID). The important consideration here is that a user account, once created, is a unique key to the network's resources. If the account is deleted and a new one is created using the same user name, the network will not recognize it as the same account and access to some resources will be lost. Think of a car key with a tag identifying the car to which it goes. If you were to destroy the key and attach the tag to a new key, you would have what appears to be the right key but would still find yourself walking home.

A major part of network administration involves the management of user accounts. An administrator will probably get to create and delete tens of thousands of accounts during his or her tenure—to say nothing of the thousands of forgotten passwords and login problems he or she will remedy.

USER NAMES AND PASSWORDS • Some of the most common features of user accounts are user names and passwords. The former provide a way of identifying the user while the latter verify the user is who he or she claims to be. You need to have policies for both!

While the concept of user names may appear quite simple, without a standard procedure for creating them, your network directory could quickly become a hodge-podge of characters resembling the graffiti on the New York subway system. A good user name should be something you would be able to determine if you knew the user's actual name, while maintaining enough complexity to allow everyone to have a unique name. The policy you select depends on the number of people in your organization and the uniqueness of their names. Some common naming conventions are first name with one or more initials of the last name, last name with one or more initials of the first name, first and middle initials plus last name, first name and last name, and last name and first name. John W. Smith, for instance could be JSMITH, JOSMITH, SMITHJ, SMITHJO, JWSMITH, JOHN-SMITH, or SMITHJOHN depending on the convention selected. There are, of course, many more ways to accomplish this. The important thing is to set a policy that can handle your needs and stick to it. When the naming convention results in an occasional duplicate name, it is common to add a number to one. We might have, for instance, JWSMITH and JWSMITH1.

While it should be easy to determine someone's user name when their given name is known, just the opposite is true for passwords. You need to set an aggressive password policy that will result in passwords that are hard to guess but easy to remember. The ideal password should be at least six to seven characters long to increase the level of difficulty of guessing.

Passwords greater than about 15 characters, however, tend to be hard to remember, resulting in users writing them next to their monitors or forgetting them and increasing your workload. A good password will also be a combination of upper and lower case alphabetic characters, numeric characters, and, where permitted by the operating system, national characters (!@#$%^&*).

Do you know what the most common password is today? It's the word *password*! This certainly doesn't portend a very secure environment, does it? Other bad password choices are names (of spouses, pets, children, companies, cars), dates, occupations, text on signs or labels you can see from your desk, or any other item that can easily be connected to you. Since many password-cracking programs are available that simply run through permutations and combinations of characters, passwords of all similar characters (e.g. common words) are a bad choice too. Sometimes users think using a common word prefixed or suffixed with a number or national character will do the trick. Knowing this, programmers have written password crackers to strip the first and last characters and treat them differently during processing. Here's an example of a good, hard-to-crack password: Iw100$sciLV. Looks hard to remember doesn't it? Well, it's actually easy to remember, but fairly hard to crack. When entering my password all I need to remember is "*I won one-hundred dollars shooting craps in Las Vegas.*" Just to make things a bit tougher, we put the dollar sign after the number in $100!

Even the best passwords should not live forever. After a while, compromise is likely; and a good network policy is to have users change their passwords on a regular basis (the most common is every thirty days). Unfortunately, most of us become very attached to our passwords and resist developing new ones. While most network operating systems allow you to set a maximum password age, it has only been recently (in NetWare 4.x and Windows NT 4.0) that the software would actually keep a list of old passwords. Before this innovation, it would be possible, for instance, to replace a password of *cat* with a new password that was also *cat*. If your NOS permits the keeping of a password history, you should definitely employ this feature.

While most NOS enforce password age and length, they do not check the actual composition of the password. If you are concerned about the security of your network, you might consider employing a password cracker to identify easy-to-crack passwords. Use this technique judiciously, however. If you are responsible for 10,000 users and 15% of them have bad passwords, the administrative load of notifying users might be more than you bargained for!

Of all the password administration duties you have, the most important is user training and education. The best password policies in the world will do no good when users tape their passwords to their monitors or share them with their office mates.

ACCOUNT LOCKOUT • All the major network operating systems (Windows NT, UNIX, NetWare) provide account lockout features. An account lockout occurs after a predetermined number of bad logon attempts. The account can be set to remain locked out until reset by an administrator or may be set to unlock after a specified time period. This feature is intended to prevent people from accessing the network using multiple attempts to crack a user password. While setting this feature to unlock the account after a specified period of time will lower your administrative workload and provide fairly good protection by introducing sufficient delay to discover the "hacker," it does not guarantee you will be notified of the potential breach. Because of this, many administrators prefer to leave the accounts locked until reset manually.

DISABLING ACCOUNTS • When someone leaves the organization for an extended period, leaving his or her account active may increase the possibility that someone could have unauthorized access to your network. Most NOS (NetWare, UNIX, and Windows NT) allow you to disable an account, leaving it in place but not active. When the employee returns, his or her account can be enabled and all their permissions will again be available.

Disabling, rather than deleting, an account after an employee's permanent departure may be desirable also. If a replacement employee will need the same access as the one who left, account management may be as simple as enabling the account and changing the name and password.

Accounts can also be set to expire after a specified amount of time. On the expiration date, the account remains, but is disabled. It may be reenabled or deleted at the administrator's discretion. This feature is most useful when dealing with temporary employees.

THE MAINTENANCE ACCOUNT • Network operating systems come with a default maintenance account (*root* in UNIX, *Administrator* in Windows NT, and *Admin* in NetWare). These accounts have full administrative rights and should be guarded against compromise. Unfortunately, their standard names make them an easy target for hacking. Since they may be renamed like any other user account, the best practice is to rename them so they don't appear to be any different from any other user. You should use normal naming conventions and avoid names that might indicate this is a special account (e.g., chief, boss, or supervisor).

Security Models

The chief reason for security is to protect network resources from unauthorized access. There are two ways (or models) commonly implemented in computer networks to apply security to resources: *share level security* and *user level security*.

SHARE-LEVEL SECURITY • Under share-level security, network resources (such as files and printers) are assigned individual passwords. All network users can see all shared resources. Any user who knows the password may access the resource. Although password policies may be easier to enforce under this model, it is difficult to track who has had access to a particular account and, because passwords are shared, the possibility of password compromise is increased. This kind of security is typically used on very small networks with no centralized administration.

USER-LEVEL SECURITY • Access to resources under user-level security is dependent on permissions granted to the user's network account. If the user has permission to access a particular resource, he or she can do so without entering any additional authentication (assuming they have already been authenticated on the network). This method allows the administrator to track resource use by user and, since user passwords are not shared (*shouldn't* be shared), this security model provides greater resource protection. This is the preferred security model and is the basis of security in most large networks.

Summary

In this chapter we provided information on users and accounts and general network administration. We planned and implemented the installation of a network upgrade and explained why the administrative and test accounts, passwords, IP addresses and configurations, and SOPs are relevant when making changes. We identified the administration after the upgrade and the practices to follow to ensure good network security.

Before we perform an upgrade or rollout what should be done? Identify the user needs. Take stock of the administrative accounts that already exist, and be certain not to remove them because they may impact your ability to use the system. Understand what is on the network and why it is being used. If you remove functionality, you may impair the entire company or part of it. What are the different servers providing in the way of File, Print, and Application functionality? What is the available network bandwidth? Will an upgrade achieve the desired effect? Have you evaluated the available security models and selected the one that will work best, or will you need to incorporate more than one security provider on the network? Will this meet the corporate security needs? Have you performed a risk assessment and reviewed security documentation to ensure you haven't missed something?

What methods of physical security do you employ? Has there been anything missing on the network. What is the history? How have the problems been solved in the past? What is the logical security model? To be authenticated on a network, users will need a user account. The important consideration here is that a user account, once created, is a unique key to the network's resources. A major part of network administration involves the management of user accounts. The chief reason for security is to protect network resources from unauthorized access.

▲ REVIEW QUESTIONS

1. *A network computer upgrade requires collecting which of the following information (Select all that apply):*
   A. User telephone extensions.
   B. Hardware bus clock speeds.
   C. Hardware issues.
   D. Existing operating system.
   E. Test accounts.
   F. Administrative accounts.
   G. SCSI data transfer rate.
   H. Server computer.

2. *Network planning helps*
   A. Continued growth of the user base.
   B. Hardware replacement.
   C. Proper operation and administration.
   D. Create IP address conflicts.

3. *User needs might include*
   A. User telephone extensions.
   B. Integrated file and print.
   C. Remote access services.

    D. SCSI data transfer rate.

    E. Both A & B.

    F. Both B & C.

4. *What is a backup domain controller used for?*

    A. A copy of all user files.

    B. A copy of all share points.

    C. A copy of all user accounts.

    D. A secondary power supply.

    E. All of the above.

5. *Two components of security include*

    A. Topical and logical security.

    B. Topical and physical security.

    C. Physical and administrative security.

    D. Logical and physical security.

6. *User authentication is provided by a security provider that maintains*

    A. User telephone extensions.

    B. Hardware bus clock speeds.

    C. Encrypted numeric identifier for each user.

    D. Existing account tabs.

    E. Server sections.

7. *The maintenance account in a UNIX system is an administrative-level account that is known as*

    A. Administrator.

    B. SuperUser.

    C. Admin.

    D. Root.

8. *A good balance between user account security and ease of administration is achieved by*

    A. Giving the administrator access to all users.

    B. Using or creating groups for resource permissions.

    C. Delegating the right to administer the network to all users.

    D. Individually assigning each user to each resource.

Maintaining the Network

Chapter Syllabus

The Physical Environment

Monitoring the System

The Virus Threat

Backup Program

Fault Tolerance

Uninterruptible Power Supply

Software Patches

Once your network is installed and good administrative procedures are in place, you will want to keep it running smoothly and efficiently. While it would be nice if you could depend on your excellent planning and network administration to keep things running while you kick back in your office to play video games and surf the net, in the real world, smooth operation depends on constant work. If you want to keep your network at peak performance, you will need to check its operation regularly, maintain a stable environment, and ensure it is protected from internal failure and external attack. (Besides, if you could spend your whole day surfing the net, you wouldn't be making those "big bucks"!)

This chapter deals with network maintenance. The context in which we use the word "maintenance" here, connotes *keeping* things working properly rather than *fixing* things that have *stopped* working properly. (We will talk about fixing things in Chapter 11, Troubleshooting.) Here, we will concentrate on ways to keep your network

327

running and the tools available to optimize and protect it. We will look at environmental factors that can lead to difficulty, discuss the importance of monitoring network systems, and discuss the virus threat and how to combat it. We will see how a back-up program, fault tolerance features, and uninterruptible power supplies can help your network contend with or recover from a host of attacks and hardware and software failures. Finally, we will see how to apply system repairs provided by software vendors to rectify detected deficiencies in your network's operating systems and applications.

After completing this chapter you will be able to do the following:

- List environmental factors that may impact your network and explain how to contend with them
- Explain why system monitoring is important and discuss ways to keep track of system activity
- Explain the impact of viruses on a network and how to minimize the threat they present
- Identify proper backup procedures and discuss the benefits of a sound backup program
- List fault tolerance methods and explain what fault tolerance can and cannot do for a network
- Explain the use and operation of an uninterruptible power supply
- Explain the function of software patches and discuss the proper procedures for their installation

The Physical Environment

A source of network trouble that is frequently overlooked is the physical environment in which the network operates. Physical issues include *line power, electrostatic discharge* (ESD), *electromagnetic interference* (EMI), *radio frequency interference* (RFI), *climate,* and *physical placement* of systems and other room contents. Physical placement can affect not only safety and convenience but may also have a significant impact on ESD, EMI, RFI, and climate.

Line Power

Most computer equipment expects its electrical power to be 117 volts AC at 60 cycles per second (Hertz). While an AC voltage between 110 and 120 volts is generally acceptable, when available power wanders beyond those limits, trouble can he expected. Power fluctuations come in two varieties: *power surges* and *power spikes*. During a power spike, the voltage rises above normal levels and returns in under a second. Unless the spike is very high, this usually doesn't result in serious damage. Power surges, on the other hand, last two seconds or more and usually cause greater damage than spikes. These phenomena may be caused by lightening, accident, human error, or malfunction at the power company. They are, unfortunately, fairly common today.

To combat against spikes and surges, you can employ *surge protectors* and *line conditioners*. Surge protectors range from inexpensive power strips equipped with a circuit breaker to more expensive, electronically controlled devices. The power strip protector is better than nothing but may not offer the best protection to your equipment. This is because the circuit breaker takes time to react to the spike or surge. By the time it trips, the damage may have already been done. Electronic surge protectors cost $30 to $50 or more but offer much better protection. They sense the power and when it exceeds the recommended level, they essentially self-destruct to break the circuit and protect the equipment.

Line conditioners offer an even better measure of protection by controlling the power coming into the system and providing current consistently within specifications. Such devices are, unfortunately, very expensive. A less expensive alternative to a line conditioner is an uninterruptible power supply (UPS). A good UPS uses a battery to power the computer (through an inverter which converts the battery's direct current to alternating current). A properly functioning UPS will always provide power meeting the specified levels. The battery keeps its charge because it is continuously charged by a charger plugged into the wall. Since the battery charger current and the current supplied to the computer should never come into contact, a properly functioning UPS will always provide safe power.

Electrostatic Discharge

Another kind of power surge comes from an electrostatic discharge (ESD). We have all experienced such static electricity—you can probably remember getting a nasty static shock after walking across a carpet and touching a doorknob on a dry winter's day. The internal circuits found in today's computer equipment operate on infinitesimal amounts of current and voltage. The nasty static shock you remember was an inconvenience to you; but if you were a computer, it could have destroyed some of your internal circuits. It could also have changed the state of information in your memory chips, resulting in data corruption and unexpected operation.

The best defense against static damage to equipment is to ensure that it is properly grounded. Additionally, it is a good idea to remove shag carpeting from areas where computer equipment is used. Installation of grounding strips and maintaining a relative humidity level of 40 to 60 percent will also help.

Electromagnetic Interference

Electromagnetic interference (EMI), occurs when computer equipment or cabling runs
through electromagnetic external electric fields. These fields typically originate from common electric motors, transformers, or generators. They can cause data transfer problems and may even cause data corruption within memory chips. It is important to ensure network cabling doesn't run through areas that would place it near a heater, air conditioner, elevator, or other common motors. Be careful when placing devices such as fans or heaters in a room containing computer equipment. If, ignoring our previous advice, you have placed your tower computers on luxurious shag carpet, any damage not caused by ESD may be caused by the EMI coming from the vacuum cleaner you run next to the computers to clean the carpet!

Radio Frequency Interference

The effects of radio frequency interference (RFI) are very similar to EMI. The chief difference is in the source. RFI comes from radio and television transmitters, two-way radios, cellular telephones, and other transmission devices. Although their RFI is small, internal components of TV sets and FM radios can also be a source of RFI. Good shielding can help reduce the effects of RFI. It is also a good idea not to use two-way radios and cell phones while sitting at the terminal. Television and FM radio receivers should be placed several feet from computer equipment.

Climate

Computer equipment runs properly under the same climatic conditions that make you comfortable. An environment of 70 degrees Fahrenheit and between 40–60% relative humidity should keep your system functioning properly. Even with good building heating, ventilating, and air conditioning (HVAC), this can be a challenge because most computer equipment generates a lot of its own heat.

While you should demand good HVAC service, you also need to place the computer equipment to make the best use of the HVAC. Placing equipment near sunny windows can raise the temperature far beyond the ambient temperature in the room. Putting a portable room heater next to a server may keep you warm in the winter but may get the equipment "hot under the collar." Placing your servers in a secure closet may protect them from unauthorized access but, unless the closet is properly ventilated, may subject them to much higher heat than they are designed for. Finally, consider the heat generated by the equipment when determining how closely to place components. Arranging all your servers such that they touch each other may result in the generation of more heat in a small area than the building's HVAC can remove. Proper climate control precludes placing equipment near any heat source, including the exhaust of another computer.

Physical Placement

If you have been paying attention during the preceding sections, you have learned a lot about how *not* to place your computer equipment. Keeping all those restrictions in mind, you should place your equipment logically and in a manner that maximizes convenience and productivity. Workstations should be placed at desks in the best ergonomic position for comfort and convenience. Common use items such as printers and plotters should be placed in areas close to the people who use them. If several printers are arranged in a "printer pool" they should be located in the same area so users don't need to wander all over the building to find where their print job "ended up this time."

Safety and security should be taken seriously too. Equipment should be located on desks and tables strong enough to support it. Computers should not be located in areas where they could be kicked or present a tripping hazard. Network cabling and power cords should be run neatly and orderly (it is preferable *not* to bundle network cable and power cords together) to prevent tripping hazards. Never run power or signal cable under carpeting, because the foot traffic over it will create wear that may result in signal loss or fire.

Monitoring the System

If no one is reporting trouble, my network must be functioning properly, right? Using this kind of approach will make you feel good for a while but when things go wrong, they may go very wrong. It is important to be on the lookout for problems, trends, and deficiencies all the time. While no one wants you to "fix things that ain't broke," you need to take a proactive approach to finding small problems before they become big ones.

Fortunately most systems offer a host of diagnostic tools to keep you going. Windows NT, for instance, offers *Performance Monitor* and *Network Monitor*. Performance Monitor allows you to monitor a host of computer and network parameters from memory and hard disk to protocol and NIC performance. The utility permits you to plot a graph, write a report, or store data in a log. You can also set alerts to warn you when a certain parameter exceeds a given value. Network Monitor permits you to examine individual packets on the network. Third party tools, such as *INTRAK System Monitor*, permit simultaneous monitoring of several NetWare or Windows NT servers. More information is available at the Web site: *http://www.intrak.com.*

In addition to monitoring tools, most operating systems and major applications write information to some sort of log. These logs may be simple text files or they may be sophisticated database applications that maintain a great deal of information. In many cases you can configure them to report a variety of information in a selection of formats. One of the best log systems is the Windows NT *Event Viewer*. Event viewer offers three logs: a *Security Log*, an *Application Log*, and a *System Log*. The Security Log reports information you have selected for monitoring. Reports of successful or unsuccessful logons or data access are typical of this log. The Application Log contains information generated by applications and the System Log contains entries originating with the operating system.

Regular reviews of these logs can reveal conditions on the computer or network that need attention. Figure 10–1, for instance, reveals a Windows NT domain logon problem on computer "Laptop." An occasional entry like this wouldn't indicate a serious problem but when this condition is noted several times or on many different machines, it might indicate a network problem. In this case, the machines are unable to locate a domain controller. If you discover something like this, your interest should be piqued. You would want to look for trends. Do we see a lot of these messages at particular times? Are they occurring during heavy logon periods? Are they confined to one network segment? You may want to use some other available analysis devices such as Network Monitor or Performance Monitor to do some further research. Ultimately, you will need to decide if the problem is caused by over use, which would require the addition of more network resources, malfunctioning equipment, or a non-optimum configuration. Anything you can do to resolve the condition before it becomes a reportable problem will keep your network running smoothly and efficiently and will keep your work-life more stable and orderly.

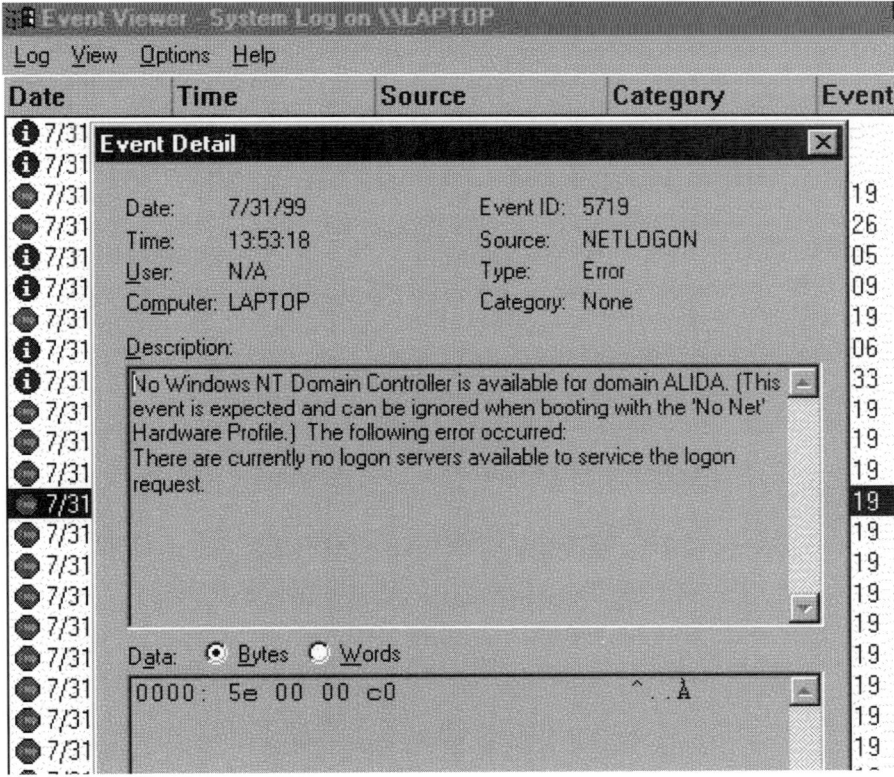

Figure 10–1 *Windows NT system log.*

When you review error logs, some definitions are very clear while others are a bit more cryptic. Are you expected to memorize a plethora of error codes and messages to keep your network running? Fortunately, the answer to this is "no." Most vendors provide Web sites that can be queried by message number of description. Additionally, there are subscription services (such as Microsoft TechNet or the MicroHouse hardware and troubleshooting CD) that provide a wealth of knowledge on CD or DVD. This information can also be searched by message number or description. Finding just the right information to explain a particular error may appear rather daunting at first but after a short time, you should get quite good at it.

The Virus Threat

Just when you think your system is secure, a tiny piece of malicious code infiltrates your network and cleans out your servers bringing your entire network to a halt. Before it did so, however, it managed to replicate itself across the network to some of your customers and infected some of your employees' home computers when they took work home on floppy disks. A far-fetched scenario from a science fiction movie? NOT! This type of scenario happens periodically and, surprisingly, on networks that should have been better prepared. While it is not possible to provide a 100 percent guarantee that you will never be infected by a computer virus, a good anti-virus program can sharply minimize the risk to your network. Such a program is built on three pillars: anti-virus policies and training, a good backup program, and anti-virus software.

Anti-virus Policies and Training

The first line of defense against virus attacks is the system's users. You should develop good and reasonable policies governing what software can be loaded on network machines and by whom. Policies concerning what can and cannot be downloaded from the Internet and when to scan a file or directory with anti-virus software will also offer a measure of protection. Good virus awareness training and a sound reporting system can ensure viruses are identified, reported, and eradicated before they spread too far. It is essential to promptly notify the system's users when a particular virus laden file has been detected to minimize the possibility of unwittingly opening or executing the file and spreading the problem.

Backup Program

Possibly the ultimate virus protection, a good backup program will permit you to recover when a virus destroys your data. Virus laden software may, however, have been backed up before it was detected. Once you have completed your system restore, it is a good idea to use your anti-virus software to scan all your data.

Anti-virus Software

When virus protection is spoken of, anti-virus software is usually the first thing that comes to mind. This is with good reason since today's virus protection software provides a great defense against infection. There are many virus protection packages available today. While antivirus programs vary in features and effectiveness, the use of any antivirus software is better than leaving your system unprotected. The general rule, "you get what you pay for," seems to apply when shopping for virus protection.

There are some features you should watch for in antivirus software. Since several new viruses are unleashed every day, you want a package that can be readily updated. It is helpful if the vendor offers a periodic update program. Your virus protection package should run in the background and be capable of checking for viruses in executable files as well as looking for macroviruses in data files such as Microsoft Word document files. A good antivirus program will run in background without interfering with other software and should be capable of checking files over the network. In addition to running in background, the software should permit you to force a scan against a particular disk or directory. Finally, antivirus software should not only detect and report a virus, it should also render the virus harmless.

Although the ability to scan files over the network is a good antivirus capability, software usually has to be functioning on the computer itself to detect a virus when a file is executed or opened. The only way to ensure your network is fully protected is to install the antivirus package on every server and workstation in the network.

Scanning Policies

As we indicated above, it is a good idea to require files downloaded or brought from off-site to be scanned for viruses before allowing them to become part of the network. This is important even if they were previously scanned, since you cannot be sure if the antivirus software used to scan them was as good as the package you're using or if it was updated with the latest virus information. Viruses have been known to come from what appeared to be some of the most secure sources imaginable. It is also a good idea to force a scan any time you suspect a virus may have infiltrated your network.

Signature Files

Files containing updated virus information are called *signature files*. These files contain information used by the antivirus software to identify and eradicate the virus. Many virus protection packages permit you to download this information from the Internet and can be configured to do so automatically. Some programs will even allow you to download the signature files to a local server from which other servers and workstations can be updated.

It is a good idea to update your signature files at least weekly. When a particularly nasty new virus is making the rounds, you should manually download the latest signature file (when it has been updated to handle the new virus) and force a scan throughout your network. This will ensure the virus didn't sneak past your antivirus software prior to the update.

Warning

Virus signature files are usually designed to work with a particular version of antivirus software. If your antivirus package has been replaced by a newer version, the new signature files may not work properly (or at all). Make sure you consult the manufacturer's documentation if any doubt exists.

Backup Program

With your network up and running, you can survey your resources and proudly reflect on the tens or hundreds of thousands of dollars worth of information technology equipment that manages the millions of dollars worth of data that your company uses every day. Sounds like a lot of money, doesn't it? When you consider what it cost to create the data and the impact on the organization if the data is suddenly lost—even for a medium sized company—the value of data stored on a computer network might easily exceed a million dollars.

Consider the cost when an unnamed insurance company had an outage about six years ago. A computer upgrade was planned during the closing week of the fiscal year. The new MIS department manager was young and aggressive. He needed to make a name in this company so he quickly learned everything he could about the operation and walked everywhere. One place, a broom closet, held shelves of network cards that the staff suggested needed to be tested. In an effort to save a few dollars, the manager purchased about 60 new computers but saved the cost of the network cards by not buying those. During the weekend before the closing week, he had his staff work Saturday to insert network cards in new machines and swap them out with machines that needed replacement on the network. There were only a few bad cards found while installing and testing. The 17-floor building held hundreds of workers who were unable to use their network at 7:36 A.M. on Monday morning. An urgent call was sent to dispatch a network analyst with a protocol analyzer to the company right away. It took four days to get the network back to proper operation because there was no indication of which machines had been switched out or which cards were bad. Related questions to ponder are as follows:

- Who paid the workers salaries for the four days while they had nothing to do?
- Who paid for the equipment and line costs?
- How much money was really saved?

As a highly qualified professional, you have made sure your network is secure. You have purchased only the most reliable components. You have ensured passwords and user accounts are secure and unauthorized use of the system is highly unlikely. You have applied good physical security practices—your server room is securely locked all the time and only those with a valid need have access. In general, you are pretty satisfied that your system will continue to provide outstanding support whenever needed.

But what if your server experiences a head crash on one of its hard drives. Or, what if a disgruntled employee manages to delete everything he or she had developed just prior to resignation? How would you handle it if a senior vice president accidentally deletes all the information pertaining to a particular account? What would you do if spring flooding puts your server room under water or if the lights from the Christmas party starts a fire that wipes out the information services wing? Is there a way to protect your company's valuable data from all these things? Of course there is! A good backup program will protect you from all these and more. Backup programs are exceptionally cheap insurance to protect your all-important data.

You will notice we didn't say "backup *system*" but, instead, used the term "backup *program*." This is because the finest data backup hardware in the world will offer absolutely no protection unless it is properly managed. The next few paragraphs will help you better understand how to make such a system work.

Backup Equipment

Although any means of copying data can provide a good backup system, backups are generally accomplished by using tape drives. Tape is a relatively inexpensive medium for data storage. The tape cartridge itself has a high capacity with a fairly small physical size. Tape drives are reliable and cheap when compared to other components or the value of your data.

Tape drives can be installed to back-up data from the local machine or over the network (although some things, such as the Windows NT Registry, can only be backed up locally). When deciding where to install tape drives, first decide what needs to be backed up, how often it will be backed up, and how long a typical backup will take. It is faster to back up locally, and local backups don't put a load on the network. It may be a good idea, then, to install a tape drive on the machine(s) that hold most of your data. You will probably want to run your backups when no one is using the network. On a small network, this may mean one tape at 7:00 P.M. in the evening. Larger networks may require more than one tape. As an example, if you calculate that backups will require 18 hours each day to complete and your organization is closed for only 12 hours a day, you will benefit from a second tape drive to cut your backup down time.

If you decide to do a network backup where you have several large servers that will be backed up by a central backup server, it's a good idea to install a second NIC in each server. You can create an isolated network segment dedicated to backup operations only. This will relieve the load on your primary network and provide a clear channel for backup operations.

What and When to Backup

It is common to say "back up what you can't afford to lose." The problem with that statement is if you could afford to lose it, it probably wouldn't (or at least shouldn't) be on your network. That being the case, it sounds like you will need to back up every one and zero in the organization—obviously an expensive proposition!

When considering what to back up, you really need to consider two things: 1) What cannot be replaced if the network fails, and 2) how often does it change. Answering these questions will tell you what to back up and how often to back it up. Much of what is on your network is executable code—operating systems and applications. While reinstalling executables is a nontrivial task, it makes little sense to expend backup time and resources on something that can simply be reinstalled. Your network is also probably rife with company records, correspondence, contact and billing information, and planning documents. If you are in the software or publishing business, you are likely to have source code or manuscripts that represent your very product. It is these items that need to be husbanded and securely backed up.

Once you know what you are going to back up, determine how often it changes. Company records or planning documents may be updated only quarterly, while correspondence and billing information may change on a daily basis. It's a good idea, then, to run a backup for the latter far more frequently than you would for the former. (A good backup program will probably have more than one scheduled backup operation.)

Users often store lots of data on their workstations. Since running a backup of every workstation in the organization might prove a bit impractical, you may want to provide each user with a server-based data storage location (such as the Windows NT *Home Folder*). If users store their critical data on the server, you can easily include this server-based data in your backup program.

Backup Methods

We have decided to back up our correspondence and billing information every day. Since not every letter changes every day, it seems like it would be a terrible waste of time and resources to recopy *every* letter and *every* bill *every* day. To prevent this duplication of effort, most backup systems provide several methods to determine what was backed up and what has changed.

Full Backup

Just as it sounds, a *full* backup copies everything you have decided should be backed up. It copies data regardless of whether the data has changed since a previous backup and marks each file it copies as having been backed up.

Copy

Copy works just like a full backup, except it doesn't mark files as being backed up.

Daily Copy

The daily copy will copy only files that have changed during the current day. Files are not marked as having been backed up.

Incremental Backup

Incremental backup copies each file you have selected for backup but only if it has changed since the last full or incremental backup. Each copied file is marked as having been backed up.

Differential Backup

Differential backup copies each file you have selected for backup, but only if it has changed since the last full or incremental backup. Files are *not* marked as having been backed up.

Backup Strategy

You should devise a backup strategy consistent with your backup needs by using the methods outlined earlier. If, for instance, you decide your data needs a daily backup, you may want to develop a weekly strategy where you would perform a full backup on Monday and incremental or differential backups throughout the rest of the week.

If you use the incremental method, each backup (after the initial full backup) will contain only the information changed that day. This will result in a fairly quick backup process. To restore data when the incremental approach has been used, you will need to restore from the full backup and from each incremental run. For example, to restore the data to Wednesday, you would restore from the Monday full backup, from the Tuesday incremental backup, and from the Wednesday incremental backup.

When using the differential method, on the other hand, each day's tape (after the initial full backup) contains everything that has changed since the full backup on Monday. Each differential tape should contain more information than the one before it. Restoration requires only the full backup tape and the most recent differential tape. To restore to Wednesday under the differential approach, you would restore from the Monday full backup and then from the Wednesday differential.

The chief difference, then, between differential and incremental backups is the time and complexity involved in running the backup and accomplishing a restore. Incremental backups will run a bit faster, since they copy less data each time, but take longer to restore because you must use every tape you made. Differential backups take longer to run on each successive day, but a restore requires only two tapes.

Warning

When restoring only a portion of data (such as a file that was inadvertently deleted), ensure that you select only the data you intend to restore. If you accidentally perform a full restore, any files changed since the last backup will be overwritten during the restore process, and recent changes will be destroyed by the process intended to protect them.

Tape Management and Storage

Tape is cheap! Don't risk your data because you want to save tape. It may be possible, for instance, to place a whole week's worth of incremental backups on the same tape (by using *append* instead of *overwrite*). If you do this, and your incremental backup tape fails, you may lose all your changes. By using multiple tapes, you will be able to get the majority of your data back even when a single tape becomes unserviceable.

In the weekly scenario we discussed previously, it might be a good idea to use two sets of tapes, employing one set every other week. In the event of an unforeseen system problem, you will have an extra backup even if it is a week old. (This may also provide a measure of insurance when an inadvertent delete isn't discovered until the following week.) If your budget allows, you may want to purchase even more tapes. While buying and storing a year's worth of tapes may be a little excessive, many organizations use enough tapes to maintain a full month of backups at any given time.

Tapes should be properly labeled and stored in a secure location. Of course, if we're concerned about fires, floods, tornadoes, or earthquakes, it might make sense to store the tapes at a remote location. The ideal way to do this is to make a second copy and store the tape off site. There are companies that will store the tapes for you or, if your company has multiple locations in the same area, tapes may be traded among the sites. If achieving this *ideal* off-site storage is beyond your capability, you should still consider some measure of remote storage. You might, for instance, store the tapes in a safe in another part of your building or find an off-site location for the previous week's backup tapes.

Regardless of where you store your tape, you should keep a record of each tape and where it is. You should record information such as the backup date, backup type, computer backed up, files backed up, and location of the backup tape(s). As we will see in the next section, some of this information can be automated.

Testing and Logging

It's a horrible feeling (and likely detrimental to job security) when you discover your backup plan doesn't work after a major loss of data. Two things can help prevent that sinking feeling: testing and logging.

Although it's a nontrivial undertaking, it is a good idea to perform periodic test restores. This usually requires configuring a test machine to receive the data—you wouldn't want to perform a restore to your production environment where recently changed data could be overwritten. To perform the test, simply use your current backup tapes and restore the test machine. Examine what is on the machine and compare it to the current environment. If you find what you expect to find, you can be confident in your backup program.

Most backup programs provide several logging options ranging from abbreviated logs that show only the date, time, and number of bytes transferred to full-logging options that include file names and any errors encountered. It is a good idea to select the full-logging option. This will show what is on the tape (to allow you to quickly locate a file or group of files to restore) and tell you how the backup went. As important as it is to create the log, logging does no good unless the logs are reviewed. *Always* review the log. If a particular file couldn't be backed up for any reason, you need to be aware of it. Information technology history is full of cases where administrators were confident that everything was working properly, only to discover—when they need to restore it—that a particular file was consistently not being backed up. Regularly checking the backup log is another solid step toward job security!

Most backup programs will not copy open files. Software that regularly maintains open files (such as database or mail systems), typically provides a means to back these files up while they are in use; but this will normally require configuration. Faithfully reviewing the backup log can alert you to open file problems and allow you to correct them before disaster strikes.

Managing the Program

As we said at the start of this section, you must have a backup *program*. The best equipment and the most eloquently written procedures can't actually make the program happen. A solid backup program requires solid management. It is critical that backups be scheduled, someone be placed in charge of accomplishing them, tapes be properly stored and inventoried, logs be checked, and tests be run. If all these elements are properly managed, your valuable data will be safe from nearly any contingency.

Study Break

Transaction Logs

> Many database-oriented programs (such as Microsoft SQL Server and Microsoft Exchange Server) write something called a *transaction log*. These logs are written each time data is changed and permit you to restore the data right up to the last change. When data is lost, the transaction log is manually or automatically applied to restored data to update it as closely as possible to the point of the failure. This will work, of course, only if the transaction log wasn't lost in the failure. When dealing with a product that uses a transaction log, pay careful attention to the documentation and make sure you write the log to the recommended location (typically on a physical drive separate from the actual database) if this is a configurable option.

Fault Tolerance

You, of course, expect your network and its resources to be operational 100 percent of the time. Unfortunately, in the real world, systems crash, controller cards fail, and hard disks self-destruct. *Fault tolerance* is a concept that will mitigate some of these problems. Fault-tolerant methods and devices are designed to provide some measure of data redundancy to prevent incapacitation when a hard drive or disk controller fails. Under fault tolerance, the system automatically recognizes a failure and provides data from the redundant store. Users may detect a change in system performance but will still be able to access the desired data.

Before we get into the details of fault tolerance, however, it is very important to make a distinction between *fault tolerance* and a *backup* program. A viable fault-tolerance methodology will permit your system to function after an unexpected drive or controller failure. It will *not* allow you to recover from malicious or inadvertent data corruption, unintended deletion, computer theft, fire, flood, nuclear war, or other disasters. Only a sound backup program with good off-site storage can help you there. Fault tolerance and sound backup programs work together to keep your network functioning and to allow it to recover in spite of a myriad of unforeseen difficulties.

Today's common fault-tolerance methods are also known as RAID. RAID is an acronym for *redundant array of inexpensive disks* and, although *inexpensive* is a relative term, this gives a clue to how fault tolerance is employed—by using additional *inexpensive* disks to store copies of our *expensive* data. RAID is implemented using both hardware and software and each has advantages. Hardware solutions tend to be very efficient and robust but are quite expensive and somewhat inflexible. Software solutions, on the other hand, are much cheaper than their hardware counterparts but are less efficient with fewer features. We will talk mostly about the software solutions since their characteristics are more standard for many implementations. The fault-tolerant concepts will, however, generally apply to both types of RAID.

Disk Mirroring

Disk mirroring is the simplest and easiest fault-tolerant system. Known as RAID1, mirroring simply uses a second disk (or partition of a second disk) to maintain an exact copy of the mirrored partition. As you can see in Figure 10–2, information written to the D: partition on Disk 0 is also written the mirror of D: on Disk 1. Should Disk 0 crash, the fault tolerance driver will sense this and provide information from the mirrored drive. (Of course, any

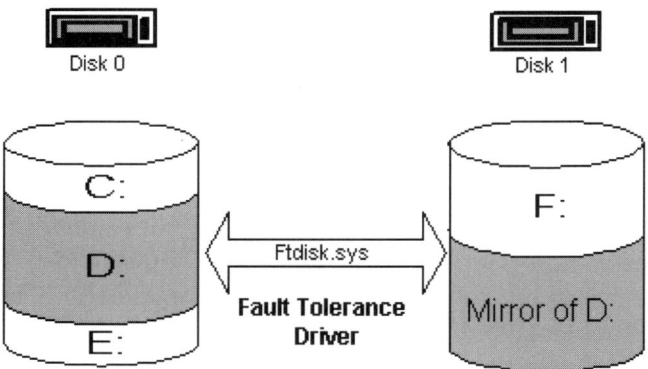

Figure 10–2 *Disk mirroring.*

information on the C: and E: partitions will be lost since they are not mirrored.) Obviously, a mirrored drive set should use two *physical* drives. Mirroring two partitions on the same drive makes no sense since they would both be lost if the drive were to fail.

Although your users are still able to obtain the desired information when a mirrored drive fails, you no longer have fault tolerance. You should correct the problem as soon as practical. To recover from the crash of a mirrored set, you would use the fault-tolerant administration software (*Disk Administrator* in Windows NT) to logically de-link the two drives (called "breaking the mirror"). You would then replace the bad drive and return to the administration software to create a new mirror set between the new drive and the remaining mirror image.

During normal operation, the fault-tolerance driver must write everything written to the mirror set twice—once on each drive. Since, however, the fault tolerant driver knows the data on both drives is identical, it can read a portion of the data from each drive simultaneously. Under normal operation, therefore, writing to a mirror set is slower than writing to a non-fault-tolerant partition; but reading is faster. If a mirrored drive were to crash, users would detect faster writes but slower reads since both read and write performance would return to that characteristic of a non-fault tolerant drive.

Because the primary drive in a mirror set can function on its own as a normal, nonfault tolerant drive, mirror sets may be used to hold software used to boot the system and initiate the fault-tolerant drivers. As we will soon see, this is not the case with other software RAID implementations.

Disk Duplexing

Mirror sets offer great protection when a disk crashes. What if the hard drive is ok but the disk controller card goes up in smoke? If we make a modification to our mirror set such that each drive is connected to its own disk controller, we have redundancy of both our drives and controllers. A failure in any single component will not prevent our users from accessing their data. This arrangement is known as *disk duplexing*.

Storage Efficiency

Mirror sets are easy to visualize and set up. They are relatively inexpensive because they require only two physical drives; but, because data is completely duplicated between the two drives, their cost per megabyte is somewhat higher than we see in other RAID options.

Stripe Set with Parity

Although more complex than a mirror set, a *stripe set with parity* offers better performance and, typically, a lower cost per megabyte. Stripe sets with parity are classified as RAID5.

Stripe Sets

Before we can understand stripe sets with parity, we need to understand basic stripe sets. Stripe sets (without parity) are sometimes referred to as RAID0. This is an unfortunate nomenclature because, as we will soon see, regular stripe sets include *no* redundancy and are *not* fault tolerant.

A stripe set is an array of at least two hard drives. Portions of the drives are combined to form a single logical drive. Data is then written evenly across the drives in 64k blocks. Since the data is written evenly, it is important that the space reserved on each drive for the stripe set is approximately the same size as that reserved on all the others. (If this is not the case, the stripe set will still work; but once the drive with the smallest allocated space is full, the stripe set will be full and any additional space in the rest of the partitions will be wasted.)

There are two main benefits from this arrangement. First, we can create a single logical drive that is much bigger than any one of our physical drives (assuming the file system in use permits large partitions). The second benefit comes from the simultaneous use of all the read/write heads on all the drives. If I have a four-drive array containing a stripe set, I now have four read/write heads working for me to transfer data to or from the device. This results in significantly increased performance over a single drive. (See Figure 10–3.)

There are some drawbacks to using a stripe set, however. A big one is the lack of fault tolerance. If any member of the drive array were to crash, the entire stripe set and *all* of its data is lost. If my stripe set employs four hard disks, my chances of experiencing a hardware failure are four times as great as with a single drive. In the case of a software implementation, the stripe set does not exist until the operating system is running and the stripe set drivers are functioning. Because of this, operating system software and file system drivers cannot reside on software-based stripe sets.

RAID5

If stripe sets provide significant performance advantages, how can we cope with the increased probability of hardware failure. The obvious answer is to provide some sort of fault tolerance, which in stripe sets is known as *stripe sets with parity* or RAID5. As you can see in Figure 10–4, a stripe set with parity is essentially the same as the stripe set; but, in addition to the data, we write parity stripes to each drive. Another difference between stripe sets and stripe sets with parity is that the latter typically requires a minimum of three hard drives.

The parity stripes on each drive contain mathematical information that can be used to help rebuild the data on any other member of the set. When a member of the set fails, the fault tolerance driver is able to use the parity data on all the other drives to "compute" the data on the failed drive and can keep the set operating without data loss.

During normal operations, a stripe set with parity has slower write performance than a normal stripe set because of the work required to compute and write the parity information. While *normal* read performance is on par

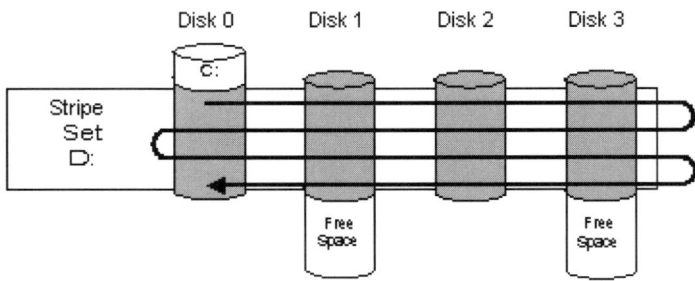

Figure 10–3   *Stripe Set.*

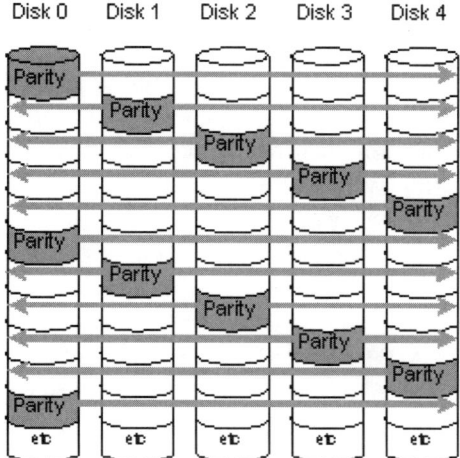

Figure 10–4 *Stripe set with parity.*

with a stripe set, when a disk fails, the stripe set with parity shows degraded read performance because of the extra time required to consistently compute the "missing" data.

Just as with a mirror set, once a stripe set with parity experiences a failure, it loses its fault-tolerance capabilities. Although users will continue to have full access to their data after the initial failure, if a second member of the stripe set with parity fails, all data is lost. Because of this, you will certainly want to recover from any failures as quickly as possible. Fortunately, this is a fairly easy task. You simply remove and replace the failed drive and use your fault-tolerance administration software to regenerate the stripe set with parity. The software will use the parity stripes and data on the remaining members to create all required information on the new drive, and your array will be fully functional once again.

In addition to enhanced input/output performance, a stripe set with parity can store data much more efficiently than can a mirror set. While a mirror set can hold only half as much data as its capacity would suggest (because it writes everything twice), a stripe set with parity can hold $(n-1)/n$ times as much data as its total capacity. In this case, "n" is equal to the number of drives in the array. For example, let's say I have a 10-drive stripe set with parity where each drive has a 100 MB partition dedicated to the set. A tenth of each drive would be taken up by parity information so the data capacity of my array would be $(10–1)/10 \times 1000$ MB or 900 MB. Compare this to a mirror set using two 500 MB drives with a maximum data capacity of 500 MB!

Like it's non-fault-tolerant counterpart, the operating system software and file system drivers cannot reside on a stripe set with parity if the set is software based. Although much more expensive, hardware-based RAID is presented to the operating system as a single drive and can contain the operating system as well as file system drivers without difficulty.

Other RAIDs

Since we've discussed RAID1 and RAID5, you are probably wondering what happened to the other numbers. RAIDs 2, 3, and 4 are similar but less advanced than RAID5. RAID2 and 3 distribute each data block across all disks in the array instead of writing a 64k block to each drive. RAID2 uses an error correction code instead of parity. RAID 3 uses parity checking but places all parity information on a single parity drive. RAID4 uses data blocks but stores parity information on a single drive like RAID3.

Sector Sparing

Sector sparing, also known as hot-fixing, can provide a measure of protection against data corruption on a single drive. If a bad sector is encountered during input or output, the fault-tolerance driver will try to move the data from the bad sector to a good sector and will lock the bad sector out. NetWare, Windows NT, and UNIX all support this feature, but it is only available on SCSI drives.

Volume Sets

Volume sets are *not* fault tolerant and are included here only to ensure you are aware of them and their lack of fault tolerance. Like a stripe set (without parity), a volume set creates a large logical drive out of smaller spaces found on multiple physical drives. As with a stripe set, the failure of any part of the volume set results in the loss of everything the volume set contained. Unlike a stripe set, data is written sequentially to the volume set and not evenly across the drives in the array. This means space allocated to the volume set need not be the same on each drive, but it also means there is no performance advantage to a volume set. As with stripe sets, operating system software and file system drivers should not be placed on volume sets. Typically, volume sets are used only to create usable drive space from several leftover fragments of a systems drives that would, otherwise, go to waste.

Hardware RAID

As we indicated at the start of this section, fault tolerance can be software or hardware based. While the overall concept doesn't vary between the two, performance and limitations can be quite different. Hardware-based RAID typically uses firmware built into the controller card instead of software-based, fault-tolerance drivers. This arrangement can make the process quite a bit faster and more efficient since the CPU doesn't have to get involved in the operation. It also typically eliminates the limitation that prevented us from loading the operating system software on a stripe set since the hardware implementation is fully functional at power up and doesn't not have to wait for the boot sequence to load appropriate drivers.

Some RAID5 hardware implementations are fully automated and contain an unused spare drive. When a member of the array fails, it is logically removed from the array and the stripe set with parity is automatically regenerated with the spare drive. Once the regeneration is complete, the administrator receives a message to remove and replace the failed drive, which will become the new unused spare. In some advanced systems, this entire process (including the drive replacement) can be accomplished without ever taking the server off line. Swapping the hard drives while the server remains online is done by using hardware that is called hot-swap or hot-swappable. In these systems, the drive electronics are built to avoid damage by removal and replacement while the system is running.

While hardware implementations are quite attractive, they can also be very expensive. A hardware solution can also require you to obtain all your server hardware from a single vendor. Once you have purchased and installed a hardware solution, you are generally committed to using it. On the other hand, when using a software solution, it is relatively easy to change your fault tolerance procedures. You may, for instance, decide to use mirroring because you only have two drives. At a later date, you could purchase an additional drive, write your mirrored data to tape, install the new drive, create a stripe set with parity, and restore the previously mirrored data to the new RAID5 array.

Uninterruptible Power Supply

What happens to your network when the power goes out or during brief power interruptions? Do your servers shutdown and restart? Is data being written to open files lost? If your servers are not connected to uninterruptible power supplies, the answer to these questions is probably "yes."

The typical uninterruptible power supply (UPS) is a battery-based system that provides a short-term power source and a service to manage a safe shutdown. There are many varieties of UPS, but the best ones communicate with the computer to which they are attached. When a power loss is detected, they immediately supply power. After a few seconds (to ensure the loss wasn't just a momentary fluctuation), they initiate processes to notify the administrator that a power failure has occurred, notify users to save their work and log off, and prevent new connections to the server. If the power remains down for a predetermined time (governed by the amount of time the UPS can provide power), a graceful system shutdown is initiated. Should the power return before the designated shutdown period, the UPS sends a "power on" notification and initiates procedures to return the system to normal operation.

When selecting and installing a UPS, make sure it can support the electrical requirements of the equipment attached to it. Refer to the product documentation to configure your operating system to work with the device. Configuration settings are typically few and simple—most depend on whether a particular signal will use a positive or negative voltage. Some UPS devices can tell the system when their batteries are about to fail. For a UPS that doesn't provide this notification, the management software can typically be configured to assume battery failure after a certain length of time and proceed accordingly.

Note

Most UPS systems communicate with the computer via the serial port. The UPS cable is, however, not a standard serial cable. Ensure you always use the cable supplied with or designated for your UPS.

Software Patches

Anyone who has been involved with information technology for more than a few minutes will not be surprised to hear that most delivered software is not perfect. As bugs are found or deficiencies noted, most software vendors build packages to correct the detected shortcomings. These corrections are called *service packs*, *fixes*, *hot-fixes*, *patches*, or *updates*, depending on what they fix and who the vendor is. Such corrections may apply to a simple application or a whole operating system, and they may correct a single problem or a host of deficiencies.

The first rule of PATCHology is "be careful." Patches are intended to fix problems and are normally tested before they are released. Having said that, they typically go through far less rigorous testing than the software they are designed to fix and may cause difficulty on certain combinations of hardware and software. You should not install any type of software correction unless you know what it fixes and actually need the fix it provides. If, for instance, the patch is designed to make your software compatible with flat-bed scanners and your network has no flat-bed scanners, you should move on to the next challenge and ignore the patch.

Where Should I Obtain Patches?

These days everyone is offering some piece of software to change or improve something. When you go looking for patches, you would be well advised to stick with the manufacturer of the software you are going to patch. If we're concerned about the degree of testing done on a patch, it stands to reason that a patch created by the manufacturer will be better tested and more reliable than one developed by a hobbyist who uploads his or her handiwork to the Internet or a bulletin board.

Manufacturers' patches are typically obtained from the manufacturers' Web sites, found on the software distribution media, available through manufacturers' support subscriptions (e.g., Microsoft TechNet), or other vendor technical bulletin or support systems.

How Can I Tell What the Patch Does and How It Will Work on My System?

Strangely enough, most patches come with documentation. The documentation is typically found in READ.ME files but may be in HTML or actually printed on paper. It is usually a good idea to read the documentation *before* installing the software. In addition to the self-contained documentation, you will likely find information on the vendor's Web site, trade publications, service bulletins, support subscriptions, and user group Web sites and bulletin boards. Although we recommended staying away from third-party patches, it is a great idea to gather third-party information concerning a vendor patch. Are there any horror stories about the patch's installation or has anyone reported that the "fix" doesn't work? Look at the manufacturer-supplied information to determine what the fix will correct and check for any warnings or recommended procedures. Check third-party information to ensure the manufactured didn't miss anything that someone else discovered. Most importantly, figure out how to determine if the patch fixed what it was supposed to fix in your system.

How Do I Install the Patch?

Patches are normally installed just as any other software, using an installation or setup program. Before you get to that step, however, ensure you have reviewed all the documentation (to include that which is in compressed files included with the patch) you can find. Once you're sure you need the patch and understand how to do the installation, you may want to do the first install on a test machine configured as closely as possible to the one you will ultimately update. As you run the installation, pay close attention to any options presented. A patch may, for instance, detect an unexpected .DLL and ask if you want to overwrite it with an older version. Typically, you would want to keep the newer release and would say "No." In any case, be sure to document your choices to ensure you can change them if the current installation fails, and you suspect you made the wrong choice.

If you complete test installation without crashing the machine, test the features the patch was designed to fix and verify all other system functions operate at least as well as they did before the patch. If testing shows that everything is functioning properly, it is time to move on to the production environment. If a problem is noted, rebuild the test machine and try the installation using different options. Repeat this process until you get the patch to function or you decide the patch will not work on your system. If you experience difficulty in making the patch function properly, you may want to contact the manufacturer's technical support department or an independent special interest group.

Before installing a patch on a production machine, take all steps necessary to ensure the machine can be returned to its original state in the event of a failed installation. This should include a full backup and any other procedures (such as the Windows NT *Emergency Repair Disk*) available. If you are going to perform the installation on a server, notify your users that the server is going down and ensure they are disconnected. Finally, when all preparations are complete, install the patch and test just as you did on the test environment.

When Will I Need to Reinstall the Patch?

Some software patches make modifications to a single piece of code, while others change code and replace a number of system support files (such as .DLLs). Operating system patches typically fit the later category. When you install a patch and later install a new feature from the original distribution disk, you run the risk of overwriting the system support files that were updated when the patch was installed. In this case, you will need to reapply the patch. Although the chances of running into trouble during the second patch installation are much less than when you ran it the first time, you cannot be absolutely sure that the combination of the newly installed features and the patch won't cause trouble. Make sure you use all normal precautions (to include a system backup) before completing the reinstallation.

Summary

This chapter presented a collection of important concerns, procedures, and tools to keep your network running properly. We started with a look at your network's physical environment and saw how the condition of the power supplied to the network, as well as climate, physical placement, and sources of radio and electromagnetic interference, can affect its operation.

We then turned our attention to system monitoring. We reviewed some of the monitoring and analysis tools available and discussed the review of error logs in some detail. Even when things appear to be operating properly, a proactive approach to detecting and correcting small deficiencies before they result in trouble reports can keep the network operating at peak efficiency.

Looking at a specific threat to our network operation, we reviewed the virus threat and saw how a good antivirus program depends on policies and training, a good backup program, and antivirus software. Antivirus software, we concluded, is only as good as its most recent update (found in signature files) and subsequent file scans.

We next looked at some data protection and recovery procedures. A good backup program depends on a well-organized plan that details what to back up, when to back up, and who will perform the backup. We reviewed the major backup methods: *copy, daily copy, full backup, incremental backup, and differential backup.* After learning how to employ these methods, we discussed the proper management and storage of the tapes that contain the backed up data. We decided that we should have enough tapes so we would not need to continually overwrite the same cartridge and discussed the benefits of off-site storage. We also saw the value of test restores and reviewing the backup log to ensure that backups are being properly completed. In general, we saw how a sound backup program, when combined with off-site tape storage, can protect our network from a multitude of mechanical, environmental, and human caused catastrophes.

While a backup program could help us recover from disaster, fault-tolerance procedures can keep our network running when disk related hardware failures occur. Fault tolerance can be hardware or software based.

While hardware-based fault tolerance is, typically, the most efficient and feature laden, the software-based variety is less expensive and more flexible. We looked principally at *disk mirroring* (RAID1) and *stripe sets with parity* (RAID5). While RAID1 systems were less expensive and easier to set up initially, RAID5 systems can have a far lower cost per megabyte of disk storage and offer better performance. After either system experiences a single failure, further fault-tolerance capabilities are lost until the hardware is replaced and the RAID 1 or 5 system reimplemented. We also looked at a fault-tolerance system called *disk duplexing* and found it to be similar to disk mirroring but with the addition of a disk controller for each mirrored drive.

Unexpected power losses can result in disk crashes, data losses, and servers going off line. To guard against such problems, you can employ an *uninterruptible power supply* (UPS). The UPS will keep your systems functioning in spite of momentary power losses and will provide sufficient power to allow a graceful shutdown during extended power failures. In addition to supplying power, a good UPS can trigger network notifications and prevent users from connecting to servers during the graceful shutdown. UPS installation and configuration is fairly simple. It is important, however, to ensure you use the proper cable to communicate with the computer's serial port (not a regular serial cable) and that the UPS is capable of providing sufficient power to all the devices connected to it. Respecting the upper wattage limit of UPS-connected equipment ensures you have sufficient shutdown power when it's needed. Don't overload, because the result may be a hard shutdown, which was what we use the UPS to avoid.

Finally, we looked at software patches (also known as service packs, fixes, hot-fixes, and updates). Patches are a way of making corrections and modifications to existing software, such as your operating systems and applications. The first rule of applying patches is to only do so if you require the feature or fix the patch provides. It is prudent to use only patches supplied by the vendor, and installation should not be undertaken until you have reviewed all the available documentation (to include third-party evaluations and trouble reports). It is a good idea to first install a patch in a test environment and evaluate its impact on the test system before installation in the active production environment. It may be necessary to reinstall the patch if you install additional features from the original software distribution package. This is because the additional features may overwrite .DLLs or other code that had been replaced by the patch.

Proper planning and administration of your network are absolutely critical to its efficient operation. Once it's running, however, it is still important to manage and monitor its activity. Unexpected hardware or software failures, virus attacks, environmental factors, or just normal growth can impede network operation or require improvement or reoptimization of equipment, software, or facilities. By taking a proactive approach to maintenance and by understanding and employing safeguards like antivirus software, fault tolerance, a sound backup program, and uninterruptible power supplies, you can guarantee your network's trouble-free performance and keep your users happy and productive.

▲ REVIEW QUESTIONS

1. *A backup program can protect your data from the following (Select all that apply):*
   A. Hardware failure.
   B. Computer theft.
   C. Fire, flood, tornadoes.
   D. Inadvertent deletion.

2. *Under a full backup, all designated files are backed up except*
   A. Executable programs.
   B. Open files.
   C. Database files.
   D. Those previously backed up.

3. *A good UPS will do the following (Select all that apply):*
   A. Run all your servers until the power returns.
   B. Send a notification that the power has gone down.
   C. Prevent users from making new connections to the server during a loss of power.
   D. Permit a graceful system shutdown.

4. *You get a trouble call from a user who claims his workstation keeps locking up. He is angry because he has had to reboot the system several times and has lost a great deal of data. When you arrive at his cubicle, you discover he has placed a large room fan on top of his computer. You suspect the trouble was caused by the following:*
   A. RFI.
   B. A power surge from the fan.
   C. EMI.
   D. High room temperature.

5. *Power surges.*

   A. Cause less damage than power spikes.

   B. Are eliminated by inexpensive circuit breaker-protected power strips.

   C. Have been nearly eliminated by today's power companies.

   D. Are best handled by power conditioners or electronic surge protectors.

6. *System error logs should be reviewed*

   A. When a problem is noted.

   B. Regularly and frequently.

   C. When a new system is installed.

   D. Annually.

7. *Fault tolerance*

   A. Provides a capability to recover data after a myriad of mishaps.

   B. Eliminates the need for regular backups.

   C. Is a hardware-based automatic backup procedure.

   D. Should be used in conjunction with a sound backup plan.

8. *Under normal RAID1 operation, writes are _____ and reads are _____ as compared to a single non-fault-tolerant disk. (Select those that apply.)*

   A. Slower; faster.

   B. Faster; slower.

   C. Slower; the same.

   D. The Same; the same.

9. *When a RAID5 system experiences a crash, reads are _____ as compared with the system prior to the crash. (Select one that applies.)*

   A. Faster.

   B. Slower.

   C. The same.

   D. Depends on how many drives crashed.

10. *You have a 10-disk, RAID5 array and have experienced malfunctions on drives 2 and 6. How would you restore the system to its fully fault-tolerant operation?*

    A. Replace drive 2, regenerate, replace drive 6, regenerate.

B. Replace drive 6, regenerate, replace drive 2, regenerate.

C. Replace both drives, and regenerate the stripe set.

D. Replace both drives, and restore from a tape.

11. *The best route to virus protection is through (Select all that apply):*

A. A good backup program.

B. Removing your network from the Internet.

C. Policy formulation and user training.

D. Antivirus software.

12. *To keep your antivirus software effective, you should*

A. Install the latest service pack as soon as it comes out.

B. Regularly obtain and install signature files.

C. Keep it server based.

D. Disable the mode that runs in background.

13. *When a new software patch is announced, you should*

A. Ignore it because it's nothing but trouble.

B. Install it right away to keep the network up to date and compatible with other network components.

C. Install it only if required by your network.

D. Install it only when upgrading operating system software.

Network Troubleshooting

▲ Chapter Syllabus

Troubleshooting Methodology

Wire to Application

Network Analysis Resources

In this chapter the discussion is wrapped around a process called troubleshooting. Troubleshooting is distinguished from maintenance because it is more than monitoring and guarding the health of your network. Now we must determine what must be done when something goes wrong. The focus of this chapter is on using a systematic method to discover, isolate, repair, and document failures. When there are problems, you should use this approach every time. Although in a perfect world, we would expect our systems to work flawlessly, providing 100% uptime, it's not likely your network will provide anything close to that without a good deal of effort on your part. If the job of network planning and implementation has been done well, there will be few times the troubleshooting process is necessary. A troubleshooting plan or checklist and the knowledge of basic troubleshooting information is essential to the task of keeping your network up and running.

After completing this chapter, you will be able to do the following:

- Use a systematic approach to identify the extent of a network problem and, given a problem scenario, select the appropriate steps to resolve it

- Determine whether a problem is attributable to the operator or the system and, given a problem scenario, select the appropriate steps to resolve it

- Describe the procedures to check for physical and logical indicators of trouble

- Determine the most likely cause or causes of the problem and select the appropriate course of action based on the information available

- Specify the tools commonly used to resolve network equipment problems and identify their purpose and function

The job of network administrator involves a considerable amount of work to properly maintain clients, servers, and other network resources. Administration tasks can be made easier through a proactive approach to network maintenance and in-depth knowledge of the network environment. Much of this in-depth knowledge is obtained through a comprehensive network documentation program.

We suggest is that you keep a record of what was changed, when it was changed, what the effect was, and how any attendant problems were resolved. Good documentation will serve as a learning tool and a method to track changes to your network. It will also help you do the same task faster the next time, help anyone that needs to know about the network, and add to your knowledge base.

While the maintenance of internetworks has become far more complex over the past 20 years, the tools for locating and correcting network problems have greatly improved. In order to take advantage of those tools, we must understand the basics of network troubleshooting and move beyond them. There is no substitute for hard work and a solid thought process. It is always best to look for the most obvious or the simplest problems first and doggedly follow your troubleshooting plan. Solid knowledge of the hardware, software, topology, gateways, routers, bridges, and hubs on your network will reap great benefit during the troubleshooting process. The best troubleshooting tool is a proactive approach to network management that eliminates trouble before it develops.

Troubleshooting Methodology

The first law of troubleshooting is to have a plan or method; the second is to follow it. Think of yourself as a cyber brain surgeon. You may have noticed that brain surgeons rarely say "OOPS" or "I guess we don't need that part."

This may sound humorous, but troubleshooting is a serious business and proper troubleshooting could mean the life or death of your systems. Troubleshooting requires a structured thought process, the ability to repeat steps over and over (even if they are boring), and the commitment to get the task completed the right way. In a short chapter we cannot cover every possible symptom, possible causes, and all solutions. We can, however, provide a *systematic approach* that creates a framework through which you may apply your systems knowledge to consistently arrive at a solution to your network's difficulties.

What is a systematic approach? A systematic approach is a series of steps that you follow each and every time there is something wrong with your network. The consistency of a routine will help you develop discipline and focus that is useful when approaching a problem of unknown origin.

Following a systematic approach means that you work from what you know to what you don't know. First define the problem, and it must be the *real* problem. For example, it is 6:00 A.M. on a typical Monday. The first user to log onto the network determines that the mail server is down and calls for help. The server outage is a symptom of the problem. What we mean by the *real* problem is the root cause. Starting with the wire and working our way up to the application, we can locate the issue and determine the true cause of the problem.

Next, develop a solution that will remove the problem completely. Clearing the collisions on a hub may fix an issue for the moment, but it will certainly return when the cards that caused the collisions start to transmit. Finally, after the problem is solved, document the work so that the past is not repeated with each new technical challenge.

STEP 1: Identify the Exact Issue

Someone has reported a problem, or an error event shows up in a log. *Identification* means to determine exactly what is going wrong. On a network you must decide whether the problem exists across the network or if it is isolated to a particular part. If the problem can be isolated to a particular network segment or component, the solution will be arrived at faster. Speed counts, as does accuracy, when you have a server down condition.

Everything you can do at this point to better define and narrow down the problem will make the rest of the troubleshooting process far easier. Can you isolate the problem to a particular workstation, workgroup, LAN, or WAN?

Let us say, for example, a particular user is complaining that he/she cannot get to the Internet. Has the user properly identified the problem or simply told you that it just doesn't work? The user probably needs to give you more information about what he/she is doing and how he/she is trying to access the Internet. Let's start with some questions: Is the user unable to get to the whole Internet or just one site? Is it a particular Web, FTP, or Gopher site or a single page on the site? Is the user new to the process or is this a person who uses the Internet every day? Is it something that is inside our network or outside? Are there other users who also cannot access the Internet? Was the connection down for a minute or two? Is this a problem that comes and goes once and a while? Is it normal behavior?

It is critical to identify the exact problem and ensure you are not just looking at a symptom. Is there a bug with the software or is this even software related? Is it perhaps hardware related? Can it be confined to a single computer or does it appear to affect all the machines on a particular network segment? Before you dash off and start ripping network cards out or troubleshooting the timing of packets on the router, STOP, and find the real issue. Step back from the problem and ask what the trouble report is really trying to tell you.

STEP 2: Recreate the Problem

Can the problem be reproduced? In order to fix the problem, you have to be able to see it. When a reported problem cannot be demonstrated, you must either assume you have a self-healing network or get more deeply into the analysis. Do we know what the trigger is for the event? Is there something that prohibits recreation of the problem such as permissions or the authority system that requires a certain login/logon privilege? Is there a log that can be checked to see what happens when trying to recreate the problem?

You have already asked what doesn't work and what should work, so this step is to ensure you can see the root cause. If *you* can't duplicate the problem, have the user perform the same steps and watch what he/she is doing. Is the user employing a very fast, unique keystroke sequence or some other unusual technique? This is not intended to cast blame on the user for problems he/she has reported; but when the problem cannot be duplicated, reintroducing the user into the scenario will help us identify the factors that helped to create the issue. Watching the user perform the steps is beneficial because it helps us understand the user process better.

Because we are observing, we are standing back from the action, and it becomes easier to identify the process and any related issues. This observation may even help you discover the root cause of the problem by itself. When trying to recreate the problem scenario, duplicate everything as accurately as possible. Don't exclude hardware, software, or procedures until you can confirm the origin of the problem. Once you actually see the problem in action, it is time to walk through the scenario and isolate the cause.

STEP 3: Isolate the Cause

The essence of troubleshooting is fixing the right problem. To make things better again, you must be able to find the real cause of the reported problem. The best way to start this process is to begin with what you know works and walk your way through the network to determine what works and what doesn't. An example on the local area network might be that two machines are unable to communicate. Start from the desktop perspective or from a server perspective, but chose one and start working from the wire up the OSI protocol stack on one side. Clearly, if you have a network with many machines and all but one can see the network, it is not likely that the server is the problem. If, on the other hand, several machines can't see the server, then you may want to start looking at the wires, hubs, protocols, and so forth. Start in the wiring closet and at the hubs that forward the signals and then move upward to the protocol configuration.

Determine if this is the first time the scenario that created the problem was attempted or if the scenario was a common practice that has worked without difficulty in the past. If it worked before, determine what has changed since the last time it worked. If this is the first time the procedure has been attempted, check to determine if the system was designed to do what the user is expecting it to do. If the problem was detected during a routine operation, you will need to determine what caused the change in system behavior. Has the user added or removed something or has there been some other software or hardware change since the last time the function worked? Is the issue always the same or does it change? Are the users doing something that is making it change?

When you suspect a problem may be user induced you should go through three steps to prove/disprove the hypothesis and try to narrow down the actual cause. First, have someone else perform the error-causing procedure on a similar workstation. If the problem does not occur, have the same individual attempt the same procedure on the workstation on which the problem was reported. If the problem is recreated during either of these steps, you can probably rule out the specific operator as a cause. In either case, the third step is to review operator procedures and ensure they are adhering to any previously established procedures. If you narrow the problem down to a specific operator, review his/her procedures. If both the operator who originally reported the problem and the operator you selected to perform the test have the same result, you will need to ensure they both used the appropriate procedures. If procedures were in accordance with organizational policies, it is time to look elsewhere for causes.

Warning

Although you have eliminated the user as a causative factor, this does not rule out a procedural problem. You may discover the problem is caused by an organizational procedure that has not kept pace with network changes. The network may be doing exactly what it was "told" to do under the circumstances, and a revision to standard procedures may be in order.

In the case of two computers on the network that can't communicate, you might find that you could create a tentative list of causes. Each action may or may not get you the connectivity you seek, so it is important that you proceed one step at a time and document along the way. A brief example is as follows:

1. Computer A or B hardware
   - Replace the wire with a known good wire
   - Replace the network card with a known good card

2. Computer A or B Software
   - IRQ, DMA, I/O base address or shared memory address configuration
   - Protocol configuration (IP address, subnet mask, default gateway, IPX network number, frame type, and so on)
   - Configuration within the computer, such as service settings

3. Wiring closet, hub, or other central switch
   - Power to the hub or Etherswitch
   - Wires or wiring changes to wall jacks
   - Settings of the network such as protocol-specific setting of IPX/SPX or TCP/IP

Study Break

An Example from the Real World

In a real world scenario not too long ago, a half-dozen engineers were attempting to understand exactly what was wrong with a particular machine. The computer was unable to communicate with the other machines on the Internet. Since this was a fairly sophisticated, Internet-capable-network installation, the highly qualified group started their troubleshooting with the machine's TCP/IP protocol settings. At the same time, an office manager, untrained in the systematic approach, picked up the end of the computer's network cable from the floor and stated: "The washing machine manual says that if the appliance doesn't work, check power cord and plug it in." Click-click, and the machine was back on the network!

This illustrates several points:

- Pick the easier solutions, and try them first.
- Always check the wires.
- Don't oversolve the problem.
- Start at the physical layer of the OSI model, and work your way up.

STEP 4: *Formulate a Correction*

This step is the one that most administrators are working through in their minds when they should be on the steps we defined previously. It is easy to get into the trap of making solutions fit the problem. If you have properly recreated the problem and isolated the cause, this step is simply "fixing what broke." If, on the other hand, you go directly to this step, your troubleshooting will be a trial-and-error process that is likely to do as much damage to the network as the initial problem.

In many cases, you will have actually formulated the correction as part of your troubleshooting process in step 3. If that is the case, this is where you step back and determine if the correction completed in the troubleshooting process is the best solution or if it needs to be implemented anywhere else within the network. If, for instance, the correction is to install a particular protocol on a workstation so it can communicate with a new server, do we need to install the same protocol on the rest of the workstations? Would it be a better idea to install a protocol compatible with the workstations on the new server?

Sometimes, even when you can completely isolate the problem, the solution is so complex that some trial and error cannot be helped. In this case, it is important to apply any corrections one at a time while noting the effect they have on the computers and the network. If a change works and the network functions properly, you have most likely corrected the problem or at least part of it. If a change doesn't work, back it out and try another change. Keep a record of what you change. It is important to keep track of what is changed and what the effect of the change is.

STEP 5: Implement the Correction

This should be a pretty straightforward step. Once you have isolated the cause and formulated the correction, you fix the problem. This may be as simple as plugging in the network wire or reinstalling a protocol or as complex as rebuilding a server or replacing a router.

STEP 6: Test the Correction

This should go without saying, but any change you make to your network has the potential to fix the problem and cause harm at the same time. First, of course, you want to ensure your corrective action really fixed the problem. Make sure you didn't fix the problem on one workstation or segment only to have it crop up elsewhere in the network.

Sometimes, even when the correction appears to have fixed the problem, it hasn't. If the problem was evidenced by a particular error message, for instance, and after implementing your fix, the error message stops, it may be possible that you have only suppressed the error message. Make sure everything related to the reported problem has been corrected.

Some repairs may completely correct the problem but result in unwanted side effects in other parts of the network. Changing an Internet protocol (IP) address of a server, for instance, may resolve an IP address conflict but may also make it impossible for other hosts to find the server unless your DNS records are updated. It is important to ensure that the rest of the system still functions as it did prior to any corrective actions undertaken. If additional problems surface, you will need to develop an alternative correction or make corrections in other parts of the network to compensate for the initial correction (as in the case of the change to the server IP address).

A final part of the test step is to remain alert for trouble reports that may be related to your change. It is not likely that you will be able to test 100 percent of the operations that occur on your network; but over the course of a few days, your users are likely to perform the majority of possible procedures. While you should never decide to let the users do your testing, their activities can certainly fill any small gaps that may remain in a good testing program.

STEP 7: Document the Problem and the Solution

As we indicated in step 6, changes made to a functional network will have a number of effects on a network. One effect might be that users won't understand how to approach the changed network.

After spending three days in correcting a problem, there is nothing worse than to hear, "Oh, yeah, that happened a couple of years ago and we fixed it the same way." If the problem and solution had been documented "a couple of years ago," you could have simply gone to the problem log and fixed the problem. Even if the problem required a different solution, the log may have pointed you to a good starting point.

Documentation can, of course, be done in a variety of ways, but thorough reporting will always pay off. Show the problem, the solution that fixed the problem, and perhaps solutions attempted that didn't fix the problem. List any unexpected side effects and their solutions too.

In addition to helping you fix future problems, good documentation is useful when a problem relating to your corrective action crops up. In that case, you will be able to refer to the documentation to help you "back" the fix out to determine if it is really a causative factor in the current situation.

Even the best documentation, of course, is no good if no one can use it. You should try to make your documentation as user friendly as possible. Building a documentation database is an excellent way of improving accessibility to the information. Such documentation would not merely be chronological but could be cross-referenced by fix, symptom, location, and any other information that would help find the information rapidly the next time something goes wrong. Be certain the documentation is available and in printed format. Having it on the server when that server is down would make the solution harder than necessary.

STEP 8: Give Feedback

Have you ever felt alone on a trouble call; and if you just had a few more pieces of information, you might be able to solve the problem? Give feedback to the operator of the equipment and give feedback to the help desk that assigned you the work to ensure that they understand the nature of the problem and what could be done about it next time.

Keep in mind that the customer is the end user in most cases. Remember to provide the end user with descriptive feedback about the origin and solution of the problem. This feedback relates directly to your credibility as a network administrator. Let the user know exactly what happened and what you did to solve the problem. Don't blame or otherwise criticize the user but let him or her know what was wrong, why it was wrong, and how the user may have had a positive or negative effect on the problem. While it is true that the network administrator's job would be much easier without users, it is users who act as the administrator's eyes and ears concerning the health of the network. In many cases, it is easier for a user to ignore, live with, or work around a problem. You want your users to take the time to properly report problems they find before the problems cause more extensive network difficulties. Good feedback will keep you and your users on the same team and will ensure that you get good feedback when you need it.

Remember, you may have made changes or corrections to your network that affect many people who didn't even know there was a problem. When making corrections that may have a far-reaching effect on the network and its users, it is always a good idea to let everyone know a change was made and what some potential effects might be.

Study Break

General Hardware Troubleshooting

START FACT FINDING

1. Users and Settings

- Who is using the computer?

- What are the user settings that affect the problem?

- Are the user settings changed from the standard?

- What permissions are required to perform this?

- Who was the last user?

- What was the last operation performed on the machine?

- Was the last user a new user or someone unfamiliar with this machine?

2. Software

- What operating system software was in use when the problem was discovered?

- What features of the software were being used?

- What service pack, NLM patch, or service level release is on the machine?

- What known problems are there with the service pack, NLM patch, or service level release?

- What applications were in use?

3. History

- Was this problem previously documented?

- How was it handled in the past?

- What is the history of the problem?

4. Backup and Recovery

- What is the status of the backup?

- Was there offsite storage?

- What is the status of the restore tape(s)?

- Was the user instructed to perform intermediate saves during the process while experiencing the problem?

- Is there another copy of the work saved elsewhere on the network?

5. Hardware Status

- Check (BIOS) settings and all options.

- Check floppy drives.

- Check CD-ROM.

- Check all power cords.

- Check any power strips.

- Check any power converter.

- Check all connections.

- Check peripherals (keyboard, monitor, mouse, printer, scanner, Iomega drive, optical drive) for proper connections.

- Check that all diskettes are removed before booting.

- Check the position of power switches to ensure that they are in the ON position.

- Check switches that may be heat sensitive (usually found inside of equipment).

- Check and run equipment (example: printer); self-test if applicable.

- Check that internal cards are seated properly (if cards were removed/replaced recently).

6. Resets

- Perform a warm or soft boot by holding down the CTRL-ALT-DEL key combination and try this before a cold boot as it is faster and places less stress on the hardware. Note: this is *not* what Windows NT uses to reboot.

- Perform a cold boot, which is also called a hard boot, by turning off the power, and wait for the hard drive to spin down and stop (about 30 seconds).

EXAMPLES OF SPECIFIC ISSUES

1. Video

Symptom:	Nothing on screen
Problem:	Brightness turned down
	Monitor turned off
	Monitor unplugged (power)
	Monitor not connected to PC
Symptom:	Cursor on screen (nothing else)
Problem:	See the boot section

2. Boot

Symptom:	System will not boot
Problem:	Floppy diskette in the drive
	ROM-BIOS settings incorrect
	Files possibly deleted or damaged on the hard drive (try to boot from floppy)

3. Floppy drive or diskette

Symptom:	System will not boot
Problem:	Not a system diskette or files missing
Symptom:	Error reported by software when saving or copying a file to diskette
Problem:	Diskette not formatted
	Diskette full
	Diskette of wrong density or type for drive

4. Keyboard

Symptom:	Key stuck or keyboard error, press F1 to continue
Problem:	Check that keyboard is plugged in and that nothing is leaning against the keyboard
Symptom:	No keyboard
Problem:	Check connection

5. Printer

Symptom:	Print fails
Problem:	Printer-to-PC cable loose
	Printer not plugged in
	Printer not turned on
	Printer not online
	Out of paper, or paper badly jammed
	Incorrect print driver

6. Modem

Symptom:	No data connection
Problem:	Cable from line to PC off, broken or loose
	Phone line dead
	Wrong COM port specified
Symptom:	Garbage on screen
Problem:	Connection issue, restart program. If this persists, try restarting computer

Wire to Application

You may remember that, at the start of this chapter, we indicated you would need a systematic approach and *solid systems knowledge* to be able to be an effective troubleshooter. This chapter concentrates on the trouble shooting system, or "road map," you follow to obtain a good solution. Just as a road map won't do much good unless you know how to start and operate your car, a systematic troubleshooting approach is little help unless you know and understand the network systems involved. With that in mind, you might consider this entire book as a troubleshooting aid. Without a good understanding of everything we've written about, you will be as unprepared for troubleshooting as you would be to head out on to Interstate 80 without your car keys and drivers license!

In addition to the general knowledge you have gathered here, you will also need to have a solid understanding of your particular network, its topology, operating system(s), connectivity devices, and applications software.

We talked earlier of walking your system to find what works and what doesn't work. We will now spend a little time looking at some of the ways we might do just that.

Go Easy Early

While the systematic approach is the key to troubleshooting, you shouldn't ignore some quick and easy things to check before you get deep into analysis. Some of them may solve the problem, while others may add to your understanding of the problem.

When a user cannot get onto the network, the 30 seconds it takes to verify his/her network cable is plugged into the computer and the NIC's indicator lights are illuminated may cut the troubleshooting process short and provide you with an opportunity to do a good stretching exercise.

Many systems have error logs that track unexpected conditions. A quick look at a log, such as the Microsoft Windows NT system or application log, may quickly reveal an easy way to isolate the problem. In Figure 11–1, for instance, we can see the workstation "laptop" was unable to renew

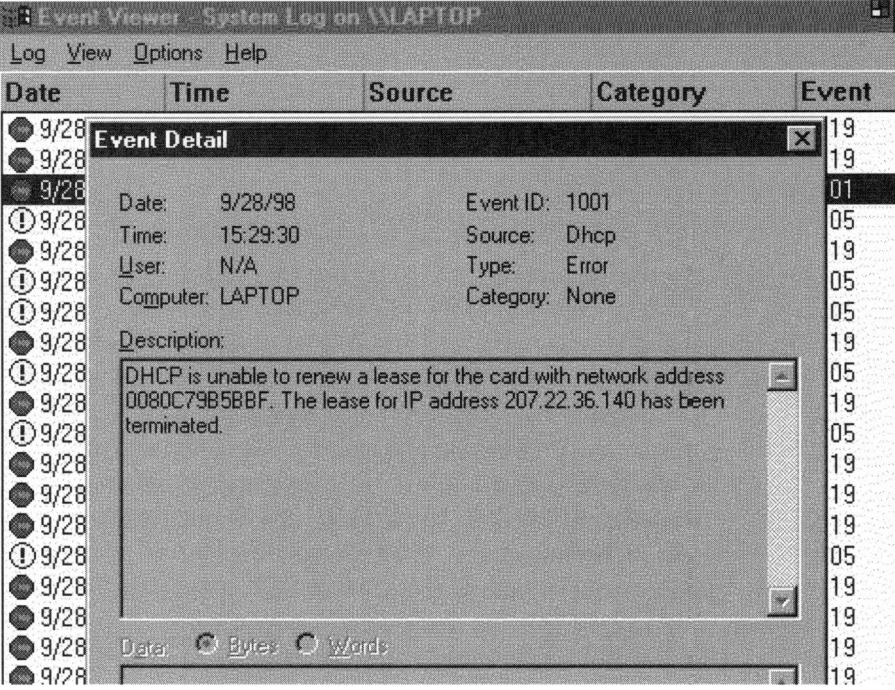

Figure 11–1 *Windows NT system log.*

its DHCP lease. With that information, we can turn our attention to areas like dynamic host configuration protocol (DHCP) connectivity and availability.

Don't forget to look for other obvious conditions too. Is the system plugged in? Are the power lights on routers, switches, modems, or other connectivity devices glowing or dark? Is there obvious physical damage to any of your network components? Do you smell smoke? We've all heard the story about the user who couldn't get his monitor to come on and complained when asked to verify if it was plugged in since it was too dark because the power was out. Don't forget to verify your installation has power in all the critical places.

Walk Through the Protocol Stack

Ok, we've looked for the obvious and came up dry. Now it's time to see where the packets are getting stuck. Start at the workstation and re-check the network cable and indicator lights on the network interface card. If the wire is OK and the lights are out, it might be a good idea to check the card. Is it properly configured and installed? Does it work? (We haven't covered NICs to any great detail up to this point, but you will find a thorough treatment of the subject a bit later in this chapter.)

If the NIC is OK and the wire is OK and you've verified connectivity all the way through the hub, switch, MSAU, or other network node through which other workstations are properly functioning, it is time to move up the protocol stack. Does the workstation have a properly configured network protocol? Is the protocol the appropriate one for connecting to the rest of the network? Are you trying to go through a router using a non-routable protocol?

If the protocol appears to be functioning properly, can the computer find the other hosts for which it is looking? If you're using TCP/IP are you having a problem with name resolution? Are any applicable WINS or DNS name servers working properly? Is the workstation configured to use the appropriate name servers? Are you using a HOST file? If so, is it up to date?

If you still haven't found the problem, another trip up the stack is in order. Is the user using a network account with the appropriate permissions to make the desired network connection? Is the operator using the appropriate logon procedure? Does the workstation have the appropriate antivirus software? Is it up to date? Does it report a virus condition?

We walked the stack from the physical layer through the application layer. While this is typically the best way to go, the reason we use people and not computers to accomplish troubleshooting is because computers sorely lack the *judgment* of a human administrator. You may have cause to suspect, for instance, a logon or virus problem. If this is the case, you shouldn't waste your time in areas you believe are OK but should go right to the most likely trouble area. Having said that, you will likely spend most of your troubleshooting time following the recommended procedure.

Network Interface Cards

The network interface card (NIC) is a common area of network difficulties. Since this is a critical link in the route a packet travels from one machine to another, problems here can take a machine off the network or take down the entire network. It may be prudent, therefore, to spend some time getting to know how these all-important devices function.

While it is fairly easy to understand that an NIC puts frames on the "wire," it is important to grasp that different NICs do this in different ways. An NIC designed to work on Ethernet won't do the job on a token ring network, nor will function very well on ARCNet. Even if an NIC is designed for a particular topology, it still needs to be able to adapt to the particular medium (coaxial cable, twisted pair, fiber-optics, etc.) and network speed. The first principle of "NICology," then, is to make sure the NIC is appropriate for the network to which it will connect. Be particularly certain that what you are putting into the computer is a network adapter and NOT a modem and vice versa. Although the difference between an RJ-11 telephone plug and an RJ-45 network plug are quite obvious, if you put an RJ-11 plug into an RJ-45 jack (which is possible), you may damage the network card beyond repair.

Data Bus Architecture

The most basic function of an NIC is to convert parallel data from the computer's data bus to serial data which can flow over the network. Since computers can have a number of different architectures, NICs come in varieties to match. Data busses found in today's most common computers, transfer 8, 16, or 32 bits at a time. Obviously, the more bits transferred simultaneously, the faster the communications are within the computer. This, however, also means more work for the NIC. Let's take a brief look at the four most common data bus architectures in use today.

INDUSTRY STANDARD ARCHITECTURE • Industry standard architecture (ISA) began as an 8-bit architecture on the original IBM personal computers. In the mid-1980s, when IBM introduced the AT, ISA was expanded to a 16-bit architecture. ISA cards fit into ISA expansion slots on the black colored bus strip inside the computer. Like the cards, ISA slots come in 8 and 16 bit varieties. Eight-bit cards can fit into 16-bit slots, but not the other way around. This type of bus is identified with a black expansion slot in the computer.

EXTENDED INDUSTRY STANDARD ARCHITECTURE • Extended industry standard architecture (EISA) was introduced in 1988. EISA provides a 32-bit data path while maintaining compatibility with the ISA standard. Both EISA and ISA cards can be put into an EISA bus, which is brown.

MICRO CHANNEL ARCHITECTURE • The micro channel architecture (MCA) and EISA both competed for market share at about the same time. Micro Channel architecture is used in the IBM PS/2 desktop and server series. It supports both 16 and 32 bit busses but is not compatible with ISA or EISA technology. MCA cards will not work in any other bus architecture.

PERIPHERAL COMPONENT INTERCONNECT • Peripheral component interconnect (PCI) is the 32-bit local bus found in most of today's Pentium computers. Not compatible with previous architectures, it is typically identified by a white expansion slot in the computer. PCI cards are intended to be plug-and-play devices that normally require little or no manual configuration.

Data Transfer and Memory

Now that we have seen the architectures through which NICs communicate with their computers, let us take a look at some of the ways this communication takes place. Part of the network response noticed by the user has to do with how fast the NIC can take data from or return data to the computer's bus. The data transfer method can have a big impact on this.

DIRECT MEMORY ACCESS • Under direct memory access (DMA), the computer can move data between the NIC's data buffer and the computer's RAM without assistance from the CPU.

SHARED ADAPTER MEMORY • Using shared adapter memory, the RAM on the NIC appears to the computer as its own. The computer accesses the NIC just as if it were part of the computer itself.

SHARED SYSTEM MEMORY • Under this method, the NIC selects a portion of the computer's memory and uses it. This is similar to shared adapter memory except, here, the NIC accesses the computer's memory as if it were part of the NIC.

BUS MASTERING • Bus mastering is an expensive technique that can speed network performance by 20 to 70%. A Bus Mastering card actually takes temporary control of the computer's bus to move data directly into RAM without using the computer's CPU. Bus mastering allows the computer to concentrate on other processing while the NIC handles network communication.

RAM BUFFERING • By placing RAM on the NIC to create a buffer, a network card can hold incoming data during periods when it (the card) cannot process packets as fast as they arrive. This prevents the NIC from becoming a network bottleneck by getting packets off the wire as quickly as possible.

Configuration Parameters

Whether a NIC is a plug-and-play device or an older type that expects to have everything configured by hand, a number of parameters must be set. Understanding these parameters is critical for installation and troubleshooting because even the best plug-and-play devices are sometimes wrong. When that happens, the card doesn't work, the network may fail, and you will need to demonstrate knowledge of factual information about the critical resources and settings in order to get things going again.

INTERRUPT REQUEST QUERY • The interrupt request query line (IRQ) represents the hardware line through which the NIC will send requests for service to the CPU. Since other devices use IRQs also, it is important to ensure a unique IRQ is selected for each device. If your NIC, for instance, uses the same IRQ as your mouse or keyboard, these devices will conflict with each other and may fail to operate all together. Common IRQs for network cards are 3, 5, 10, 11, and 15, but you must consult the NIC's documentation to ensure it can support the selected IRQ and that the IRQ you select is not being used by another device. Table 11.1 shows the commonly assigned IRQs for an Intel-based computer.

BASE I/O PORT • The base I/O port address specifies the channel used by a device to exchange information with the CPU. Like the IRQ, this value must be unique or conflicts and malfunctions will follow. Typical NIC addresses are 300 to 30F and 310 to 31F. It is critical, however, to consult the documentation for your NIC and computer to ensure these are available and correct. You will also need to know if the card supports auto assignment of these addresses or if they must be set manually with jumpers or a software program.

BASE MEMORY ADDRESS • NICs that use shared system memory need to know where to look for that memory. The *base memory address* tells the NIC where to look. Also referred to as the "RAM start address," the typical value for this parameter is D8000 (sometimes annotated without the final zero as "D800"). Obviously, NICs that do not use any system RAM do not need a base memory address.

Table 11.1 *Common IRQs for Intel-based (80286 or later) computers*

IRQ	Function
0	System Timer
1	Keyboard
2	EGA/VGA
3	Available (if not used by COM2/COM4)
4	COM1/COM3
5	Available (if not used by LPT2 or a sound card)
6	Floppy disk controller
7	LPT1
8	Real time clock
9	EGA/VGA
10	Available
11	Available
12	Mouse (PS/2)
13	Math Coprocessor
14	Hard disk controller
15	Available (if not used by a secondary hard disk controller)

DIRECT MEMORY ACCESS CHANNEL • Cards using direct memory access must be configured with a *direct memory access channel* or *DMA channel*. DMA Channels are typically 1–7 and should be configured in accordance with the NIC documentation.

RING SPEED • Most token-ring networks operate at 4 or 16 Mbps and many token-ring NICs may be configured to either speed. If you are operating on a token-ring network, ensure your card is set to the correct speed if it is capable of both.

TRANSCEIVER TYPE • As we discussed in Chapter 1, the *transceiver* is the part of the NIC that actually transmits and receives signals to and from the medium. Some NICs (typically those that work with Thicknet and Thinnet) have an on-board transceiver but can also work with an external transceiver. These cards typically have both a BNC and AUI port. If you are using such a card, ensure it is set to use the appropriate transceiver. You should also note that in a combination card (i.e., a card with multiple connector types) you may have to use jumpers or a software utility to set the correct output type.

Configuration Devices

NIC parameters are important but how do we ensure they are set properly or correct them if they aren't? The most common configuration methods are jumpers, DIP switches, EEPROMs, and plug-and-play technology. To set these properly, you *must* consult the NIC's documentation and may need to decipher markings on the printed circuit board. Let's take a brief look at these configuration types.

JUMPERS • Perhaps the simplest configuration method, jumpers consist of a set of pins protruding from the NIC accompanied by a small block that is pushed onto the pins to make contact between them. Parameters are changed by removing the block from the pins it connects and placing it on a set that will bring about the desired value. Jumper blocks are small and easily lost—they are best removed and inserted through the use of tweezers or needle-nosed pliers

DIP SWITCHES • This common circuit board device performs essentially the same function as the jumper but is a bit more expensive and has no small parts to lose. "DIP" stands for *dual inline package* and is descriptive of the parallel rows of pins through which the device is connected to the circuit board. The switches can be moved back and forth to either connect or disconnect pairs of wires on the board just as the jumper block connected or disconnected pins. To achieve the proper configuration, set the DIP switches in accordance with the NIC documentation. It is sometimes necessary to use the small awl-like tool supplied in the A+ kits, nail punch, ballpoint pen, small screwdriver, or similar device to move the tiny switches.

EEPROM CHIPS • If you don't like taking a pen or tweezers to your circuit cards, the EEPROM chip is for you! EEPROM stands for *electrically erasable programmable read-only memory*, which can store the configuration parameters in a small onboard chip. To configure a card equipped with EEPROM chips, you simply load the configuration software that came with the card and enter your settings at the keyboard. The computer and EEPROMs do the rest! If you ever need to remove the settings, you can short the leads—which is to touch the two ends together creating a circuit that discharges the EEPROM memory—and start over.

PLUG AND PLAY • Most everyone has heard of plug and play (PnP) by now. With plug and play you simply insert the card and the system ensures everything is properly configured, right? Well, the only people who really believe that would seem to be in marketing. While the PnP standard can make installation and configuration a breeze, when the entire system is not PnP compliant, great frustration can follow. If, for instance, a PnP device wants a particular IRQ, it will check all the other PnP devices to ensure the IRQ is available and configure itself accordingly. The difficulty occurs when there is a non-PnP device already using the setting that couldn't speak for itself when the PnP card went IRQ shopping. When this happens, you are faced with the dreaded *IRQ conflict*! Resolution for this type of problem typically involves re-configuring the non-PnP device so it doesn't conflict with the newly added resource or removing one or both of the conflicting devices and replacing them with better behaved cards. Although we used IRQ as an example, conflicts may arise over any common parameter.

Diagnostics and Testing

NIC is installed and we should determine if it is functioning properly. What should you do? It's best to look at the simplest problems and methods first. A good start, therefore, is to determine if you can communicate over the network. If everything appears OK, you have probably done well. If your computer still appears to be a stand-alone machine, ensure you have the proper network protocol installed and that it is properly configured. (As we saw in Chapter 6, if you are using TCP/IP, you can ping the loop-back address—127.x.x.x—to ensure the protocol is properly installed.)

In addition to common sense and "can I see you" diagnostics, many hardware vendors supply diagnostics that check both the NIC's hardware and the software drivers supporting it. Many of the newer cards permit you to run the diagnostics during installation. These packages typically test the NIC, the drivers, and the network wire and report the status of each.

Vendor supplied after-installation diagnostic software can perform similar functions to help troubleshoot problems that arise over time. Some packages even do analysis across the network by placing components in more than one computer. These diagnostics can send packets across the network to monitor a number of performance areas. (This is the same concept as using the TCP/IP ping utility but is typically based on the manufacturer's proprietary protocol.)

LOOPBACK CHECKS • What if I need to check my NIC and I have serious doubts about the functionality of the network itself? A hardware/software diagnostic for 10BASE-T networks will permit you to make your NIC "talk to itself" to verify its operation. A hardware loopback connector is attached to the NIC's port. This connector is simply an RJ-45 plug that has been wired to make the data channel loop back to the NIC by shorting pins 1 and 3 and pins 2 and 6. With the loopback connector in place, you can load and run the NIC's loopback diagnostic software for a full report.

Network Analysis Resources

Now that we have a solid understanding of how our network systems function and are ready to use a systematic troubleshooting approach, let's take a look at some other resources available to make troubleshooting easier.

Crossover Cables

You will remember that we mentioned a *loopback* connector in the previous section. A similar device, called a *crossover cable,* can be used on twisted-pair networks to analyze operation beyond the local NIC. A crossover cable is simply a UTP cable with pins 1 and 2 on each connector connected to pins 3 and 6 on the opposite connector. Wired in this way, the cable can be used to connect two computers directly without going through a hub. By using a crossover cable, you can eliminate hubs and other network devices and verify the operation of a single pair of computers.

Warning

If you construct a crossover cable, ensure you mark it appropriately. Using a crossover cable thought to be a normal network cable we find that it will, of course, introduce some unexpected network problems.

Tone Generator/Tone Locator

Earlier we said you might want to trace your wiring to ensure everything is routed and connected properly. Once the wire goes through the wall and mixes with the rest of the network wiring, how do you determine which cable is which in the wiring closet? The answer to this question is a *tone generator.* Tone generators connect to UTP wires and send an electronic signal down a particular pair. Another device, called a *tone locator,* detects these signals and lets you know when you've found the correct pair. You don't need to connect the tone locator since it works by induction. The louder the tone, the closer you are to the desired pair of conductors.

This pair of devices is sometimes referred to as "fox and hounds." The tone generator is the fox, "running" down the wires, while the tone locator represents the hounds "sniffing" out the fox. In most of the modern cable test scenarios, the two devices are in one unit, which is used for wire identification and not to test for continuity or ground fault.

Time-Domain Reflectometers

A frequent cause of network malfunction is broken or disconnected network cables. While you can use the "fox and hounds" to find a particular wire, you probably would be happier to find which wire is broken. *Time-domain reflectometers* (TDRs) work much like sonar. They send a pulse capable of detecting breaks, shorts, and other imperfections down the wire. A good TDR can locate a problem within a few inches.

Protocol Analyzers

The ultimate in network analysis is the *protocol analyzer*. A protocol analyzer typically has a built-in TDR and is able to monitor network traffic at the frame level. Working across the OSI model, these analyzers can check the entire network from cabling and interface cards to operating system software and applications. A good protocol analyzer can even identify an individual computer that is sending bad packets or which is flooding the network with traffic and slowing the network. Some of the most popular protocol analyzers are the Hewlett-Packard Network Advisor, Network General Sniffer, and Novell LANalyzer™

Summary

This chapter provided a framework through which we can use our systems knowledge to diagnose and correct network problems. We studied a troubleshooting methodology that employed an eight step systematic approach: 1) *Identify the exact issue*, 2) *Recreate the problem*, 3) *Isolate the cause*, 4) *Formulate a correction*; 5) *Implement the correction*, 6) *Test the correction*, 7) *Document the problem and solution*, 8) *Give feedback*. By following the eight steps, we ensured we knew what was wrong, what caused the problem, and how to fix it. We then fixed the problem and tested our fix to make sure it corrected the problem while doing no harm to the existing network. Finally, we documented what we had done and let our users know what we did.

Knowing how to proceed in the troubleshooting process requires not only the understanding of the systematic approach but a good solid background in how the network functions. In addition to this final chapter, the entire book should be considered a troubleshooting resource. When embarking on a troubleshooting task, it is sometimes prudent to look for some obvious problems such as fire, flood, and power failure before going through a more detailed analysis. Don't forget to check that the wire is connected and look for power and activity lights. Remember to look at any available logs or other analysis aids.

When analyzing a network problem, it may be helpful to start at the physical layer and work up to the application layer, considering issues such as connectivity, protocols, network permissions, and viruses.

We spent some time looking at the workings of the network interface card. We looked at the cards' data bus architecture and how it relates to converting parallel data to serial data. We reviewed ISA, EISA, MCA, and PCI technologies and then looked at how NICs exchange data with the computer. The data access methods we reviewed were *direct memory access, shared adapter memory, shared system memory,* and *bus mastering.* Many of these methods permit exchange of data between the computer and NIC with no processing overhead. We reviewed *IRQs, base I/O port, base memory address,* and other configuration parameters, which must be properly (and uniquely) configured for proper operation. We examined the actual configuration methods for a network card to include *jumpers, DIP switches,* and *EEPROM chips,* and looked at NIC diagnostic aids such as *loopback checks.*

We completed the chapter by taking a look at some network troubleshooting resources such as *crossover cables, tone generators, tone locators, time-domain reflectometers,* and *protocol analyzers.*

▲ REVIEW QUESTIONS

1. *When a user reports a problem, your first concern is to*
   A. Identify the exact problem.
   B. Patch the problem so the network continues to operate.
   C. Train the user in problem reporting.
   D. Recreate the problem.

2. *When you suspect a problem may be induced by a user, you should do as follows (Select all that apply):*
   A. Have someone else attempt the error-causing problem on another machine.
   B. Have someone else attempt the error-causing problem on the machine on which the problem was observed.
   C. Retrain the user.
   D. Review operator procedures to ensure they are adhering to previously established policies.

3. *When formulating a correction you should*
   A. Pick a solution that fits the problem.
   B. Embark on a trial and error process that will ultimately solve the problem.
   C. Keep a record of anything you have done to the network.
   D. Apply all possible corrections to get the network up as quickly as possible.

4. *Select all that apply: You should test your correction to*

    A. Ensure you have fixed the problem.

    B. Measure by how much you have improved network efficiency.

    C. See if you have fixed any other preexisting problems.

    D. Determine if your fix has caused any other network problems.

5. *Problems and solutions should be documented to*

    A. Provide a record of operator problems.

    B. Form a basis for network administrator advancement.

    C. Make the troubleshooting job easier next time.

    D. Be used in litigation against the operating system or hardware vendor.

6. *The most obvious problem causes should be*

    A. Ignored, since it is not likely IT professionals would miss obvious clues.

    B. Reviewed during the appropriate step of the systematic approach.

    C. Checked first.

    D. Checked only after a thorough analysis of all possible problem factors.

7. *Extended industry standard architecture is compatible with the following:*

    A. All database architectures.

    B. Industry standard architecture.

    C. Micro channel architecture.

    D. Peripheral component interconnect.

8. *Your computer will not function on the network. You check the network wire, and it appears to be connected properly. You look at the NIC and see no activity lights. When you review the NIC's settings you discover the following: Base I/O Port, 320; Base Memory, D800; IRQ, 8; Transceiver, external. Where do you expect the problem?*

    A. In the protocol since the card is properly configured.

    B. External transceiver was selected with no external transceiver connected.

    C. IRQ is incorrect.

    D. Base memory is off by a power of 10.

9. *A crossover cable*

    A. Is used to connect two networks together to rule out router problems.

    B. May be used in place of standard UTP to analyze computer/hub problems.

    C. Must be used when analyzing MSAU problems.

    D. Can connect two computers directly.

10. *Select all that apply: Protocol analyzers*

    A. Test only frames going to or from a particular computer.

    B. May include a TDR.

    C. Can identify "problem" computers.

    D. Cannot test wiring problems.

11. *A user reports that he is unable to connect to the server "Server1." You go to his workstation and find you can successfully ping Server1's IP address. You suspect*

    A. The user doesn't know how to connect to Server 1.

    B. The user's workstation cannot get a DHCP lease.

    C. The network name servers are down.

    D. The user reported a transitory problem.

12. *You are in charge of a small 10BASE-2 computer network. Although this is characteristically a very stable network with no significant problems, one morning the network fails to operate. You are able to quickly identify the problem (network doesn't work) and have no problem reproducing it. It is time to isolate the cause. What do you suspect it the most likely cause of the problem?*

    A. Server power failure.

    B. Malfunctions in one or more computers.

    C. Break in the network cable.

    D. Protocol mismatch between the server and workstations.

    E. Name server malfunction.

Chapter Review Questions & Answers

Chapter 1 Questions

1. *What are the two major types of LANs?*
   - A. Sneakernet and NETBIOS.
   - B. Server based and client server.
   - C. Peer-to-peer and server based.
   - D. Centralized and remote.

2. *Which type of LAN is better for a large company?*
   - A. Sneakernet.
   - B. NetBIOS.
   - C. Server based.
   - D. Peer-to-peer.

3. *Who is the central administrator in a peer-to-peer LAN?*
   - A. No one.
   - B. The proxy administrator.
   - C. The server administrator.
   - D. The person using NWADMIN.

4. *What is the main advantage of peer-to-peer networking?*
   A. Requires more planning.
   B. Requires multiple segments.
   C. Requires no servers.
   D. Requires only one administrator.

5. *What are the main advantages of a server-based network? (Select all that apply.)*
   A. Greater freedom for the user.
   B. Increased security.
   C. Less standardization.
   D. No centralization of protocols.

6. *What is topology?*
   A. Packet transfer process that includes encapsulation.
   B. A form of routing.
   C. Multiple network cards.
   D. The physical arrangement of the equipment or the logical flow of the traffic on the wires.

7. *What are the three most common topology designs?*
   A. Bus, star, token ring.
   B. Ring, star, bus.
   C. Bus, closed loop, token ring.
   D. Standard bus, looped bus, star.

Chapter 1 Answers

1. *C; Peer-to-peer and server-based systems are the two major types of LANs.*

2. *C; A server-based LAN is better for a large company to centralize administration and security.*

3. *A; No one is the central administrator in a peer-to-peer LAN.*

4. *C; Requires no servers because each workstation can serve out files and resources.*

5. *A & B; Greater freedom for the user because he/she can log on anywhere. Increased security because the security, profiles, and policies are centrally administered.*

6. *D; The physical arrangement of the equipment or the logical flow of the traffic on the wires.*

7. *B; Ring, star, and bus are the three most common topology designs.*

Chapter 2 Questions

1. *A Server computer*
   - A. Holds databases, files, messaging systems, and management console products.
   - B. Permits users to log on and access resources found on other computers.
   - C. Is a machine a user operates to perform word processing, electronic mail, and other related tasks.
   - D. Must have a redirector.

2. *Novell NetWare server products support the following (select all that apply):*
   - A. ARCnet and token ring networks.
   - B. Unix and Apple environments.
   - C. Ethernet networks.
   - D. IBM and OS/2.

3. *NetWare 3.x is*
   - A. A monolithic application.
   - B. ODI compliant.
   - C. NDIS compliant.
   - D. Microsoft networking compliant.

4. *The Novell Bindery is*
   - A. A NetWare 3.x function that permits the use of multiple servers for user logon.
   - B. A NetWare 4.x feature that allows NetWare domains to look like Internet domains.

    C. A NetWare 3.x feature that creates a preferred server.

    D. A NetWare 5.x feature that creates a preferred server.

5. *NetWare 4.x NDS*

    A. Relies on primary and backup domain controllers.

    B. Is the networking protocol that must be installed on clients to permit them to connect to the server.

    C. Maintains network information in a hierarchical tree.

    D. Provides enhanced features for the bindery.

6. *Windows NT fault-tolerance support includes the following (select all that apply):*

    A. RAID1.

    B. RAID2.

    C. RAID3.

    D. RAID4.

    E. RAID5.

7. *Windows NT Server services include the following (select all that apply):*

    A. Client services for NetWare.

    B. Gateway services for NetWare.

    C. Message retrieval services for NetWare.

    D. File and print services for NetWare.

8. *Select all that apply: Windows NT directory services*

    A. Are based on a domain structure.

    B. Maintain a SAM database.

    C. Are found under a default tree and context.

    D. Require a primary domain controller.

9. *Windows 2000 Server is*

    A. The server equivalent to the Windows 95/98 operating system.

    B. The follow-on product to Windows NT 4.0 Server.

    C. A y2k compliant version of Windows NT 4.0 Server.

    D. A client program for accessing NetWare 2000 software.

10. *Select all that apply: Active Directory Services*

    A. Eliminate BDCs from Windows 2000 networks.

    B. Create a hierarchical database.

    C. Work with an automated DNS product.

    D. Maintain the distinction between Windows 2000 domains and Internet domains.

11. *UNIX operating systems*

    A. Come in only one variation.

    B. Are found in many varieties because the product is always being improved and rereleased.

    C. Are found in many varieties because many vendors provide a proprietary version to go with their hardware.

    D. Are outdated and no longer used in major networks.

12. *Select all that apply: Linux*

    A. Was the forerunner of UNIX.

    B. Is a new UNIX version that has had slow acceptance with software vendors.

    C. Is the next version of Apple networking.

    D. Has found solid support in Web-related operations.

13. *OS/2*

    A. Provides connectivity between Windows NT and Apple networks.

    B. Is still found in many large networks performing gateway functions.

    C. Is a Novell/IBM product designed to compete with Windows 2000.

    D. Is not a NOS.

14. *Select all that apply: Windows 95/98 and Windows NT Workstation*

    A. Are not suited as client operating systems, unless they run with Windows NT Server.

    B. Have nearly identical graphical user interfaces.

    C. Operate with TCP/IP only.

    D. Do not support 16-bit software.

15. *Once server and client software has been installed and the machines connected with the appropriate hardware, what two items must be functioning on the client to provide a network connection?*

    A. Network monitor.

    B. Redirector.

    C. Protocol.

    D. Remote access server.

Chapter 2 Answers

1. *A; Server computers hold databases, mail servers, and other network re-sources. Users use client computers to access these server-based resources.*

2. *A, B, C, D; NetWare supports all these networking environments.*

3. *B; NetWare supports the open datalink interface (ODI) standard which means it can work with a range of network adapter cards. ODI is one of the standards that permit the use of adapters without regard to proprietary specifications. This means the NOS is not monolithic. The NDIS standard applies chiefly to Microsoft products.*

4. *C; The Bindery is a NetWare 3.x feature. The Bindery permits only a single server for logon, known as the preferred server.*

5. *C; NetWare 4.x features NetWare Directory Services (NDS). This was a replacement for the Bindery and allowed the storage of network informa-tion in a hierarchical tree structure.*

6. *A, E; Windows NT provides RAID 1 (mirror sets) and RAID 5 (stripe set with parity)*

7. *A, B, D; Windows NT supports all listed services except message retrieval services for NetWare (which we made up).*

8. *A, B, D; Windows NT networks are based on a Windows NT domain that uses a primary domain controller and one or more backup domain con-trollers to manage the network. User accounts are stored in the security accounts manager (SAM) database. The term default tree and context per-tains to connectivity with NetWare Directory Services.*

9. *B; Windows 2000 was originally named Windows NT 5.0. This new release will use Windows NT architecture and features Active Directory Services.*

10. *A, B, C; The Windows 2000 active directory services work with all peer-level domain controllers (DCs) which effectively eliminates the backup*

domain controller (BDC) concept from Windows 2000. Unlike the Windows NT predecessors, the active directory database is hierarchical. Active directory services works with the automated DNS to integrate the network with the Internet and makes the Windows 2000 domain name the same as the Internet domain name.

11. *C; The many varieties of UNIX operating systems were designed to fit customer needs back when hardware and software were generally proprietary with very little cross-vendor applicability. Customers are still purchasing these products for their utility, strength, security, and fault tolerance.*

12. *B, D; Linux is a UNIX variant that has not had the support necessary from the application community but has received widespread acceptance for Internet-based work and among hobbyists*

13. *B; OS/2 was created as a Microsoft/IBM joint venturE. Although the NOS did not attract a wide following of software developers and never won a significant market share, it was a robust operating system. You will likely find OS/2 somewhere in the installed base of most large organizations. The NOS is frequently used, for example, as a gateway for older mail systems.*

14. *Windows 95/98 and Windows NT Workstation are particularly suited as network clients for a variety of network operating systems using a number of protocols. Their nearly identical graphical user interface provides excellent uniformity between the products and permits quick user training. They provide support to a variety of 16- and 32-bit software.*

15. *B, C; To communicate with a server, the client must use a network protocol available on the server and a redirector compatible with the networking environment.*

Chapter 3 Questions

1. *What are the four layers of the DoD Model?*
    A. Application, transport, internet, and network.
    B. Application, transport, network, and data.
    C. Application, transport, network, and physical.
    D. Application, central, transport, and remote.

2. *Which layer in the DoD Model is responsible for pulling frames off and putting them on the wire?*

    A. Application.

    B. Transport.

    C. Data.

    D. Network.

    E. Internet.

3. *Which layer provides connectionless delivery, routing, fragmentation and reassembly?*

    A. Application.

    B. Transport.

    C. Central.

    D. Network.

    E. Internet.

4. *What five protocols are used at, and map to, the Internet layer?*

    A. GGP, IGRP, ICMP, PARP, and IP.

    B. IGMP, RARP, ARP, ICMP, and IP.

    C. ARP, IP, PARP, ICMP and IGMP.

    D. IP, PARP, ARP, ICMP and IGMP.

5. *When a host recognizes that the source and destination addresses are on the same LAN, it will do the following:(Select one):*

    A. Apply a decrement of at least 1 and forward the datagram directly to the host.

    B. Forward the datagram directly to the host.

    C. Reject the datagram for having the same source and destination network numbers.

    D. Suspend processing until the LAN ID is resolved.

6. *When a host recognizes that the source and destination addresses are on different LANs, it will do the following (Select one):*

    A. Reject the datagram for having incorrect network numbers.

    B. Suspend the processing until the LAN ID is resolved.

    C. Forward the datagram directly to the host.

    D. Forward the datagram to the default gateway.

7. *What is encapsulation?*

    A. A tunneling protocol that can be used on bus, star, and token ring networks.

    B. A process for tunneling through the layers to provide for Ethernet and token ring compatibility with the OSI and DoD models.

    C. A process where the data is wrapped with layer-specific information.

    D. A process for wrapping the layers with the data to place more information in a frame than could otherwise be transmitted.

8. *At what layer of the OSI model does the NIC operate as it exchanges data with the wire?*

    A. Network.

    B. Transport.

    C. Session.

    D. Data link.

9. *What is an interprocess communication?*

    A. A tunneling protocol that can be used on bus, star, and token ring networks.

    B. The way that programs communicate with one another.

    C. The way an application can encapsulate data.

    D. A process for tunneling through the layers to provide for Ethernet feedback.

10. *What is a socket?*

    A. A tunneling protocol.

    B. The Ethernet connector that permits hub attachment.

    C. A connection-oriented interprocess communication.

    D. Transport layer host ID that is used to identify each computer.

    E. Network layer host ID that is used to identify each process.

11. *IEEE 802.2 introduces the specification for the following (select one):*

    A. Logical link control.

    B. Connection-oriented interprocess communication.

    C. Tunneling protocols.

    D. Encrypted datagram, media access controlled Ethernet.

Chapter 3 Answers

1. C; *Application, transport, network and physical.*

2. D; *The network, or lowest layer, is responsible for putting frames on and pulling frames off the wire.*

3. E; *The Internet layer provides connectionless delivery, routing, fragmentation and reassembly.*

4. B; *The five protocols that are used at, and map to, the DoD Internet layer are IGMP, RARP, ARP, ICMP, and IP.*

5. B; *Forward the datagram directly to the host.*

6. D; *Forward the datagram to the default gateway.*

7. C; *Encapsulation is a process where the data is wrapped with layer-specific information.*

8. D; *The layer of the OSI model at which the NIC operates as it exchanges data with the wire is the data link layer.*

9. B; *Interprocess communication is the way that programs communicate with each other on a LAN.*

10. C; *A socket is a connection-oriented interprocess communication (usually expressed as an IP address:port number combination).*

11. A; *The IEEE 802.2 introduces the logical link control specification.*

Chapter 4 Questions

1. What is used to connect coaxial cable over long distances to strengthen the signal?

    A. A barrel connector.

    B. A long continuous cable.

    C. A repeater.

    D. A hub.

    E. A terminator.

2. *What is the maximum distance that thin coaxial cable is able to carry signal without noticeable attenuation?*

    A. 185 m.

    B. 200 m.

    C. 500 m.

    D. 2 km.

3. *What technology or connector type is used for thick coaxial cable?*

    A. BNC T connector.

    B. RJ-45 connector.

    C. RJ-11 connector.

    D. AUI connector.

    E. SC connector.

    F. ST connector.

4. *Both ends of an AUI cable should always be* _____

    A. Male-female.

    B. Female-female.

    C. Male-male.

    D. Genderless.

5. *Which of the following BNC connectors are used to connect devices to thin coaxial bus? (Refer to Figure 4–35.)*

    A. A.

    B. B.

A   B   C

Figure 4–35 *Cable connectors.*

    C. C.

    D. A and B.

    E. B and C.

    F. A and C.

6. *What is the transmission rate that twisted pair Cat. 4 is capable of?*

    A. 4 Mbps.

    B. 10 Mbps.

    C. 16 Mbps.

    D. 20 Mbps.

    E. 100 Mbps.

7. *True or False. When wiring a twisted pair cable, it is not important to connect specific wires to specific pins in the RJ-45 connector. The only concern is that wires of the same colors are connected to the same pins on both ends of the cable.*

    A. True.

    B. False.

8. *What is the drawback of using multimode fiber?*

    A. Since modes can potentially travel along different paths, bouncing different numbers of times, they will arrive at the other end of the cable at different times. This is called mode dispersion, and this limits the maximum speed and lengths of the cable.

    B. The diameter of the glass is smaller than in a single-mode cable, making it difficult to work with.

    C. Multimode cables require using lasers, making the technology more expensive.

    D. Multimode fiber is more difficult to vampire tap, because you need to do this with each mode individually.

9. *What does MM 62.5/125 stand for?*

    A. The internal cylinder is 62.5 micron in diameter and the cladding diameter is 125 micron.

    B. The minimum allowed transmission speed allowed is 62.5 Mbps the maximum is 125 Mbps.

    C. The minimum distance between nodes is 62.5 meters, the maximum is 125 meters.

D. The propagation delay for this network should be no more than 125 µs, and one-way propagation delay should be no more than 62.5 µs.

10. *You need to connect 10 computers in location A and 15 computers in location B. Locations A and B are separated by 130 meters. You do not want to use any active connectivity equipment in this area and want to minimize the costs of the project. What cable type would you use?*

    A. Twisted pair.

    B. Fiber optic cable.

    C. Thick coaxial cable.

    D. Thin coaxial cable.

11. *What term is not related to the other three?*

    A. CSMA/CD.

    B. Token passing.

    C. Demand priority.

    D. BNC.

12. *10BASE-T uses only _____ for transmitting and receiving the signal.*

    A. Two fiber optic cables.

    B. Two twisted pairs (4 wires).

    C. Four twisted pairs (8 wires).

    D. Ten twisted pairs (20 wires).

13. *100BASE-T4 uses only _____ for transmitting and receiving the signal.*

    A. Four fiber optic cables.

    B. Two twisted pairs (4 wires).

    C. Four twisted pairs (8 wires).

    D. Ten twisted pairs (20 wires).

14. *Will the Ethernet network displayed in Figure 4–36 work?*

    A. No.

    B. Yes, but only if the network is 10BASE-T.

    C. Yes, but only if the network is 10BASE-T or 100BASE-TX.

    D. Yes, in all cases.

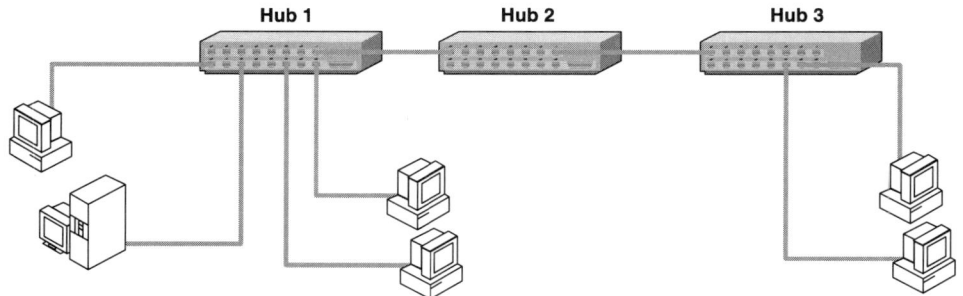

Figure 4–36 *Ethernet network.*

15. *Will the fast Ethernet network displayed in Figure 4–37 work?*

    A. No.

    B. Yes, only if the concentrators are class I repeaters.

    C. Yes, only if the concentrators are class II repeaters.

    D. Yes, in all cases.

16. *You want to expand a network, which was built with thick coaxial cable. You already have 3 segments, and you plan to add 3 more. You plan to use thicknet only. Is it possible to do this using 10BASE-5 repeaters?*

    A. Yes.

    B. No.

17. *What is the propagation delay in fast Ethernet?*

    A. 25.6 µs.

    B. 2.56 µs.

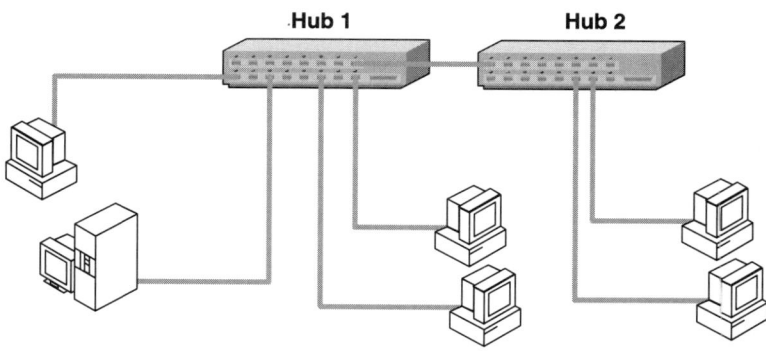

Figure 4–37 *Fast ethernet network.*

    C. There is no propagation delay concept in Ethernet. Only token passing has this concept.

    D. Propagation delay depends on the class of repeater being used.

18. *A token ring network is logically a ring but physically a*

    A. Star.

    B. Bus.

    C. Token Bus.

    D. MSAU.

19. *The active monitor in token ring is*

    A. The first station that joins the ring.

    B. MSAU.

    C. A special device.

    D. Active monitor concept does not exist it token ring.

20. *ARCNET uses _____ method as media access control.*

    A. Token passing.

    B. CSMA/CD.

    C. CSMA/CA.

    D. Demand priority.

Chapter 4 Answers

1. *C; A repeater is used to connect coaxial cable over long distances to strengthen the signal.*

2. *A; The maximum distance that thin coaxial cable is able to carry signals without noticeable attenuation is 185m.*

3. *D; The AUI connector type is used for thick coaxial cable.*

4. *A; Both ends of an AUI cable should always be male-female. Transceivers require power to operate and if connected by female/female connector, both devices will try to draw power from each other; and the configuration will not function.*

5. *A; The correct BNC connector to use for attaching devices to thin coaxial bus is a T connector. See Figure 4–8.*

6. C; *Category 4 twisted pair is capable of transmission rates of up to 16 Mbps.*

7. B; *False. Wiring order is important because certain wires in the twisted pair cable are used for sending data while others are used for receiving it.*

8. C; *Multimode cables require equipment that makes the technology expensive.*

9. A; *Multimode fiber is usually marked as MM 62.5/125. MM stands for multimode, 62.5 micron is the diameter of the glass core and 125 micron is the diameter of the cladding.*

10. C; *Thick coaxial cable would be the best choice because of it's ability to carry signals farther. Keep in mind that Location A and Location B both have segment lengths that add to the computation of the total length. Fiber would not keep the cost low.*

11. D; *BNC is not related to the other terms. It is a connector type, while the others are media access methods.*

12. C; *Typically, twisted pair cable has four twisted pairs or eight wires.*

13. C; *100BASE-T4 uses only four twisted pairs (8 wires) for transmitting and receiving the signal.*

14. A; *Uplink channels are used to connect hubs, not ports.*

15. D; *Yes in all cases, if the uplink port is used.*

16. B; *5–4–3 rule is a good rule of thumB. The longest path a signal should travel between the most distant computers should not exceed four hubs and five cable segments.*

17. A; *If you add propagation delays from all devices in the network, this value should not exceed 25.6 μs.*

18. A; *A token ring network is logically a ring but physically a star.*

19. A; *The active monitor in token ring is usually selected at initialization time and is usually the first station to access the ring.*

20. A; *ARCNET uses a token-passing method of media access control.*

Chapter 5 Questions

1. *Select all that apply: You might want to expand your LAN to*

A. Connect two or more LANs.

B. Make use of repeaters, routers, and gateways.

C. Segment the existing LAN to overcome limitations of LAN technologies.

D. Connect it to other foreign systems and environments.

2. *The rule that states that there may be a maximum of 30 nodes per Ethernet segment is*

A. A firm rule that is true and which must be followed in all cases.

B. Incorrect.

C. An empirical rule that provides a good guideline but which is not as accurate as determining the network utilization value.

D. Only applicable in networks using coaxial cable (10BASE-2; 10BASE-5).

3. *Repeaters*

A. Operate at the physical layer and provide packet synchronization.

B. Operate at the data link layer and provide frame synchronization.

C. Operate at the data link layer and provide bit synchronization.

D. Operate at the physical layer and provide bit synchronization.

4. *A multiport repeater*

A. Functions as a bridge.

B. Can work as a bridge or a router.

C. Is really a repeater hub.

D. Uses parallel processing to speed up data transfer.

5. *Select all that apply to classical bridges.*

A. Operate at the data link layer of OSI model.

B. Can overflow due to excessive traffic.

C. Can make intelligent decisions to propagate frames more efficiently when multiple paths to the destination exist.

D. Have higher processing overhead than routers.

6. *The process called flooding occurs*

A. When repeater receives a broadcast packet.

    B. When repeater gets a packet with an unknown MAC address.

    C. When the protocol being used is nonroutable.

    D. Flooding is not defined for repeaters.

7. *What happens when a bridge receives a packet with a destination MAC address that is not present in the bridge table?*

    A. Bridge discards the packet.

    B. Bridge propagates the packet to all its ports.

    C. Bridge propagates the packet to all its ports except the port from which the packet came.

    D. Bridge does not examine MAC addresses of incoming frames and cannot make decisions based on that criterion.

8. *Why is it so undesirable when a switch drops frames due to excessive traffic on its ports?*

    A. Because packet loss cannot be recovered at the lower layers of the OSI model and can be detected only at the higher layers by transport- and application-level protocols, with all the overhead associated with this process.

    B. Because switches request the frame retransmission and stop further operations until they receive the requested packet.

    C. Because a lost frame means that the file or message this frame is part of will become corrupt.

    D. This is not a problem at all. Switches do not drop frames because of their high performance. Only bridges do that.

9. *You install network monitoring software on one of the computers connected to a dedicated port of a 3COM switch. The other 100 computers in your network are connected to the same switch. You read in the documentation that this monitoring software allows you to capture all packets by switching the network adapter to the promiscuous mode allowing it to process all the packets it sees. Will you be able to monitor network traffic from all computers in your network?*

    A. No.

    B. Yes.

10. *Which type of switching technology can detect corrupted frames?*

    A. Cut through.

    B. Store and forward.

    C. Full duplex.

    D. Half duplex.

11. *A network consists of 40 workstations and 1 server, as pictured in Figure 5–14. Users often use multimedia applications that are run from the server and consume a large amount of bandwidth, causing delays to other computers. Through the use of network monitoring software, you discover your network experiences a high level of collisions because users access the server simultaneously to download large multimedia files. You decide to substitute a 10BASE-T hub with a 10BASE-T switch. How will this affect the situation?*

    A. The performance will dramatically increase and delays will be eliminated.

    B. There will be a slight performance improvement, delays become less frequent.

    C. This will not change the situation. Performance will stay on the same level.

    D. Performance will decrease. Delays will become even longer.

12. *You have a large 10BASE-5 network that consists of four segments connected by three repeaters. You decide to substitute two repeaters with one router and one bridge. How many collision domains will your network have?*

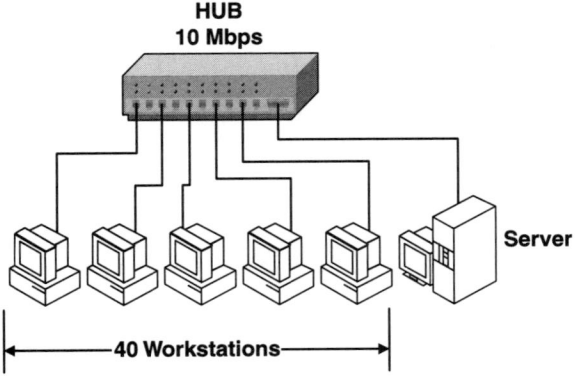

Figure 5–14   *Client/server network.*

  A. 1.

  B. 2.

  C. 3.

  D. Collision domains are not defined for 10BASE-5 networks since they use token passing technology, which prevents collisions.

13. *At what layer of the OSI model do routers work?*

  A. Physical.

  B. Data link.

  C. Network.

  D. Transport.

  E. Network and transport.

  F. Data link and network.

  G. All of the above.

14. *How does a router propagate the packets it receives?*

  A. By examining the destination MAC address and consulting its routing table.

  B. By examining the network ID portion of the network address and consulting its routing table.

  C. By propagating packets to all its ports.

  D. By examining the network address and, if no decision can be made based on this, examining the MAC address.

15. *Assume that the network uses classical hubs: Will the fast Ethernet type network pictured in Figure 5–15 work?*

  A. No.

  B. Yes.

  C. Yes, if this is 100BASE-T4 network.

  D. Yes, if this is 100BASE-TX network.

16. *The 10 Mbps network with a classic hub pictured in Figure 5–16 has low performance due to the high network utilization level. Client computers constantly access the corporate server to download large CAD files, thus producing network delays. You want to improve performance, but keep the migration costs as low as possible. Hence, you*

  A. Upgrade the link from the hub to the server to 100 Mbps.

  B. Implement a full duplex connection between the hub and the server.

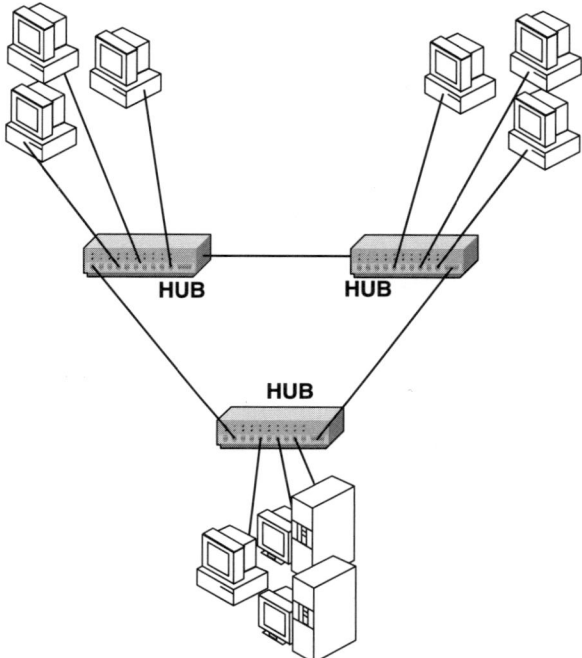

Figure 5–15 *Fast ethernet network.*

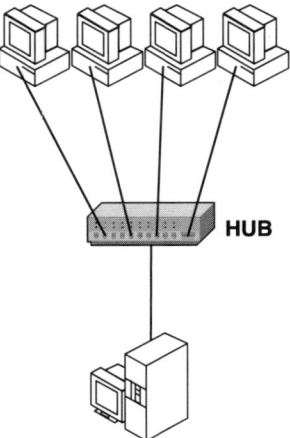

Figure 5–16 *10 Mbps network.*

    C. Substitute a switch for the hub.

    D. Replace the hub with a switch and implement a 100 Mbps full duplex connection to the server.

17. *Your Ethernet bus-type network running only the NetBEUI protocol experiences a large number of broadcast messages. You want to segment the network using two routers to reduce broadcast messages. How will this affect your network?*

    A. The entire network will stop functioning.

    B. The network will continue to operate and the level of broadcast messages will be reduced.

    C. The network will continue to operate but the level of broadcast messages will not be reduced, since routers are transparent for broadcasts.

    D. The network will be broken into three segments that are not able to communicate with each other.

18. *You have two networks: one is an SNA-type network and one is Microsoft based. What type of device would you use to connect these networks to let them talk to each other?*

    A. Repeater.

    B. Bridge.

    C. Router.

    D. Gateway.

19. *You need to connect a Microsoft network and a Novell NetWare network. Two solutions have been suggested: either install a gateway or install client software on all Microsoft-based computers. Which solution offers better performance?*

    A. Gateway solution.

    B. Client software on each Microsoft-based computer.

    C. Both solutions have the same performance.

    D. Microsoft and Novell NetWare networks cannot talk to each other since they use completely different sets of protocols.

20. *At what speed does T1 operate?*

    A. 1.544 Mbps.

    B. 128 Kbps.

    C. 64 Kbps.

    D. 10 Mbps.

21. *What is the size of the ATM cell?*

    A. From 64 to 1,542 bytes.

    B. 53 bytes.

    C. 1 KB.

    D. 64 bytes.

22. *What ISDN channel is capable of data transmissions?*

    A. A channel.

    B. B channel.

    C. C channel.

    D. D channel.

Chapter 5 Answers

1. *A, C, D; While you will likely use repeaters, routers, and gateways in expanding a network, this was not given as a reason for undertaking such an expansion.*

2. *C; The empirical 30 node rule is not as accurate in today's computing environment as actually calculating the network utilization value.*

3. *D; Repeaters operate at the physical layer of the OSI model and provide bit synchronization—they do not recognize frames.*

4. *C; A multiport repeater is simply a conventional hub with a repeater feature.*

5. *A, B; Bridges can overflow due to excessive traffic and operate at the data link layer. However, bridges cannot make intelligent decisions like routers do, and they have better performance than routers because they work at the lower layer of the OSI model.*

6. *D; Flooding is the process of propagating a packet to all ports of the device when the device's table has no entry for the destination MAC address or when the packet is a broadcast packet. A repeater always performs bit synchronization between all ports, so the flooding process is not defined for a repeater.*

7. C; *When a bridge receives a packet with the unknown destination MAC address, the bridge propagates the packet to all its ports except the port the packet came from.*

8. A; *Discarding (or losing) a frame is very undesirable, since it cannot be recovered at the lower layers of the OSI model through the LAN protocols. Packet loss is detected only at the higher layers of the OSI model where the processing overhead is higher. The retransmission of the lost packet may occur after dozens of seconds.*

9. A; *The switch will filter network traffic and network monitoring software will not see the conversation of other computers unless they broadcast.*

10. B; *The entire incoming frame is captured, an address lookup occurs to resolve the outgoing port, and a cyclic redundancy check (CRC) is performed. Because of the full buffering, this technique provides higher levels of error detection since corrupt frames can be detected and discarded, while valid frames are processed, queued, and transmitted.*

11. D; *The performance will decrease because substituting a switch for a hub will not solve the problem of the funnel. Instead, it will raise it to the next layers of the OSI model. Obviously the switch eventually will start dropping packets. In this case we would rather have collisions that could be recovered on the data link layer than a packet loss that is detected at the transport layer or above.*

12. C; *Both routers and bridges segment network into collision domains.*

13. C; *Routers work at the network layer of the OSI model.*

14. B; *Routers work only on the network layer of the OSI model, so that they access only the network address. They check the network address against their routing table to make routing decisions.*

15. A; *The network will not work since it has loops. Repeaters will continuously propagate the same packet around the circle, thus creating a constant collision.*

16. D; *The only possible choice that improves performance is putting in a switch and upgrading the server link. The solution of upgrading the link and using a hub will not work since hubs cannot connect segments with different speeds.*

17. D; *NetBEUI is non routable and will not work across routers. The network will be split into separate segments.*

18. *D; Gateways repackage and convert data going from one environment to another.*

19. *B; Because gateways operate at higher layers of the OSI model, they incur extra overhead to process the low layer addressing, extract data, and then repackage the data into the new protocol stacks. Installing connectivity software on all client computers is more performance advantageous.*

20. *A; T1 operates at the speed of 1.544 Mbps.*

21. *B; An ATM cell is 53 bytes long. 5 bytes for the header 48 bytes for data.*

22. *B; The B-channel service operates at 64 kbps and is meant to carry user data.*

Chapter 6 Questions

1. *Which of the following utilities is used to capture network traffic for analysis?*

    A. IPCONFIG.

    B. PING.

    C. Network Monitor.

    D. Performance Monitor.

    E. LPD.

2. *Select all that apply: Which utility (utilities) is (are) NOT used for TCP/IP printing?*

    A. LPR.

    B. PING.

    C. LPQ.

    D. telnet.

3. *Which of the following function as both client and server applications on Windows NT 4.0?*

    A. PING.

    B. IPCONFIG.

    C. FTP.

    D. REXEC.

4. *Select all that apply: Why is it important to obtain the most recent RFC on the particular topic?*

    A. RFC numbers are not replaced.

    B. RFC numbers are reviewed and changed weekly.

    C. New RFC are created with new numbers.

    D. RFC number corresponds to its publishing date.

5. *TCP/IP is really*

    A. One protocol.

    B. Two protocols: TCP and IP.

    C. More than two protocols.

    D. A set of rules published in RFCs.

6. *Which of the following is used to connect to other hosts in TCP/IP networks? (Choose two.)*

    A. IPCONFIG.

    B. FTP.

    C. PING.

    D. telnet.

7. *Choose all that apply: What parameters are used to configure Microsoft TCP/IP on Windows NT 4.0?*

    A. IP address.

    B. Subnet mask.

    C. Internal network number.

    D. The maximum speed of the WAN link.

8. *What protocol handles the resolution of Media Access Control addresses to IP addresses on your network?*

    A. Ping.

    B. ARP.

    C. IP.

    D. ICMP.

9. *What protocol reports errors associated with IP traffic?*

    A. IGMP.

    B. ICMP.

      C. ARP.

      D. TCP.

10. *What is the class of address 194.226.192.52?*

      A. Class A.

      B. Class B.

      C. Class C.

      D. Class D.

      E. Class E.

11. *How many bits does the IP address occupy?*

      A. 8 bits.

      B. 16 bits.

      C. 32 bits.

      D. 64 bits.

12. *What class of network has 254 hosts per network?*

      A. Class A.

      B. Class B.

      C. Class C.

      D. None of the above.

13. *Which of the following are invalid for network ID?*

      A. All 0's.

      B. 127.

      C. All 1's.

      D. 100.

      E. 195.

14. *What class network is 10.0.0.0?*

      A. Class A.

      B. Class B.

      C. Class C.

      D. Class D.

15. *What is the network ID for 200.0.0.1?*

      A. 200.

B. 200.0.

C. 200.0.0.

D. 200.0.0.1.

16. *You are setting up TCP/IP on a computer in a small company. Can you assign this computer the IP address of 127.56.10.45?*

A. Yes.

B. No, because this is a special purpose IP address.

C. No, because the network ID is all 1's.

D. No, because this is class A IP address and it is suitable for large enterprises only.

17. *You physically move a DHCP client computer to a new subnet, but it fails to function on the network. What might account for this?*

_____

18. *What can you use to determine the current DHCP client configuration?*

19. *Linda wants to view the NetBIOS name cache on her computer. What should she type on the command line?*

A. arp -a.

B. nbtstat –c.

C. ping.

D. netstat –c.

E. nbtstat –r.

20. *Lynn manages a large network that relies on LMHOSTS files for name resolution. One of her users complains that the time required to connect to remote hosts has become excessivE. Lynn examines the user's LMHOSTS file and discovers a large number of #PRE and #DOM tagged entries in the file. What can Lynn do to increase the speed with which the LMHOSTS file is read?*

A. Move all the #PRE and #DOM tagged entries to the top of the file.

B. Delete the #PRE tag from every #DOM tagged entry.

C. Move the #PRE and #DOM tagged entries to the bottom of the file.

D. Delete all the #PRE and #DOM entries.

21. *Your network uses a DHCP server to assign IP addresses and WINS information. You want to ensure your computers use WINS before resorting to broadcast name resolution. What node should you specify in the DHCP options?*

    A. P-node.

    B. B-node.

    C. H-node.

    D. M-node.

22. *Mike changed the NetBIOS scope value on the WINS address tab for several of his computers. What effect did this have on those machines?*

    A. Forced them to use the WINS database.

    B. Permitted their names to preload into the group's NetBIOS cache.

    C. Preloaded their names into the corresponding HOSTS file.

    D. Prevented them from communicating with machines not configured with that scope value.

23. *Sandy will use FTP to retrieve files from a UNIX server. Her computer is not a DNS client. What can she use to connect to the UNIX machine? (Select all that apply.)*

    A. WINS.

    B. LMHOSTS.

    C. DHCP.

    D. HOSTS.

24. *When Vicky uses the command "ftp FileSrv" she connects to a UNIX server on a remote network. When she types "ftp 122.36.5.22," however, the operation fails. What is the likely cause of the problem?*

    A. The UNIX server's LMHOSTS file has entries that conflict with Vicky's HOSTS file.

    B. Vicky does not have IP permissions on the UNIX server.

    C. 122.35.5.22 is not the IP address of an FTP server.

    D. FTP will not work with IP addresses.

Chapter 6 Answers

1. *C; Network monitor is used to capture network traffic for analysis. IP-CONFIG shows configuration. PING tests connectivity. Performance monitor provides the tool for sampling utilization of processes, and LPD is the line printer daemon.*

2. *B, D; PING and telnet are not used for TCP/IP printing.*

3. *C; FTP has two functions—one as client and the other as a server application on Windows NT 4.0 server.*

4. *C; New RFCs are created with new numbers, so that it is always important to obtain the most recent RFC to ensure compliance with the emerging standards.*

5. *C; TCP/IP is really more than two protocols. It includes several utilities, and TCP/IP utilities can be logically divided into several groups based on their purpose: data transfer utilities, remote execution utilities, printing utilities, and diagnostic utilities.*

6. *B, D; FTP and telnet are used to connect to remote hosts.*

7. *A, B; The required parameters used to configure TCP/IP on Microsoft Windows NT 4.0 include the IP address and subnet mask.*

8. *B; Address resolution protocol (ARP) displays and modifies the cache of locally resolved IP addresses to media access control (MAC) addresses.*

9. *B; ICMP reports errors associated with IP traffiC.*

10. *C; 194.226.192.52 is a class C address.*

11. *C: IP addresses occupy 32 bits.*

12. *C; Class C networks have 254 hosts per network.*

13. *C; All 1s indicates a broadcast.*

14. *A; 10.0.0.0 is a class A network (restricted or reserved from use on the Internet).*

15. *C; The network ID is 200.0.0—the host ID is 1.*

16. *B; No. IP addresses beginning with 127 are special purpose IP addresses that are normally used for loop-back testing.*

17. *Most likely cause is that the DHCP client had already received its leased address on the old subnet. Renegotiation of the IP address is based on the lease expiration time, which may not occur for some time.*

18. *IPCONFIG/all or WINIPCFG is used to determine DHCP client configuration.*

19. *Nbtstat -c will retrieve NetBIOS names from the cache and display them. She would use nbtstat –n to show her local machine namE.*

20. *C; To increase efficiency it is best to put the computers you access most frequently at the top of the list and entries tagged with **#PRE** at the bottom. Since #PRE tagged entries are cached at TCP/IP initialization, they will be read from the list only once (at initialization).*

21. *C; Under an H-node, a system first attempts P-node resolution. Should that fail, the system seeks resolution through B-node broadcasts. The H-node not only provides a comprehensive resolution plan, it limits network traffic by ensuring broadcasts are used only as a last resort.*

22. *D; When scope IDs are not used, NetBIOS names must be unique throughout the entire network; with scope IDs, names must be unique only within the scope. NetBIOS resources within the scope, however, are not able to communicate with resources outside their own scope using NetBIOS over TCP/IP*

23. *A, B, D; Non-WINS entries can be placed in the WINS database making WINS a good choicE. LMHOSTS is ONLY possible if the remote host has NetBIOS helper software such as SAMBA but it is also a good choice. DHCP does not resolve names and would be an invalid choicE. HOSTS file is the proper method in a mixed environment.*

24. *C; If any part of the fully qualified domain name is misspelled or wrong, the ping will not work.*

25. *C; The address is not the IP address of that FTP server.*

Chapter 7 Questions

1. *You run IPCONFIG on your Windows NT Server computer and get the following output:*

```
C:\WINNT>ipconfig
Windows NT IP Configuration
```

```
Ethernet adapter Elnk31:
    IP Address. . . . . . . . . : 0.0.0.0
    Subnet Mask . . . . . . . . : 0.0.0.0
    Default Gateway . . . . . . :
```

What is the most likely cause of this?

   A. Duplicate subnet mask.

   B. TCP/IP is not installed on this computer.

   C. Default gateway is missing.

   D. This computer was unable to get the IP address from the DHCP server.

2. *Which utility is used to identify the subnet mask?*

   A. Network Monitor.

   B. IPCONFIG.

   C. PING.

   D. Event Log.

3. *Which address symbolizes the loopback address?*

   A. 127.0.0.1.

   B. 255.255.255.255.

   C. 255.255.0.0.

   D. 0.0.0.0.

   E. 176.20.0.10.

4. *Your computer is configured to use WINS, DNS, HOSTS, and LMHOSTS files for name resolution. You launch a command prompt and try to ping your neighbor's computer (located in the same subnet) by using its Net-BIOS name (ping mctcomp). The ping command hangs for about a minute and then gives you four successful pings. What is the most likely reason on such a delay?*

   A. DNS server is unreachable.

   B. WINS server is unreachable.

   C. The broadcast name resolution is a very slow method.

   D. PING cannot use NetBIOS names.

5. *You are the administrator of the network that is illustrated in Figure 7–8.*

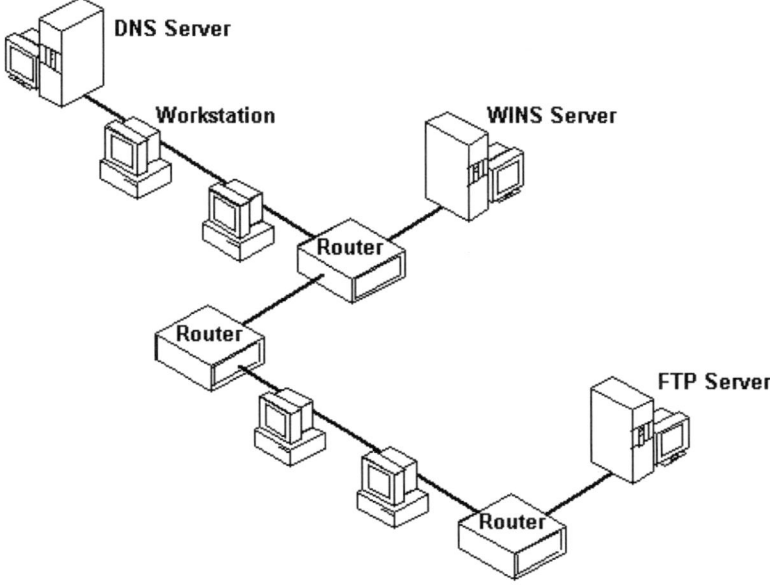

Figure 7–8 *Network example.*

Using FTP client software, your workstation cannot connect to the FTP server in the remote subnet. You can, however, connect to the FTP server by using Windows NT Explorer. What is the most likely reason for this behavior?

   A. The computer running FTP server is down.

   B. Your workstation does not have the default gateway.

   C. Your workstation is not configured to use DNS.

   D. Your workstation has a duplicate IP address.

6. *You can successfully ping all workstations in your subnet and most remote subnets in your Intranet. You cannot, however, ping all remote subnets in your Intranet. All other computers are able to ping each other. What is the most likely reason for this problem?*

   A. Your computer has an invalid subnet mask.

   B. Your computer has a duplicate IP address.

   C. The router is down.

   D. Your computer is not using WINS.

7. *Which utility would you use to check how your computer registers its Net-BIOS name?*

   A. NBTSTAT.

   B. NETSTAT.

   C. NSLOOKUP.

   D. IPCONFIG.

8. *You use Microsoft Network Monitor and you discover that your computer sends an ARP request for the default gateway address every time it attempts to contact another machinE. What could be the problem?*

   A. Your workstation is not TCP/IP enabled.

   B. Your workstation does not use DNS.

   C. Your workstation has an invalid subnet mask.

   D. There is no problem, this is normal.

9. *Your computer has an invalid subnet mask. Which statement(s) is (are) true?*

   A. Your computer cannot communicate with all other computers.

   B. Your computer can only communicate with remote computers.

   C. Your computer can only communicate with local computers.

   D. Your computer possibly cannot communicate with some or all computers.

10. *You try to map a network drive to the computer named RED, that is located on the remote subnet, but you fail. Your computer is not WINS enabled, but it uses an LMHOSTS filE. You check the TCP/IP configuration and discover that your computer has received valid TCP/IP parameters from the DHCP server. What should you check next?*

    A. Check that the DHCP server is turned on and functional.

    B. Check that an entry for computer RED is present and has the correct mapping in the LMHOSTS file.

    C. Check that your computer is NOT using broadcasts for name resolution.

    D. Check if computer RED is WINS enabled.

11. *A user is complaining that she is not able to connect to the corporate file server with Windows NT Explorer. From her computer you check that you are able to ping the corporate file server's IP address. What else should you check? (select all that apply)*

A. Check that the route to the corporate file server is configured.

B. Check that the user's computer is configured to use WINS.

C. Check that the user's computer has a valid LMHOSTS file.

D. Check that the user's computer has a valid subnet mask.

12. *You are the administrator of the network shown in Figure 7–9. You are sitting at the computer named WKS1. You are able to access all computers in your Intranet, but you are not able to access server RED. What is the most likely reason for this?*

A. DHCP Server is in another network segment.

B. WINS Server is in another network segment.

C. No route is configured to the subnet with server RED.

D. File LMHOSTS is corrupted.

13. *You can successfully ping Mary's computer; but when you use the **net use** command to connect to it, you fail. You check that you are able to FTP her computer by name. What should you check next? (select all that apply)*

A. Check that Mary's computer is NetBIOS enabled.

B. Check that your computer uses DNS.

C. Check that both computers are using the same scope ID.

D. Check that the link between these two computers is not broken.

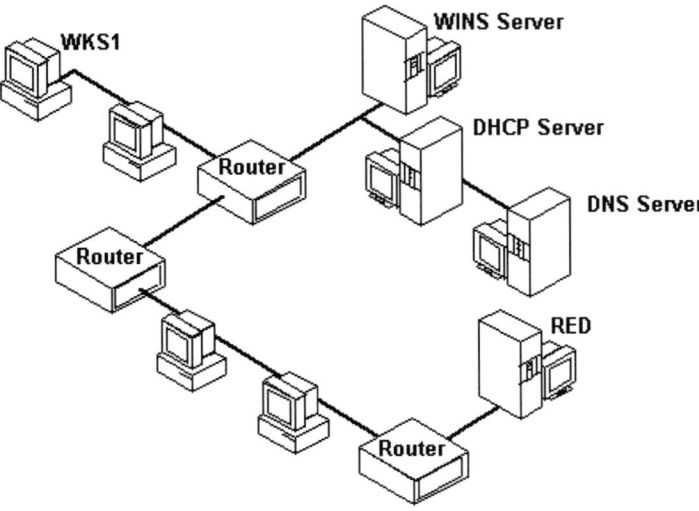

Figure 7–9 *Network example.*

14. *You suspect that your computer has a duplicate IP address. Which utility can you use to check it?*

   A. Network Monitor.

   B. Performance Monitor.

   C. Event Viewer.

   D. Server Manager.

15. *When you type the command* **net use z: \\SRV\Public** *on your Windows NT computer, you connect to the computer named SRV. But when you use FTP SRV, you connect to the computer named RED. What is the most likely reason of this problem?*

   A. LMHOSTS file is missing.

   B. HOSTS file has an invalid entry.

   C. LMHOSTS file has duplicate entries.

   D. Server SRV is not a WINS client.

16. *Sandy's TCP/IP network has grown significantly in recent months, and the job of managing TCP/IP configuration on all the network computers has taken valuable time from her other network management duties. What should Sandy install to reduce her workload?*

   A. Netmon.

   B. DHCP.

   C. SNMP.

   D. WINS.

   E. A Default Gateway.

Chapter 7 Answers

1. *D; The computer was unable to get an IP address from the DHCP server.*

2. *B; IPCONFIG is used to identify IP address and subnet mask.*

3. *A; 127.0.0.1 is typically used for the loopback address.*

4. *A; DNS server is unreachable is the most likely reason.*

5. *C; Your workstation is not configured to use DNS. FTP resolves using DNS and your client must also.*

6. *D; The computer is not using WINS for resolution.*

7. *A; NBTSTAT –n would produce the required result.*

8. *B; Your workstation does not use DNS.*

9. *A; Binary means that the likelihood of communication nears zero. If the subnet mask is wrong, your computer appears on another network and will not be able to reach other computers.*

10. *B; Check that an entry for computer RED is present and has the correct mapping in the LMHOSTS filE.*

11. *B; C; Checking resolution methods is the next step of this troubleshooting problem.*

12. *C; No route has been configured to the subnet would be the most likely reason. DHCP will not resolve names, and name resolution is needeD. WINS server or LMHOSTS will resolve if configured.*

13. *C; Check that the computers are both using the same scope ID.*

14. *C; Event Viewer is the only way to find out about a duplicate address since the other utilities require the network services be started. With a duplicate address on a Microsoft-based network, the second computer fails to start network services.*

15. *B; Hosts file has an invalid entry.*

16. *B; DHCP would provide leased IP addresses and reduce the amount of configuration required at each desktop.*

Chapter 8 Questions

1. *The most common remote access hardware is*
    A. A remote access server.
    B. X.25 PAD.
    C. Modem.
    D. NIC.

2. *Select all that apply: An asynchronous modem is*
    A. Less expensive than a synchronous modem.

    B. Faster than a synchronous modem.

    C. More expensive than a synchronous modem.

    D. Slower than a synchronous modem.

3. *Sandy installs an asynchronous internal modem and configures it to use the COM3 port. After the installation, her mouse operates erratically. What could account for this?*

    A. The modem is using too much power.

    B. The mouse is plugged into the COM3 external port.

    C. The mouse uses COM1 which shares an IRQ with COM3.

    D. The mouse has failed coincidentally with the modem installation since there is no way a mouse and modem would conflict.

4. *Modems can be configured through*

    A. The Windows NT MODEMCONFIG.EXE utility.

    B. Returning them to the factory for resetting.

    C. The AT command, which alters information in the modem's S-registers.

    D. The AT command which alters information in the system registry.

5. *Select all that apply: Modem transmission rates depend primarily on*

    A. The system's maximum port speed.

    B. The CPU speed.

    C. The modem's baud rate.

    D. Modem data compression.

6. *Internal and external modems will always have the same maximum port speed when installed on the same system.*

    A. True.

    B. False.

7. *Parity*

    A. Is used to determine if a transmitted word was received correctly.

    B. Is used to alter the transmission rate.

    C. Is used to determine where a word starts and stops.

    D. Is not used in asynchronous modem transmissions.

8. *Select all that apply: PSTN connections*

    A. Always provide a digital connection.

    B. Are available almost anywhere in the world.

    C. Provide a guaranteed path from source to destination.

    D. May not be available during peak traffic periods.

9. *Select all that apply: ISDN connections*

    A. Always provide a digital connection.

    B. Are available almost anywhere in the world.

    C. Provide a maximum bandwidth of 128Kbps.

    D. Should be used for dedicated, around-the-clock connections.

10. *Linda wants to dial into a Novell Network NetWare connect server. The Novell LAN uses IPX/SPX only. What remote access protocol should Linda use?*

    A. NWLink.

    B. SLIP.

    C. PPP.

    D. DLC.

11. *Select all that apply: PPP is superior to SLIP because*

    A. It is smaller and simpler.

    B. Provides automatic configuration and encrypted authentication.

    C. Is universally supported by platforms and applications.

    D. Provides data compression and automated logon.

12. *If you needed to set up a VPN, which protocol would you use?*

    A. SLIP.

    B. PPTP.

    C. DLC.

    D. Ethernet snap.

Chapter 8 Answers

1. *C; The most common remote access hardware is the modem.*

2. *A, D; Asynchronous modems are less expensive and less complex than synchronous modems. Transmitted start and stop bytes add to the transmission overhead, however, making asynchronous modems slower than their synchronous counterparts.*

3. *C; COM1 and COM3 both use IRQ 4; the modem should be installed on COM4 to resolve the conflict.*

4. *C; Hayes compatible modems are configured by altering information in their S-Registers. This is accomplished through use of the AT command.*

5. *A, C, D; Modem transmission rate depends on the maximum port speed and the modem speeD. The modem speed is determined by its speed of oscillation (baud) and data compression.*

6. *B; The maximum port speed of an external modem is governed by the UART chip controlling the serial port to which the modem is connected. Internal modems have an on-board UART chip.*

7. *When parity checking is employed, the parity bit makes the number of ones in a transmitted word odd or even or is always set to one or zero (depending on the parity type). This gives the receiving computer a clue about what the transmitted word looked like and helps it determine if any data was received in error.*

8. *B, D; The public switched telephone network (PSTN) is a public system available almost anywhere in the world. Because it is switched, the path and line quality is not guaranteed. There are more customers than telephone lines and a line may not be available when demand is high.*

9. *A; The integrated digital services network (ISDN) provides guaranteed digital service and up to twenty-four 64Kbps channels. It is not as universally available as PSTN and is a dial-up service not intended for 24-hour operation.*

10. *C; Linda needs to use IPX/SPX on the network. The only remote access protocols listed are SLIP and PPP. Since SLIP uses only TCP/IP, PPP is the correct choice.*

11. *B, D; PPP provides automated logon capability, data compression, automatic configuration, and encrypted authentication. The only down side to PPP is that it is more complex and larger than SLIP and not all platforms and applications are designed to support it. (Of course, many of the newer*

applications, such as the Windows NT Remote Access Server, support only PPP.)

12. *A virtual private network (VPN) can be set up on the Internet through use of the point-to-point tunneling protocol (PPTP).*

Chapter 9 Questions

1. *A network computer upgrade requires collecting which of the following information (check all that apply):*
   A. User telephone extensions.
   B. Hardware bus clock speeds.
   C. Hardware issues.
   D. Existing operating system.
   E. Test accounts.
   F. Administrative accounts.
   G. SCSI data transfer rate.
   H. Server computer.

2. *Network planning helps:*
   A. Continued growth of the user base.
   B. Hardware replacement.
   C. Proper operation and administration.
   D. Create IP address conflicts.

3. *User Needs might include*
   A. User telephone extensions.
   B. Integrated file and print.
   C. Remote access services.
   D. SCSI data transfer rate.
   E. Both A & B.
   F. Both B & C.

4. *What is a backup domain controller used for?*
   A. A copy of all user files.
   B. A copy of all share points.

  C. A copy of all user accounts.

  D. A secondary power supply.

  E. All of the above.

5. *Two components of security include*

  A. Topical and logical security.

  B. Topical and physical security.

  C. Physical and administrative security.

  D. Logical and physical security.

6. *User authentication is provided by a security provider that maintains*

  A. User telephone extensions.

  B. Hardware bus clock speeds.

  C. Encrypted numeric identifier for each user.

  D. Existing account tabs.

  E. Server sections.

7. *The maintenance account in a UNIX system is an administrative-level account that is known as*

  A. Administrator.

  B. SuperUser.

  C. Admin.

  D. Root.

8. *A good balance between user account security and ease of administration is achieved by*

  A. Giving the administrator access to all users.

  B. Using or creating groups for resource permissions.

  C. Delegating the right to administer the network to all users.

  D. Individually assigning each user to each resource.

Chapter 9 Answers

1. *C, D, E, F, H; A great deal of information is absolutely essential. Knowing what operating system and whether it can be upgraded is imperative. For example, knowing the telephone extensions of users adds little value and*

would not be important unless the telephone system was interfaced with the network via a VOIXX or other telephone system interface. Administrative and test accounts are critical information, and the server computer information is also important to note.

2. *B, C; Network planning helps the administrator deal with hardware replacement and continued operation and administration of the network.*

3. *F; File, print, and remote access are three typical requirements that users have of a network.*

4. *C; A backup domain controller is used for central administration because it maintains a copy of all user accounts.*

5. *D; Logical and physical security are two components of general security.*

6. *C; The use of an encrypted numeric identifier for each user is how security is maintained.*

7. *D: The maintenance account in a UNIX system is called root.*

8. *B; The use of groups for assigning resource permissions makes administration easier and maintains security.*

Chapter 10 Questions

1. *Select all that apply: A back-up program can protect your data from*
    A. Hardware failure.
    B. Computer theft.
    C. Fire, flood, tornadoes.
    D. Inadvertent deletion.

2. *Under a full backup, all designated files are backed up except*
    A. Executable programs.
    B. Open files.
    C. Database files.
    D. Those previously backed up.

3. *Select all that apply: A good UPS will*
    A. Run all your servers until the power returns.

    B. Send a notification that the power has gone down.

    C. Prevent users from making new connections to the server during a loss of power.

    D. Permit a graceful system shutdown.

4. *You get a trouble call from a user who claims his workstation keeps locking up. He is angry because he has had to reboot the system several times and has lost a great deal of data. When you arrive at his cubicle, you discover he has placed a large room fan on top of his computer. You suspect the trouble was caused by.*

    A. RFI.

    B. A power surge from the fan.

    C. EMI.

    D. High room temperature.

5. *Power surges*

    A. Cause less damage than power spikes.

    B. Are eliminated by inexpensive circuit breaker-protected power strips.

    C. Have been nearly eliminated by today's power companies.

    D. Are best handled by power conditioners or electronic surge protectors.

6. *System error logs should be reviewed*

    A. When a problem is noted.

    B. Regularly and frequently.

    C. When a new system is installed.

    D. Annually.

7. *Fault tolerance*

    A. Provides a capability to recover data after a myriad of mishaps.

    B. Eliminates the need for regular backups.

    C. Is a hardware-based automatic backup procedure.

    D. Should be used in conjunction with a sound backup plan.

8. *Under normal RAID1 operation, writes are _____ and reads are _____ as compared to a single non-fault-tolerant disk.*

    A. Slower; faster.

    B. Faster; slower.

    C. Slower; the same.

    D. The same; the same.

9. *When a RAID5 system experiences a crash, reads are _____ as compared with the system prior to the crash.*

    A. Faster.

    B. Slower.

    C. The same.

    D. Depends on how many drives crashed.

10. *You have a ten-disk RAID5 array and have experienced malfunctions on drives 2 and 6. How would you restore the system to its fully fault-tolerant operation?*

    A. Replace drive 2, regenerate, replace drive 6, regenerate.

    B. Replace drive 6, regenerate, replace drive 2, regenerate.

    C. Replace both drives and regenerate the stripe set.

    D. Replace both drives and restore from a tape.

11. *Select all that apply: The best route to virus protection is through*

    A. A good backup program.

    B. Removing your network from the Internet.

    C. Policy formulation and user training.

    D. Antivirus software.

12. *To keep your antivirus software effective, you should*

    A. Install the latest service pack as soon as it comes out.

    B. Regularly obtain and install signature files.

    C. Keep it server based.

    D. Disable the mode that runs in background.

13. *When a new software patch is announced, you should*

    A. Ignore it because it's nothing but trouble.

    B. Install it right away to keep the network up to date and compatible with other network components.

    C. Install it only if required by your network.

    D. Install it only when upgrading operating system software.

Chapter 10 Answers

1. *A, B, C, D; A properly managed backup program can protect your data from nearly every imaginable calamity*

2. *B; A full backup will copy all designated files regardless of update status. Backup software, however, does not typically copy files which are open during the backup.*

3. *B, C, D; Good UPS devices typically alert the network, prevent server access, and permit a graceful shutdown when the power goes out. A single, typical, battery-based UPS will not likely have sufficient power to run all your servers, however, nor will it be able to supply power for more than a few minutes.*

4. *B; It is likely the problem was caused by electromagnetic interference (EMI) originating in the room fan's motor.*

5. *D; Power surges cause more damage than power spikes. The best protection against surges is a power conditioner or a good electronic surge protector.*

6. *B; Although you would certainly review the log after installing new equipment or when a problem is noted, the best answer here is to review the logs regularly and frequently. By doing so you can take a proactive approach to keep your network running!*

7. *C; Fault tolerance will help you stay up after a hard disk or controller malfunction but should be used in conjunction with a good backup plan to permit sound data security.*

8. *A; When a mirror set (RAID1) is operating normally, each piece of data must be written twice but reads may be made simultaneously from both drives.*

9. *B; When a stripe set with parity loses a drive, the information previously stored on the inoperative drive must be "computed" from the remaining parity stripes which makes reads much slower.*

10. *D; When a stripe set with parity loses more than one drive, all data is lost. The only way to recover here is to rebuild the stripe set with parity and restore the data from a tape backup*

11. *A, B, D; Although many viruses are transmitted over the Internet, removing the network from the Internet is neither practical nor a guarantee*

viruses won't infiltrate the network through other means. A good antivirus program is based on user training and policy formulation, a good backup program, and antivirus software.

12. *B; Since new viruses are created every day, you should obtain regular updates in the form of signature files, for your antivirus software.*

13. *C; Software patches provide fixes for reported deficiencies. They should be installed, after testing, if they will correct a problem on, or provide a feature needed by, your network. If a patch does not provide you with anything constructive, you should avoid installation since side effects may cause unwanted problems.*

Chapter 11 Questions

1. *When a user reports a problem, your first concern is to*
  A. Identify the exact problem.
  B. Patch the problem so the network continues to operate.
  C. Train the user in problem reporting.
  D. Recreate the problem.

2. *You should Select all that apply: When you suspect a problem may be user induced,*
  A. Have someone else attempt the error-causing problem on another machine.
  B. Have someone else attempt the error-causing problem on the machine on which the problem was observed.
  C. Retrain the user.
  D. Review operator procedures to ensure they are adhering to previously established policies.

3. *When formulating a correction you should*
  A. Pick a solution that fits the problem.
  B. Embark on a trial-and-error process that will ultimately solve the problem.
  C. Keep a record of anything you have done to the network.
  D. Apply all possible corrections to get the network up as quickly as possible.

4. *Select all that apply: You should test your correction to*

    A. Ensure you have fixed the problem.

    B. Measure by how much you have improved network efficiency.

    C. See if you have fixed any other preexisting problems.

    D. Determine if your fix has caused any other network problems.

5. *Problems and solutions should be documented to*

    A. Provide a record of operator problems.

    B. Form a basis for network administrator advancement.

    C. Make the troubleshooting job easier next time.

    D. Be used in litigation against the operating system or hardware vendor.

6. *The most obvious problem causes should be*

    A. Ignored since it is not likely IT professionals would miss obvious clues.

    B. Reviewed during the appropriate step of the systematic approach.

    C. Checked first.

    D. Checked only after a thorough analysis of all possible problem factors.

7. *Extended industry standard architecture is compatible with*

    A. All database architectures.

    B. Industry standard architecture.

    C. Micro channel architecture.

    D. Peripheral component interconnect.

8. *Your computer will not function on the network. You check the network wire and it appears to be connected properly. You look at the NIC and see no activity lights. When you review the NICs settings, you discover the following: Base I/O Port, 320; Base Memory, D800; IRQ, 8; Transceiver, external. Where do you expect the problem?*

    A. In the protocol since the card is properly configured.

    B. External transceiver was selected with no external transceiver connected.

    C. IRQ is incorrect.

    D. Base memory is off by a power of ten.

9. *A crossover cable*

    A. Is used to connect two networks together to rule out router problems.

    B. May be used in place of standard UTP to analyze computer/hub problems.

    C. Must be used when analyzing MSAU problems.

    D. Can connect two computers directly.

10. *Select all that apply: Protocol Analyzers*

    A. Test only frames going to or from a particular computer.

    B. May include a TDR.

    C. Can identify problem computers.

    D. Cannot test wiring problems.

11. *A user reports that he is unable to connect to the server "Server1." You go to his workstation and find you can successfully ping Server1's IP address. You suspect*

    A. The user doesn't know how to connect to Server 1.

    B. The user's workstation cannot get a DHCP lease.

    C. The network name servers are down.

    D. The user reported a transitory problem.

12. *You are in charge of a small 10BASE-2 computer network. Although this is characteristically a very stable network with no significant problems, one morning the network fails to operate. You are able to quickly identify the problem (network doesn't work) and have no problem reproducing it. It is time to isolate the cause. What do you suspect it the most likely cause of the problem?*

    A. Server power failure.

    B. Malfunctions in one or more computers.

    C. Break in the network cable.

    D. Protocol mismatch between the server and workstations.

    E. Name server malfunction.

Chapter 11 Answers

1. A; The first step in the systematic approach to trouble shooting is to identify the exact problem. You can't fix a problem unless you know exactly what you need to fix.

2. A, B, D; Although retraining the user may be appropriate at some point, choices A, B, and D reflect the appropriate procedures to determine if a problem may be user induceD.

3. C; You should always record any changes you make to the network. This will help you back the changes out if they don't work and will show what worked if you solve the problem.

4. A, D; Testing should ensure the problem was solved without causing any additional network problems.

5. C; Documenting your problems and solutions will provide a reference to use when a similar network problem is detected.

6. C; It is always best to check the most obvious problems first.

7. B; EISA was designed to be compatible with ISA.

8. C; IRQ 8 is typically assigned to the real time clock. This will result in an IRQ conflict with the NIC.

9. D; Crossover cables are used to connect two computers directly to test their connectivity, thus eliminating other network devices, such as hubs, from the analysis.

10. B, C; The ultimate network analysis tool, a protocol analyzers typically include a time-domain reflectometer (TDR) and can even identify computers transmitting bad frames.

11. C; If the user could not connect to the server by name but you could connect by IP address, suspect a name resolution problem. Likely causes are malfunctioning name servers (DNS, WINS) or an improperly configured workstation that cannot find a name server.

12. C; It is always best to start with the physical layer and with the most obvious or easiest-to-correct problem first. In this case, we know that an entire 10BASE-2 network will fail if the cable is broken or disconnected, making a broken cable the most obvious and, perhaps, the easiest to find. Cable breaks are also at the physical layer making this clearly the place to start!

Network-Related Terms

Abstract Syntax: A description of a data structure that is independent of machine-oriented structures and encoding.

Account Policy: Controls how passwords and other authentication criteria are used in a network.

ACE: Advanced Certified Engineer.

ACK: An acknowledgement signal.

ACSE: Association Control Service Element. The method used in OSI for establishing a call between two applications.

Address Mask: A bit mask used to select bits from an Internet address for subnet addressing. The mask is 32 bits long and selects the network portion of the Internet address and one or more bits of the local portion. Sometimes called subnet mask.

Address Resolution: A means for mapping network layer addresses onto media-specific addresses. See ARP.

ADMD: Administration Management Domain. An X.400 Message Handling System public service carrier. Examples: MCImail and ATTmail in the U.S., British Telecom Gold400mail in the U.K. Together the ADMDs in all countries worldwide provide the tX.400 backbone. See PRMD.

Advanced RISC Computing (ARC): A standard for computers based on a RISC processor.

AEC: Authorized Education Center (SCO/UNIX).

AFP: AppleTalk Filing Protocol.

Agent: In the client-server model, the part of the system that performs information preparation and exchange on behalf of a client or server application. See NMS, DUA, MTA.

AHS: Advanced Hardware Supplement (latest drivers and peripheral support).

American National Standards Institute (ANSI): US organization of industry and business groups involved in the development of communications and trade standards.

ANSI: American National Standards Institute. The U.S. standardization body. ANSI is a member of the International Organization for Standardization (ISO).

AOW: Asia and Oceania Workshop. One of the three regional OSI implementors workshops, equivalent to OIW and EWOS.

APC: Advanced Product Center.

API: Application Program Interface. A set of calling conventions defining how a service is invoked through a software package.

Application Layer: The top-most layer in the OSI Reference Model providing such communication services as electronic mail and file transfer.

ARC: See Advanced RISC Computing.

ARP: Address Resolution Protocol. The Internet protocol used to dynamically map Internet addresses to physical (hardware) addresses on local area networks. Limited to networks that support hardware broadcast.

ARPA: Advanced Research Projects Agency. For a time called DARPA, the U.S. government agency that funded the ARPANET.

ARPANET: A packet switched network developed in the early 1970s. The "grandfather" of today's Internet. ARPANET was decommissioned in June 1990.

Attribute: The form of information items provided by the X.500 Directory Service. The directory information base consists of entries, each containing one or more attributes. Each attribute consists of a type identifier together with one or more values. Each directory Read operation can retrieve some or all attributes from a designated entry.

Autonomous System: Internet (TCP/IP) terminology for a collection of gateways (routers) that fall under one administrative entity and cooperate using a common interior gateway protocol (IGP). See subnetwork.

Backbone: The primary connectivity mechanism of a hierarchically distributed system. All systems which have connectivity to an intermediate system on the backbone are assured of connectivity to each other. This does not prevent systems from setting up private arrangements with each other to bypass the backbone for reasons of cost, performance, or security.

Baseband: Characteristic of any network technology that uses a single carrier frequency and requires all stations attached to the network to participate in every transmission. See broadband.

Big-Endian: A format for storage or transmission of binary data in which the most significant bit (or byte) comes first. The reverse convention is called little-endian.

Bit Time: The time required to receive and store a bit

Bit: Short for binary digit. Either a 1 or 0. Eight bits make up a byte, while four bits comprise a nyble.

BITNET: Because It's Time NETwork. An academic computer network based originally on IBM mainframe systems interconnected via leased 9600 bps lines. BITNET has recently merged with CSNET, The Computer+Science Network (another academic computer network) to form CREN: The Corporation for Research and Educational Networking. See CSNET.

BNC: British Naval Connector. A coaxial cable connector that is inserted into another similar connector of opposite gender and locked with a quarter turn.

BOC: Bell Operating Company. More commonly referred to as RBOC for Regional Bell Operating Company. The local telephone company in each of the seven U.S. regions.

Bottleneck: A particular hardware or software component that is found to be the principle cause of network or system degradation

Bridge: A device that connects two or more physical networks and forwards packets between them. Bridges can usually be made to filter packets, that is, to forward only certain traffic. Related devices are:: repeaters, which simply forward electrical signals from one cable to another, and full-fledged routers, which make routing decisions based on several criteria. In OSI terminology, a bridge is a Data Link Layer intermediate system. See repeater and router.

Broadband: Characteristic of any network that multiplexes multiple, independent network carriers onto a single cable. This is usually done using frequency division multiplexing. Broadband technology allows several networks to coexist on one single cable; traffic from one network does not interfere with traffic from another since the "conversations" happen on different frequencies in the "ether"—rather like the commercial radio system.

Broadcast Storm: A condition that occurs when the number of broadcast messages on a network exceeds the capacity of the network to handle them.

Broadcast: A packet delivery system where a copy of a given packet is given to all hosts attached to the network. Example: Ethernet.

Broadcast: A transmission simultaneously sent to more than one target.

BSD: Berkeley Software Distribution. Term used when describing different versions of the Berkeley UNIX software, as in "4.3BSD UNIX."

Buffer: RAM set aside to temporarily hold data pending some sort of processing.

Byte: Unit of data comprising eight bits.

Catenet: A network in which hosts are connected to networks with varying characteristics, and the networks are interconnected by gateways (routers). The Internet is an example of a catenet. See IONL.

CCR: Commitment, Concurrency, and Recovery. An OSI application service element used to create atomic operations across distributed systems. Used primarily to implement two-phase commit for transactions and non-stop operations.

CCITT: International Consultative Committee for Telegraphy and Telephony. A unit of the International Telecommunications Union (ITU) of the United Nations. An organization with representatives from the Post Telegraph and Telecommunications (PTT) committees of the world. CCITT produces technical standards, known as "Recommendations," for all internationally controlled aspects of analog and digital communications. See X Recommendations.

Client-Server Model: A common way to describe network services and the model user processes (programs) of those services. Examples include the name-server/name-resolver paradigm of the DNS and file-server/file-client relationships such as NFS and diskless hosts.

CLNP: Connectionless Network Protocol. The OSI protocol for providing the OSI Connectionless Network Service (datagram service). CLNP is the OSI equivalent to Internet IP, and is sometimes called ISO IP.

CLTP: Connectionless Transport Protocol. Provides for end-to-end transport data addressing (via Transport selector) and error control (via checksum), but cannot guarantee delivery or provide flow control. The OSI equivalent of UDP.

CMIP: Common Management Information Protocol. The OSI network management protocol.

CMOT: CMIP Over TCP. An effort to use the OSI network management protocol to manage TCP/IP networks.

Connectionless: The model of interconnection in which communication takes place without first establishing a connection. Sometimes (imprecisely) called datagram. Examples: LANs, Internet IP and OSI CLNP, UDP, ordinary postcards.

Connection-Oriented: The model of interconnection in which communication proceeds through three well-defined phases: connection establishment, data transfer, connection release. Examples: X.25, Internet TCP and OSI TP4, ordinary telephone calls.

Core Gateway: Historically, one of a set of gateways (routers) operated by the Internet Network Operations Center at BBN. The core gateway system forms a central part of Internet routing in that all groups must advertise paths to their networks from a core gateway, using the Exterior Gateway Protocol (EGP). See EGP, backbone.

COS: Corporation for Open Systems. A vendor and user group for conformance testing, certification, and promotion of OSI products.

COSINE: Cooperation for Open Systems Interconnection Networking in Europe. A program sponsored by the European Commission, aimed at using OSI to tie together European research networks.

CREN: See BITNET and CSNET.

CSMA/CA: Carrier Sense Multiple Access with Collision Avoidance. The access method used by local area networking technologies such as AppleTalk.

CSMA/CD: Carrier Sense Multiple Access with Collision Detection. The access method used by local area networking technologies such as Ethernet.

CSNET: Computer+Science Network. A large computer network, mostly in the U.S. but with international connections. CSNET sites include universities, research labs, and some commercial companies. Now merged with BITNET to form CREN. See BITNET.

CTEC: Certified Training and Education Center (Microsoft). Formerly known as ATEC.

DARPA: Defense Advanced Research Projects Agency. The U.S. government agency that funded the ARPANET.

Data Link Layer: The OSI layer that is responsible for data transfer across a single physical connection, or series of bridged connections, between two Network entities.

DCA: Defense Communications Agency. The government agency responsible for the Defense Data Network (DDN).

DCE: Distributed Computing Environment. An architecture of standard programming interfaces, conventions, and server functionalities (e.g., naming, distributed file system, remote procedure call) for distributing applications transparently across networks of heterogeneous computers. Promoted and controlled by the Open Software Foundation (OSF), a consortium led by HP, DEC, and IBM. See ONC.

DDN: Defense Data Network. Comprises the MILNET and several other DoD networks.

DECnet: Digital Equipment Corporation's proprietary network architecture.

DHCP: See Dynamic Host Configuration Protocol

DIP Switch: Dual Inline Package Switch. A type of switch, commonly found on printed circuit boards, that consists of one or more rocker switches typically used to set hardware properties.

DNS: Domain Name System. The distributed name/address mechanism used in the Internet.

Domain: In Microsoft networking, a collection of computers sharing a common Security Accounts Management Database. Members of a domain may access resources throughout the domain with a single user name, password, and set of access permissions.

Domain: In the Internet, a part of a naming hierarchy. Syntactically, an Internet domain name consists of a sequence of names (labels) separated by periods (dots), e.g., "tundra.mpk.ca.us." In OSI, "domain" is generally used as an administrative partition of a complex distributed system, as in MHS Private Management Domain (PRMD), and Directory Management Domain (DMD).

Dotted Decimal Notation: The syntactic representation for a 32-bit integer that consists of four 8-bit numbers written in base 10 with periods (dots) separating them. Used to represent IP addresses in the Internet, as in: 192.67.67.20.

DSA: Directory System Agent. The software that provides the X.500 Directory Service for a portion of the directory information base. Generally, each DSA is responsible for the directory information for a single organization or organizational unit.

DUA: Directory User Agent. The software that accesses the X.500 Directory Service on behalf of the directory user. The directory user may be a person or another software element.

Dynamic Host Configuration Protocol (DHCP): Provides automatic TCP/IP configuration to DHCP client computers.

EARN: European Academic Research Network. A network using BITNET technology connecting universities and research labs in Europe.

EGP: Exterior Gateway Protocol. A reachability routing protocol used by gateways in a two-level internet. EGP is used in the Internet core system. See core gateway.

Encapsulation: The technique used by layered protocols in which a layer adds header information to the protocol data unit (PDU) from the layer above. As an example, in Internet terminology, a packet would contain a header from the physical layer, followed by a header from the network layer (IP), followed by a header from the transport layer (TCP), followed by the application protocol data.

End System: An OSI system which contains application processes capable of communicating through all seven layers of OSI protocols. Equivalent to Internet host.

Entity: OSI terminology for a layer protocol machine. An entity within a layer performs the functions of the layer within a single computer system, accessing the layer entity below and providing services to the layer entity above at local service access points.

ES-IS: End system to intermediate system protocol. The OSI protocol by which end systems announce themselves to intermediate systems.

EUnet: European UNIX Network.

EUUG: European UNIX Users Group.

EWOS: European Workshop for Open Systems. The OSI Implementors' Workshop for Europe. See OIW.

FARNET: Federation of American Research NETworks.

FDDI: Fiber Distributed Data Interface. An emerging high-speed networking standard. The underlying medium is fiber optics, and the topology is a dual-attached, counter-rotating token ring. FDDI networks can often be spotted by the orange fiber "cable."

File Transfer Protocol (FTP): A protocol intended to transfer files between computers over a network.

FIPS: Federal Information Processing Standard.

Fire Wall: A barrier in a bridge, router, or gateway to filter data frames based on a particular criterion to prevent unauthorized access to the network on either or both sides

Flame: To express strong opinion and/or criticism of something, usually as a frank inflammatory statement in an electronic message.

FNC: Federal Networking Council. The body responsible for coordinating networking needs among U.S. Federal agencies.

Fragmentation: The process in which an IP datagram is broken into smaller pieces to fit the requirements of a given physical network. The reverse process is termed reassembly. See MTU.

Frame: Parcel of information sent over a network as a single unit. Often used interchangeably with the term "packet."

FRICC: Federal Research Internet Coordinating Committee. Now replaced by the FNC.

FTAM: File Transfer, Access, and Management. The OSI remote file service and protocol.

FTP: File Transfer Protocol. The Internet protocol (and program) used to transfer files between hosts. See FTAM.

Gateway: The original Internet term for what is now called router or more precisely, IP router. In modern usage, the terms "gateway" and "application gateway" refer to systems which do translation from some native format to another. Examples include X.400 to/from RFC 822 electronic mail gateways. See router.

GB: See Gigabyte.

Gigabyte: 1,024 Megabytes.

GOSIP: Government OSI Profile. A U.S. government procurement specification for OSI protocols.

Groupware: A product to facilitate interaction by multiple users working simultaneously. Commonly involves activities such as messaging, scheduling, and conferencing.

Hardware Compatibility List (HCL): Lists what hardware will work with a particular operating system.

HCL: See Hardware Compatibility List.

HTML: See Hypertext Markup Language.

HTTP: See Hypertext Transport Protocol.

Hypertext Markup Language: Language used for writing pages on the World Wide Web.

Hypertext Transport Protocol: Procedure for transferring World Wide Web pages over the network.

IAB: Internet Activities Board. The technical body that oversees the development of the Internet suite of protocols (commonly referred to as "TCP/IP"). It has two task forces (the IRTF and the IETF), with each charged with investigating a particular area.

ICMP: Internet Control Message Protocol. The protocol used to handle errors and control messages at the IP layer. ICMP is actually part of the IP protocol.

IEEE: See Institute of Electrical and Electronics Engineers.

IESG: Internet Engineering Steering Group. The executive committee of the IETF.

IETF: Internet Engineering Task Force. One of the task forces of the IAB. The IETF is responsible for solving short-term engineering needs of the Internet. It has over 40 Working Groups.

IGP: Interior Gateway Protocol. The protocol used to exchange routing information between collaborating routers in the Internet. RIP and OSPF are examples of IGPs.

IGRP: Internet Gateway Routing Protocol. A proprietary IGP used by Cisco System's routers.

Impedance: Resistance to alternating current in a wire. Measured in Ohms.

Institute of Electrical and Electronics Engineers (IEEE): Organization of engineering and electronics professionals. This organization has produced a number of network standards to include IEEE 802.3 standards for physical and data link layers of the OSI model.

INTAP: Interoperability Technology Association for Information Processing. The technical organization which has the official charter to develop Japanese OSI profiles and conformance tests.

Intermediate System: An OSI system which is not an end system, but which serves instead to relay communications between end systems. See repeater, bridge, and router.

International Standards Organization: Organization of standard-setting groups from around the world. The US member group is the American National Standards Institute (ANSI). The OSI Reference Model was developed by ISO.

Internet Address: A 32-bit address assigned to hosts using TCP/IP. See dotted decimal notation.

Internet: (note the capital "I") The largest internet in the world consisting of large national backbone nets (such as MILNET, NSFNET, and CREN) and a myriad of regional and local campus networks all over the world. The

Internet uses the Internet protocol suite. To be on the Internet you must have IP connectivity, i.e., be able to Telnet to—or ping—other systems. Networks with only e-mail connectivity are not actually classified as being on the Internet.

internet: A collection of networks interconnected by a set of routers which allow them to function as a single, large virtual network.

IONL: Internal Organization of the Network Layer. The OSI standard for the detailed architecture of the network layer. Basically, it partitions the network layer into subnetworks interconnected by convergence protocols (equivalent to internetworking protocols), creating what Internet calls a catenet or internet.

IP Datagram: The fundamental unit of information passed across the Internet. Contains source and destination addresses along with data and a number of fields which define such things as the length of the datagram, the header checksum, and flags to say whether the datagram can be (or has been) fragmented.

IP: Internet Protocol. The network layer protocol for the Internet protocol suite.

IRTF: Internet Research Task Force. One of the task forces of the IAB. The group responsible for research and development of the Internet protocol suite.

ISDN: Integrated Services Digital Network. ISDN combines voice and digital network services in a single medium, making it possible to offer customers digital data services as well as voice connections through a single "wire." The standards that define ISDN are specified by CCITT.

IS-IS: Intermediate system–to–Intermediate system protocol. The OSI protocol by which intermediate systems exchange routing information.

ISO: See International Standards Organization.

ISODE: ISO Development Environment. A popular implementation of the upper layers of OSI. Pronounced eye-so-dee-eee.

JANET: Joint Academic Network. A university network in the United Kingdom.

Jumper: Device for connecting points of an electronic circuit. Typical jumpers found on printed circuit boards consist of pins connected by a small plastic and metal block or a piece of wire.

JUNET: Japan UNIX Network.

KA9Q: A popular implementation of TCP/IP and associated protocols for amateur packet radio systems.

KB: See Kilobyte

Kermit: A popular file transfer and terminal emulation program.

Kilobyte: 1,024 Bytes

LAEC: Lotus Authorized Education Center

Little-Endian: A format for storage or transmission of binary data in which the least significant byte (bit) comes first. See Big-Endian.

Lost Token: Error condition on a token ring network where the token has been stopped and is not available on the ring.

Mail Exploder: Part of an electronic mail delivery system which allows a message to be delivered to a list of addressees. Mail exploders are used to implement mailing lists. Users send messages to a single address (e.g., hacks@somehost.edu) and the mail exploder takes care of delivery to the individual mailboxes in the list.

Mail Gateway: A machine that connects two or more electronic mail systems (especially dissimilar mail systems on two different networks) and transfers messages between them. Sometimes the mapping and translation can be quite complex, and generally it requires a store-and-forward scheme whereby the message is received from one system completely before it is transmitted to the next system with suitable translations.

Martian: Humorous term applied to packets that turn up unexpectedly on the wrong network because of bogus routing entries. Also used as a name for a packet which has an altogether bogus (non-registered or ill-formed) Internet address.

MB: See Megabyte

Megabyte: 1,024 Kilobytes

MHS: Message Handling System. The system of message user agents, message transfer agents, message stores, and access units which together provide OSI electronic mail. MHS is specified in the CCITT X.400 series of recommendations.

MIB: Management Information Base. A collection of objects that can be accessed via a network management protocol. See SMI.

MILNET: MILitary NETwork. Originally part of the ARPANET, MILNET was partitioned in 1984 to make it possible for military installations to have reliable network service, while the ARPANET continued to be used for research. See DDN.

MTA: Message Transfer Agent. An OSI application process used to store and forward messages in the X.400 Message Handling System. Equivalent to Internet mail agent.

MTU: Maximum Transmission Unit. The largest possible unit of data that can be sent on a given physical medium. Example: The MTU of Ethernet is 1,500 bytes. See fragmentation.

Multicast: A special form of broadcast where copies of the packet are delivered to only a subset of all possible destinations. See broadcast.

Multi-Homed Host: A computer connected to more than one physical data link. The data links may or may not be attached to the same network.

NAEC: Novell Authorized Education Center.

Name Resolution: The process of mapping a name into the corresponding address. See DNS.

NetBIOS: Network Basic Input Output System. The standard interface to networks on IBM PC and compatible systems.

Network Address: See Internet address or OSI Network Address.

Network Layer: The OSI layer that is responsible for routing, switching, and subnetwork access across the entire OSI environment.

NFS(R): Network File System. A distributed file system developed by Sun Microsystems which allows a set of computers to cooperatively access each other's files in a transparent manner.

NIST: National Institute of Standards and Technology. (Formerly NBS). See OIW.

NMS: Network Management Station. The system responsible for managing a (portion of a) network. The NMS talks to network management agents, which reside in the managed nodes, via a network management protocol. See agent.

NOC: Network Operations Center. Any center tasked with the operational aspects of a production network. These tasks include monitoring and control, trouble-shooting, user assistance, and so on.

Node: A network device which can communicate with other network devices (e.g., clients, servers, bridges, routers, repeaters).

Noise: Electrical interference which degrades signal transmission.

NSAP: Network Service Access Point. The point at which the OSI network service is made available to a transport entity. The NSAPs are identified by OSI network addresses.

NSF: National Science Foundation. Sponsors of the NSFNET.

NSFNET: National Science Foundation NETwork. A collection of local, regional, and mid-level networks in the U.S. tied together by a high-speed backbone. NSFNET provides scientists access to a number of supercomputers across the country.

Ohm: Unit of electrical resistance. One ohm is equal to one volt divided by one ampere.

OIW: Workshop for implementors of OSI. Frequently called NIST OIW or the NIST Workshop, this is the North American regional forum at which OSI implementation agreements are decided. It is equivalent to EWOS in Europe and AOW in the Pacific.

ONC(tm):   Open Network Computing. A distributed applications architecture promoted and controlled by a consortium led by Sun Microsystems.

OSI Network Address: The address, consisting of up to 20 octets, used to locate an OSI transport entity. The address is formatted into an initial domain part which is standardized for each of several addressing domains, and a domain specific part which is the responsibility of the addressing authority for that domain.

OSI Presentation Address: The address used to locate an OSI application entity. It consists of an OSI network address and up to three selectors, one each for use by the transport, session, and presentation entities.

OSI: Open Systems Interconnection. An international standardization program to facilitate communications among computers from different manufacturers. See ISO.

OSPF: Open Shortest Path First. A "proposed standard" IGP for the Internet. See IGP.

Packet Assembler/Disassembler (PAD):   Breaks large pieces of data into packets—typically for use with the X.25 protocol.

Packet Switching: Delivery system that relays packets through a computer network over the best available path. All packets in a particular message do not necessarily take the same route.

Packet: Parcel of information sent over a network as a single unit. Often used interchangeably with the term frame.

PAD: See Packet Assembler/Disassembler

PCI: Protocol Control Information. The protocol information added by an OSI entity to the service data unit passed down from the layer above, all together forming a protocol data unit (PDU).

PDU: Protocol Data Unit. This is OSI terminology for "packet." A PDU is a data object exchanged by protocol machines (entities) within a given layer. PDUs consist of both protocol control information (PCI) and user data.

Permanent Virtual Circuit (PVC): Similar to leased lines but the customer only pays for the time he/she actually uses the line.

Physical Layer: The OSI layer that provides the means to activate and use physical connections for bit transmission. In plain terms, the physical layer provides the procedures for transferring a single bit across a physical media.

Physical Media: Any means in the physical world for transferring signals between OSI systems. Considered to be outside the OSI model, and therefore sometimes referred to as "layer 0." The physical connector to the media can be considered as defining the bottom interface of the physical layer, i.e., the bottom of the OSI reference model.

Piercing Tap: A coaxial cable connector that pierces the cable's insulating layer to make contact with the shield and core conductors.

Ping: Packet internet groper. A program used to test reachability of destinations by sending them an ICMP echo request and waiting for a reply. The term can be used as a verb: "Ping host X to see if it is up!"

Plenum: Space between the ceiling and upper floor in many buildings. Used for the circulation of climate controlling air.

Port: The abstraction used by Internet transport protocols to distinguish among multiple simultaneous connections to a single destination host. See selector.

POSI: Promoting Conference for OSI. The OSI "800-pound gorilla" in Japan. Consists of executives from the six major Japanese computer manufacturers and Nippon Telephone and Telegraph. They set policies and commit resources to promote OSI.

PPP: Point-to-Point Protocol. The successor to SLIP, PPP provides router-to-router and host-to-network connections over both synchronous and asynchronous circuits. See SLIP.

Presentation Address: See OSI Presentation Address.

Presentation Layer: The OSI layer that determines how application information is represented (i.e., encoded) while in transit between two end systems.

PRMD: Private Management Domain. An X.400 Message Handling System private organization mail system. Example: NASAmail. See ADMD.

Protocol: A formal description of messages to be exchanged and rules to be followed for two or more systems to exchange information.

Proxy ARP: The technique in which one machine, usually a router, answers ARP requests intended for another machine. By faking its identity, the router accepts responsibility for routing packets to the real destination.

Proxy ARP allows a site to use a single IP address with two physical networks. Subnetting would normally be a better solution.

Proxy: The mechanism whereby one system fronts for another system in responding to protocol requests. Proxy systems are used in network management to avoid having to implement full protocol stacks in simple devices, such as modems.

PSN: Packet Switch Node. The modern term used for nodes in the ARPANET and MILNET. These used to be called IMPs (interface message processors). PSNs are currently implemented with BBN C30 or C300 minicomputers.

PVC: See Permanent Virtual Circuit.

RAID: See Redundant Array of Inexpensive Disks.

RARE: Reseaux Associes pour la Recherche Europeenne. European association of research networks.

RARP: Reverse Address Resolution Protocol. The Internet protocol a diskless host uses to find its Internet address at startup. RARP maps a physical (hardware) address to an Internet address. See ARP.

RBOC: Regional Bell Operating Company. See BOC.

Reduced Instruction Set Computer: A microprocessor design based on a limited number of relatively simple CPU instructions. RISC computers tend to carry out these simplified instructions very rapidly.

Redundant Array of Inexpensive Disks (RAID):   Set of methods for hard disk fault tolerance.

Repeater: A device that propagates electrical signals from one cable to another without making routing decisions or providing packet filtering. In OSI terminology, a repeater is a physical layer intermediate system. See bridge and router.

RFC: Request for Comments. The document series, begun in 1969, which describes the Internet suite of protocols and related experiments. Not all (in fact very few) RFCs describe Internet standards, but all Internet standards are written up as RFCs.

RFS: Remote File System. A distributed file system, similar to NFS, developed by AT&T and distributed with their UNIX System V operating system. See NFS.

RIP: Routing Information Protocol. An interior gateway protocol (IGP) supplied with Berkeley UNIX.

RIPE: Reseaux IP Europeenne. European continental TCP/IP network operated by EUnet. See EUnet.

RISC: See Reduced Instruction Set Computer.

Rlogin: A service offered by Berkeley UNIX which allows users of one machine to log into other UNIX systems (for which they are authorized) and interact as if their terminals were connected directly. Similar to Telnet.

ROSE: Remote Operations Service Element. A lightweight RPC protocol, used in OSI message handling, directory, and network management application protocols.

Router: A system responsible for making decisions about which of several paths network (or Internet) traffic will follow. To do this, it uses a routing protocol to gain information about the network and algorithms to choose the best route based on several criteria known as "routing metrics." In OSI terminology, a router is a network layer intermediate system. See gateway, bridge, and repeater.

RPC: Remote Procedure Call. An easy and popular paradigm for implementing the client-server model of distributed computing. A request is sent to a remote system to execute a designated procedure, uses arguments supplied, and returns the result to the caller. There are many variations and subtleties, resulting in a variety of different RPC protocols.

RS: Release Supplement. The current update package to a shipping product.

RS-232:   A standard adopted by the Electrical Industries Association specifying lines and signal characteristics used in serial transmission.

RTSE: Reliable Transfer Service Element. A lightweight OSI application service used above X.25 networks to handshake application PDUs across the session service and TP0. Not needed with TP4 and not recommended for use in the U.S. except when talking to X.400 ADMDs.

SAP: Service Access Point. The point at which the services of an OSI layer are made available to the next higher layer. The SAP is named according to the layer providing the services: e.g., Transport services are provided at a transport SAP (TSAP) at the top of the transport layer.

SCSI: See Small Computer System Interface.

Selector: The identifier used by an OSI entity to distinguish among multiple SAPs at which it provides services to the layer above. See port.

SES: Software Enhancement Service. Quarterly delivery of support and updated products.

Session Layer: The OSI layer that provides means for dialogue control between end systems.

SGMP: Simple Gateway Management Protocol. The predecessor to SNMP. See SNMP.

SLIP: Serial Line Internet Protocol. An Internet protocol used to run IP over serial lines such as telephone circuits or RS-232 cables interconnecting two systems. SLIP is now being replaced by PPP. See PPP.

SLS: Support Level Supplement. Emergency fix for a particular bug. (These are combined into a quarterly RS.)

Small Computer System Interface (SCSI): An ANSI standard high-speed parallel interface used to connect microcomputers to peripheral devices.

SMDS: Switched Multimegabit Data Service. An emerging high-speed networking technology to be offered by the telephone companies in the U.S.

SMI: Structure of Management Information. The rules used to define the objects that can be accessed via a network management protocol. See MIB.

SMTP: Simple Mail Transfer Protocol. The Internet electronic mail protocol. Defined in RFC 821, with associated message format descriptions in RFC 822.

SNA: See Systems Network Architecture

SNA: Systems Network Architecture. IBM's proprietary network architecture.

SNMP: Simple Network Management Protocol. The network management protocol of choice for TCP/IP-based internets.

SOS: SCO Online Support (system).

SPAG: Standards Promotion and Application Group. A group of European OSI manufacturers which chooses option subsets and publishes these in a "Guide to the Use of Standards." (GUS).

SQL: Structured Query Language. The international standard language for defining and accessing relational databases.

SSE: System Security Enhancement.

SSL: Software Support Library.

Subnet Mask: See address mask.

Subnetwork: A collection of OSI end systems and intermediate systems under the control of a single administrative domain and utilizing a single network access protocol. Examples: private X.25 networks, collection of bridged LANs.

Systems Network Architecture (SNA): An IBM-developed communications framework that defines network functions to permit different types of computers to exchange data.

TA: Technical Articles

TCP: Transmission Control Protocol. The major transport protocol in the Internet suite of protocols, providing reliable, connection-oriented, full-duplex streams. Uses IP for delivery. See TP4.

Telnet: The virtual terminal protocol in the Internet suite of protocols. Allows users of one host to log into a remote host and interact as normal terminal users of that host.

Three-Way-Handshake: The process whereby two protocol entities synchronize during connection establishment.

TLS: Technical Library Supplement.

TP0: OSI Transport Protocol Class 0 (Simple Class). This is the simplest OSI transport protocol, useful only on top of an X.25 network (or other network that does not lose or damage data).

TP4: OSI Transport Protocol Class 4 (Error Detection and Recovery Class). This is the most powerful OSI transport protocol, useful on top of any type of network. TP4 is the OSI equivalent to TCP.

Transceiver: Transmitter-receiver. The physical device that connects a host interface to a local area network, such as Ethernet. Ethernet transceivers contain electronics that apply signals to the cable and sense collisions.

Transport Layer: The OSI layer that is responsible for reliable end-to-end data transfer between end systems.

UA: User Agent. An OSI application process that represents a human user or organization in the X.400 Message Handling System. Creates, submits, and takes delivery of messages on the user's behalf.

UDP: User Datagram Protocol. A transport protocol in the Internet suite of protocols. UDP, like TCP, uses IP for delivery; however, unlike TCP, UDP provides for exchange of datagrams without acknowledgements or guaranteed delivery. See CLTP.

UUCP: UNIX-to-UNIX Copy Program. A protocol used for communication between consenting UNIX systems.

VCD: Vendor Contributed Driver.

World Wide Web: HTTP-based Internet multimedia service.

WWW: See World Wide Web

X Recommendations: The CCITT documents that describe data communication network standards. Well-known ones include: X.25 Packet Switching standard, X.400 Message Handling System, and X.500 Directory Services.

100BASE-FX Ethernet, 125
100BASE-T4 Ethernet, 124–125
100BASE-TX Ethernet, 124
100VG-AnyLAN, 126–127
10BASE-2 Ethernet, 122
10BASE-5 Ethernet, 120–121
10BASE-FL Ethernet, 122
10BASE-T Ethernet, 118–120
5-4-3 rule, 121, 123

ABEND (abnormal end), 31
Access methods, 112–115
Account creation, 317–318
Account lockout, 322
Active communication equipment, 88
Address classes, 215–220
Addressing, 76, 77
    See also Hardware addresses; IP addresses.
Admin, 322
Administration. See Network administration.
Administrative accounts, 310–311
Administrator, 322
ADSL (asymmetric or asynchronous digital
    subscriber line), 182–183
Advanced NetWare 86, 24–25
Advanced NetWare 286, 24–25
AM (active monitor), 130–131
AND, 223
Anti-virus policies and training, 334
Anti-virus software, 334–335
Apache Web Server, 50
APIs (applications programming interfaces),
    70, 73–74, 211, 231
AppleTalk, 42, 170
Application layer
    DoD four-layer model, 70–72, 74
    OSI model, 73–74, 79, 81–83
Application Log, 332
Applications, 310

ARCHIE, 200
ArcNet, 132–134
ArcNet Plus, 132
ARP (address resolution protocol), 69, 200,
    204–206, 222, 245, 255, 256
ASIC (application specific integrated circuit), 160
Asymmetric data rates, 292
Asynchronous modems, 287, 288
AT command, 290
ATM (Asynchronous Transfer Mode), 179–181
AT&T, 176
Attenuation, 92, 117, 123
AUDITCON, 34
AUI cables, 93
AUI connectors, 92, 94, 95

Backbones, 17–19
Backup program, 317, 334, 336–343
Bandwidth, 111–112
Banyan-Vines servers, 56
Baseband transmission, 91
Base I/O port, 376
Base memory address, 376
Baud, 291
Baudot, Jean Marie Emile, 291
BDC (backup domain controllers), 45, 317
Binary notation, 211–213
BIND, 197–199
BINDERY, 27
Binding, 67
Block suballocation, 29
BNC cable connectors, 94–98
B-node, 237
Bound DHCP client, 226
Bridgeable protocols, 170
Bridges, 88, 151–159
Broadband transmission, 91
Broadcast node, 237
Broadcast traffic isolation, 168

Brouters, 171
Browmon, 255
Browstat, 255
BSD (Berkley Software Distribution), 49
Bus mastering, 375–376
Bus topology, 12–14

Cables, 13–17, 87–112
    access methods and, 112–115
    attenuation and, 92
    baseband transmission over, 91
    broadband transmission over, 91
    choosing, 110–112
    coaxial. *See* Coaxial cable.
    comparison of, 112
    fiber optic. *See* Fiber optic cable.
    impedance and, 90
    network architecture and. *See* Network architecture.
    twisted-pair. *See* Twisted-pair cable.
Cascaded star topology, 15, 16
Cause of problem, isolation of, 363–365
CDE (common desktop environment), 49
CDM (custom device module), 29
Cell switching, 180–181
Checkpoints, 75–76
Circuit switching, 175
Cladding, 107
Class A IP addresses, 216, 218
Class B IP addresses, 216–218
Class C IP addresses, 217, 218
Class D IP addresses, 217, 218
Class E IP addresses, 217, 218
Classes, IP address, 215–220
Client32, 56
Client for Microsoft Networks, 56
Client operating systems, 53–57
Clients, 24
Climate, 330–331
CMR-common mode rejection, 99
Coaxial cable, 13–14, 89–99
    ArcNet and, 134
    compared with other cables, 112
    connectors, 92–99

Ethernet and, 120–122
    thick (thicknet), 13, 91–92, 112, 117, 120–121
    thin (thinnet), 13–14, 112, 117
Collision domains, 149, 152, 162, 163
Compression, 75
Computer Browser Service, 43
Computer equipment placement, 331
Concentrators, 88, 104, 125
Connectors
    coaxial cable, 92–99
    fiber optic cable, 109–110
    in token ring architecture, 128–130
    twisted pair cable, 101–104
ConsoleOne, 36
Contention method, 114
Controlled Access implementation, 34
Copy, 339
Correction formulation, 365
Correction implementation, 366
Correction testing, 366
CRC, 158
Crossover cables, 380
Crosstalk, 101, 111
Cryptography, 38
CSLIP, 298
CSMA/CA (carrier-sense multiple access with collision advance), 114, 116
CSMA/CD (carrier-sense multiple access with collision detection), 113–114
CSU/DSU (channel service unit/data service unit), 177–178

Daemons, 198, 274
Daily copy, 339
Data bits, 293–294
Data bus architecture, 374–375
Data compression, 291
Data formatting, 74–75
Datagrams, 69–70
Data link frame structure, 149–150
Data link layer, OSI model, 74, 76–79, 81, 83
Data link layer devices, 151
Datapoint Corporation, 132

Data transfer and memory, 375–376
Data transfer utilities, TCP/IP, 198
DDR (dial on demand routing), 176
DEC (Digital Equipment Corporation), 66, 116, 157, 170
DECnet, 170
Default gateways, 172, 225, 261
Default subnet masks, 222, 223
Demand priority method, 115
DET (Directory Entry Table), 32
DFS 2000 (Distributed File System), 46–47
DHCP (Dynamic Host Configuration Protocol), 43, 224–230, 373
DHCPACK, 226, 227
DHCPDISCOVER, 225–227
DHCP Manager, 227, 228
DHCPNACK, 227
DHCPOFFER, 225
DHCP relay agents, 228–229
DHCPREQUEST, 226
Diagnostic utilities, TCP/IP, 198, 200–203
Dial backup, 176
Dial-up services, 176
Differential backup, 339, 340
Differential Manchester encoding, 129–130
Digital data service, 177–178
DIP switches, 378
Directory services
    Microsoft Windows NT Server 4.0, 45
    Microsoft Windows 2000 Server, 47–48
    Novell NetWare 4.1, 30, 33–34
    Novell NetWare 5, 37
    Novell NetWare 3.1x, 27
    UNIX, 51–52
Disabling accounts, 322
Disk duplexing, 32, 345
Disk mirroring, 343–345
Disk quotas, 46
DLC (Data Link Control, 42
DMA (direct memory access), 375, 377
DNA (digital network architecture), 66
DNS (domain name system), 44, 47, 80, 225, 237, 244–246

Documentation, 5, 366–367
DoD (Department of Defense) four-layer model, 65, 67–72, 74
DOS support, 57
Dotted decimal notation, 211–213
Drop cables, 92
DSL (digital subscriber line), 182–183
Dual-cable solution, 91
Duplicate IP addresses, 224
Dynamic routers, 169

EEPROM chips, 377
EIA/TIA (Electronic Industries Association and Telecommunication Industry Association) 568
    Commercial Building Wiring Standards, 100, 103, 104
EISA (extended industry standard architecture), 375
EMI (electromagnetic interference), 330
Encapsulation, 82–83, 203–204
Encoding methods, 117–118
Encryption, 74, 75
EPPs (Ethernet packet processors), 160
Error checking and correction, 75, 76
Error logs, 332–333, 372–373
ESD (electrostatic discharge), 329–330
Ethernet, 78, 81, 116–127, 149–150
Event log, 255
Event Viewer, 273, 332, 333

Fast Ethernet standards, 124–126
FAT (File Allocation Table), 32
Fault tolerance, 343–349
    Microsoft Windows NT Server 4.0, 41
    Microsoft Windows 2000 Server, 46–47
    Novell NetWare 4.1, 31–33
    UNIX, 51
FC (fiber channel) support, 48
Feedback, 367–368
Fiber optic cable, 107–110
    ArcNet and, 134
    compared with other cables, 112
    connectors, 109–110

Fiber optic cable (*cont.*)
    Ethernet and, 122, 125
    token ring architecture and, 131, 132
Fieldbus technology, 132
File compression, 29
Finger utility, 200
Flooding, 155
"Fox and hounds," 380
FQDN (fully qualified domain name), 242, 245
Frame relay, 178–179, 297–298
Frames, 68, 69, 76–77, 117–118, 180
Frame structure, 149–150
FreeBSD, 52
FTP (file transfer protocol), 70, 71, 80, 195, 198, 272
Full backup, 339
Full duplex, 75, 164–166
Funneling, 163–164

Gateways, 171–174
    default, 172, 225, 261
    routers referred to as, 170
GRE (generic routing encapsulation), 301, 302
Grounding, 330
GSNW (Gateway Services for NetWare), 173
GUI (graphical user interface), 197

Half duplex, 75, 165
HAM (host adapter module), 29
Hardware
    requirements, 4–5, 310
    troubleshooting, 368–371
Hardware addresses, 69, 77, 82
Hayes compatible modems, 290
HDLC (high-level data-link control), 81
HDSL (high-speed digital subscriber line), 183
Headend, 91
Hewlett-Packard, 126
H-node, 238
Host ID, 214–215, 220
HOSTNAME, 200
Host name resolution, 241–246, 270–272
HOSTS file, 236–237, 243–244, 270
Host-to-host layer. *See* Transport layer.
Hot fix, 32

Hotmail.com SMTP to HTTP gateway, 173
HTTP (hypertext transfer protocol), 195
Hubs
    repeater, 118–120, 147–149, 166
    in star topology, 14–16
    switching, 166
HVAC (heating, ventilating, and air condition-ing), 330–331
Hybrid node, 238

IAB (Internet Advisory Board), 301
IANA (Internet Assigned Numbers Authority), 211
IBM Corporation, 127
IBM Operating System/2, 53–57
ICMP (Internet control message protocol), 69, 195, 202, 206, 274
Identification of problem, 361–362
IDSL (ISDN digital subscriber line), 183
IEEE (Institute of Electrical and Electronic Engineers), 66, 118, 124, 127
IEEE (Institute of Electrical and Electronic Engineers) 802 model, 80–82
IFCONFIG, 197, 199–201, 230, 256, 257, 259
IGMP (Internet group management protocol), 69, 206
Impedance, 90
Incremental backup, 339, 340
Installation, network, 310–316
Intel Corporation, 116
Internal termination, 97
International Telecommunications Union, 291
Internet Architecture Board, The, 195
Internet Engineering Task Force, 225
Internet layer, DoD four-layer model, 69–70, 72, 74
Internet Society, The, 195
InterNIC (Internet Information Center), 70
INTRAK System Monitor, 332
Intranet Ware, 29–30
I/O addresses, 289
IP (Internet protocol), 69, 79, 81, 169, 207
IP addresses, 69–70, 76, 202, 203, 205, 211–230
    automating assignment using DHCP, 224–230
    classes, 215–219

dotted decimal notation, 211–213
host ID, 214–215, 220
host name resolution and, 242–246
IPng (IPv6), 219–220
NetBIOS name resolution and, 235–241
network ID, 214–215, 220
network installation and, 311
subnet masks, 221–224
troubleshooting problems with, 259–260
IPCONFIG, 201, 229–230, 255, 257–259
IPng (IPv6), 219–220
IP-to-IP gateway, 173–174
IPTRACE, 257
IPX (NetWare Internet Packet Exchange), 79, 81, 169
IRL (inter-repeater link), 121
IRQ (interrupt request query line), 289, 376–379
ISA (industry standard architecture), 374–375
ISC (Internet Software Consortium), 227
ISDN (integrated services digital network), 181–182, 296–297
ISDN Anywhere, 296
ISDN modems, 296
ISO (International Standards Organization), 66, 72

Jam signal, 148
Jumpers, 378

Kerberos protocol, 48
Keyed connectors, 101

LAN (local area network) expansion equipment, 146–174
bridges, 151–159
brouters, 171
gateways, 171–174
repeaters, 147–149
routers, 167–171
switches, 159–167
LANs (local area networks), 3, 4
connecting to other foreign systems and environments, 145–146
connecting two or more, 142–143
expansion equipment. *See* LAN expansion equipment.
peer-to-peer, 4, 6–8
reasons for expanding, 142–146
segmenting, 143–145
server-based, 8–11
Lasers, 108
LAVA (Los Alamos Vulnerability and Risk Assessment), 318
LCP (link control protocol), 300
LEDs (light emitting diodes), 108
Licensing, 5
Line conditioners, 329
Line power, 328–329
Linux, 50
LLC (logical link control) sublayer, 81, 82
LMHOSTS file, 236, 238–241, 244, 267–269
LOAD utility, 197–199
Local broadcast, 236, 244
Local host name, 243
Logging, backup, 341–342
Logical security, 319–323
Logical topologies, 12–13
LOGIN script, 27
Logs
as monitoring tool, 332–333
transaction, 342
troubleshooting and, 372–373
LONG.NAM, 30–31
Loopback address, 203, 261
Loopback checks, 379
Loops, 157–158
LPD (line printer daemon), 199
LPQ (line printer queue), 199
LPR (line printer remote), 199
LPRM (line printer remove), 199
LRAM (Livermore Risk Analysis Methodology), 318

MAC (media access control) address, 82, 151, 153–156, 159, 160, 222
Macintosh, services for, 44
MAC (media access control) sublayer, 81–82
Maintenance. *See* Network maintenance.
Maintenance accounts, 322

ManageWise, 36–37

Manchester encoding, 117–118
  differential, 129–130

Mapping. *See* Name resolution.

Matrix, 160–161

MCA (micro channel architecture), 375

Media access delays, 143, 144

Memory, NICs and, 375–376

Memory requirements
  Microsoft Windows NT Server 4.0, 40, 41
  Microsoft Windows 2000 Server, 46
  Novell NetWare 4.1, 31
  Novell NetWare 5, 35
  Novell NetWare 3.1x, 25–26
  UNIX, 50–51

Mesh topology, 12–13, 17, 18

MIC (medium interface connector), 128–130

MicroHouse hardware and troubleshooting
  CD, 333

Microsegmentation, 164

Microsoft Directory Service Migration Tool, 48

Microsoft enhanced b-node, 237

Microsoft name resolution methods, 236–241,
  244–245

Microsoft Network Monitor, 274–279, 332

Microsoft redirectors, 55–56

Microsoft SNA Server, 40

Microsoft SNMP service, 255

Microsoft TCP/IP diagnostic utilities, 255

Microsoft TechNet, 333

Microsoft Windows. *See* Windows entries.

MicroSure Self Assessment, 318

MINIRISK, 318

Mixed node, 238

M-node, 238

Mode dispersion, 108

Models
  concept of, 64–65
  origins of, 65–66

Modems, 286–294, 296

MONITOR, 27

Monitoring the system, 331–333

MPR (multi protocol router), 264

MSAUs (multistation access units), 128–129

MS-Network Client, 57

Multimode fiber optic cable, 108, 109, 117, 131,
  132

Multiplexers, 88

Name cache, 235

Name discovery, 233

Name registration, 232

Name release, 233

Name resolution
  host, 241–246, 270–272
  NetBIOS. *See* NetBIOS.
  testing, 267–272

Name resolution nodes, 237

Name scopes, 233–235

NAT (network address translator), 174

NBFP (NetBIOS frames protocol), 231

NBNS (NetBIOS name server), 232, 235–236,
  244

NBTSTAT, 200, 241, 255, 268–269

NCP (NetWare Core Protocol), 55, 80, 81

NDIS (Network Driver Interface Specification),
  42, 67

NDS (NetWare directory services), 30, 33–34

NetBEUI (NetBIOS extended user interface),
  42, 71, 170

NetBIOS (network basic input/output system),
  70–71, 80, 81, 230–241
  common names, 232
  name discovery, 233
  name registration, 232
  name release, 233
  name resolution, 235–241
  name resolution problems, 267–269
  names, defined, 231–232

NetBT (NetBIOS over TCP/IP), 231

NETSTAT, 200, 255, 256, 265, 270–272

NetWare Connect, 29

NetWare redirectors, 56

Network adaptor cards, 88

Network administration, 309–324
  account creation, 317–318
  backup, 317
  installation, 310–316

maintenance. *See* Network maintenance.
security, 318–323
Network analysis resources, 379–381
Network architecture, 116–134
ArcNet, 132–134
Ethernet, 78, 81, 116–127, 149–150
token ring, 127–132
Network ID, 214–215, 220
Networking, 1–20
defined, 2–4
planning, 4–5, 9–10
topologies. *See* Topologies.
types of networks, 5–11
Network interface layer, DoD four-layer model,
68–69, 72, 74
Network layer, OSI model, 74, 76, 79, 81
Network maintenance, 316–318, 327–355
backup program, 317, 334, 336–343
fault tolerance, 343–349
monitoring, 331–333
physical environment, 328–331
UPS (uninterruptible power supply), 329,
349–350
virus threat, 334–336
Network Monitor, 44, 255, 274–279, 332
Network operating systems. *See* NOS.
Network planning, 4–5, 9–10, 312–315
Network services
Microsoft Windows NT Server 4.0, 42–45
Microsoft Windows 2000 Server, 47
Novell NetWare 4.1, 33
Novell NetWare 5, 36–37
Novell NetWare 3.1x, 26–27
UNIX, 51
Network troubleshooting, 359–382
hardware in general, 368–371
methodology, 360–368
network analysis resources, 379–381
wire to application walk-through, 371–379
Network utilization, 144–145
NETX, 57
NFS (network file system), 56
NICs (network interface cards), 67, 69, 77,
373–379

NIS (Network Information System), 51
NMBLOOKUP, 256
Nonroutable protocols, 170
NOS (network operating systems), 23–59
clients, 53–57
defined, 23–24
Microsoft Windows NT Server 4.0, 39–45
Microsoft Windows 2000 Server, 45–48
network installation and, 310
Novell NetWare, 24–39
OS/2 (IBM Operating System/2), 53
UNIX, 49–52
Novell Client for Windows 3.x, 56
Novell NetWare, 24–39, 44–45
Novell NetWare 2.12, 25
Novell NetWare 3.1x, 25–29
Novell NetWare 4.1, 29–35
Novell NetWare 5, 35–39
Novell SNMP agent, 257
Novell TCP/IP diagnostic utilities, 257
NSLOOKUP, 200, 256, 270
NTFS2000 (New Technology File System ver-
sion 2000), 46
NWADMIN (NetWare Administrator), 317
NWLink, 42
NWPA (NetWare peripheral architecture), 29

ODI (Open Datalink Interface), 26–28, 67
Open Server, 52
Open wire, 13
Operating systems. *See* NOS.
Oracle, 50
OS/2 (IBM Operating System/2), 53
OSI (open systems interconnect) model, 72–83
OS2.NAM, 31

Packet loss, 158–159
Packets, 68, 69
Packet switching, 175–176, 176, 178
PAD (X.25 Packet Assembler/Disassembler),
297
Parity, 293–294
Passive communication equipment, 88
Password cracker, 321

Passwords, 7, 311, 318, 320–323
Patches, 350–353
Patch panels, 104–106
PC Card, 29
PCI (peripheral component architecture), 375
PDC (primary domain controller), 45
Peer-to-peer LANs, 4, 6–8
Peer-to-peer node, 237
Performance Monitor, 255, 273–274, 332
Physical environment, maintenance of,
    328–331
Physical layer, OSI model, 74, 77–79, 81, 83
Physical placement, 331
Physical security, 318–319
Physical topologies, 13–17
PING (Packet Internet Groper), 201–203,
    255–257, 261–264, 266
Planning networks, 4–5, 9–10, 312–315
Plenum-grade cabling, 89
Plenums, 89
Plug and play, 377–378
P-node, 237
Point-to-point links, 175
Ports, 71, 208–211, 288–289
Port speed, 291
Positive name query response, 233
Power spikes, 329
Power surges, 329
PPP (point-to-point protocol), 299–301
PPTP (point-to-point tunneling protocol),
    301–302
Preferred server, 27
Presentation layer, OSI model, 74–75, 79,
    81–83
Primary rate ISDN, 296
Printing utilities, TCP/IP, 198, 199
Problem identification, 361–362
Problem recreation, 362–363
Promiscuous mode, 274–275
Propagation delay, 119, 126, 142
Protocol analyzers, 381
Protocols
    client connection to server and, 55
    defined, 66

DoD model and, 67–72
Microsoft Windows NT Server 4.0, 42
OSI model and, 78–80
remote access, 298
routable and nonroutable, 169–170
troubleshooting, 373–374
PSTN (public-switched telephone network),
    294–295
PVC-coated coaxial cables, 89
PVCs (permanently established virtual circuits),
    176

RAA/SYS (Risk Analysis System), 318
RAID (redundant array of inexpensive disks),
    31, 41, 343–349
RAM buffering, 376
RAM start address, 376
RARP (reverse address resolution protocol), 69
RAS (remote access service), 44
RCONSOLE (NetWare Remote Console), 28
RCP (remote copy protocol), 198
READ.ME files, 351
Recreation of problem, 362–363
Redirectors, 55–56, 75, 80
Registry, editing to specify smaller packet size,
    266–267
Relative humidity, 330
Remote connectivity, 285–305
    media, 294–298
    modems, 286–294
    protocols, 298–302
    software, 286
Remote execution utilities, TCP/IP, 198, 199
Repackaging, 76, 153
Repeater hubs, 118–120, 147–149, 166
Repeaters, 88
    in Ethernet networks, 118, 120–123, 125, 148
    features of, 147–149
Replica synchronization process, 34
Restores, test, 341
Retransmission, 75–76
REXEC (remote execution), 199
RFCs (Requests for Comments), 195–196, 225
RFI (radio frequency interference), 330

RG-58 group of coaxial cables, 90
Ring speed, 377
Ring topology, 12, 16–17
RI/RO (ring-in/ring-out) ports, 128
RISC (reduced instruction set computer), 160
RISKPAC, 318
RiskWatch, 318
RJ-11 connectors, 104
RJ-45 connectors, 101–104
Root, 322
Routable protocols, 169–170
ROUTE, 200, 255, 256, 265
Routers, 88, 167–171
Route tracing utilities, 265–266
Routing problems, 264–266
Routing table, 168–169
RPC (remote procedure call), 52
RRAS (routing and remote access service), 47
RSH (remote shell), 199
RSHD (remote shell daemon), 198

Safety, 331
SAM (security accounts manager), 45
Samba suite, 235
SAP (Service Advertising Protocol), 80, 81
SAR (System Activity Reporter), 256
SATAN, 52, 318
Scanning policies, 335
SC connectors, 109–110
Scopes
    DHCP, 227–228
    NetBIOS, 233–235
SDSL (symmetric digital subscriber line), 183
Sector sparing, 348
SECURE CONSOLE, 27–28
SECURE.NFC SET, 34
Security, 318–323, 334–336
Security Log, 332
Security services
    Microsoft Windows 2000 Server, 48
    Novell NetWare 4.1, 34
    Novell NetWare 5, 37–38
    Novell NetWare 3.1x, 27–28
    UNIX, 52

Segments, 17–19, 149
Serial ports, 288–289
Server-based networks, 8–11
Servers, 24
Session, 75
Session communication problems, 272
Session layer, OSI model, 74–76, 79, 81, 83
SFT (server fault tolerance), 31
Shared adapter memory, 375
Shared system memory, 375
Share-level security, 323
Shielding, 89
SID (security identifier), 320
Signature files, 335–336
Simplex data flow, 75
Single-cable solution, 91
Single mode fiber optic cable, 108, 109
SLIP (serial line Internet protocol), 298–299
SMB (Server Management Blocks), 80, 81
SMB (server message blocks), 55, 173
SMP (Symmetric Multiprocessing), 32–33
SMS (Storage Management Services), 30
SMS (Systems Management Server), 274–275
SMTP (simple mail transfer protocol), 71, 173,
    195
SNMP (simple network management protocol),
    71
Sockets, 70, 71, 196–197, 210–211
Software
    anti-virus, 334–335
    remote access, 286
    requirements, 4–5
Software patches, 350–353
SOP (standard operating procedures),
    311–312
Source quench messages, 206
Source-route bridging, 153
Source-route transparent bridging, 153
SPX (sequenced packet exchange), 80, 81, 169
S-registers, 290
STA (spanning tree algorithm), 157–158
Standard Ethernet, 91–92
Standards, 63–84
    defined, 64–65

Standards (*cont.*)
  DoD (Department of Defense) four-layer
    model, 65, 67–72, 74
  encapsulation, 82–83
  IEEE 802 model, 80–82
  networking models and, 65–66
  for NICs (network interface cards), 67
  OSI (open systems interconnect) model,
    72–83
  protocols, 66
  TCP/IP, 195–196
Star bus topology, 15, 16
StarOffice, 52
Start bits, 293
Star topology, 12, 14–16
Static routers, 169
ST connectors, 109
Stop bits, 293–294
Store-and-forward switches, 161–162
STP (shielded twisted pair) cable, 101,
  131–132
Stripe set with parity, 345–348
Subnet masks, 221–224, 260–261
Subnetwork, 168
Sun Microsystems, 49–50, 52
Sun Solaris, 49–50
Sun Solaris Easy Access Server, 50
Surge protectors, 329
SVC (switched virtual circuits), 176
Switched 56, 178
Switches, 88, 159–167
Switching hubs, 166
Switching matrix, 160–161
Synchronous modems, 287–288
Systematic approach, 361, 371
System Log, 332, 333
System Log files, 256
Sytek Corporation, 230

T1, 176–177, 297
T3, 297
Tape backup, 317, 337–338, 340–341
Taps, 13
T-connectors, 13–14, 92, 95–97

TCP (transmission control protocol), 66, 70,
  80, 81, 173–174, 207–208
TCPCON, 257
TCPDUMP, 256
TCP/IP (transmission control protocol/Internet
    protocol), 193–247
  advantages of, 196–197
  architecture, 203–211
  basic information, 195–203
  default gateways, 172
  defined, 195
  DoD model and, 69–71
  host name resolution, 241–246
  IP addresses. *See* IP addresses.
  Microsoft Windows NT Server 4.0 and, 42
  name scopes, 233–235
  NetBIOS. *See* NetBIOS.
  OSI model and, 79
  routability and, 169, 170
  standards, 195–196
  troubleshooting. *See* TCP/IP troubleshooting.
  UNIX and, 51, 56
  utilities and services, 197–203
TCP/IP (transmission control protocol/Internet
    protocol) troubleshooting, 253–279
  configuration checking, 257–259
  diagnostic tools overview, 254–256
  general considerations, 254
  guidelines, 256–258
  IP address problems, 259–261
  IP communications testing, 261–267
  name resolution testing, 267–272
  tools, 272–279
TDRs (time-domain reflectometers, 380–381
Telephone network, public-switched, 294–295
Telnet, 71, 199
Terminators, 13
Test accounts, 311
Test restores, 341
TFTP (trivial file transfer protocol), 195, 198
Thick (thicknet) coaxial cable, 13, 91–92, 112,
  117, 120–121
Thin (thinnet) coaxial cable, 13–14, 90, 94, 95,
  112, 117

Three-way handshake, 208
Token holding time, 115
Token passing, 114–115
Token Ring, 78, 81
Token ring architecture, 127–132
Tone generator, 380
Tone locator, 380
Topologies, 11–19
  defined, 11
  logical, 12–13
  physical, 13–17
  segments and backbones, 17–19
Total internal reflection, 108
TPCON, 257, 266
TPING, 203, 257
TRACEROUTE, 200, 256, 265–266
TRACERT, 255, 265
Transaction logs, 342
Transceiver cables, 92
Transceivers, 92, 93, 377
Transitional bridging, 153
Transmission layer. *See* Transport layer.
Transmission speed, 111–112
Transparent bridging, 153
Transport layer
  DoD four-layer model, 70, 72, 74
  OSI model, 74, 76, 79, 81, 83
Troubleshooting. *See* Network troubleshooting;
  TCP/IP troubleshooting.
Trusted Computer System Evaluation Criteria,
  34
Trusted Network Interpretation, 34
TSAs (target service agents), 30
Tunnel, 301, 302
Twisted-pair cable, 15, 98–107
  ArcNet and, 134
  classes of, 100–101
  compared with other cables, 112
  connectors, 101–104
  Ethernet and, 118–120, 124–125
  token ring architecture and, 131–132

UART (universal asynchronous receiver-
  transmitter), 291

UDP (user datagram protocol), 70, 80, 81, 206,
  209
UID (user identifier), 320
University of California, Berkeley, 271, 298
UNIX Operating Systems, 49–52
UNIX redirectors, 56
UNIX System V, 49
UNIX TCP/IP diagnostic utilities, 256
UPS (uninterruptible power supply), 329,
  349–350
User authentication, 319–320
User-level security, 323
User names, 320
User needs, 4
UTP (unshielded twisted pair) cable, 100, 102,
  103, 131, 132, 134

V series standards, 291–292
Vampire connectors, 13
Vampire taps, 92, 93
Variable-length frames, 180
VDSL (very high speed digital subscriber line),
  183
Virtual circuits, 176
Virus threat, 334–336
VLM (very large memory), 46
Volume sets, 348

Wallplates, 105–106
WANs (wide area networks), 3, 141, 174–185
  defined, 142, 175
  devices, 176–183
  expanding LANs to. *See* LAN expansion
    equipment.
  technologies, 175–176
WDM (Win32 Device Manager Model), 48
Well-known ports, 208, 209
Windows 2000 Active Directory Services, 46–47
Windows 2000 Enterprise Edition, 46
Windows 2000 Server, 45–48
Windows 2000 Server Configuration Wizard, 48
Windows 95/98, 53–54
Windows Dial-Up Networking software, 286
Windows NT Event Viewer, 273, 332, 333

Windows NT Performance Monitor, 255, 273–274, 332
Windows NT Remote Access Server software, 286, 301
Windows NT Resource Kit, 255
Windows NT Routing and Remote Access Server software, 286
Windows NT Server 4.0, 39–45
Windows NT Server 4.0 DHCP Manager, 228, 229
Windows NT 4.0 Workstation, 53–55
Windows sockets, 70, 71, 196–197
WINIPCFG, 201
WINS (Windows Internet naming service), 225, 235, 236, 244

Wizards, 315
  Microsoft Windows 2000 Server, 48
  Novell NetWare 4.1, 34–35
  Novell NetWare 5, 39
Wntipcfg, 255
Workstations, 24
Workstation Service, 56

X.25 packet switching, 176, 178, 179, 297
Xerox Corporation, 116
Xerox Palo Alto Research Center, 116
XNSS, 170

Yes, Tested and Approved program, 28

ZENworks, 37

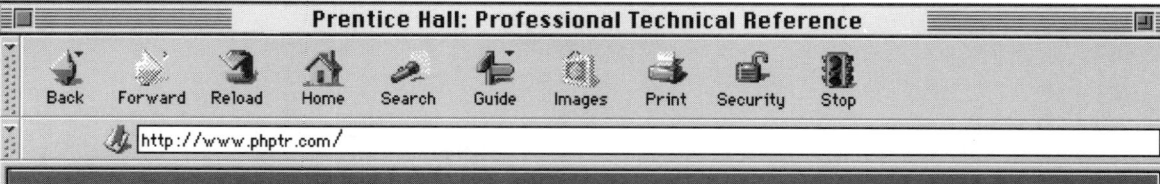